REVIEW TEXT IN
COMPREHENSIVE ENGLISH

(Three and Four Years)

By HAROLD LEVINE

Chairman of English,
Richmond Hill High School,
New York City

Dedicated to Serving Our Nation's Youth

AMSCO SCHOOL PUBLICATIONS, Inc.
315 Hudson Street   New York, N.Y. 10013

PREFACE

The paramount goal of this text is to give as much help as possible —but help with understanding—to students reviewing high school English and preparing for the New York State Comprehensive Examination. The author and editors have spared no effort to make explanations clear, hints and suggestions genuinely useful, and practice exercises thorough and abundant. Problems often treated superficially in the past (for example, how to choose the best title of a reading-comprehension passage), are discussed in this book in concrete terms that students can readily comprehend and apply. Composition skills are presented in a practical, easy-to-understand manner. Detailed step-by-step procedures, including critiques of numerous pieces of pupils' writing, are used to build up the student's skill to plan and write better compositions and better literature-discussion essays. Comparably thorough treatment is given in other examination areas: vocabulary, spelling, correct usage, punctuation, capitalization, library and reference skills, magazines, newspapers, parliamentary procedure, etc. Students looking for worthwhile reading selections, or desiring to review selections already read, will be helped by the concise comments on more than three hundred recommended works. Teachers will be interested in the presentations based on successful classroom experience, and they will surely welcome the generous supply of exercises and past Regents examinations.

This text is intended to help students pass the Comprehensive Examination and, beyond that, as an English handbook, to promote overall competence in the most vital subject in the curriculum—English.

—Harold Levine

CONTENTS

Chapter 1

THE VOCABULARY TEST (QUESTION 1)

THE IMPORTANCE OF VOCABULARY

A good vocabulary identifies you as a superior student. It indicates that you have probably done considerable reading. It strongly suggests that you have the word power to function on a high level in thinking, understanding others, and expressing your own ideas.

Quite properly, the New York State Regents Comprehensive Examination in English places heavy emphasis on vocabulary. The vocabulary test (question 1—maximum weight fifteen points) is not the only measure of your word power. Other parts of the examination that test your vocabulary are the reading test (question 3—twenty points), the literature-discussion test (questions 5a and 5b—twenty points), and the composition test (question 6—thirty points).

The following examinations, in which you are likely to have a personal stake, also lay heavy stress on vocabulary:

Preliminary Scholastic Aptitude Test and
Scholastic Aptitude Test (both administered by the College Entrance Examination Board)
National Merit Examination
New York State Regents Scholarship Examination
civil service examinations

For examination purposes—and more vitally, for your success and happiness in school, on the job, and in your relations with others—you should resolve to give daily attention to improving your vocabulary.

TYPICAL REGENTS VOCABULARY TEST

The vocabulary test measures your ability to select the synonym of a word from a group of five choices. It is a challenging test, as you will discover by doing the sample test below. But first cover the answers that have been inserted on the lines at the right.

1

JANUARY 1961

On the line at the right of *each* group below, write the *number* of the word or expression that most nearly expresses the meaning of the italicized word.   [15]

a obnoxious .... (1) dreamy   (2) visible   (3) angry   (4) daring   (5) objectionable ...   a. ....5....

b verbatim ...... (1) word for word   (2) at will   (3) without fail   (4) in secret   (5) in summary ....   b. ....1....

c entice .... (1) inform   (2) observe   (3) permit   (4) attract   (5) disobey ....   c. ....4....

d acclaim .... (1) discharge   (2) excel   (3) applaud   (4) divide   (5) speed ...   d. ....3....

e turbulence .... (1) treachery   (2) commotion   (3) fear   (4) triumph   (5) overflow   e. ....2....

f defer .... (1) discourage   (2) postpone   (3) empty   (4) minimize   (5) estimate ....   f. ....2....

g adage .... (1) proverb   (2) supplement   (3) tool   (4) youth   (5) hardness ...   g. ....1....

h ensue .... (1) compel   (2) remain   (3) absorb   (4) plead   (5) follow ....   h. ....5....

i zenith .... (1) lowest point   (2) compass   (3) summit   (4) middle   (5) wind direction ....   i. ....3....

j hypothetical .. (1) magical   (2) visual   (3) two-faced   (4) theoretical   (5) excitable ....   j. ....4....

k superficial .... (1) shallow   (2) unusually fine   (3) proud   (4) aged   (5) spiritual ..   k. ....1....

l disparage ..... (1) separate   (2) compare   (3) refuse   (4) belittle   (5) imitate ...   l. ....4....

m protagonist ... (1) prophet   (2) explorer   (3) talented child   (4) convert   (5) leading character ....   m. ....5....

n ludicrous ..... (1) profitable (2) excessive (3) disordered (4) ridiculous (5) undesirable .... *n.* ...4...

o intrepid ...... (1) moist (2) tolerant (3) fearless (4) rude (5) gay .... *o.* ...3...

ANALYSIS OF THE VOCABULARY TEST

Analysis shows that the vocabulary test is difficult, except for the student who has read widely and is precise in his thinking. It is difficult because:

1. The words you have to define are offered in isolation, not in context. How much easier it would be if in question *o*, for example, you were to be confronted with "intrepid explorer," instead of merely "intrepid"!

2. The choices offered usually contain traps for the unwary. There are two principal ways in which you may be misled:

a. Related but Inexact Definitions. Example 1: in question *e*, the student who is careless in his thinking may hastily select "overflow" as the answer because he may associate it with "turbulence." True, "turbulence" may be present when there is an "overflow," but "overflow" does not mean "turbulence." The answer is "commotion."

Example 2: In question *a*, "angry" and "daring" are related to the correct definition because they suggest reasons for which a person may be considered "obnoxious," but only "objectionable" is an exact synonym.

These two examples should convince you that, even if you know the meaning of the test word, you may sometimes choose the wrong synonym. You must carefully weigh each alternative and select the one "that most nearly expresses the meaning," as the directions state.

b. Sound Traps. Example 1: In question *n*, students may be trapped into choosing "profitable" as the synonym for "ludicrous." Why? The explanation is that the "lu" and "cr" of "ludicrous" may beguile them into thinking of "lucrative," which means "profitable." The correct answer is "ridiculous." Beware of sound traps!

Example 2: In question *g*, students may select "supplement." Why? They may be misled by the sound "ad" in "adage." This may prompt them to choose "supplement," on the reasoning that a supplement is something added. The correct synonym is "proverb." The vocabulary test is rife with such subtle sound traps.

Caution: Do not conclude from the foregoing that a similarity in sound is necessarily a trap. Notice that the synonym for "*ob*noxious" in question *a* is "*ob*jectionable," and the synonym for "hypoth*etical*" in question *j* is "theor*etical*."

HOW TO CHOOSE THE CORRECT SYNONYM

1. Since the test words are presented without context, your first step should be to *recall a context in which you have seen or heard or used the word.* Examples:

A court stenographer makes a *verbatim* (question *b*) account of testimony.
We had to *defer* (question *f*) our picnic to next Sunday.
Who knows what will *ensue* (question *h*) next?

2. Be precise. A related or approximate definition will not do. Make sure that your choice "most nearly expresses the meaning" of the test word. (See 2*a*, page 3.)

3. Should you find that a word is completely unfamiliar to you, try breaking it down into its component parts—prefix, root, and suffix. This is discussed in the pages that follow.

PREFIXES, ROOTS, SUFFIXES

You should memorize the meanings of common prefixes, roots, and suffixes because they form countless words in our language. Notice how a knowledge of prefixes, roots, and suffixes can help you to answer these typical Regents vocabulary questions:

QUESTION 1: *revocation* .... (1) certificate   (2) repeal   (3) animation   (4) license   (5) plea
ANSWER: repeal
EXPLANATION: *revocation* contains the following:

re—a prefix meaning "back"
vocat—a root meaning "call"
ion—a suffix meaning "act or result of"

Therefore, *revocation* means "act or result of calling back," or *repeal*.

QUESTION 2: *loquacious* .... (1) grim   (2) stern   (3) talka-
tive   (4) lighthearted   (5) liberty-loving
ANSWER: talkative
EXPLANATION: *loquacious* contains the following:

loqu—a root meaning "talk"
ous—a suffix meaning "full of"

Therefore, *loquacious* means "full of talk," or *talkative*.

LATIN PREFIXES

PREFIX	MEANING	SAMPLE WORDS
a, ab	away, from	avert, abduct
ad	to	adhere
ante	before	anteroom
bi	two	bicycle
circum	around	circumnavigate
com (con, col, etc.)	together	compete, convoke, collect
contra	against	contradict
de	from	deduce
dis	apart	disperse
e, ex	out	emit, expel
extra	beyond	extraordinary
in	not, in, into	insignificant, invade
inter	between	interrupt
intra	within	intramural
ob	against	object
per	through, thoroughly	permeate, perfection
post	after	postwar
pre	before	predict
pro	forward	progress
re	again, back	reprint, recall
retro	backward	retrospect
semi	half	semicivilized
sub	under	submerge
super	above	supernatural
trans	across	transcontinental
ultra	beyond, excessively	ultraconservative

LATIN ROOTS

ROOT	MEANING	SAMPLE WORDS
ag, act	do	agent, react
cad, cas	fall	cadence, casualty
cap, cept	take, hold	capture, receptacle
ced, cess	go	secede, procession
cid, cis	kill, cut	suicide, incision
cred, credit	believe	incredible, creditor
cur(r), curs	run	current, cursory
dict	say	predict
duc, duct	lead	reduce, conduct
fact	make	manufacture
fer	carry	ferry
flect, flex	bend	deflect, inflexible
grad, gress	go, step	graduate, progress
ject	throw	projectile
junct	join	junction
leg, lect	choose, read	legible, select
loqu, locut	speak, talk	loquacious, elocution
mit(t), miss	send	remit, mission
mov, mot, mob	move	remove, promote, mobile
ped	foot	pedestrian
pel(l), puls	drive	expel, repulse
pend, pens	hang	pendant, suspense
pon, posit	put	exponent, position
port	carry	transport
rupt	break	eruption
scrib, script	write	inscribe, manuscript
sequ, secut	follow	sequel, consecutive
spect	look	retrospect
sta	stand	stationary
tang, tact	touch	tangible, intact
termin	end	terminal
tract	drag, draw	extract
ven, vent	come	convene, advent
vid, vis	see	provident, vision
vinc, vict	conquer	invincible, victory
voc, vocat	call	vocal, vocation
volv, volut	roll, turn	revolve, evolution

EXERCISE A

Each of the italicized words below is made up of a prefix and a root discussed previously. Define each word and then check your definitions with the dictionary.

1. a *circumspect* person
2. Don't *involve* me.
3. an *abject* beggar
4. *Repel* the attack.
5. a *disruptive* force

6. to *intercede* in a quarrel
7. an *eloquent* speaker
8. *Eject* that rowdy.
9. an *incisive* reply
10. a vicious *obloquy*

EXERCISE B

Construct word families (at least five words to a family) with each of the following roots. Then check your results with the dictionary. Example:

ag, act (do): agent, actor, inactive, agency, transaction

1. cap, cept (take)
2. cur(r), curs (run)
3. duc, duct (lead)
4. mit(t), miss (send)
5. mov, mot, mob (move)

6. ped (foot)
7. pel(l), puls (drive)
8. port (carry)
9. scrib, script (write)
10. vid, vis (see)

GREEK PREFIXES AND ROOTS

PREFIX OR ROOT	MEANING	SAMPLE WORDS
a, an	not, without	atheist, anonymous
anthropo	man	anthropology
anti	against	antislavery
astro	star	astronomer
auto	self	autobiography
biblio	book	bibliography
bio	life	biology
chromo, chromato	color	chromophotography, polychromatic
chrono	time	chronology
cosmo	world	cosmopolitan
cracy	government	bureaucracy
demo	people	democracy
eu	well, good	eulogize, euphony

PREFIX OR ROOT	MEANING	SAMPLE WORDS
geo	earth	geography
graph	write	telegraph
hydro	water	hydrosulfuric
hyper	excessively	hypercritical
log	word, speech	dialog
logy	science	biology
meter	measure	perimeter
micro	small	microfilm
mono	one	monolog
onym	name	pseudonym
pan	all	Pan-American
patho	suffering, disease	pathology
peri	around, about	periphery
phil, phile, philo	love	philately, Anglophile, philosophy
phobe, phobia	fear	Anglophobe, claustrophobia
phone, phono	sound	telephone, phonograph
poly	many	polygon
pseudo	false	pseudonym
psycho	mind	psychology
scope	see	periscope
soph	wisdom	sophisticated
syn, sym	with	synchronize, symphony
tele	far off	television
theo	God	theology
thermo	heat	thermonuclear

EXERCISE C

Test your skill. First define each word below, using your knowledge of Greek prefixes and roots. (Each of the words has two such components.) Then check your definitions with the dictionary.

1. monolog
2. psychology
3. perimeter
4. democracy
5. anonymous
6. bibliophile
7. hydrophobia
8. monotheism
9. geology
10. philanthropy

SUFFIXES

SUFFIX	MEANING	SAMPLE WORDS
-able, -ible	capable of being	lovable, visible
-ance, -ence, -cy, -ty	act of or state of being	appearance, independence, infancy, generosity
-ary, -ic, -ical	having to do with	revolutionary, rustic, musical
-ate, -ize, -fy	to make	liberate, pauperize, magnify
-er, -or, -ant, -ent, -ian, -ist	one who	teacher, donor, servant, resident, comedian, pianist
-ion, -age, -(a)tion, -ment	act or result of	union, marriage, conversation, judgment
-ish, -like	resembling a	clownish, childlike
-less	without	senseless
-ous, -y	full of	perilous, risky
-ship	office, skill	kingship, penmanship

EXERCISE D

In this final exercise, make use of your knowledge of suffixes, as well as of prefixes and roots. Define each of the following words by giving the meaning of each of its component parts. Then check your results with the dictionary.

Example: The word "eruption" is made up of "e" (out), "rupt" (break), and "ion" (act of). It means "the act of breaking out."

1. incredible
2. convocation
3. porter
4. terminate
5. psychologist
6. victor
7. inscription
8. psychopathic
9. visualize
10. polychromatic

HOW TO BUILD A GOOD VOCABULARY

The New York State Education Department sums up some of the best thinking on this question when it recommends *wide reading* plus *the dictionary habit* as the principal methods for vocabulary expansion.

1. Wide Reading. As you read for pleasure or information in literary works and good newspapers or magazines, you encounter unfamiliar words. Many of these you may be able to define by using the two methods we have already discussed:

a. Using the Context. This means getting the definition of a strange word from the words that surround it (the context).

b. Using Word Analysis. This is the process of getting the meaning of the unfamiliar word by breaking it down into its component parts (prefix, root, suffix).

2. The Dictionary Habit. There will, of course, be many words that will yield to neither of the above methods; in these cases you must refer to the dictionary. By all means develop the habit of consulting the dictionary. In later years you will come to realize that few habits are so important and rewarding.

a. Purchasing a Dictionary. It is imperative that you own a good desk dictionary. The New York State Education Department offers this list of desk dictionaries, arranged alphabetically, without indication as to relative merit. You may be able to inspect these in your school or public library before you buy one.

DESK DICTIONARIES

The American College Dictionary. Random House.

Funk & Wagnalls New College Standard Dictionary. Funk & Wagnalls.

Thorndike-Barnhart High School Dictionary. Scott, Foresman.

Webster's New Collegiate Dictionary. G. & C. Merriam.

The Winston Dictionary; Advanced Edition. Holt, Rinehart, & Winston.

b. Emphasis on Using New Words. Don't make the mistake of looking up a new word, putting its meaning down in your vocabulary notebook, and then letting it go at that! You will never make much progress in word power if that is all you do. You must consciously, deliberately, *use* the new word in your speaking and writing. Make it a point to *use* new vocabulary as soon as possible in appropriate situations—in chats with friends, in classroom discussions, in letters and compositions you write. If a new word remains unused in your vocabulary notebook, it is soon forgotten; only by "exercising" the new word will you succeed in making it part of your active vocabulary.

c. Differentiating Commonly Confused Words. In the following pairs of words, one is frequently mistaken for the other. Eliminate the confusion by looking up the meaning of each of these words and using it in a complete (written) sentence:

1. soliloquy, monolog
2. allusion, illusion
3. continual, continuous
4. libel, slander
5. effect, affect
6. hypercritical, hypocritical
7. ingenious, ingenuous
8. notorious, famous
9. respectfully, respectively
10. translucent, transparent

d. Tracing Word Histories. This can be one of the most fascinating ways of building your vocabulary. Do you know, for example, that "boycott" was actually the name of an Irish land agent, Captain Charles C. Boycott? Because he refused to lower the rents and evicted many tenants, the inhabitants organized a campaign of retaliation. They would have no dealings with him, and they prevented him from dealing with anyone, even to purchase food. Since that time (1880), to "boycott" has meant to follow a policy of refusing to deal in any way (with a person, group, or nation) as a punitive measure.

Using an unabridged dictionary, record in your notebook the original meaning of the following words:

1. ambition
2. assassin
3. belfry
4. bonfire
5. candidate
6. chapel
7. congregation
8. curfew
9. neighbor
10. tantalize

VOCABULARY NOTEBOOK EXERCISE

In your notebook write (1) the definition and (2) a short illustrative sentence for each of the words in the list below. Check your definitions with the dictionary. Arrange your notebook as follows:

WORD	DEFINITION	ILLUSTRATIVE SENTENCE
onslaught	attack	The enemy began a massive *onslaught*.
impartial	just	A judge should be *impartial*.
import	meaning	I did not get the *import* of your remark.

1. fictitious
2. proximity
3. siphon
4. placid
5. intern
6. fluctuate
7. dilemma
8. writhe
9. rudiment
10. invariable
11. consensus
12. annals

13. prerogative
14. pensive
15. allot
16. impeach
17. glib
18. prevaricate
19. utilitarian
20. jargon
21. condole

22. chaotic
23. irate
24. appraisal
25. insurgent
26. tremulous
27. celerity
28. facade
29. scrutinize
30. dexterous

31. cardiac
32. instigate
33. rescind
34. maudlin
35. volition
36. immunity
37. posterity
38. arrogance
39. enmesh

40. vivacious
41. deft
42. coalition
43. prudent
44. garrulous
45. genial
46. evasive
47. pomp
48. jostle

MATCHING TESTS IN VOCABULARY

Match the vocabulary words in column *A* with their definitions in column *B*.

1

Column A
a. traditional
b. compulsion
c. sinister
d. nullify
e. longevity
f. surveillance
g. rendition
h. permeate
i. innocuous
j. incarcerate

Column B
1. imprison
2. penetrate
3. close watch
4. force
5. customary
6. destroy
7. interpretation
8. long life
9. harmless
10. evil

2

Column A
a. inflexible
b. salvage
c. succumb
d. precision
e. cult
f. integrity
g. docile
h. relentless
i. consternation
j. commend

Column B
1. stern
2. dismay
3. unyielding
4. praise
5. save
6. honesty
7. yield
8. accuracy
9. obedient
10. sect

3

Column A	Column B
a. ethics	1. customers
b. zealousness	2. exaggeration
c. clientele	3. destructive
d. chronology	4. earnestness
e. articulation	5. fixed idea
f. autocratic	6. moral principles
g. obsession	7. time sequence
h. vestige	8. enunciation
i. hyperbole	9. trace
j. subversive	10. dictatorial

4

Column A	Column B
a. deteriorate	1. doctrine
b. adolescent	2. frank
c. antagonist	3. weaken
d. dilute	4. agree
e. abridge	5. shorten
f. candid	6. youthful
g. concur	7. sagacity
h. capitulate	8. opponent
i. dogma	9. surrender
j. acumen	10. depreciate

5

Column A	Column B
a. melancholy	1. suffocation
b. vogue	2. fashion
c. massive	3. universe
d. asphyxia	4. elastic
e. accelerate	5. pithy saying
f. cosmos	6. quicken
g. epigram	7. gloomy
h. prophylactic	8. weighty
i. loquacious	9. voluble
j. resilient	10. preventive

6

Column A	Column B
a. felony	1. departure
b. decoy	2. crime
c. dazing	3. grip
d. enthusiastic	4. ardent
e. grapple	5. wickedness
f. aggravate	6. understand
g. exodus	7. intensify
h. fathom	8. stunning
i. laconic	9. lure
j. iniquity	10. concise

7

Column A	Column B
a. skepticism	1. compute
b. detour	2. doubt
c. callous	3. spying
d. calculate	4. boundless
e. espionage	5. assumption
f. amalgamate	6. spice
g. hypothesis	7. coax
h. incalculable	8. go around
i. cajole	9. unfeeling
j. condiment	10. unite

8

Column A	Column B
a. guile	1. inactive
b. dormant	2. flood
c. proxy	3. skillful
d. aptitude	4. approach
e. deluge	5. group of voters
f. fortitude	6. agent
g. sheath	7. deceit
h. electorate	8. pluck
i. approximation	9. scabbard
j. adroit	10. ability

9

Column A	Column B
a. affiliate	1. unruffled
b. deflate	2. industrial magnate
c. nonchalant	3. associate
d. desperate	4. bottle
e. tycoon	5. rash
f. caustic	6. askew
g. cache	7. hiding place
h. astute	8. shrewd
i. awry	9. stinging
j. cruet	10. reduce

FORMER REGENTS QUESTIONS

Write the **number** of the word or expression that most nearly expresses the meaning of the italicized word.   [10]

[Illustration: *sadden*—(1) cheer   (2) turn back   (3) make unhappy   (4) refuse   (5) welcome   . . 3 . .]

1

a. foil . . . . (1) defeat   (2) punish   (3) accuse   (4) pray   (5) return

b. prevalent . . . . . (1) brilliant   (2) mediocre   (3) previous   (4) occurring often   (5) occurring seldom

c. contemplate . . . (1) recall   (2) consider   (3) respect   (4) commit   (5) distribute

d. crystallize . . . . (1) overwhelm completely   (2) lead to confusion   (3) assume definite form   (4) blame   (5) glamorize

e. sorcery . . . . (1) ancestry   (2) grief   (3) acidity   (4) filth   (5) witchcraft

f. retrospect . . . . (1) withdrawal   (2) review of the past   (3) very severe punishment   (4) prediction   (5) self-examination

g. veneer . . . . (1) respect   (2) arrival   (3) poison   (4) summons   (5) gloss

h. subsidize . . . . . (1) store for later use   (2) aid with public money   (3) place under military control   (4) check   (5) ridicule in public

i. ominous . . . . . . (1) devouring everything   (2) all-inclusive   (3) having two meanings   (4) foreboding   (5) vegetable

j. inadvertently . . (1) actually   (2) harmlessly   (3) heedlessly   (4) angrily   (5) confidently

2

a. authorize . . . . . (1) compose   (2) self-educate   (3) permit   (4) manage   (5) complicate

b. versatile . . . . . . (1) imaginative   (2) many-sided   (3) proud   (4) upright   (5) self-centered

c. *opportune* ....(1) self-confident   (2) rare   (3) frequent   (4) timely (5) contrasting

d. *inconsistent* ...(1) insane   (2) senatorial   (3) undeviating   (4) contradictory   (5) faithful

e. *acrid* ....(1) agricultural   (2) athletic   (3) extremely tasty (4) fierce   (5) bitterly irritating

f. *futility* ....(1) loyalty   (2) evil   (3) faith   (4) hatred   (5) uselessness

g. *metaphor* .....(1) unrhymed poetry   (2) change of structure   (3) part of a foot   (4) implied comparison   (5) signal light

h. *static* ....(1) not moving   (2) referring to the state   (3) itemized (4) clear   (5) pointed

i. *tentative* .....(1) formal   (2) experimental   (3) affectionate   (4) tight (5) progressive

j. *forestall* ......(1) dispossess   (2) overshadow   (3) anticipate   (4) establish   (5) prepare

3

a. *designate* .....(1) draw   (2) expel   (3) permit   (4) name   (5) repeat

b. *bipartisan* ....(1) adhering to views of one party   (2) prejudiced (3) representing two parties   (4) bisected   (5) narrow

c. *fervor* ....(1) artistic ability   (2) hatred   (3) kindness   (4) intense feeling   (5) coldness

d. *elusive* ....(1) helpful   (2) baffling   (3) abundant   (4) lessening (5) expanding

e. *exploit* ....(1) utilize   (2) favor   (3) expel   (4) pool   (5) labor

f. *anecdote* .....(1) equipment   (2) remedy for poison   (3) brief narrative   (4) inquiry   (5) hysteria

g. *usurp* ....(1) seize by force   (2) accompany   (3) become useful (4) move cityward   (5) return

h. *wily* ....(1) stubborn   (2) graceful   (3) nervous   (4) insignificant   (5) crafty

i. *nomenclature* ..(1) election   (2) system of names   (3) morality (4) grammar   (5) migration

j. *acquiesce* .....(1) provide   (2) share   (3) climb   (4) submit (5) proceed

4

a. *crucial* ....(1) technical   (2) decisive   (3) ill-natured   (4) inelegant   (5) greatly distorted

b. *implicate* .....(1) please   (2) expect   (3) involve   (4) trick (5) ambush

c. *domestic* .....(1) internal   (2) alien   (3) untrained   (4) political (5) beneficial

d. *audacious* ....(1) daring   (2) fearful   (3) indifferent   (4) attentive (5) wicked

e. *buoyant* ......(1) unwise   (2) cheerful   (3) alarming   (4) uncertain (5) juvenile

f. *gaunt* ....(1) stiff   (2) white   (3) repulsive   (4) harsh-sounding (5) lean

g. *phobia* .... (1) temper   (2) disease   (3) puzzle   (4) dream
(5) fear

h. *diversity* ..... (1) amusement   (2) discouragement   (3) variety   (4) mistrust   (5) confusion

i. *presumptuous* .. (1) forward   (2) foreshadowing   (3) costly   (4) renewable   (5) unhealthful

j. *enigmatic* .... (1) sarcastic   (2) skillful   (3) puzzling   (4) healthy
(5) like an insect

5

a. *dwindle* ...... (1) hang loosely   (2) deceive   (3) fight   (4) share
(5) decrease

b. *forthright* .... (1) direct   (2) constitutional   (3) unpleasant   (4) polite
(5) accidental

c. *vigilant* ...... (1) forceful   (2) immoral   (3) alert   (4) sightless
(5) many-sided

d. *confirmation* .. (1) trust   (2) suspense   (3) encounter   (4) restraint
(5) proof

e. *prevail* .... (1) introduce   (2) misjudge   (3) rescue   (4) triumph
(5) overestimate

f. *aloof* .... (1) hard   (2) imaginary   (3) reserved   (4) happy
(5) willing

g. *unscrupulous* .. (1) unprincipled   (2) unbalanced   (3) careless   (4) disfigured   (5) obstinate

h. *profound* ..... (1) deep   (2) disrespectful   (3) plentiful   (4) positive
(5) expert

i. *pretext* .... (1) argument   (2) excuse   (3) preliminary examination
(4) first glimpse   (5) sermon

j. *infer* .... (1) surprise   (2) hope   (3) disagree   (4) conclude
(5) shift quickly

6

a. *controversial* .. (1) faultfinding   (2) pleasant   (3) debatable   (4) ugly
(5) talkative

b. *ghastly* .... (1) hasty   (2) furious   (3) breathless   (4) deathlike
(5) spiritual

c. *belligerent* .... (1) worldly   (2) warlike   (3) loudmouthed   (4) furious
(5) artistic

d. *proficiency* .... (1) wisdom   (2) oversupply   (3) expertness   (4) advancement   (5) sincerity

e. *compassion* ... (1) rage   (2) strength of character   (3) forcefulness
(4) sympathy   (5) uniformity

f. *dissension* .... (1) treatise   (2) pretense   (3) fear   (4) lineage
(5) discord

g. *intimate* ...... (1) charm   (2) hint   (3) disguise   (4) frighten
(5) hum

h. *berate* .... (1) classify   (2) scold   (3) underestimate   (4) take
one's time   (5) evaluate

i. *dearth* .... (1) scarcity   (2) width   (3) affection   (4) wealth
(5) warmth

j. *meditate* ..... (1) rest   (2) stare   (3) doze   (4) make peace
(5) reflect

7

a. *bondage* ......(1) poverty   (2) redemption   (3) slavery   (4) retirement   (5) complaint

b. *agility* ....(1) wisdom   (2) nimbleness   (3) agreeableness   (4) simplicity   (5) excitement

c. *abdicate* .....(1) achieve   (2) protest   (3) renounce   (4) demand   (5) steal

d. *stifle* ....(1) talk nonsense   (2) sidestep   (3) depress   (4) smother   (5) stick

e. *edict* ....(1) abbreviation   (2) lie   (3) carbon copy   (4) correction   (5) decree

f. *amity* ....(1) ill will   (2) hope   (3) pity   (4) friendship   (5) pleasure

g. *coercion* ......(1) force   (2) disgust   (3) suspicion   (4) pleasure   (5) criticism

h. *abash* ....(1) embarrass   (2) encourage   (3) punish   (4) surrender   (5) overthrow

i. *taciturn* ......(1) weak   (2) evil   (3) tender   (4) silent   (5) sensitive

j. *remiss* ....(1) memorable   (2) neglectful   (3) useless   (4) prompt   (5) exact

8

a. *stagnant* .....(1) inactive   (2) alert   (3) selfish   (4) difficult   (5) scornful

b. *mandatory* ....(1) insane   (2) obligatory   (3) evident   (4) strategic   (5) unequaled

c. *infernal* ......(1) immodest   (2) incomplete   (3) domestic   (4) second-rate   (5) fiendish

d. *exonerate* ....(1) free from blame   (2) warn   (3) drive out   (4) overcharge   (5) plead

e. *arbiter* ....(1) friend   (2) judge   (3) drug   (4) tree surgeon   (5) truant

f. *enmity* ....(1) boredom   (2) puzzle   (3) offensive language   (4) ill will   (5) entanglement

g. *discriminate* ..(1) fail   (2) delay   (3) accuse   (4) distinguish   (5) reject

h. *derision* ......(1) disgust   (2) ridicule   (3) fear   (4) anger   (5) heredity

i. *exultant* ......(1) essential   (2) elated   (3) praiseworthy   (4) plentiful   (5) high-priced

j. *ostensible* ....(1) vibrating   (2) odd   (3) apparent   (4) standard   (5) ornate

9

a. *abhor* ....(1) hate   (2) admire   (3) taste   (4) skip   (5) resign

b. *dutiful* ....(1) lasting   (2) sluggish   (3) required   (4) soothing   (5) obedient

c. *zealot* ....(1) breeze   (2) enthusiast   (3) vault   (4) wild animal   (5) musical instrument

d. *magnanimous*   (1) high-minded   (2) faithful   (3) concerned   (4) individual   (5) small

e. *cite* ....(1) protest   (2) depart   (3) quote   (4) agitate   (5) perform

f. *oblivion* ......(1) hindrance   (2) accident   (3) courtesy   (4) forgetfulness   (5) old age

g. *cardinal* ......(1) independent   (2) well-organized   (3) subordinate   (4) dignified   (5) chief

h. *deplete* ......(1) restrain   (2) corrupt   (3) despair   (4) exhaust   (5) spread out

i. *supersede* ....(1) retire   (2) replace   (3) overflow   (4) bless   (5) oversee

j. *sporadic* ......(1) bad-tempered   (2) infrequent   (3) radical   (4) reckless   (5) humble

10

a. *neutralize* ....(1) entangle   (2) strengthen   (3) counteract   (4) combat   (5) converse

b. *insinuate* .....(1) destroy   (2) hint   (3) do wrong   (4) accuse   (5) release

c. *diminutive* ....(1) proud   (2) slow   (3) small   (4) watery   (5) puzzling

d. *plight* ....(1) departure   (2) weight   (3) conspiracy   (4) predicament   (5) stamp

e. *illicit* ....(1) unlawful   (2) overpowering   (3) ill-advised   (4) small-scale   (5) unreadable

f. *benign* ....(1) contagious   (2) fatal   (3) ignorant   (4) kindly   (5) decorative

g. *reverie* ....(1) abusive language   (2) love song   (3) backward step   (4) daydream   (5) holy man

h. *apprehensive* ..(1) quiet   (2) firm   (3) curious   (4) sincere   (5) fearful

i. *recoil* ....(1) shrink   (2) attract   (3) electrify   (4) adjust   (5) enroll

j. *guise* ....(1) trickery   (2) request   (3) innocence   (4) misdeed   (5) appearance

Chapter 2

THE SPELLING TEST (QUESTION 2)

THE IMPORTANCE OF SPELLING

If you think that spelling is not too important because the spelling test (question 2) is usually worth only five points, you are making a serious mistake. Don't forget that your spelling is tested also in your composition and discussion-type literature answers, which together are worth fifty points. When you receive your test paper, you will notice the following statement on page 1 in bold type:

"No paper seriously deficient in English composition will be accepted for Regents credit."

One of the reasons for which the examiners may consider your paper "seriously deficient in English composition" is a marked spelling deficiency.

Looking beyond the examination, you will find that in your career as a student, and later in your social and business activities, the ability to spell correctly will spare you needless pain and embarrassment and earn you respect.

TYPICAL REGENTS SPELLING TEST

The Regents spelling test measures your ability to recognize misspelled words and to rewrite them correctly. Try this typical test. Then check your spellings with the correct ones on the lines at the right.

JANUARY 1961

In each of the following, (1) through (10), only one of the words is misspelled. In *each* case spell correctly on the line at the right the misspelled word.   [5]

(1) argueing, baggy, contagious, knives, shepherd   (1) arguing

(2) civillian, primeval, uncanny, trigonometry, be-
witches . . . .   (2) civilian

(3) thousandth, unreleived, canine, vengeful, obit-
uary . . . . (3) unrelieved

(4) dissapprove, apologetic, truancy, theologian,
statuesque . . . . (4) disapprove

(5) cadence, millinery, lonliness, caramel, burglar-
ize . . . . (5) loneliness

(6) perpetuate, colleague, familiar, mannerism,
ajournment . . . . (6) adjournment

(7) publicity, promontory, bureaucracy, patriarch,
sacrafice . . . . (7) sacrifice

(8) abandonment, righteous, wiry, critisize, use-
fulness . . . . (8) criticize

(9) loosely, breakage, symtom, angrily, bridle . . . . (9) symptom

(10) vindictive, satchel, transferable, preliminary,
obstinite . . . . (10) obstinate

ANALYSIS OF THE SPELLING TEST

The words misspelled in the test above fall into these categories:

a. **Some words conform to spelling rules. Examples:**

QUESTION 1: argueing, baggy, contagious, knives, shepherd
   ANSWER: arguing
     RULE: Drop silent *e* before a suffix starting with a vowel. (See
top of page 25, rule 1.)

QUESTION 2: civillian, primeval, uncanny, trigonometry, bewitches
   ANSWER: civilian
     RULE: Do not add a letter when attaching a suffix. (See page 27,
rule 2.)

QUESTION 3: thousandth, unreleived, canine, vengeful, obituary
   ANSWER: unrelieved
     RULE: Write *i* before *e*, except after *c*. (See page 23, *ie* and *ei*
rules.)

QUESTION 4: dissapprove, apologetic, truancy, theologian, statuesque
   ANSWER: disapprove
     RULE: Do not add a letter when attaching a prefix. (See top of
page 27, rule 1.)

QUESTION 5: cadence, millinery, lonliness, caramel, burglarize
   ANSWER: loneliness
     RULE: Keep silent *e* before a suffix starting with a consonant. (See page 25, rule 2.)

NOTE:

lone + *ly* = *lonely* (Silent *e* is kept.)
lonely + *ness* = *loneliness* (See page 24, rule 1.)

b. **Some words are misspelled because they are carelessly pronounced.** (See page 30.)

QUESTION 9: loosely, breakage, symtom, angrily, bridle
   ANSWER: symptom

c. **Some words are difficult to spell because they contain a silent letter.** (See page 31.)

QUESTION 6: perpetuate, colleague, familiar, mannerism, ajournment
   ANSWER: adjournment

d. **Some words present individual difficulties and require special study.** (See the spelling lists on pages 33-36.)

QUESTION 7: publicity, promontory, bureaucracy, patriarch, sacrafice
   ANSWER: sacrifice

QUESTION 8: abandonment, righteous, wiry, critisize, usefulness
   ANSWER: criticize

QUESTION 10: vindictive, satchel, transferable, preliminary, obstinite
   ANSWER: obstinate

HOW TO IMPROVE SPELLING

In this chapter we will discuss five ways to improve spelling:

      A. Use Spelling Rules
      B. Pronounce Words Correctly
      C. Use Step-by-Step Drill
      D. Use Mnemonic Devices
      E. Study Spelling Lists

A. USE SPELLING RULES

Here is a quick review of some helpful spelling rules. Notice that they fall into these groups: rules for spelling a sound, lengthening words, forming contractions, forming plurals, forming possessives.

RULES FOR SPELLING A SOUND

1. The *-ful* rule

The sound *full* at the end of a word is spelled with only one *l*. Examples: careful, graceful, healthful, hopeful, teaspoonful, etc.
Exception: the word *full* itself.

2. The *-ceed* or *-cede* rule

There are only three verbs in the English language ending in *-ceed*. All other verbs with that sound end in *-cede*.

-ceed: succeed, proceed, exceed
-cede: secede, recede, intercede, concede, accede, cede, precede, antecede

Exception: super*sede*. This is the only verb ending in *-sede*.

3. The *ie* and *ei* rules

To help you to recognize when *i* comes before *e* (believe, relief, grief) and when *e* comes before *i* (receive, deceit, receipt), master the following rule and its exceptions:

Write *i* before *e*

(Examples: achieve, belief, brief, chief, fiend, fierce, grief, piece, shriek, siege, yield, etc.)

Except after *c*

(After *c*, the rule is reversed; we write *e* before *i*. Examples: ceiling, conceit, conceive, deceit, deceive, perceive, receipt, receive, etc.)

Or when sounded like *ay*
As in *neighbor* or *weigh*.

(In such cases, too, we write *e* before *i*. Examples: freight, reign, sleigh, vein, weight, etc.)

Master these seven common exceptions, each of which has *e* before *i*: either, neither, foreigner, height, leisure, seize, weird.

Rules for Lengthening Words

Let us briefly review what is meant by *vowels* and *consonants*, since we shall be using these terms frequently in the rules that follow.

Vowels are the letters *a, e, i, o,* and *u.* All the other letters of the alphabet are called *consonants*.

1. Lengthening words ending in *y*

Rule 1: If there is a consonant before the *y*, change *y* to *i* before adding a suffix (*-ed, -er, -est, -ful, -ness, -less,* etc.).

hurry—hurried	pity—pitiful
silly—sillier	heavy—heaviness
icy—iciest	mercy—merciless

Exception 1: Except before *-ing*.

hurry—hurrying	pity—pitying
try—trying	worry—worrying

Exception 2: Learn these special exceptions:

dry—dryness, dryly	baby—babyish
shy—shyness, shyly	lady—ladylike

Rule 2: If there is a vowel before the *y*, do not change the *y* before adding a suffix.

joy—joyful	annoy—annoying
allay—allayed	obey—obeyed
convey—conveying	stray—straying

Exceptions:

say—said	lay—laid
day—daily	pay—paid

2. Lengthening words ending in *c* when adding *ed, er, ing,* or *y*

Rule: Insert a *k* after the *c* (to keep the *c* from being pronounced as *s*).

picnic—picnicked, picnicking, picnicker
mimic—mimicked, mimicking
frolic—frolicked, frolicking
traffic—trafficked, trafficking
panic—panicked, panicky

3. Lengthening words ending in silent *e*

Rule 1: Drop silent *e* before a suffix starting with a vowel.

love—lovable, loving	move—movable, moving
shape—shaping	force—forcible, forcing
use—using, usage	write—writing

Exception 1: Words ending in *ce* and *ge* keep the final *e* before a suffix beginning with *a* or *o*.

notice—noticeable	advantage—advantageous
service—serviceable	courage—courageous
manage—manageable	outrage—outrageous

Exception 2:

canoe—canoeing	acre—acreage
hoe—hoeing	mile—mileage
shoe—shoeing	singe—singeing

Rule 2: Keep silent *e* before a suffix starting with a consonant.

arrange—arrangement	fierce—fiercely, fierceness
care—careful, careless	nine—nineteen, ninety

Exceptions:

acknowledge—acknowl-edgment	argue—argument
due—duly	true—truly
awe—awful	nine—ninth
judge—judgment	whole—wholly

4. Doubling final consonants when lengthening words

Rule 1: Double a final consonant in a one-syllable word before a suffix beginning with a vowel.

```
stop—stopped, stopping, stopper
run—running, runner
hit—hitting, hitter
plan—planned, planning, planner
wet—wetter, wettest, wetting
slip—slipped, slipping, slipper, slippery
```

Exception 1: If the final consonant is preceded by two vowels, do not double it.

>   sail—sailed, sailing
>   kneel—kneeled, kneeling

Exception 2: If the final consonant is preceded by another consonant, no doubling occurs.

>   halt—halted, halting
>   talk—talked, talking

Rule 2: Double a final consonant in an *accented* syllable at the end of a word of two or more syllables before a suffix beginning with a vowel.

>   refer′—referred, referring, referral
>   compel′—compelled, compelling
>   recur′—recurred, recurring, recurrence
>   regret′—regretted, regretting, regrettable
>   commit′—committed, committing, committee

Note: The rule does not apply when the final consonant is in an *unaccented* syllable.

>   cred′it—credited, crediting, creditor
>   deb′it—debited, debiting
>   lim′it—limited, limiting
>   of′fer—offered, offering, offerer
>   gal′lop—galloped, galloping

Exception 1: The rule does not apply when the consonant is preceded by two vowels.

>   contain—contained, containing, container
>   recoil—recoiled, recoiling
>   appeal—appealed, appealing
>   curtail—curtailed, curtailing
>   abstain—abstained, abstaining, abstainer

Exception 2: The rule does not apply when the consonant is preceded by another consonant.

>   enlist—enlisted, enlisting
>   condemn—condemned, condemning, condemnable
>   conduct—conducted, conducting, conductance

5. Lengthening words by prefixes or suffixes

Rule 1: Do not omit or add a letter when attaching a prefix to a word. Keep all the letters of the prefix and all the letters of the word.

PREFIX		WORD		LENGTHENED WORD
mis	+	spell	=	misspell
dis	+	satisfy	=	dissatisfy
dis	+	appoint	=	disappoint
un	+	natural	=	unnatural

Rule 2: Do not omit or add a letter when attaching a suffix to a word. Keep all the letters of the word and all the letters of the suffix.

WORD		SUFFIX		LENGTHENED WORD
accidental	+	ly	=	accidentally
barren	+	ness	=	barrenness
final	+	ly	=	finally
allot	+	ment	=	allotment

Exceptions: See the eight exceptions beginning with *acknowledgment* on page 25.

RULE FOR FORMING CONTRACTIONS

Rule: When contracting two words, insert an apostrophe in the space where a letter (or letters) has been lost.

does	+	not	=	doesn't
it	+	is	=	it's
they	+	will	=	they'll
you	+	have	=	you've
I	+	am	=	I'm
we	+	are	=	we're
she	+	would	=	she'd

RULES FOR FORMING PLURALS

1. Most nouns form their plurals by adding *s* or *es* to the singular.

chair—chairs
tree—trees
box—boxes
church—churches

2. The plurals of nouns ending in *y* preceded by a consonant are formed by changing *y* to *i* and adding *es.*

city—cities
liberty—liberties

lady—ladies
prophecy—prophecies

3. The plurals of nouns ending in *y* preceded by a vowel are formed by adding *s.*

essay—essays
monkey—monkeys

journey—journeys
survey—surveys

Exception: words ending in *-quy,* as soliloquy—soliloquies.

4. The plurals of most nouns ending in *o* preceded by a vowel are formed by adding *s.*

cameo—cameos
radio—radios
studio—studios

folio—folios
ratio—ratios
patio—patios

5. The plurals of most nouns ending in *o* preceded by a consonant are formed by adding *es.*

potato—potatoes
tomato—tomatoes
embargo—embargoes
echo—echoes

veto—vetoes
motto—mottoes
Negro—Negroes
hero—heroes

Exceptions: banjos, pianos, solos, sopranos.

6. The plurals of most nouns ending in *f* are formed by adding *s.*

brief—briefs
proof—proofs
belief—beliefs

staff—staffs
sheriff—sheriffs
chief—chiefs

Exceptions: Change *f* or *fe* to *v* and add *es.*

life—lives
knife—knives
leaf—leaves

half—halves
thief—thieves
loaf—loaves

7. A few everyday nouns form their plurals by means of a change in spelling, instead of adding *s* or *es*.

foot—feet	ox—oxen
tooth—teeth	man—men
mouse—mice	woman—women
louse—lice	oasis—oases
child—children	goose—geese

8. A few irregular nouns have the same spelling for the singular as for the plural.

trout	deer
sheep	series
species	moose

9. Hyphenated nouns form their plural by adding *s* to the principal word (*not* to the end of the phrase).

mother-in-law—mothers-in-law
editor-in-chief—editors-in-chief
court-martial—courts-martial

RULES FOR FORMING POSSESSIVES

1. To form the possessive of singular nouns, add an apostrophe and *s*.

SINGULAR NOUNS	POSSESSIVE CASE
boy	boy's hat
friend	friend's book
child	child's toy
James	James's mother

2. To form the possessive of plural nouns ending in *s*, add the apostrophe alone (') after the *s*.

PLURAL NOUNS	POSSESSIVE CASE
girls	girls' lockers
ladies	ladies' dresses
students	students' projects
players	players' averages

3. To form the possessive of plural nouns that do not end in *s*, add the apostrophe and *s*.

PLURAL NOUNS	POSSESSIVE CASE
men	men's clothes
women	women's handbags
mice	mice's tails
sheep	sheep's wool

4. To form the possessive of hyphenated nouns, put the apostrophe and *s* after the last word.

SINGULAR NOUNS	POSSESSIVE CASE
brother-in-law	brother-in-law's
editor-in-chief	editor-in-chief's

Note: Possessive pronouns (*yours, his, hers, its, ours, theirs,* and *whose*) do *not* require an apostrophe.

That boat is *ours* (not *our's*).
That dog is *hers* (not *her's*).
Her hair lost *its* (not *it's*) gloss.
　But:
It's all over. (Here *it's* is correct because it means *it is*, the apostrophe standing for the missing *i*.)

B. PRONOUNCE WORDS CORRECTLY

Careless pronunciation often results in careless spelling. If you have been misspelling any of the words below, it is most likely the result of your leaving out a sound or inserting one that doesn't belong. Form the habit of pronouncing these words correctly (check with the dictionary, if in doubt) and you will have no trouble in spelling them correctly.

Antarctic	February	probably
Arctic	government	recognize
athletics	hindrance	sarsaparilla
candidate	incidentally	surprise
champion	interesting	symptom
chocolate	library	temperature
disastrous	mischievous	visualize

Caution: Sometimes correct pronunciation is not a sure spelling guide, as certain words have a "silent" letter that is not pronounced. Master these spellings:

silent *b:* debt, plumber, subtle
silent *d:* all *adj-* words: adjourn, adjust, etc.
silent *n:* column, hymn, solemn
silent *p:* pneumonia, psychology, receipt
silent *s:* viscount, corps (the *p* is silent too)
silent *t:* bankruptcy, mortgage, wrestle
silent *w:* answer, sword

C. USE STEP-BY-STEP DRILL

When you study a new word, carefully follow this step-by-step method recommended by the New York State Education Department.

1. Pronounce the word. Use it correctly in a sentence.

2. See the word. Say it by syllables. Say the letters in order.

3. Close your eyes and spell the word. Check your spelling to be sure that it is correct.

4. Write the word correctly. Form every letter carefully, especially *i*'s and *e*'s, *a*'s and *o*'s.

5. Cover the word and write it. If the spelling is correct, cover the word and write it again.

6. If you make a mistake during step 5, repeat the previous steps before repeating step 5.

D. USE MNEMONIC DEVICES

A *mnemonic* (the first *m* is silent) device is a trick of association that helps you to remember.

Example: The following mnemonic devices may help you to remember when the correct spelling is *principle* and when it is *principal*. (The associated or similar elements have been italicized.)

1. A princip*le* is a ru*le*.
2. A princi*pal* (the head of a school) ought to be a *pal*.
3. A princip*al* street is a m*a*in street.

When you have unusual difficulty in spelling a word, try to invent a mnemonic device. No matter how farfetched or ridiculous the association may be, if it can help you to spell correctly it is a good mnemonic device. Here are some additional mnemonics that have proved helpful:

WORD	MNEMONIC DEVICE
beginning	the be*ginning* of the *inning*
believe	Don't be*lie*ve that *lie!*
calendar	Janu*ar*y and Febru*ar*y are in the calend*ar*.
friend	a fri*end* to the *end*
parallel	*All* rails are par*all*el.
piece	a *pie*ce of *pie*
privilege	It is a pr*ivi*lege to have two eyes (*i*'s) and a *leg*.
stationary	Station*ar*y means st*a*nding still.
stationery	Station*er*y is writing pap*er*.
there	*There, here, where* all refer to place.
women	*Women* are *wo*(e) to *men!*

SPELLING TEST

Supply the missing letters in the following 50 words:

1. sep — rate	18. am — ng	35. notic — able
2. fug — tive	19. begi — ing	36. courag — ous
3. for — gner	20. gramm — r	37. int — esting
4. def — nition	21. di — appoint	38. poss — ble
5. transfe — ed	22. di — atisfied	39. parti — ular
6. Yours tru —	23. exist — nce	40. stud — ing
7. Yours respect — ly	24. nece — arily	41. practic — y
8. n — ghbor	25. b — siness	42. princip — l
9. ac — demic	26. d — scription	43. princip — e
10. commer — al	27. appear — nce	44. immediat — ly
11. bel — ve	28. re — ommend	45. opin — on
12. commi — ee	29. p — chology	46. occa — ionally
13. conven — nce	30. absolut — y	47. benefi — ed
14. oc — red	31. indef — nitely	48. penn — less
15. privil — ge	32. advis — ble	49. picnic — ing
16. acco — odate	33. forc — ble	50. misch — vous
17. soc — ty	34. servic — ble	

E. STUDY SPELLING LISTS

Spelling lists are a valuable aid because they present words that have proved troublesome to many students. Here are two important lists for you to review and master.

THE ONE HUNDRED SPELLING DEMONS

ache	done	making	they
again	don't	many	though
always	early	meant	through
among	easy	minute	tired
answer	enough	much	tonight
any	every	none	too
been	February	often	trouble
beginning	forty	once	truly
believe	friend	piece	Tuesday
blue	grammar	raise	two
break	guess	read	used
built	half	ready	very
business	having	said	wear
busy	hear	says	Wednesday
buy	heard	seems	week
can't	here	separate	where
choose	hoarse	shoes	whether
color	hour	since	which
coming	instead	some	whole
cough	just	straight	women
could	knew	sugar	won't
country	know	sure	would
dear	laid	tear	write
doctor	loose	their	writing
does	lose	there	wrote

A Regents Preparation Spelling List

The following words were presented in misspelled form on past Regents Examinations. They are reprinted here, correctly spelled, for two reasons: (1) to give you an idea of the level of difficulty of the Regents spelling test, and (2) to acquaint you with an excellent list of useful words carefully selected by the New York State Education Department.

abandoning	anchored	bibliography	cholera
abbreviate	announcement	bicycle	civilian
absence	annual	bigamy	clearance
absolutely	anthology	bituminous	collegiate
abutting	anticipate	blizzard	combustible
academic	antique	bolster	commercial
accessible	apartment	boycotted	committee
accession	apparently	brief	committing
accidentally	appetite	brilliance	comparative
accommodate	apprehension	bulletin	competition
accuracy	appropriation	burglaries	competitors
achievement	approximately		concerning
achieves	aquarium	cafeteria	conclusively
acknowledge	architecture	calendar	condemned
acquaintance	arguing	callous	conferring
acquisition	argument	callus	confidential
adage	ascending	campaign	congressional
adequate	assassination	candidacy	conscious
adjourn	assistance	career	consequently
adjournment	assurance	carnival	conservatory
advantageous	athletic	carriage	constant
advisable	attendants	category	contemptuous
affirmative	authentic	cathedral	controversial
aggravate	auxiliary	caucus	conveyance
aggregate	average	cauliflower	copies
agitation		cavalry	copyright
allotment	balloon	ceiling	cordial
alphabetical	banana	cellophane	coronation
amateur	bankruptcy	cemetery	corridor
ambassador	beneficial	challenge	corrugated
amendment	benefit	chancellor	courageous
anatomy	besieged	changeable	criminal
ancestry	betrayal	chauffeur	criticize

curiosity
cylinder

dazzling
decided
deferred
definite
delegate
delicious
delinquent
description
descriptive
deteriorate
dimension
dirigible
disappeared
disappoint
disapprove
discernible
disciplinary
disease
disillusioned
dispatch
disperse
dissatisfied
dissolve
duped

efficiency
eighth
embarrassment
embassies
emphasis
emphasizes
encourage
engagement
enormous
entrance
envelop
envelope
environment
equipping

evaporate
excellent
excitement
exhaustion
exhibition
existence
expedition
extracurricular
extravagant

fascinate
fatiguing
feasible
feminine
fertile
fervent
fickle
fictitious
fiendish
fierce
filial
forecast
foresight
forfeit
forty-fourth
frostbitten

gallery
gaseous
grateful
grease
guardian

handicapped
handkerchief
handwriting
height
heroes
humiliate
humorists
humorous
hybrid

hypnotize

icing
illegal
illegally
illness
imagine
immaculate
immature
immediately
immovable
inadequate
inconceivable
inconvenience
indebtedness
indefinite
independence
indifferent
influential
information
institute
instrumental
insurance
integrity
intelligible
intensified
interpretation
interrupt
interview
intimate
intriguing

juvenile

kindergarten
kindliness

larceny
lavender
legend
legitimate
liability

lieutenant
literally
loneliness
loyalty
lubricant
lynch

magnificent
maintain
management
marmalade
masterpiece
mattress
medicine
memorandum
merchandise
merely
millionaire
misappropriating
mischievous
misdemeanor
misunderstood
monkeys
municipal
murderer

narrative
neither
nineteenth
ninety
notary
notoriety

obstacles
obstinate
occasion
occupancy
occurrence
offering
omitted
opponents
opportunity

oppression
ordinarily
original
organization
orphaned
overrule
outrageous

pageant
papal
parachute
paradise
paradoxical
parallel
paralysis
parliaments
partially
pedigree
peninsula
pennant
permanent
persevere
phrenologist
physical
physician
pianos
pleasant
poise
politician
porcelain
portiere
possession
poultice
poultry
prairie
precedence
preceding
precipice
predecessor

predominant
prefabricate
prejudice
preliminary
preparation
prevalent
primarily
prisoner
privileges
professional
proficiency
promptness
propaganda
proprietor
purchase

rabid
rearmament
rearrangement
rebellion
rebuttal
reciprocate
recognize
recommendation
reconciliation
recruit
referee
regretting
rehearsal
religious
relinquish
renewal
repetitious
resemblance
responsible
restaurant
rheumatism
rhythm

righteous

sacrifice
salaries
saucy
scenery
schedule
seance
secretarial
seize
senatorial
session
settlement
severity
sieges
similar
sincerity
softening
soliciting
solos
sophisticated
spectacular
spiritualist
sponsor
standard
standardize
statistical
statistics
stunning
submitting
subsidy
successful
suffrage
superb
superintendent
surgeon
surgery
surprising
suspense

symptom

tableaux
tariff
telegram
temperature
tendency
tragedy
tragic
transparent
treachery
tremendous
troupe
truthfulness
tyranny

unbearable
unconscious
undecided
unmanageable
unrelieved
unscheduled
unveiling

vacant
vaccinate
valuable
vegetable
vertical
village
vinegar
virtue
visualize
voluble
volunteer

warrior
whistle
wield

FORMER REGENTS QUESTIONS

In each of the following, (1) through (10), only one of the words is misspelled. In *each* case spell correctly the misspelled word.   [5]

1

(1) strenuous, deceive, salaried, carreer, mislaid
(2) khaki, survival, laboratory, intensefied, stature
(3) tedious, rellinquish, peddle, pasteurize, dissuade
(4) parashute, hiccup, argument, physics, opponent
(5) anesthetic, virtuoso, consecrate, afirmation, alcohol
(6) sophistacated, predisposed, taboo, regimentation, professor
(7) explosive, galery, idol, keynote, confident
(8) eloquence, specimen, beggar, dazling, mysterious
(9) plaintiff, degree, hostility, cauterize, anchered
(10) quarantine, proverbial, adaptation, disernment, stupidity

2

(1) recognition, valleys, pervade, engagment, economy
(2) examiner, graphic, mentality, partialy, haven
(3) morbid, narrative, sanguine, chide, imposition
(4) kindlyness, imaginary, homespun, sluggish, attic
(5) appended, softning, reminisce, fantastic, emphasized
(6) detestable, severety, technique, bequest, sympathetic
(7) credence, alienated, envirorment, disgusted, geometric
(8) accompanying, benefited, conveyence, loosely, legitimate
(9) spectaculer, essentially, flinching, worthiness, strategist
(10) inanimate, pottery, lavander, appendix, accidentally

3

(1) pleasent, sophomore, happiness, foreign, knowledge
(2) personify, disinherit, concoct, canditate, sacrament
(3) nonsense, reverent, decieded, hazard, lieutenant
(4) regreting, malady, dependent, jealous, lobster
(5) continuous, whistling, accredit, leisure, promtness
(6) contaminate, forcible, messenger, tarriff, circuit
(7) secretive, primer, hypnatize, accede, sundry
(8) superstition, anguish, brillance, lithe, christening
(9) collegeate, maritime, consonant, hazy, erosion
(10) legacy, statistics, management, appropriate, pedegree

4

(1) interference, controllable, merchandise, inquiries, patience
(2) parrot, visible, barrel, wholehearted, baloon
(3) irrigate, rivalry, seniority, evaperate, stony
(4) remorseful, acquittal, austerity, tangible, submiting
(5) hankerchief, implement, nationalism, umbrella, laboratory
(6) imaculate, withhold, fractional, dentistry, pilgrimage
(7) amateurish, corrider, interpreter, granary, humorous
(8) fashionable, echoes, vacuum, achieve, embarrased
(9) salvos, anniversary, multiple, condemmed, recollect
(10) herald, grippe, notify, ancestery, evacuate

5

(1) vacent, universities, apparatus, humiliate, trespass
(2) proffesional, summaries, witnesses, prescription, stubbornness
(3) settlment, obliterate, bounteous, diligent, delicacy
(4) caress, ascertain, eigth, measuring, positively
(5) suddenness, accademic, predictability, chaplain, khaki
(6) juvinile, anxiety, perseverance, complexion, council
(7) scarcity, statistics, authenic, technical, dimensions
(8) spryness, restaraunt, solicit, explanatory, recoup
(9) enumerated, drastic, enterance, utmost, notary
(10) prophecy, achievement, margarine, purify, enormus

6

(1) aggravate, villiage, despair, hereditary, conscience
(2) preservation, revelation, blithely, chassis, temperture
(3) symbolism, orphanned, nondescript, malicious, diminutive
(4) marionette, volunteer, exhilaration, literaly, analytical
(5) uncompromising, artifice, vacinate, purport, strident
(6) calories, preliminary, carnaval, prescribe, syllabus
(7) substantial, goddesses, harnessed, derisive, approximitly
(8) condenser, usefulness, unvieling, hustling, atomic
(9) whereabouts, cocksure, billiard, calous, surgeon
(10) contemptous, reaffirm, mileage, itinerary, rummage

7

(1) simultaneous, haggard, celestial, epoch, appartment
(2) surgeon, acknowlege, structural, systematic, pitiable
(3) diameter, symphony, fertilizer, explicit, anouncement
(4) volanteer, diseased, rejoicing, merger, manufacturer
(5) documentary, fantasy, suffrage, boycoted, strategy
(6) apparently, strengthened, desperse, macadam, catapult
(7) acquaintance, persecute, physics, indefinate, artificial
(8) reconciliation, incorrigible, laboratory, sectarian, vigilance
(9) congenital, rearangment, summation, guttural, luscious
(10) likelihood, grudging, nuisance, pyramid, rightous

8

(1) missunderstood, career, artificially, acquired, thoroughly
(2) apprentices, decision, oppresion, familiar, urgency
(3) annoyance, themselves, tripped, convenient, beseiged
(4) warrant, evasion, indiffrent, suffuse, quizzical
(5) extension, embellish, humerous, worrisome, pyramid
(6) curiosity, sincerety, extraordinary, monitor, persuasive
(7) maneuver, parallel, resistance, tolerance, benificial
(8) grotesque, impetuous, gaiety, vineger, processional
(9) protectorate, delinquint, ratified, scrutinize, legendary
(10) delegation, injunction, obsolete, senitorial, alkali

9

(1) ilegally, masquerade, surgeon, spinach, nuisance
(2) assignment, medecine, equality, tidal, ammunition
(3) secratarial, fidelity, immediately, treachery, preferred
(4) abreviate, strategy, thoroughfare, dissolve, compulsion
(5) scandalous, bathe, encouragment, merciless, assortment
(6) exquisite, agravate, complexion, emphasis, dismissal
(7) unschedualed, analysis, predominant, homogenized, approximately
(8) sorority, extension, converse, language, occassion
(9) condemnation, grandeur, canopy, outragious, aspirin
(10) compliance, potential, unmanagable, constraint, coroner

10

(1) correspondence, pliable, precipice, reconize, supervisory
(2) imovable, cubicle, headache, urgency, exemption
(3) promoter, verbal, weild, ostrich, planned
(4) clarify, playwright, glossary, paralell, officially
(5) stetistical, feigned, grammatical, hygienic, analyzing
(6) permanent, replica, twentieth, personnel, discriptive
(7) alluded, stationery, privelege, sociability, molasses
(8) allege, repititious, intercede, assimilate, congratulatory
(9) sedative, allay, fiscal, truthfullness, transit
(10) disiplinary, altimeter, judiciary, linguist, gymnastics

Chapter 3

THE READING COMPREHENSION TEST (QUESTION 3)

THE IMPORTANCE OF READING

Consider how important reading is. If you read well, you will be able to continue your education throughout life solely by reading. You will be able to succeed in college. (If you cannot read well, you will almost certainly have to drop out.) You will probably advance more rapidly in your chosen employment, business, or profession. You will be better informed and, therefore, more intelligent as a citizen. You will be able to enjoy the leisure reading of good books. Your friends will find you a more interesting person. In a very real sense, your future success and happiness require that you be able to read well.

As you might expect, the Comprehensive English Examination attaches major importance to reading. It tests reading in two ways:

1. Every question on the examination is, in a way, a reading test, since you must be able to understand what each question calls for before you can answer it successfully.

2. The examination includes a separate reading comprehension test worth twenty points.

TYPICAL READING COMPREHENSION TEST

To help you in your study of the reading comprehension test, we have added two features in reprinting the typical test below:

1. We have numbered every sentence in each passage to facilitate reference.

2. We have fully discussed and answered the questions asked about each passage before going on to the next passage.

Below *each* of the following passages you will find several questions or incomplete statements about the passage. Each question or statement is followed by five words or expressions numbered 1 through 5. Select the word or expression that most satisfactorily completes *each in accordance with the meaning of the passage*. The correct answers have been inserted in brackets at the end of the questions. [Two credits for each correct title; one credit for each other correct completion.]　　[20]

JANUARY 1960

Passage a

[1]American women have been maneuvered back into the kitchen. [2]The evidence is unmistakable: a flurry of specialized cookbooks, a kaleidoscope of luscious food pages in magazines, and, even in the most ordinary kitchen, mingled odors of garlic, sesame and coriander.

[3] The situation is more insidious than it appears. [4]In many communities homemade mayonnaise has more feminine prestige than mink, and the zealous housewife can lose face finally and terribly by leaving the eel out of the bouillabaisse. [5]Cooking has become roughly competitive.

[6]Perversely, this is happening in an era when kitchens are entering the pushbutton stage; foods are premixed, prebreaded, prefried—everything but predigested, and the meat-tenderizer people are working on *that* goal.

[7]One rather pat sociological explanation is that the direct expenditure of money on food is no longer impressive. [8] Time is now the valued commodity, and frequently the modern cook lavishes hours and effort, rather than vulgar old money, in order to hold up her head.

QUESTION: The title below that best expresses the ideas of this passage is:
1 The importance of foreign foods
2 New savings through cooking
3 Time versus money
4 Precooked foods
5 The new interest in cooking . . . . [5]

ANSWER EXPLAINED: Every sentence in the passage deals with title 5 (The new interest in cooking). (For further help in selecting the best title, see pages 51-54.)

WRONG CHOICES: 1 and 2 are not discussed in the passage.
3 is discussed in S8, *but only in relation to the new interest in cooking.*
4 is suggested only in S6.

QUESTION: The author implies that American women have gone back to the kitchen as a result of   (1) their desire to please their husbands   (2) the new conveniences for cooking   (3) their study of sociology   (4) their desire to keep up with their neighbors   (5) their interest in spices . . [4]

ANSWER EXPLAINED: The following statements support 4 as the correct answer:

(S4) "mayonnaise has more feminine *prestige* than mink" and "the zealous housewife can *lose face*"

(S5) "Cooking has become roughly *competitive.*"

(S8) "the modern cook lavishes hours and effort, rather than vulgar old money, in order to *hold up her head*"

WRONG CHOICES: 1 and 3 are not discussed in the passage.

2—"Perversely" in S6 tells us that American women have gone back to the kitchen *in spite of* (not as a result of) the new conveniences for cooking.

5—S2 tells us that American women are using spices—not that they have returned to the kitchen because of their interest in them.

QUESTION: The tone of the passage indicates that the attitude of the author toward his subject is one of (1) amusement (2) indifference (3) reverence (4) severe criticism (5) outspoken defense [1]

ANSWER EXPLAINED: The author's use of words clearly indicates that he is having fun with his subject.

(S1) By "maneuvered back," he jokingly discusses the return of American women to the kitchen as if it were a military defeat.

(S4) His comparison of two such widely different things as "mayonnaise" and "mink" is obviously comic. So, too, is "the zealous housewife can lose face finally and terribly by leaving the eel out of the bouillabaisse."

(S6) He pokes fun at modern food processing: "foods are premixed, prebreaded, prefried —everything but predigested, and the meat-tenderizer people are working on *that* goal."

(S8) "vulgar old money" is further proof that the attitude of the author toward his subject is one of amusement.

WRONG CHOICES: 2, 3, 4, and 5 are not supported by the passage.

QUESTION: The author of this passage makes the point that in many communities (1) people are spending too little money on food (2) "pushbutton" kitchens are undesirable (3) people are using meat tenderizers for purposes other than that for which they were intended (4) mink coats are no longer an absolute measure of social prestige (5) the modern cook values her time too much to spend needless hours in the kitchen .... [4]

ANSWER EXPLAINED: The following statement in S4 supports 4 as the correct answer: "In many communities homemade mayonnaise has more feminine prestige than mink."

WRONG CHOICES: 1, 2, 3, and 5 are not stated in the passage.

Passage b

[1]Nevertheless, there is such a voluble hue and cry about the abysmal state of culture in the United States by well-meaning, sincere critics that I would like to present some evidence to the contrary. [2]One is tempted to remind these critics that no country has ever achieved the complete integration of *haute culture* into the warp and woof of its everyday life. [3]In the wishful memories of those who moon over the passed glories of Shakespeare's England, it is seldom called to mind that bearbaiting was far more popular than any of Master Shakespeare's presentations. [4]Who cares to remember that the same Rome that found a Juvenal proclaiming *mens sana in corpore sano* could also watch an Emperor Trajan celebrate his victory over Decebalus of Dacia in 106 A.D. with no fewer than 5,000 pairs of gladiators matched to the death? [5]And this in the name of amusement!

QUESTION: The title that best expresses the ideas of this passage is:
1 The hue and cry of the critics
2 Reflections on culture
3 Dangers in contemporary criticism
4 The world's amusements
5 Everyday life .... [2]

ANSWER EXPLAINED: Every sentence in the passage contains a *reflection on culture*.

S1 refers to a reflection on culture in the United States with which the author disagrees.

S2 is the author's reflection on culture in general in past history.

S3 is his reflection on the culture of England in Shakespeare's time.

S4 and S5 are his reflection on the culture of Rome in Juvenal's time.

WRONG CHOICES: 1, 3, 4, and 5 are too general and fail to "cover" enough of the passage.

1 does not say what the "hue and cry" is about. It is very vague.

3 —The passage deals with the specific topic of culture—not with the general area of contemporary criticism. S1 points out an error (not a danger) in contemporary criticism.

4 —We cannot, on the basis of the two amusements discussed (bearbaiting in S3 and gladiatorial combats in S4), say that this passage deals with the entire world's amusements.

5 is too general. The passage deals specifically with *reflections on culture* of everyday life.

QUESTION: The paragraph preceding this passage most probably discussed   (1) the increased interest of Americans in public affairs   (2) the popularity of Shakespeare during his lifetime   (3) the interest of Americans in the arts   (4) the duties of a literary critic   (5) Juvenal's contributions to poetry . . . . [3]

ANSWER EXPLAINED: The introductory word "Nevertheless" (S1) tells us that the preceding paragraph most probably discussed a topic which is the opposite of "the abysmal state of culture in the United States" (S1). Of the five choices offered, the only "opposite" one is 3 (*the interest of Americans in the arts*).

WRONG CHOICES: 1, 2, 4, and 5 are all wrong answers because they are not "opposites" of "the abysmal state of culture in the United States."

QUESTION: According to the passage, those who criticize the level of culture in America are (1) amusing (2) outspoken (3) unappreciated (4) sarcastic (5) popular .... [2]

ANSWER EXPLAINED: In S1, *voluble* (meaning "characterized by ease and smoothness of utterance") and *hue and cry* (meaning "shouts of protest") prove that those who criticize the level of culture in America are *outspoken,* choice 2.

WRONG CHOICES: 1, 3, 4, and 5 are not supported by the passage.

QUESTION: The author's attitude toward culture is essentially (1) despairing (2) realistic (3) distorted (4) uncritical (5) childish .... [2]

ANSWER EXPLAINED: Unlike the critics (S1), the author feels that no nation can be completely cultured. He proves this by showing how, in the past, highly cultured people like Shakespeare and Juvenal lived with deplorably uncultured contemporaries (S3 and S4). The author's attitude, based on the lessons of history, is therefore *realistic,* answer 2.

WRONG CHOICES: 1, 3, 4, and 5 are not supported by the passage.

QUESTION: One can conclude from the passage that (1) the masses instinctively recognize artistic achievement (2) the popularity of culture depends on economic factors (3) human nature has not changed too much over the years (4) "a sound mind in a sound body" ought to be America's educational goal (5) Americans do not appreciate intelligence .... [3]

ANSWER EXPLAINED: Some human beings in the past were so depraved as to be able to enjoy bearbaiting (S3) and gladiatorial fights to the death (S4). Some humans today lack culture, too, as hinted by "the abysmal state of culture in the United States" (S1). From these circumstances one can conclude that *human nature has not changed too much over the years,* choice 3.

WRONG CHOICES: 1, 2, 4, and 5 are not supported by the passage.

Passage c

[1]There is controversy and misunderstanding about the proper functions of juvenile courts and their probation departments. [2]There are cries that the whole process produces delinquents rather than rehabilitates them. [3]There are speeches by the score about "getting tough" with the kids. [4]Another large group thinks we should be more understanding and gentle with delinquents. [5]This distrust of the services offered can be attributed in large part to the confusion in the use of these services throughout the country.

[6]On the one hand, the juvenile courts are tied to the criminal court system, with an obligation to decide guilt and innocence for offenses specifically stated and formally charged. [7]On the other, they have the obligation to provide treatment, supervision and guidance to youngsters in trouble, without respect to the crimes of which they are accused. [8]These two conflicting assignments must be carried out—quite properly—in an informal, private way, which will not stigmatize a youngster during his formative years.

[9]And, as the courts' preoccupation with the latter task has increased, the former (that of dispensing justice) has retreated, with the result that grave injustices are bound to occur.

QUESTION: The title below that best expresses the ideas of this passage is:

1 Grave injustices
2 A problem for today's teenagers
3 Rehabilitating youthful criminals
4 Fitting the punishment to the crime
5 Justice for juvenile offenders .... [5]

ANSWER EXPLAINED: Every sentence in the passage deals with some aspect of 5.

WRONG CHOICES: 1 is too general. An improvement would be "Grave injustices against juvenile offenders," but even this more specific title can be supported only by S2 and the end of S9.

2 —The passage deals with a problem for society as a whole—not just for today's teenagers. Besides, the passage does not deal in general with teenagers, but more specifically with: delinquents (S2 and S4), youngsters formally charged with crimes (S6), youngsters in trouble (S7), etc.

3 is only one of the main topics in the passage. Another important one is judging the guilt or innocence of accused youngsters. A title like 5, which combines both of these topics, would be much better.

4 is too general. An improvement would be "Fitting the punishment to the crime for juvenile offenders." But this more specific title would still not "cover" the topic of rehabilitation, which gets major attention in the passage (S2, 7, 8, and 9).

QUESTION: The author contends that public distrust of juvenile courts is primarily the result of   (1) resentment on the part of those convicted by them (2) the dual function of these courts   (3) lack of a sufficient number of probation officers (4) injustices done by the courts   (5) the cost of keeping up the courts .... [2]

ANSWER EXPLAINED: In S5 the author states: "This distrust of the services offered (by the juvenile courts) can be attributed in large part (primarily) to the confusion in the use of these services . . ." In S6, 7, and 8, he indicates that the confusion is the result of "*two* (dual) conflicting assignments" (functions) of these courts: "to decide guilt and innocence" (S6), and "to provide treatment, supervision and guidance" (S7). The evidence in S5-8 clearly establishes 2 as the correct answer.

WRONG CHOICES: The passage does not indicate that public distrust of the juvenile courts is primarily the result of 1, 3, 4, or 5.

QUESTION: The passage suggests that the author   (1) is familiar with the problem   (2) is impatient with justice   (3) sides with those who favor leniency for juvenile offenders   (4) regards all offenses as equally important   (5) favors maximum sentences at all times .... [1]

ANSWER EXPLAINED: S2, 3, and 4 indicate that the author is acquainted with three points of view in the controversy over the proper functioning of the juvenile courts. S5, 6, 7, and 8 show that he knows the reasons for the misunderstanding and distrust of the courts; they also show that he knows how the courts should function. S9 implies that he has studied the juvenile courts over a period of time. The passage as a whole, therefore, strongly suggests that the author *is familiar with the problem,* answer 1.

WRONG CHOICES: 2, 3, 4, and 5 are not supported by the passage.

QUESTION: The tone of this passage is   (1) highly emotional   (2) highly personal   (3) optimistic   (4) calm   (5) sarcastic .... [4]

ANSWER EXPLAINED: The author believes neither in "getting tough" (S3) nor in being "more understanding and gentle with delinquents" (S4). He neither attacks nor distrusts the courts; he tries to understand them. Instead of finding fault, he is more interested in arriving at a solution of the problem, as S8 shows. The tone of this passage may therefore properly be described as 4, *calm.*

WRONG CHOICES: 1 may describe the attitude of those who hold the beliefs expressed in S2 and S3. It certainly does not describe the author's attitude, nor the tone of the passage as a whole.

2 —Nowhere in the passage does the author use *I, me, my, myself,* etc., or say anything of a personal nature.

3 —The passage does not indicate that a solution to the problem will surely be found or that it will be easy.

5 is not supported by the passage.

Passage d

¹The economic struggle in America continues; but it seems apparent that the struggle is no longer between the giant segments of our society, but within them. ²Battles for power and control are being fought within some of the large corporations, enlivened by wars in which the big prizes are stockholders' votes or proxies. ³Similarly, struggles for power are taking place within the large labor organiza-

tions. [4]In each case public opinion seems to be playing an increasingly important part, judging by the dramatic efforts being made to inform the people about the partisan positions. [5]And so long as the battleground involves public favor, moderation seems neither implausible nor unnatural.

QUESTION: The title below that best expresses the ideas of this passage is:
1 The people in power
2 A compromise in disputes between labor and capital
3 The importance of votes and proxies
4 Public influence in internal industrial conflicts
5 The need for moderation in economic disputes .... [4]

ANSWER EXPLAINED: S1-3 describe "internal industrial conflicts." S4 and S5 tell of "public influence" in these conflicts.

WRONG CHOICES: 1 and 2 are not discussed in the passage.
3 deals with a very small part of the passage—the end of S2.
5 —The passage mentions "moderation" (S5) but says nothing about the *need* for it.

QUESTION: According to this passage, the economic struggle in America is currently   (1) between government and industry   (2) between capital and labor   (3) within both capital and labor   (4) between large and small corporations   (5) among stockholders and workers .... [3]

ANSWER EXPLAINED: S2 discusses struggles within capital. S3 discusses struggles within labor.

WRONG CHOICES: 1, 2, 4, and 5 are not discussed.

QUESTION: As used in this passage, the word "partisan" (line 9) means   (1) revolutionary   (2) important   (3) unfavorable   (4) unusual   (5) opposing .... [5]

ANSWER EXPLAINED: Even if you do not know the meaning of "partisan," the passage compels you to choose *opposing*. The words "economic struggle" (S1), "Battles for power and control" (S2), and "struggles for power" (S3) imply that opposing sides are present. S4 indicates that each opposing side is informing the public of its position in an effort to win public support. "Partisan" positions must therefore mean 5, *opposing* positions.

WRONG CHOICES: 1, 2, 3, and 4 are not supported by the passage, and they are not synonyms for "partisan."

CHALLENGING NATURE OF READING PASSAGES

The passages in the reading comprehension test are not at all like the ones we ordinarily encounter in novels or short stories. They are *expository* (explanatory) passages. Passage *a,* you will notice, *explains* a new trend in cooking; passage *b explains* some beliefs about culture. Every one of the passages in this typical reading comprehension test *explains* or teaches and is therefore expository.

Be on your guard when you read expository materials. Such materials call for slower and more careful reading than fiction. Be especially alert for (1) the *main idea* of the passage and (2) the *specific facts* that support the main idea.

AN EXPOSITORY PASSAGE FREQUENTLY REQUIRES SEVERAL READINGS TO BE FULLY UNDERSTOOD.

NEED FOR PROPER MENTAL APPROACH

In seeking the right answer, be guided only by what is printed in the passage. Rigidly exclude from your mind any previous information you may have about the topic in the passage. Suppose, for example, you are confronted with a selection about stamp collecting. Suppose, further, that you have been a stamp collector for several years and have read several books and articles on this subject. Beware! Do not allow any outside information to influence you in your search for the correct answer.

BE GUIDED ONLY BY THE TEXT OF THE PASSAGE YOU ARE READING.

DOUBLE IMPORTANCE OF TITLE QUESTIONS

The reading comprehension test is worth twenty credits. Notice that our typical test (pages 41-50) has only sixteen questions. Each of these is worth one credit, except title questions, which are worth *two* credits.

Surprising as it may seem, you may correctly answer twelve of sixteen reading questions and yet fail the reading comprehension test. If you cannot select the four best titles, you lose eight credits. This reduces your maximum score to twelve (out of twenty) or 60%, which is below passing for the reading comprehension test.

PAY SPECIAL ATTENTION TO TITLE QUESTIONS.

SELECTING THE BEST TITLE

To select the best title, read the passage through carefully (several readings are often necessary). Follow the main thought as it develops from topic sentence, through supporting details, to concluding sentence. Then patiently examine the five suggested titles, one by one, to determine which one best sums up the ideas of the passage as a whole.

To help you analyze a passage and choose the best title, here is a valuable clue. It was discovered by studying many passages and questions like those that appear on the typical reading comprehension test. The clue is simply this: *the best title is the title describing the thought of more of the passage than any of the other suggested titles.*

From this clue, we get a helpful method for locating the best title. We shall call it the "yardstick" method. According to this method, reread the passage sentence by sentence, *putting down the title to which each sentence belongs.* When you have finished, "measure" the extent (count the lines) of the passage described by title 1. Then do the same for titles 2, 3, 4, and 5. The title describing the thought of the greatest number of lines is probably the best of the five titles. (You should, of course, always verify your answer by using the "double checks" explained on pages 53-54.)

USING THE "YARDSTICK" METHOD

Let us now learn how to analyze a passage and find the best title by the "yardstick" method. For this purpose we have reprinted the title question and passage *a* from the typical reading comprehension test on page 41.

The Question:

> The title below that best expresses the ideas
> of this passage is:
> 1 The importance of foreign foods
> 2 New savings through cooking
> 3 Time versus money
> 4 Precooked foods
> 5 The new interest in cooking ...... ( )

The Passage Analyzed:

American women have been maneuvered back into the kitchen. The
All-important topic sentence clearly belongs to title 5.   *This*

evidence is unmistakable: a flurry of specialized cookbooks, a kaleido-
sentence gives evidence for American women's return to kitchen; therefore

scope of luscious food pages in magazines, and, even in the most
it belongs to title 5.

ordinary kitchen, mingled odors of garlic, sesame and coriander.

The situation is more insidious than it appears. In many communities
Refers to return to kitchen; therefore title 5.   *This sentence gives de-*

homemade mayonnaise has more feminine prestige than mink, and the
tails about new interest in cooking; therefore title 5.

zealous housewife can lose face finally and terribly by leaving the eel

out of the bouillabaisse. Cooking has become roughly competitive.
                                   Describes new interest in cooking; therefore title 5.

Perversely, this is happening in an era when kitchens are entering
The word "this" means new interest in cooking; therefore whole sentence

the pushbutton stage; foods are premixed, prebreaded, prefried—
belongs to title 5.   *But this part of the sentence may be interpreted as*

everything but predigested, and the meat-tenderizer people are work-
belonging also to title 4.

ing on *that* goal.

One rather pat sociological explanation is that the direct expenditure
Explains   new   interest   in   cooking;   therefore   title 5.   But   discusses

of money on food is no longer impressive. Time is now the valued
role of money; therefore also title 3.   *Sentence   belongs   to   title*

commodity, and frequently the modern cook lavishes hours and effort,
3 or, better still, title 5. It discusses time versus money—but only in

rather than vulgar old money, in order to hold up her head.
relation to the new interest in cooking.

The Answer:

According to the above analysis, the extent of the passage covered
by each title is as follows:

> 1 (The importance of foreign foods)—0 lines
> 2 (New savings through cooking)—0 lines
> 3 (Time versus money)—4 lines
> 4 (Precooked foods)—2 lines
> 5 (The new interest in cooking)—16 lines

Title 5 obviously is the best title because it describes more of the
thought of the passage than titles 1, 2, 3, or 4.

VERIFYING THE ANSWER: "DOUBLE CHECKS"

As with all problems, you should verify your choice for the best title
by applying as many "double checks" as possible. Here are a few good
suggestions:

a. CHECK THE THOUGHT OF THE TOPIC AND CONCLUD-
ING SENTENCES WITH THE THOUGHT OF THE SELECTED
TITLE.

Example: In passage *a* (page 41), the topic sentence informs us
that American women are back in the kitchen. The final sentence
emphasizes an important point about the new interest in cooking: the
modern cook tries to impress others by the time, not the money, she
spends in cooking. Both of these key sentences support title 5 (The
new interest in cooking).

b. CHECK TO SEE THAT THE SELECTED TITLE IS NOT TOO BROAD FOR THE PASSAGE.

Example: In passage *b* (page 43), title 4 (The world's amusements) is obviously too broad. The passage discusses *only two* so-called "amusements" (bearbaiting and gladiatorial combats). It would be folly to select 4 (The world's amusements) as the best title.

c. CHECK TO SEE THAT THE SELECTED TITLE IS NOT TOO NARROW FOR THE PASSAGE.

Example: In passage *c* (page 46), title 3 (Rehabilitating youthful criminals) is too narrow to cover the whole passage. True, rehabilitation is one of the main topics in the passage. But there is another—dispensing justice—and title 3 does not cover that.

d. USE THE PROCESS OF ELIMINATION. Do not put down your selected answer on the examination paper unless you have carefully considered and eliminated every wrong answer.

ANSWERING ONE-POINT READING QUESTIONS

Most of the one-point (non-title) questions ask you to locate information stated or implied in the passage. The rule for answering such questions is simple: never guess. Before you write the answer on your examination paper, make sure that you have located supporting evidence in the passage. As a check, go over each wrong answer to make sure that it is not supported by the passage.

Example: Review the explanation for the correct answer to the following question (page 49): "According to this passage, the economic struggle in America is currently . . ."

ANSWERING QUESTIONS ABOUT TONE

When you are asked a question about the tone of a passage, it is usually helpful to study the author's choice of words.

Example: Review the explanation for the correct answer to the following question (page 42): "The tone of the passage indicates that the attitude of the author toward his subject is one of . . ."

Study Suggestion: Before answering any of the reading questions in the tests that follow, reread this chapter carefully. Pay special attention to the thinking used in getting the correct answers to the typical reading comprehension test. Then try to use the same thinking in similar questions in the following tests.

FORMER REGENTS QUESTIONS

At the right of *each* of the following passages you will find one or more questions or incomplete statements about the passage. Each question or statement is followed by five words or expressions numbered 1 through 5. Select the word or expression that most satisfactorily completes *each in accordance with the meaning of the passage* and write its *number* in the parentheses. [Two credits for each correct title; one credit for each other correct completion.]   [20]

1

a. Lithography is the art of drawing with a greasy substance, usually crayon, on a stone, metal, or paper surface, and then printing. It is based on the fact that grease attracts grease and is repelled by water. It is the most direct of all the graphic arts, for in practising it the artist first sees the exact value of each line that he draws and then has his drawing reproduced so accurately that it may truly be said to have been multiplied. In making either an etching, a process in which a drawing is engraved on a metal plate through a thin film of wax, or a woodblock, in which the drawing is carved in wood, the artist must wait for a print to estimate his work fairly. When a lithograph is made, the artist's drawing grows in definite values under his eyes and he can make changes in it as he works.

The title below that best expresses the ideas of this passage is:
1. Advantages of lithography
2. How etchings and woodblocks are made
3. Crayon and stone in art
4. Modern graphic arts
5. Basic principles of art ...... ( )

A great advantage of lithography as a means of reproducing drawings is that it (1) is quicker and neater than other methods (2) gives faithful reproductions (3) requires a metal plate (4) requires no special materials (5) is less expensive than other methods .... ( )

Many artists like to use lithography to reproduce their drawings because they (1) know in advance the value of each picture (2) often get unexpected results (3) get higher prices for lithographs than for etchings (4) can get clearer enlargements (5) can make alterations and corrections .... ( )

b. How are symphony orchestras launched, kept going, and built up in smaller communities? Recent reports from five of them suggest that, though the pattern changes, certain elements are fairly common. One thing shines out; enthusiasm is essential. Also, aside from the indispensable instrumentalists who play, the following personalities, either singly, or preferably in combination, seem to be the chief needs: a conductor who wants to conduct so

The title below that best expresses the ideas of this passage is:
1. Skepticism concerning community music
2. The changing pattern of community music
3. Making a community orchestra a success
4. The personalities of local music
5. Five symphony orchestras .... ( )

badly he will organize his own orchestra if it is the only way he can get one; a manager with plenty of resourcefulness in rounding up audiences and finding financial support; an energetic community leader, generally a woman, who will take up boosting the orchestra as a hobby; and generous visiting soloists who will help draw those who are skeptical that anything local can be good.

c. But the weather predictions which an almanac always contains are, we believe, mostly wasted on the farmer. He can take a squint at the moon before turning in. He can "smell" snow or tell if the wind is shifting dangerously east. He can register forebodingly an extra twinge in a rheumatic shoulder. With any of these to go by, he can be reasonably sure of tomorrow's weather. He can return the almanac to the nail behind the door and put a last stick of wood in the stove. For an almanac, a zero night or a morning's drifted road —none of these has changed much since Poor Richard wrote his stuff and barns were built along the Delaware.

d. The most important influences in raising the standard of living of modern times, and indeed of all times, are scientific progress and the invention of mechanical devices. A hundred years ago the average hourly output of a laborer in the United States was valued at 27 cents. Today the laborer's average hourly production is worth $1.32, or five times as much. Yet he is not five times as strong, nor does he work five times as hard. The answer to his increased productivity lies, in part, in his use of better tools and of mechanical power. The latter accounts for 92 per cent of the energy used in our present wonderful productivity.

Visiting soloists are necessary in community musical organizations because (1) they contribute their financial support   (2) they are generous toward skeptics   (3) they encourage local talent   (4) they increase attendance   (5) they are better than the local musicians . . . . . . ( )

The title below that best expresses the ideas of this passage is:
1. The farmer as weather prophet
2. The farmer uses the almanac
3. Guessing tomorrow's weather
4. Getting ready for the night
5. Unchanged weather predictions
. . . . ( )

The author implies that in predicting weather there is considerable value in   (1) reading the almanac   (2) placing a last stick of wood in the stove   (3) sleeping with one eye on the moon   (4) noting rheumatic pains   (5) keeping the almanac behind the door . . . . . ( )

The title below that best expresses the ideas of this passage is:
1. Effect of mechanical power on the standard of living
2. Importance of good tools in industry
3. Progress of inventions
4. Better tools and higher wages
5. Study of our wonderful productivity . . . . ( )

The author indicates that   (1) an increase in man's physical strength results in greater productivity   (2) labor's total progress has been made in the last century   (3) tools and mechanical power are both important in production   (4) the standard of living results from better living conditions   (5) the source of energy for most of our productivity is tools . . . . ( )

e. It is not easy to draw on a canvas the man whose nature is large and central, without cranks or oddities. The very simplicity of such souls defies an easy summary, for they are as spacious in their effect as daylight or summer. Often we remember friends by a gesture, or a trick of expression, or by a favorite phrase. But with Nelson I do not find myself thinking of such idiosyncrasies. His presence warmed and lit up so big a region of life that in thinking of him one is overwhelmed by the multitude of things that he made better by simply existing among them. If you remove a fire from the hearth you will remember the look, not so much of the blaze itself, as of the whole room in its pleasant glow.

The title below that best expresses the ideas of this passage is:
1. Portraying a noble nature
2. The idiosyncrasies of friends
3. The beauty of a room in firelight
4. Overwhelmed by Nelson
5. Remembering friends by their tricks of expression .... ( )

The passage implies that   (1) Nelson was a complex person   (2) Nelson lived an outdoor life   (3) gestures are the most important memories of friends   (4) the queer individual is easily described   (5) when the fire is out, you cannot remember the blaze .... ( )

f. One of the most urgent problems in teaching handwriting is presented by the left-handed child. The traditional policy has been to attempt to induce all children to write with their right hands. Parents and teachers alike have an antipathy to the child's using his left hand. On the other hand, psychologists have shown beyond a doubt that some persons are naturally left-handed and that it is much more difficult for them to do any skillful act with the right hand than with the left hand. Some believe, furthermore, that to compel a left-handed child to write with his right hand may make him nervous and may cause stammering. There seem to be some cases in which this is true, although in the vast majority of children who change over, no ill effects are noticed. In addition to these difficulties, left-handedness sometimes seems to cause mirror writing—writing from right to left—and reversals in reading, as reading "was" for "saw."

The title below that best expresses the ideas of this passage is:
1. Nervous aspects connected with handwriting
2. Teaching handwriting
3. The problems of the left-handed child
4. A special problem in teaching handwriting
5. Stammering, mirror writing and reversals .... ( )

The author implies that   (1) parents should break children of left-handedness   (2) left-handed children need special consideration   (3) left-handed persons are inclined to stutter   (4) left-handed persons are not more brilliant than right-handed ones   (5) left-handed persons are less skillful than right-handed ones .... ( )

The traditional policy in teaching handwriting has   (1) dismayed the experts   (2) resulted in failure to learn to write   (3) aimed at mirror writing   (4) made many children skillful with both hands   (5) resulted in unsolved problems .... ( )

2

a. The propaganda of a nation at war is designed to stimulate the energy of its citizens and their will to win, and to imbue them with an overwhelming sense of the justice of their cause. Directed abroad, its purpose is to create precisely contrary effects among citizens of enemy nations and to assure to nationals of allied or subjugated countries full and unwavering assistance.

The title below that best expresses the ideas of this passage is:
1. Propaganda's failure
2. Designs for waging war
3. Influencing opinion in wartime
4. The propaganda of other nations
5. Citizens of enemy nations and their allies .... ( )

This passage implies that a nation's wartime propaganda is   (1) dangerous to its nationals   (2) useful to some of its enemies   (3) unjustified   (4) doubtful procedure   (5) varied .... ( )

b. The rattler is our national snake, or would be if we had a national snake. Benjamin Franklin wanted to see it on the Great Seal. Maine, New Hampshire and Vermont seem to be the only states which are practically free of it, though rumors come down from time to time of rattlers having strayed across into southern Vermont. The rattler varies from the great diamond-backs down to pygmies no larger than garter snakes. Our local variety, the timber rattler, suns itself on the rock ledges of the mountains of Massachusetts, New York, New Jersey and Pennsylvania. To the west of us is the territory of the massasauga, a rattler which grows to two or three feet.

The title below that best expresses the ideas of this passage is:
1. Snakes from Maine to New York
2. Ben Franklin's design for the Great Seal
3. A widely distributed snake
4. Reptiles of New England and the West
5. Snakes rampant .... ( )

The paragraph implies that rattlesnakes   (1) are on the Great Seal (2) are unknown in Vermont   (3) appear in more than two sizes   (4) of the smallest size are garter snakes (5) migrate by way of Vermont
.... ( )

c. We now know that what constitutes practically all of matter is empty space; relatively enormous voids in which revolve with lightning velocity infinitesimal particles so utterly small that they have never been seen or photographed. The existence of these particles has been demonstrated by mathematical physicists and their operations determined by ingenious laboratory experiments. It was not until 1911 that experiments by Sir Ernest Rutherford revealed the architecture of the mysterious atom. Moseley, Bohr, Fermi, Mil-

The title below that best expresses the ideas of this passage is:
1. The work of Sir Ernest Rutherford
2. Empty spaces in matter
3. Atoms, molecules and space
4. Notable scientists
5. The structure of matter
.... ( )

The center of the atom, according to this passage,   (1) contains one electron   (2) has not yet been seen by the naked eye   (3) was seen as early as 1911   (4) is about

likan, Compton, Urey, and others have also worked on the problem. Matter is composed of molecules whose average diameter is about 1/125 millionth of an inch. Molecules are composed of atoms so small that about five million could be placed in a row on the period at the end of this sentence. Long thought to be the ultimate, indivisible constituent of matter, the atom has been found to consist roughly of a proton, the positive electrical element in the atomic nucleus, surrounded by electrons, the negative electric elements swirling about the proton.

d. One man's productivity, however, varies greatly from country to country. It depends on the amount of assistance the average worker is given in the form of machinery—that is to say, on the horsepower per head. It depends also—and this may be a point of growing importance—on the spirit and stamina of the workers. The industrial workers of certain countries have been working under heavy strain for many years. During that time they have been badly fed. Moreover, the countries referred to have become dependent in a significant degree on slave labor, the inefficiency of which is notorious.

e. Remembering the experiences of many so-called "modern" artists of the past, it is not surprising that in our time their story should have been repeated. We too have had and have many artists who have ventured forth into new and at first unaccepted ways of painting. Not all artists who have turned their backs upon accepted ways are great painters. Some very poor pictures have been created by our own modern artists. To but few, in any generation, is given that ability, that genius, which lies behind a truly fine picture. Yet from the experimenting of today already there have emerged some great paintings.

the size of a period   (5) might be photographed under microscopes

. . . . (   )

The paragraph indicates that the atom (1) is the smallest particle   (2) is very little larger than a molecule (3) has been seen   (4) is composed of several particles   (5) is empty space . . . . (   )

Scientists agree that molecules are (1) huge compared with electrons (2) voids   (3) the most mysterious particles   (4) not divisible (5) not basically composed of electric elements . . . . (   )

The title below that best expresses the ideas of this passage is:
1. Machinery makes the difference
2. Horsepower per head
3. Worker productivity
4. Countries and workers
5. The importance of spirit and stamina . . . . (   )

The author implies that   (1) workers have neglected their health   (2) slaves are weak   (3) machinery adds one horsepower to each worker (4) working under strain reduces output   (5) one man counts little

. . . . (   )

The title that best expresses the ideas of this paragraph is:
1. Great painters of the past
2. Types of modern paintings
3. Disadvantages of contemporary art
4. Breaking artistic tradition
5. The public's interest and influence in art . . . . (   )

The author implies that among artists of the past, some few have made fine paintings because they   (1) were more modern than their predecessors (2) were encouraged by the people at large   (3) possessed genius (4) followed the teachings of the

Rulers no longer control art; and art galleries since the French Revolution have belonged to the people. This of course has been an encouragement to art.

f. Supporters of television believe that it will introduce the public on a mass scale to the best in the visual arts which, up to now, have either been too expensive or too remote for most to enjoy. As a mass medium, television necessarily will have to cater to majority tastes, but at the same time it will be confronted with a more critical audience than the radio, if only for one reason. The eye reacts more sharply—favorably or unfavorably—than the ear.

masters   (5) overcame the criticism by the public .... (   )

The title below that best expresses the ideas of this passage is:
1. A mass medium
2. Majority tastes and the entertainment field
3. The critical influence of eye and ear
4. Television displaces radio
5. Television's future .... (   )

The author implies that   (1) television should not cater to majority tastes   (2) television audiences are more intelligent than radio audiences (3) the reaction of the eye is usually favorable   (4) artistically, television will prove to be a blessing   (5) all the arts have been very expensive for the public .... (   )

3

a. Underlying historical events which influenced two great American peoples, citizens of Canada and of the United States, to work out their many problems through the years with such harmony and mutual benefit constitute a story which is both colorful and fascinating. It is a story of border disputes, questions and their solutions, for certainly the controversies and wars of the early years of Canada and the northern colonies of what now is the United States, and after 1783 their continuation through the War of 1812, scarcely constituted a sound foundation for international friendship. The fact too that great numbers of Loyalists fled to Canada during the Revolutionary period, combined with the general Loyalist sentiment of the citizens of Canada, both of French and British extraction, might well have brought about historical antipathy between the two coun-

The title below that best expresses the ideas of this passage is:
1. A proud record
2. Our northern neighbor
3. Cooperation with Canada
4. Our northern boundary line
5. The role of the Loyalists in Canada .... (   )

Disagreements between Canada and the United States   (1) did not occur after 1800   (2) were solved in every case   (3) constituted a basis for friendship   (4) were solved principally to America's advantage   (5) resulted from the presence of natural barriers ... (   )

The writer considers the period before 1812   (1) an insurmountable barrier   (2) a time of geographical disputes   (3) the definer of our differences   (4) a cementer of

tries, such as often has proved insurmountable in similar circumstances in other parts of the world.

Yet it is a fact that solutions were found for every matter of disagreement that arose and, as it is, the two nations have been able to work out a peaceful result from the many difficulties naturally arising in connection with a long and disputed boundary line, in many cases not delineated by great natural barriers.

b. An airplane equipped with the turbo-jet engine is not efficient at low altitudes; its best performance may be around 40,000 feet. It will accelerate slowly and will usually require longer runways for take-off. It has no propellers to be reversed to slow the aircraft down after landing, and is less efficient for ground control. Its fuel consumption, on a relative basis, is much higher than that of a turbo-prop installation. It is capable of very high speeds.

c. Lumbering in the Northwest in the early days was often a two-fisted business, in which one would say that neither the lumber barons nor the lumberjacks had learned a thing from the wastage, the fires, the boom-and-bust days, and stump counties of eastern history. Nothing, that is, except greatly increased efficiency at whirlwind exploitation. But that was in a cruder age, in the days when labor troubles went to the shooting stage, when pirates on Puget Sound stole whole rafts of timber, when fires burned over forests the size of many a European principality, and when the Forest Service was jeered at and obstructed. Those days are gone. Progressive companies now hire their own trained foresters and follow practical conservation. Well-located lumber towns have become permanent cities with fine schools and churches. Employees are usually married, eat the best of

our Canadian friendship   (5) the period that settled our northern boundary . . . .   (   )

The title below that best expresses the
   ideas of this passage is:
1. The turbo-jet
2. Advances in aviation
3. An efficient airplane
4. A relative of the turbo-prop
5. Equipment for the turbo-jet
   . . . .   (   )

The turbo-jet is probably superior to the turbo-prop   (1) in military use   (2) at low altitudes   (3) in fuel consumption   (4) in climbing ability   (5) at altitudes of seven to eight miles . . . .   (   )

The title below that best expresses the
   ideas of this passage is:
1. Forestry today
2. The good old days
3. Lessons of history
4. Lumber baron and lumberjack
5. Improvement in the lumber industry . . . .   (   )

Early methods of lumbering were   (1) unplanned   (2) impractical   (3) pugnacious   (4) extravagant   (5) magnificent . . . .   (   )

food, and own their homes. Fire is fought like the Devil.

d. When a shortage of aluminum threatened this country some time ago, Kodak engineers set about to find a substitute for it to be used in reflectors for flash photography, which were made completely of that defense-vital metal.

Featuring a mirror-bright finish, the new product, called the Lumaclad reflector, is made by vacuum-depositing a minute quantity of aluminum on a clear Tenite II plastic shell. The resulting shiny finish enables the Lumaclad reflector to give up to 50 per cent more reflectivity than is provided by reflectors of the satin finish type. Another advantage of this plastic-based reflector is that it is flexible, but cannot be dented. Currently in production, the Lumaclad reflector is being distributed in connection with the less expensive line of Kodak cameras.

The title below that best expresses the ideas of this passage is:
1. Aluminum shortage
2. Kodak's contribution
3. Research in photography
4. A shortage in World War II
5. The new plastic flash reflector
.... (   )

The writer implies that in flash photography   (1) the new plastic reflector is inflexible   (2) 50% of all cameras use aluminum reflectors   (3) the new reflectors are not ready for distribution   (4) plastic surfaces give greater reflectivity   (5) aluminum is the best material for reflecting light .... (   )

The author implies that   (1) Kodak camera sales have boomed   (2) the new reflector is superior to others   (3) plastic reflectors cost too much for use in most cameras   (4) in the past aluminum shortages have been frequent   (5) the experiment involves too much defense-vital material .... (   )

e. There is no absolute formula which will solve the problem of the poet in America. In an industrial and commercial civilization, his career will always be a compromise. Things are better than they were at the turn of the century, and neither the poet nor his well-wishers covet for him a life withdrawn into indolence and ease. What is wanted is a way of life not destructive of the work he was meant to do.

The title below that best expresses the ideas of this passage is:
1. A way of life
2. Poet's compromise
3. The poet's problem
4. A formula for poetry
5. Making life easier for poets
.... (   )

It is characteristic of poets to   (1) wish to be active   (2) search for a formula   (3) desire to compromise   (4) dislike exhausting work   (5) desire financial gain ..... (   )

f. It takes no calendar to tell root and stem that the calm days of midsummer are here. Last spring's sprouted seed comes to fruit. None of these

The title below that best expresses the ideas of this passage is:
1. The appeal of spring
2. The march of time

things depends on a calendar of the days and months. They are their own calendar, marks on a span of time that reaches far back into the shadows of time. The mark is there for all to see, in every field and meadow and treetop, as it was last year and ten years ago and when the centuries were young.

The time is here. This is that point in the great continuity when these things happen, and will continue to happen year after year. Any summer arrives at this point, only to lead on to the next and the next, and so to summer again. These things we can count on; these things will happen again and again, so long as the earth turns.

3. Earth cycles
4. The beauty of wild flowers
5. The continuity of nature .... (   )

The passage indicates that the author experiences a feeling of   (1) frustration   (2) fear of the forces of nature   (3) pessimism   (4) regret at the rapid passage of time (5) serene confidence .... (   )

4

a. Once every year Kansas City is host to a convention of the world's largest aggregation of juvenile capitalists. On no other occasion is so much teenage wealth seen under one roof. The 8,000 youngsters from forty-eight states and territories who assemble here every October are delegates of Future Farmers of America, a national organization composed of 340,000 members. The prosperous boys who meet here have accumulated their own wealth as farmers and farm operators. Their individual net worth ranges through varying degrees of affluence up to as much as $50,000 for some of the boys.

What's more, they earned it during their high school years or immediately afterwards. Each boy is eligible to be a member of Future Farmers until he reaches twenty-one. He enters the ranks by enrolling in an agricultural class under a well-trained teacher in the school he is attending.

The title below that best expresses the ideas of this passage is:
1. Prosperity
2. Young capitalists
3. Farming enterprises
4. Agriculture aids education
5. The need for more agriculture education .... (   )

The author implies that   (1) all high schools offer agricultural training   (2) many of the boys have earned $50,000 since graduation (3) a boy does not necessarily have to be a trained farmer   (4) the entire United States is represented in this organization   (5) "juvenile capitalists" is the world's largest organization .... (   )

The author states that   (1) 340,-000 is the maximum number of members   (2) each year the convention is held in the same city   (3) only boys earning a certain amount may be delegates   (4) once a member, a boy is always a member until he becomes 21   (5) any boy between 18 and 21 years of age may join the organization .... (   )

b. Readers took their first trip to the moon 1800 years ago via two stories by Lucian of Samosata, who may therefore properly be called the father of science fiction. In one of his tales, titled "True History," the trip was accidental: a ship sailing in mysterious waters west of the Pillars of Hercules was blown to the moon by a sudden storm. In the other the trip was premeditated. Its hero, Icaromenippus, undertook long training with the wings of large birds, finally became airborne and flapped to his destination. For more than fourteen centuries Lucian remained the only story-teller to write of a trip into space, largely because astronomy had slipped back to the idea that the earth was not only the center of the universe but that all other planets were immaterial.

The title below that best expresses the ideas of this passage is:
1. Lucian's stories
2. Visiting stellar space
3. The decline of astronomy
4. Beginnings of science fiction
5. The history of a trip to the moon
.... ( )

Icaromenippus' trip was accomplished through (1) careful planning (2) the gods of chance (3) a fortuitous storm (4) the help of Hercules (5) the courage of Lucian .... ( )

The writer attributes the lack of stories about interplanetary travel to centuries of (1) ignorance and conceit (2) stubbornness and pride (3) emphasis upon astrology (4) neglect of Lucian's tales (5) interest in other kinds of stories
.... ( )

c. The six year old is about the best example that can be found of that type of inquisitiveness that causes irritated adults to exclaim, "Curiosity killed the cat." To him, the world is a fascinating place to be explored and investigated quite thoroughly, but such a world is bounded by the environment in which he or the people he knows live. It is constantly expanding through new experiences, which bring many eager questions from members of any group of first graders, as each one tries to figure out new relationships—to know and accept his place within the family, the school, and the community—to understand all around him. There are adults who find it quite annoying to be presented with such rank inquisitiveness. But this is no purposeless prying, no idle curiosity! It is that quality, characteristic of the successful adult, inherent in the good citizen—intellectual curiosity.

The title below that best expresses the ideas of this passage is:
1. A new-found world
2. New relationships
3. Wonders of growth
4. Purposeless prying
5. Curiosity—six-year-old style
.... ( )

The author states that a successful adult inherently exhibits (1) irritation (2) questioning (3) curiosity (4) comprehension of change (5) understanding of machines .... ( )

In this passage the author's attitude toward children is one of (1) despair (2) confidence (3) indifference (4) sharp criticism (5) exaggerated optimism .... ( )

d. The submarine is as much a "Yankee notion" as the telephone and telegraph, the cotton gin, the steamship, the electric light, the airplane, the talking machine, and the great American doughnut. At least the first working submarines—the grandfathers of the great undersea leviathans that pretty much control the seven seas today—were conceived, built, and manned by Americans. To claim that the submarine is one hundred per cent American in origin would be a bit extreme, because early, always interesting but almost invariably unsuccessful experiments were made before America was even discovered. In fact, fragmentary records of submarine experiments go as far back as 1184 B.C. when, Aristotle states, some sort of diving bell device was used at the Siege of Troy. And Alexander the Great is reputed to have "sat in a watertight bell and defied the whale."

The title below that best expresses the ideas of this passage is:
1. Yankee ingenuity
2. Leviathans of the seven seas
3. The submarine, an American invention
4. The American doughnut and other inventions
5. Successful ancestors of the submarine . . . . ( )

The author implies that (1) the doughnut was as great an invention as the cotton gin (2) early experimenters with the submarine were easily discouraged (3) the talking machine was not a very important invention (4) the diving bell of 1184 B.C. was a submarine (5) submarines do not control the seas today . . . . ( )

e. Since 1750, about the beginning of the Age of Steam, the earth's population has more than tripled. This increase has not been an evolutionary phenomenon with biological causes. Yet there was an evolution—it took place in the world's economic organization. Thus, 1,500,000,000 more human beings can now remain alive on the earth's surface, can support themselves by working for others who in turn work for them. This extraordinary tripling of human population in six short generations is explained by the speeded-up economic unification which took place during the same period. Thus most of us are now kept alive by this vast cooperative unified world society. Goods are the great travelers over the earth's surface, far more than human beings. Endlessly streams of goods crisscross, as on Martian canals, with hardly an inhabited spot on the globe unvisited.

The title below that best expresses the ideas of this passage is:
1. Modern phenomena
2. The Age of Steam
3. Increasing population
4. Our greatest travelers
5. Our economic interdependence . . . . ( )

A generation is considered to be (1) 20 years (2) 25 years (3) 33 years (4) 40 years (5) dependent on the average age at marriage . . . . ( )

The writer considers trade necessary for (1) travel (2) democracy (3) political unity (4) self-preservation (5) the theory of evolution . . . . ( )

The basic change which led to the greatly increased population concerns (1) a revolution (2) economic factors (3) biological factors (4) an increase in travel (5) the growth of world government . . ( )

5

a. Three English officers and a group of natives were hunting for two lions which had made a raid upon a village the night before. In the course of the day one of the pair was killed, but the other escaped to the jungle. Proceeding cautiously, after a few steps the lieutenant saw the lion and instantly fired, thus enraging the beast so that it rushed toward him at full speed. Captain Woodhouse saw the movement and knew that if he tried to get into a better position for firing, he would put himself directly in the way of the charge; so he decided to stand still, trusting that the lion would pass close by him unaware, when he could perhaps shoot to advantage. But he was deceived. The furious animal saw him, and flew at him with a dreadful roar. In an instant, the rifle was broken and thrown out of the captain's hand, his left arm at the same moment being seized by the claws and his right by the teeth of his antagonist.

b. Air Research Centers at various sites in the United States use balloons in the study of the atmosphere 50,000 to 100,000 feet above the ground. The balloons are unmanned, but carry a number of instruments. They aim to find the answers to questions about wind patterns, temperatures, pressures and turbulence in the upper-air regions as yet unexplored. Balloons are preset to reach specific altitudes and to remain there the desired length of time. As they are carried along with the wind stream, delicate instruments radio back—or telemeter—the pertinent data. Radio direction-finding stations track the balloon in transit and record the telemetered data concerning altitudes, identification of the particular balloon, rate of its ballast consumption and so on. By accurately tracking and plotting the balloon in flight, it is easy to determine the direction of the wind currents carrying the balloon along.

The title below that best expresses the ideas of this passage is:
1. Hunting
2. The captain's misjudgment
3. Raid upon a village
4. Escape to the jungle
5. Revenge for his mate's death ( )

According to the passage, which one of the following occurred? (1) The lion killed the captain. (2) The lieutenant's gun jammed. (3) The lieutenant wounded the lion. (4) The captain's rifle proved useless. (5) The natives stayed to guard the village .... ( )

The captain's mistake was that he (1) trusted the lion (2) shot to poor advantage (3) believed the lion would not notice him (4) thought that his officers would protect him (5) tried to get into a better position for firing .... ( )

The title below that best expresses the ideas of this passage is:
1. Gathering meteorological data
2. Weather at 50,000 feet
3. Plastic technicians
4. Real flying saucers
5. Aviation research .... ( )

The purpose of a radio in a balloon is to (1) relay information from other instruments to earth (2) allow the pilot to contact the Center (3) control the balloon's rate of ascent (4) plot the direction of wind currents (5) track the balloon in flight .... ( )

The balloons of the Air Research Center (1) are similar to rockets (2) are valuable instruments of war (3) may detect use of the hydrogen bomb (4) rise to the altitudes indicated by the experimenters (5) are launched from a central point in the United States .... ( )

c. In the gush of admiration for the beautifully redone interior of the White House the public has largely lost sight of the new look about its eighteen acres of grounds. Old cedars and elms dating back to John Quincy Adams' occupancy of the White House have been refurbished. New trees, bushes, gardens and walks have appeared where shacks and building materials marred the landscape during the four years of the restoration. Although one group of tourists recently complained of a few stalks of onion grass in the pansy beds, most Washington visitors agree that the White House grounds never looked more colorful and impressive.

The title below that best expresses the ideas of this passage is:
1. The White House gardens
2. A flaw in the landscape
3. Refurbishing the gardens
4. Improved setting for the White House
5. The new White House interior ( )

The writer indicates that (1) tourists complain about the plantings (2) the old gardens were more attractive than the new (3) the White House is visited by more tourists than before (4) some of the trees go back to the days of an early President (5) reconstruction of the White House was a very expensive undertaking . . . . ( )

d. Wherever there is an actively developing culture with sufficient number of specialists capable of thinking in advance of their fellows, discoveries of a similar nature tend to occur at the same time. Whatever may be the deficiencies of our Western civilization, there is no doubt that it is one of the most actively developing cultures there has ever been, and the degree of simultaneous discovery is evidence of this. A recently published work cites over two hundred examples in the realm of medicine alone. Moreover, this trend continues. To mention only one recent invention of great importance: jet propulsion of airplanes was being developed secretly both in England and Germany during the years just prior to 1939, and parallel researches were also proceeding in Italy.

The title below that best expresses the ideas of this passage is:
1. Advances in medicine
2. Jet propulsion in Europe
3. Simultaneous discovery
4. Importance of specialists
5. Our backward civilization . . ( )

The civilization referred to in the passage is that of the (1) Far East (2) Western Hemisphere (3) Mediterranean region (4) Western Hemisphere and Europe (5) Middle East and Europe ( )

The author implies that (1) discoveries are on the wane (2) America pioneered in jet propulsion (3) Oriental culture is inferior to Western (4) Western civilization has improved medicine (5) Western countries have an excess of specialists . . . . ( )

e. Today in America vast concourses of youth are flocking to our colleges, eager for something, just what they do not know. It makes much difference what they get. They will be prone to demand something they can immedi-

The title below that best expresses the ideas of this passage is:
1. Why pupils go to college
2. Foreign languages for culture
3. The need for vocational training
4. The shepherd and his student flock

ately use; the tendency is strong to give it to them: science, economics, business administration, law in its narrower sense. I submit that the shepherds should not first feed the flocks with these. I argue for the outlines of what used to go as a liberal education—not necessarily in the sense that young folks should waste precious years in efforts, unsuccessful for some reason I cannot understand, to master ancient tongues; but I speak for an introduction into the thoughts and deeds of men who have lived before them, in other countries than their own, with other strifes and other needs. This I maintain, not in the interest of that general cultural background, which is so often a cloak for the superior person, the prig, the snob and the pedant. But I submit to you that in some such way alone can we meet and master the high-power salesman of political patent medicines.

5. The importance of a liberal education .... ( )

One purpose of a college education should be to help students to (1) achieve political wisdom (2) become good salesmen (3) develop their talents (4) find their individual interests (5) become future leaders .... ( )

Many students entering college desire to study (1) other countries (2) history and law (3) cultural subjects (4) "practical" subjects (5) too many subjects ...... ( )

The writer stresses the study of (1) other cultures (2) foreign languages (3) politics and medicine (4) business administration (5) general culture .... ( )

6

a. But there is more to the Library of Congress for the American dream than merely the wise appropriation of public money. The Library of Congress could not have become what it is today, with all the generous aid of Congress, without such a citizen as Dr. Herbert Putnam at the directing head of it. He and his staff have devoted their lives to making the four million and more books and pamphlets serve the public to a degree that cannot be approached by any similar great institution in the Old World. Then there is the public that uses these facilities. As one looks down on the general reading room, which alone contains ten thousand volumes that may be read without even the asking, one sees the seats filled with silent readers, old and young, rich and poor, black and white, the executive and the laborer, the general and the private, the noted scholar and the schoolboy, all reading at their own library provided by their own democracy.

The title below that best expresses the ideas of this passage is:
1. Wise use of public funds
2. An institution of democracy
3. Intelligent use of books
4. Generosity of Congress to the public
5. The Old World and the new ( )

The author implies that the Library of Congress is unlike libraries of Europe in that its collections (1) are more easily accessible (2) are in better condition (3) are more valuable (4) are steadily growing in size (5) reveal the spirit of democracy .... ( )

The author indicates that the general reading room (1) should be more fully used (2) should be modernized (3) is used to capacity (4) is too large for practical use (5) should adopt the best features of Old World libraries .... ( )

According to the author, the greatest factor in the present success of the Library of Congress is (1) the spacious general reading room (2) money appropriated by Congress (3) contributions of laborer and executive alike (4) capable leadership (5) an outstanding book collection .... ( )

b. The Greek language is a member of the Aryan or Indo-European family and its various dialects constitute the Hellenic group. It was probably spoken in Europe and Asia at least 1,500 years before the Christian Era by Greeks with classical learning. Later it was a universal language among the cultured classes, just as Latin afterward became the medium of international communication. During the Dark Ages Greek was little known to Western Europe, except in monasteries, although it remained the language of the Byzantine Empire. The emigration of the Greeks to Italy after the fall of Constantinople, and during the century preceding, gave a new impetus to the study of the Greek language, and the revival of learning gave it the place it has ever since occupied.

The title below that best expresses the ideas of this passage is:
1. The Greek language
2. Greece, past and present
3. Importance of the Greek dialects
4. Greek, the universal language
5. An interesting language ... ( )

A result of Greece's being the center of classical learning was that (1) it built great schools (2) its citizens were all cultured (3) Greek was the universal language among the cultured classes (4) Greek was not important during the Dark Ages (5) Greek displaced Latin .... ( )

The Greek language (1) was probably spoken in Europe as early as 1500 B.C. (2) was introduced into Europe by way of Constantinople (3) was responsible for the revival of learning (4) became dominant in Italy (5) had more dialects than Latin .... ( )

c. The hearty laugh, Chesterton maintained, cannot be had without touching the heart. I do not know why touching the heart should always be connected only with the idea of touching it to compassion or a sense of distress. The heart can be touched to joy and triumph; the heart can be touched to amusement. But all our comedians are tragic comedians. These later fashionable writers are so pessimistic in bone and marrow that they never seem able to imagine the heart ever having any concern with mirth. When they speak

The title below that best expresses the ideas of this passage is:
1. Arousing compassion
2. The right place for a man's heart
3. Laughter and sympathy
4. Tragic humor
5. Touching the heart ...... ( )

References to the heart should always be connected with (1) the pangs and disappointments of the emotional life (2) genuine emotional experience (3) feelings of joy and triumph (4) compassion or a sense

of the heart, they always mean the pangs and disappointments of the emotional life. When they say that a man's heart is in the right place, they mean, apparently, that it is in his boots.

of distress   (5) extreme gaiety
.... ( )

Fashionable writers today always produce   (1) pessimistic, heartless pangs   (2) sarcasm mixed with joy (3) witticisms and pangs of regret (4) comedy and pessimism   (5) sad or unhappy emotional effects
.... ( )

d. The English are a heterogeneous and contradictory race with conservative tendencies. While progress is the aim of every Englishman, he nevertheless distrusts and resents change. When he goes to bed, he insists that his mattress shall be supported by a symphony of springs that is the newest word in comfort, but when he wakes up in the morning he requires that the view from his bedroom window shall be the same as it was yesterday and for centuries of yesterdays before that. Thus it is that Great Britain is a land in which the past is always becoming the present, in which history is inescapably part of the picture of today, and thus it is that Great Britain has become a storehouse of treasures that are both the work of nature and the work of man.

The title below that best expresses the ideas of this passage is:
1. History and the British
2. The losing battle of the past
3. The contradictory British
4. Great Britain, noblest work of nature and of men
5. No escape from tradition .. ( )

The passage implies that Englishmen (1) oppose progress   (2) are careless of their ancient natural beauties (3) are favorable to changes   (4) are a race of few and unvaried characteristics   (5) enjoy luxuries ( )

e. Yet the fact remains that as enthusiasm for Shakespearean drama has increased, the tendency has been steadily away from realism and spectacle and steadily toward a rediscovery of the Shakespearean play in conditions resembling its first staging. It has, for instance, been realized that the alternation of scenes—swift scenes following the major crises, gay scenes switching the mood from sadness, comedy breaking in on dire tragedy—enormously enhances the emotional effect of the whole play. Shakespeare wrote his plays to be acted at a single stretch. The alternation of scene and mood is like the orchestration of a symphony, the climaxes carefully prepared in subsidiary themes, the tension heightened or re-

The title below that best expresses the ideas of this passage is:
1. Shortening Shakespeare's plays
2. Modern trends in stage design
3. Decline of the picture-frame set
4. Appropriate Shakespearean staging
5. Revival of interest in Shakespeare
.... ( )

The emotional effect in Shakespeare's plays result from   (1) tension (2) realism   (3) contrasts   (4) mood music   (5) elaborate spectacles .... ( )

Certain scenes in a Shakespearean play are written to   (1) provide a musical theme   (2) decrease production costs   (3) provide relaxed, the movement quickened or slowed to suit the general rhythm of the drama. It follows that Shakespeare cannot be successfully confined on a stage within a picture-frame set statically fixed throughout the three-quarters of an hour allotted to each act. The stage must be one on which the quick succession of scenes and rapid alternation of moods is technically possible.

lief for the actors   (4) contribute to a desired effect   (5) show Shakespeare's versatility ..... ( )

7

a. Television is still too new to have had a pronounced influence on opera. However, those who saw the first televised opera, *Pagliacci,* given by the NBC on March 10, 1940, will not have forgotten the closeup of Tonio's face in the Prologue. To see the comedian's tear-filled eyes gave the musical expression greater intensity than would have been possible in the theater. Television offers the same advantages as the motion picture for conveying minute details of facial expression and gesture more intimately than can be done from the opera stage. The day soon will come when this new door will be opened wide to receive opera.

The title below that best expresses the ideas of this passage is:
1. Closeups in movies
2. The future of television
3. Superiority of television over the theater
4. Prospects for opera in television
5. Pathos in Italian opera .... ( )

According to the passage, to see a singer's facial expressions in closeup (1) reduces opera to the folk level of motion pictures   (2) distracts the listener   (3) enhances the effect of the music   (4) enlivens a television commercial   (5) is more pathetic to watch than his gestures
.... ( )

The writer seems to believe that television   (1) has the advantages of motion picture techniques   (2) has brought opera to more listeners than the theater has   (3) will encourage the singing of *Pagliacci* in English   (4) will not be able to find commercial sponsors for opera (5) can reproduce the magnitude of the opera stage .... ( )

b. We were about a quarter mile away when quiet swept over the colony. A thousand or more heads periscoped. Two thousand eyes glared. Save for our wading, the world's business had stopped. A thousand avian personalities were concentrated on us, and the psychological force of this was terrific.

The title below that best expresses the ideas of this passage is:
1. Our shore birds
2. A quiet colony
3. Judgment day
4. Waiting
5. An unwelcome intrusion ... ( )

Contingents of homecoming feeders, suddenly aware of four strange specks moving across the lake, would bank violently and speed away. Then the chain reaction began. Every throat in that rookery let go with a concatenation of wild, raspy, terrorized trumpet bursts. With all wings now fully spread and churning, and quadrupling the color mass, the birds began to move as one, and the sky was filled with the sound of judgment day.

The passage indicates that the writer (1) was a psychologist   (2) observed the fear of the flying birds (3) was terrified at the sounds (4) crossed the lake by boat   (5) went alone to the rookery .... (   )

According to the passage, when they first noticed the visitors, the birds of the colony   (1) flew away   (2) became very quiet   (3) churned their wings   (4) set up a series of cries   (5) glared at the homecoming birds .... (   )

The reaction of the visitors to the experience described in this passage was probably one of   (1) impatience   (2) fear   (3) anger (4) awe   (5) sadness .... (   )

c. "Sticks and stones can break my bones,
But names will never hurt me."

No doubt you are familiar with this childhood rhyme; perhaps, when you were younger, you frequently invoked whatever protection it could offer against unpleasant epithets. But like many popular slogans and verses, this one will not bear too close scrutiny. For names *will* hurt you. Sometimes you may be the victim, and find yourself an object of scorn, humiliation, and hatred just because other people have called you certain names. At other times you may not be the victim, but clever speakers and writers may, through name calling, blind your judgment so that you will follow them in a course of action wholly opposed to your own interests or principles. Name calling can make you gullible to propaganda which you might otherwise readily see through and reject.

The title below that best expresses the ideas of this passage is:
1. An object of scorn
2. An unusual course of action
3. The foolishness of rhymes
4. Verbal assassination
5. The clever speaker .... (   )

Name calling may make you more susceptible to   (1) childhood rhymes   (2) biased arguments (3) sticks and stones   (4) invoked protection   (5) unpleasant epithets .... (   )

The author evidently feels that slogans and verses are frequently (1) invoked by gullible writers (2) humiliating to their authors (3) disregarded by children   (4) misunderstood by clever speakers (5) an over-simplification of a problem .... (   )

d. Despite the many categories of the historian, there are only two ages of man. The first age, the age from the beginnings of recorded time to the present, is the age of the cave man. It is

The title below that best expresses the ideas of this passage is:
1. The historian at work
2. The dangers of all-out war
3. The power of world anarchy

the age of war. It is today. The second age, still only a prospect, is the age of civilized man. The test of civilized man will be represented by his ability to use his inventiveness for his own good by substituting world law for world anarchy. That second age is still within the reach of the individual in our time. It is not a part-time job, however. It calls for total awareness, total commitment.

4. Mankind on the threshold
5. The decline of civilization .. ( )

The author's attitude toward the possibility of man's reaching an age of civilization is one of   (1) limited hope   (2) complete despair   (3) marked uncertainty   (4) complacency   (5) anger .... ( )

e. Had Leonardo da Vinci seen the plain evidence of upward winds—the evidence of flying leaves and soaring birds—the air age might have begun in his time, and the airplane would have developed along with the sailing vessel. For these upward winds also explain the sailing of gliders. A glider is nothing but a wood-and-fabric replica of a hawk; there is nothing in it that Leonardo could not have designed, built, and flown. It used to be that motorless airplanes could fly only over carefully selected sites, where a steep hillside faced a strong wind and deflected it upward. But today, with no new equipment but a clear mental image of these upward winds, men can fly without motors for hundreds of miles across country, even across flat plains, without machine power of any kind, riding on these updrafts.

The title below that best expresses the ideas of this passage is:
1. Updrafts
2. A wood-and-fabric bird
3. Da Vinci's invention
4. The power of imagination
5. The limitations of gliders ...( )

Gliders can soar only   (1) over plateaus   (2) by riding the winds   (3) for short distances   (4) in mountainous country   (5) over carefully surveyed areas ...... ( )

The author's treatment of his material may best be described as   (1) quaintly humorous   (2) completely carefree   (3) predominantly factual   (4) utterly pessimistic   (5) bitterly sarcastic ( )

8

a. The white man lapsed easily into an Indian. The mountain man's eye had the Indian's alertness, forever watching for the movement of boughs or grasses, for the passage of wildlife downwind, something unexplained floating in a a stream, dust stirring in a calm, or the configuration of mere scratches on a cottonwood. His ear would never again hear church bells or the noises of a farm, but, like the Indian's, was tuned to catch any sound in a country where every sound was provisionally a death warning. He dressed like an Indian, in blankets, robes, buckskins, and mocca-

The title below that best expresses the ideas of this passage is:
1. Signs of an enemy
2. In praise of the Indian
3. Characteristics of a traitor
4. The white man turned Indian
5. Disadvantages of Indian life ( )

The senses of the Indian were sensitively attuned to   (1) the movement of animals through the bushes   (2) the ringing of church bells   (3) the noises on a farm   (4) the sounds of the war whoop   (5) a few distinct sounds only .... ( )

sins. He lived like an Indian in bark huts or skin lodges. He thought like an Indian, propitiating the demons of the wild, making medicine, and consulting the omens.

b. All this activity and taking of responsibility runs right down into the smallest villages. There are at least 200,-000 organizations, associations, clubs, societies, and lodges in the United States, along with innumerable social groups and *ad hoc* committees formed for specific causes. Except for the few intellectuals who don't believe in "joining," and the very, very poor who can't afford to, practically all adult Americans belong to some club or other, and most of them take part in some joint effort to do good. This prodigious army of volunteer citizens, who take time from their jobs and pleasure to work more or less unselfishly for the betterment of the community, is unique in the world. It is, in a way, the mainspring as well as the safeguard of democracy. For the volunteers are always ready to work and fight for what they think is right.

c. Today in a time of great confusion and fierce disagreement, and also a time of great opportunity for all who are disposed to make their profit of that confusion, we who use words have a heavy responsibility. We need illimitable boldness in our seeking of truth, and great generosity of feeling and imagination in our approach to our task of giving it concrete and moving expression. But we need the greatest care in our choice of the words we use that they may first of all be accurate and fair,

The author states that the mountain man was (1) homesick (2) patriotic (3) humble (4) alert (5) learned .... ( )

This passage suggests that the Indian is (1) careless (2) antisocial (3) contemptuous of the whites (4) a lover of his family (5) superstitious .... ( )

The title below that best expresses the ideas of this passage is:
1. The busy citizen and his activities
2. The joiner
3. Group action in a democracy
4. Soldiers as civilians
5. America's smallest communities .... ( )

An *ad hoc* committee is one appointed (1) under parliamentary rules (2) to enlist volunteers (3) for a particular service (4) on a permanent basis (5) to supervise other organizations .... ( )

The author states that Americans who join clubs are interested in (1) the welfare of society (2) making friends (3) a unique organization (4) using their leisure profitably (5) maintaining American leadership .... ( )

The title below that best expresses the ideas of this passage is:
1. Taking advantage of confusion
2. The need for disagreement
3. Truth-seeking aspect of words
4. Confusion and limitation of words
5. A duty of writers and speakers .... ( )

The writer believes that (1) most Americans lack imagination (2) writers must be fearless (3) all Americans stand for justice for all

that they may meet the classic American test of "justice to all."

d. English folk singers have adopted a conventional method of singing. During the performance the eyes are closed, the head is upraised, and a rigid expression of countenance is maintained until the song is finished. A short pause follows the conclusion, and then the singer relaxes his attitude and repeats in his ordinary voice the last line of the song, or its title. This is the invariable ritual on formal occasions. It does not proceed from any lack of appreciation. The English peasant is by nature a shy man and undemonstrative, and on ceremonious occasions, as when he is singing before an audience, he becomes very nervous and restrained, and welcomes the shelter afforded by convention.

e. The American Revolution is the only one in modern history which, rather than devouring the intellectuals who prepared it, carried them to power. Most of the signatories of the Declaration of Independence were intellectuals. This tradition is ingrained in America, whose greatest statesmen have been intellectuals—Jefferson and Lincoln, for example. These statesmen performed their political function, but at the same time they felt a more universal responsibility, and they actively defined this responsibility. Thanks to them there is in America a living school of political science. In fact, it is at the moment the only one perfectly adapted to the emergencies of the contemporary world, and one which can be victoriously opposed to communism. A European who follows American politics will be struck by the constant reference in the press and from the platform to this political philosophy, to the historical events through which it was best expressed, to

(4) "Justice for All" is a classic American essay (5) a majority wish to make a profit from confusion .... ( )

The title below that best expresses the ideas of this passage is:
1. Country music festivals
2. Traditional music
3. A changing ritual of song
4. An unappreciative audience
5. A helpful custom .... ( )

The English folk singer has adopted a conventional method of singing chiefly because of his (1) pride (2) reserved nature (3) relaxed attitude (4) dislike of customs (5) desire to please .... ( )

The tone of this passage is best described as (1) matter-of-fact (2) pleading (3) argumentative (4) depressing (5) ironic .... ( )

The title below that best expresses the ideas of this passage is:
1. Fathers of the American Revolution
2. Jefferson and Lincoln—ideal statesmen
3. The basis of American political philosophy
4. Democracy versus communism
5. The responsibilities of statesmen .... ( )

According to this passage, intellectuals who pave the way for revolutions are usually (1) honored (2) misunderstood (3) destroyed (4) forgotten (5) elected to office .... ( )

Which statement is true according to the passage? (1) America is a land of intellectuals. (2) The signers of the Declaration of Independence were all well educated. (3) Jefferson and Lincoln were revolution-the great statesmen who were its best representatives.

aries. (4) Adaptability is a characteristic of American political science. (5) Europeans are confused by American politics . . . . ( )

9

a. Self-contained diving suits have made it possible for a diver to explore the depths without the local authorities' knowing very much about it. Should he be lucky enough to discover a wreck, a diver can recover the less cumbersome fragments, bronzes, marble, or bits of statuary, without attracting official attention. Today one can indulge in a secret treasure hunt right down to the seabed with the added advantage that it is far harder to keep a watch on sunken treasure than it is to protect excavations on shore. So the modern despoiler is as great a pest to the serious archaeologist at sea as he is on land. In Egypt and Syria he has deprived us of invaluable data. He nearly always ransacks his objective to take away some portable trophy which he thinks valuable, he keeps his treasure house a secret, and we must blame him for the appearance of various objects impossible to date or catalog.

The title below that best expresses the ideas of this passage is:
1. Recovering ships
2. Modern diving suits
3. The irresponsible explorer
4. Cataloging long-lost objects
5. Concealing the truth in the Near East . . . . ( )

The passage suggests that the author is (1) opposed to excavations on shore (2) sympathetic to the officials (3) sympathetic to the divers (4) opposed to investigations in Syria and Egypt (5) opposed to the despoilers' cataloging their finds . . . . ( )

It is to the amateur archaeologist's advantage that local authorities (1) protect his findings on land (2) allow him to keep portable treasures (3) provide catalogs of underwater treasures (4) are sometimes unaware of his diving activities (5) are ignorant of the true value of sunken treasures . . . . ( )

b. All museum adepts are familiar with examples of *ostrakoi,* the oystershells used in balloting. As a matter of fact, these "oystershells" are usually shards of pottery, conveniently glazed to enable the voter to express his wishes in writing. In the Agora a great number of these have come to light, bearing the thrilling name, Themistocles. Into rival jars were dropped the ballots for or against his banishment. On account of the huge vote taken on that memorable day, it was to be expected that many ostrakoi would be found, but the interest of this collection is that a number of these ballots are inscribed in an

The title below that best expresses the ideas of this passage is:
1. An odd method of voting
2. Themistocles, an early dictator
3. Democracy in the past
4. Political trickery—past and present
5. The diminishing American politician . . . . ( )

An obol, as used in the passage is evidently (1) an oystershell (2) a Greek coin (3) a promise of bread (4) a complimentary remark (5) an appointive public office . . . . ( )

identical handwriting. There is nothing mysterious about it! The Boss was on the job, then as now. He prepared these ballots and voters cast them—no doubt for the consideration of an obol or two. *The ballot box was stuffed.*

How is the glory of the American boss diminished! A vile imitation, he. His methods as old as Time!

The author suggests that the verdict against Themistocles was to a certain extent (1) justified   (2) mysterious (3) predetermined   (4) unpopular (5) unimportant . . . . (   )

The tone of the last paragraph is (1) matter-of-fact (2) self-righteous (3) complimentary   (4) insincere (5) sarcastic . . . . (   )

c. Windstorms have recently established a record which meteorologists hope will not be equaled for many years to come. Disastrous tornadoes along with devastating typhoons and hurricanes have cost thousands of lives and left property damage totaling far into the millions. The prominence these storms have held in the news has led many people to ask about the difference between the three. Is a typhoon the same as a hurricane? Is a tornado the same as a typhoon? Basically, there is no difference. All three consist of wind rotating counterclockwise (in the Northern Hemisphere) at a tremendous velocity around a low-pressure center. However, each type does have its own definite characteristics. Of the three the tornado is certainly the most treacherous. The Weather Bureau can, with some degree of accuracy, forecast the typhoon and the hurricane; however, it is impossible to determine where or when the tornado will strike. And out of the three, if one had a choice, perhaps it would be safer to choose to withstand the hurricane.

The title below that best expresses the ideas of this passage is:
1. Recent storms
2. Record-breaking storms
3. Predicting windstorms
4. Treacherous windstorms
5. Wind velocity and direction . (   )

Which is *not* common to all of the storms mentioned?   (1) fairly accurate forecasting   (2) violently rotating wind   (3) high property damage   (4) loss of human lives (5) public interest . . . . (   )

The author indicates that   (1) typhoons cannot be forecast   (2) the Southern Hemisphere is free from hurricanes   (3) typhoons are more destructive than hurricanes (4) hurricanes are not really dangerous   (5) tornadoes occur around a low-pressure center . . . . (   )

d. A large number of Shakespeare's soliloquies must be considered as representing thought, not speech. They are to make the audience understand what is passing through the mind of the character, not what, under the circumstances, he would have said aloud. A maiden would not say aloud Juliet's speech, "Gallop apace, you fiery-footed steeds," which represents the secret passion of her body and soul. And her soliloquy

The title below that best expresses the ideas of this passage is:
1. Gesture and changes in the voice
2. The difficulties of Shakespearean actors
3. Misunderstanding the Shakespearean play
4. Revealing thought through the soliloquy
5. Unfolding the plot through the soliloquy . . . . (   )

when she takes the drug is also a representation of her thoughts; it was not spoken in reality. The dramatist is compelled to put it into words and the actress to speak it—but to add to it gesture or great changes in the voice or outward show is to mistake altogether the idea of the dramatist.

The writer assumes that (1) actors have used poor enunciation (2) *Romeo and Juliet* is the most popular play by Shakespeare (3) his readers are familiar with Shakespeare's plays (4) many people dislike Shakespeare (5) Shakespeare is only for "highbrows" . . . . ( )

Which statement can be made on the basis of the passage? (1) The role of Juliet is more difficult than other roles. (2) The role of Juliet is only one example of the point made. (3) Audiences have no feeling for characterization. (4) Shakespeare was an incompetent dramatist in some respects. (5) There are too many soliloquies in Shakespeare's plays . . . . ( )

e. To keep clear of concealment, to keep clear of the need of concealment, to do nothing which he might not do out on the middle of Boston Common at noonday—I cannot say how more and more it seems to me to be the glory of a young man's life. It is an awful hour when the first necessity of hiding anything comes. The whole life is different thenceforth. When there are questions to be feared and eyes to be avoided and subjects which must not be touched, then the bloom of life is gone. Put off that day as long as possible. Put it off forever if you can.

The title below that best expresses the ideas of this passage is:
1. A time for concealment
2. Noonday on Boston Common
3. A code for living
4. Penalties for procrastination
5. Youth vs. age . . . . ( )

The author recommends (1) being aboveboard (2) living for the present (3) avoiding necessity (4) living by example (5) being careful in discussion . . . . ( )

10

a. A legendary island in the Atlantic Ocean beyond the Pillars of Hercules was first mentioned by Plato in the *Timaeus*. Atlantis was a fabulously beautiful and prosperous land, the seat of an empire nine thousand years before Solon. Its inhabitants overran part of Europe and Africa, Athens alone being able to defy them. Because of the impiety of its people, the island was de-

The title below that best expresses the ideas of this passage is:
1. A persistent myth
2. Geography according to Plato
3. The first discoverers of America
4. Buried civilizations
5. A labor of Hercules . . . . . . ( )

According to the passage, we may most safely conclude that the inhabit-

stroyed by an earthquake and inundation. The legend may have existed before Plato and may have sprung from the concept of Homer's Elysium. The possibility that such an island once existed has caused much speculation, resulting in a theory that pre-Columbian civilizations in America were established by colonists from the lost island.

ants of Atlantis   (1) were known personally to Homer   (2) were ruled by Plato   (3) were a religious and superstitious people   (4) used the name Columbia for America   (5) left no recorded evidence of their existence . . . . (   )

According to the legend, Atlantis was destroyed because the inhabitants (1) failed to obtain an adequate food supply   (2) failed to conquer Greece   (3) failed to respect their gods   (4) believed in Homer's Elysium   (5) had become too prosperous . . . . (   )

b. Readers in the past seem to have been more patient than the readers of today. There were few diversions, and they had more time to read novels of a length that seems to us now inordinate. It may be that they were not irritated by the digressions and irrelevances that interrupted the narration. But some of the novels that suffer from these defects are among the greatest that have ever been written. It is deplorable that on this account they should be less and less read.

The title below that best expresses the ideas of this passage is:
1. Defects of today's novels
2. Novel reading then and now
3. The great novel
4. The impatient reader of novels
5. Decline in education . . . . . (   )

The author implies that   (1) authors of the past did not use narration to any extent   (2) great novels are usually long   (3) digressions and irrelevances are characteristic of modern novels   (4) readers of the past were more capable   (5) people today have more pastimes than formerly . . . . (   )

c. Throughout extensive areas of the tropics the tall and stately primeval forest has given way to eroded land, scrub and the jumble of secondary growth. Just as the virgin forests of Europe and North America were laid low by man's improvidence, so those of the tropics are now vanishing—only their destruction may be encompassed in decades instead of centuries. A few authorities hold that, except for government reserves, the earth's great rain forests may vanish within a generation. The economic loss will be incalculable, for the primary rain forests are rich sources of timber (mahogany, teak)

The title below that best expresses the ideas of this passage is:
1. Scene of evolution
2. Virgin forests today
3. Products of the rain forests
4. Importance of the rain forests
5. Man's waste of natural resources

Concerning the rain forests, man still lacks knowledge of their   (1) rate of disappearance   (2) exact geographic locations   (3) value as sources of timber   (4) need for protective foliage   (5) potential commercial development . . . . (   )

and such by-products as resins, gums, cellulose, camphor and rattans. No one, indeed, can compute their resources, for of the thousands of species that compose the forest cover, there are only a few whose physical and chemical properties have been studied with a view to commercial use.

Most important of all, the primeval rain forest is a reservoir of specimens, a dynamic center of evolution whence the rest of the world's plant life has been continually enriched with new forms. These extensive reserves must be defended from the acquisitive hand of man, whose ruthless ax would expose them to the ravages of sun and rain.

The resources of the rain forests are (1) incalculable   (2) purely chemical   (3) somewhat limited (4) uncommercial   (5) of interest only to scientists .... (   )

The second sentence of the passage suggests that   (1) man has been unlucky   (2) no virgin forests have been replanted   (3) man has become more wasteful   (4) tropical rain forests have vanished   (5) forests in North America were destroyed in a period of ten years .. (   )

The primary reason for conservation of the great rain forests is that they (1) are areas of botanical evolution (2) are not ready for man's ruthless ax   (3) are the chief source of income for governments   (4) provide major sources of material for chemical industries   (5) need further development before they can be utilized commercially .... (   )

As used in the passage, the word "primeval" (second paragraph, first line) means   (1) of first importance   (2) commercial   (3) gorgeous   (4) untouched   (5) thick .... (   )

The ideas of the author would probably be most strongly supported by (1) lumber company representatives (2) conservationists and botanists (3) chemical manufacturers   (4) government representatives   (5) the "man on the street" .... (   )

d. The reasons for the do-it-yourself movement are apparent. An ever-reduced work week means more and more leisure time, and we have to fill waking hours that might otherwise go empty. Now automation threatens us with an even greater number of idle hours. Then, the postwar housing boom, which for the first time in our history has made us really a nation of homeowners,

The title below that best expresses the ideas of this passage is:
1. Leisure time activities
2. A nation of homeowners
3. The pride of ownership
4. Rising wages
5. Economy-inspired activity .. (   )

According to the author, many members of the do-it-yourself group

makes us home-conscious. It is one thing to let someone else's lawn go bad, another when you yourself are the owner and the weeds are no one's but your own. There's another reason too, like that of the fellow who explained there were a hundred reasons why he didn't want to build a squash court: "The first is that a court costs $100,000 . . . the other ninety-nine don't matter!" So it is with do-it-yourself—the best answer to rising costs of labor in a number of trades.

(1) have developed a new interest in community affairs (2) find it hard to pay for home repairs and renovations (3) are scientific gardeners (4) now favor automation (5) avoid using machine tools (   )

The do-it-yourself movement can best be explained as being the result of (1) a variety of postwar economic factors (2) increased use of power tools (3) a general relaxing of credit restrictions (4) a trend toward a lower standard of living (5) increased employment in specialized trades . . . . (   )

According to the passage, which statement is true? (1) More homes than apartment houses are being erected. (2) Homeowners are now building squash courts. (3) Automation will decrease the number of homeowners. (4) Homeowners may have more leisure time in the future. (5) The lawns of rented homes are usually neglected . . . . (   )

Chapter 4

THE CORRECT USAGE TEST: GRAMMAR (QUESTION 4)

THE IMPORTANCE OF CORRECT USAGE

A knowledge of correct English usage will help you to solve many language problems. It will enable you to use *who* and *whom* correctly. It will guide you in making verbs agree with their subjects, and pronouns with their antecedents. It will serve as a safeguard against gross errors, such as double negatives and dangling constructions. On written examinations it will help you to get better grades. In personal interviews it will help you to make a favorable impression on important people: your prospective employer, your college interviewer, and others.

Do not be misled by the fact that the Regents Comprehensive Examination in English allots only five credits to its correct usage test. Your skill in correct usage will be rated also in your written answers to the twenty-credit literature-discussion test and the thirty-credit composition test. For these reasons you should carefully go over the helpful review of correct usage in the following pages.

TYPICAL REGENTS CORRECT USAGE TEST

JANUARY 1961

In each of the following sentences that is incorrect, underline the word or expression that is incorrectly used and indicate your correction in the space provided. If a sentence is correct as it stands, place a *C* in the space provided. Do not change any correct part of a sentence.   [5]

(1) I couldn't hardly believe that he would desert the cause.   (1) could

(2) I found the place in the book more readily than she.   (2) C

(3) A good example of our American outdoor activities are sports.   (3) is

(4) My point of view is much different from your's.   (4) yours

(5) The cook was suppose to use two spoonfuls of dressing for each serving.   (5) supposed

82

ANALYSIS OF THE CORRECT USAGE TEST

Note that the directions state: "Do not change any correct part of a sentence." If you do, you will lose credit. Correct the error only.

QUESTION 1: I *couldn't* hardly believe that he would desert the cause.
ANSWER: *could*
REASON: The *n't* (in *couldn't*) is unnecessary because *hardly* is a negative word.

QUESTION 2: I found the place in the book more readily than she.
ANSWER: C (correct)
REASON: *she* is the subject of the verb *did* understood. (I found the place in the book more readily than she *did*.)

QUESTION 3: A good example of our American outdoor activities *are* sports.
ANSWER: *is*
REASON: The verb *is* must be singular to agree with its subject *example*, which is singular.

QUESTION 4: My point of view is much different from *your's*.
ANSWER: *yours*
REASON: Possessive pronouns (*yours, his, hers, its, ours, theirs, whose*) never have an apostrophe.

QUESTION 5: The cook was *suppose* to use two spoonfuls of dressing for each serving.
ANSWER: *supposed*
REASON: The helping verb *was* requires the past participle *supposed*.

A REVIEW OF CORRECT USAGE

The following pages will review the principles of correct usage that have been involved in test after test.

A.   PRONOUNS

More Regents usage questions deal with pronouns than with any other usage topic because pronouns are troublesome words. For example, most pronouns have one form as a subject, another form as an object, and a third as a possessive.

AS SUBJECT (*Nominative Case*)	AS OBJECT (*Objective Case*)	AS POSSESSIVE (*Possessive Case*)
I	me	my, mine
you	you	your, yours
he	him	his
she	her	her, hers
it	it	its
we	us	our, ours
they	them	their, theirs
who	whom	whose
whoever	whomever	whosever

TYPICAL QUESTIONS ON PRONOUNS

Questions preceded by an asterisk (*) are actual Regents questions but with this modification: the source of error is called to the attention of the student, and both the correct and incorrect forms are presented in parentheses, the correct form being italicized.

Rule 1: A pronoun used as a subject takes the nominative case.

*QUESTION 1: I know of no other person in the club who is more kind-hearted than (*she*, her).

ANSWER EXPLAINED: *she* is subject of the understood verb *is*. (I know of no other person in the club who is more kind-hearted than she *is*.)

HINT: Mentally supply the understood verb. It will help you choose the correct pronoun.

*QUESTION 2: (*Who*, Whom) do you believe is the most capable?

ANSWER EXPLAINED: *Who* is subject of the verb *is*.

HINT: Ignore interrupting expressions like *do you believe* (*do you suppose, think, say,* etc.). They do not affect the case of *who* and *whom*.

*QUESTION 3: He voted against (*whoever*, whomever) favored that proposal.

ANSWER EXPLAINED: *whoever* is subject of the verb *favored*.

HINT: Don't choose *whomever* in the belief that it is the object of the preposition *against*. It isn't. The object of *against* is the entire clause *whoever favored that proposal.*

Exception to Rule 1: A pronoun used as the subject of an infinitive takes the objective case.

(The infinitive is the form of the verb preceded by *to*: *to be, to tell, to read,* etc.)

QUESTION 4: Father expects Fred and (I, *me*) to pass.

ANSWER EXPLAINED: *me* (together with *Fred*) is the subject of the infinitive *to pass*—not the object of *expects*. The entire phrase *Fred and me to pass* is the object of *expects.*

HINT: In an instance like this, construct two sentences. Then combine them for the correct answer.
Sentence 1: Father expects Fred to pass.
Sentence 2: Father expects *me* (not *I*) to pass.
Answer: Father expects Fred and *me* to pass.

Rule 2: A pronoun used as a predicate nominative takes the nominative case.

[A noun or pronoun after some form of *to be* (*is, was, might have been,* etc.) is called a predicate nominative.]

*QUESTION 5: It was (*we*, us) girls who swept the gym floor after the dance.

ANSWER EXPLAINED: *we* is a predicate nominative after the verb *was.*

HINT: Remember that the verb *to be*, in all of its forms, is the same as an equal sign (=). Whatever case comes before it (practically always nominative case) must also follow it:

| It | was | we. |
| (nominative) | = | (nominative) |

Rule 3: A pronoun used as object of a verb, object of a preposition, or indirect object takes the objective case.

*QUESTION 6: "(Who, *Whom*) can you send to help us?" inquired Aunt May.

ANSWER EXPLAINED: *Whom* is object of the verb *can send.*

HINT: With a *who-whom* question, change the word order: You can send *whom* to help us? Obviously, *you* is subject and *whom* is object of *can send.*

*QUESTION 7: The lawyer promised to notify my mother and (I, me) of his plans for a new trial.

ANSWER EXPLAINED: *me* (together with *mother*) is object of the infinitive *to notify*.

HINT: In a case like this, construct two sentences. Then combine them for the correct answer.

> Sentence 1: The lawyer promised to notify my mother.
>
> Sentence 2: The lawyer promised to notify *me* (not *I*).
>
> Answer: The lawyer promised to notify my mother and *me* of his plans for a new trial.

*QUESTION 8: It is always a pleasure for (we, us) boys to visit a firehouse.

ANSWER EXPLAINED: *us* is object of the preposition *for*.

HINT: When a pronoun is combined with a noun (*we boys, we girls,* etc.), temporarily omit the noun.

> Noun omitted: It is always a pleasure for *us* (not *we*) to visit a firehouse.
>
> Noun added: It is always a pleasure for *us* boys to visit a firehouse.

*QUESTION 9: All the pupils except George and (she, her) plan to order the book.

ANSWER EXPLAINED: *her* (together with *George*) is object of the preposition *except*. (*Except* is a preposition as are *to, by, of, for, with,* etc. Prepositions are followed by the objective case.)

HINT: In a case like this, construct two sentences. Then combine them for the correct answer.

> Sentence 1: All the pupils except George plan to order the book.
>
> Sentence 2: All the pupils except *her* (not *she*) plan to order the book.
>
> Answer: All the pupils except George and *her* plan to order the book.

QUESTION 10: Grandfather gave my sister and (I, *me*) a year's subscription to a news magazine.

ANSWER EXPLAINED: *me* (together with *my sister*) is the indirect object of the verb *gave*.

HINT: In a case like this, construct two sentences. Then combine them for the correct answer.

> Sentence 1: Grandfather gave my sister a year's subscription.
>
> Sentence 2: Grandfather gave *me* (not *I*) a year's subscription.
>
> Answer: Grandfather gave my sister and *me* a year's subscription.

Rule 4: A pronoun used in apposition with a noun is in the same case as that noun.

QUESTION 11: Two contestants, Martha and (*she*, her), were disqualified by the judges.

ANSWER EXPLAINED: The pronoun *she* must be in the nominative case because it is in apposition with the noun *contestants*, which is in the nominative case.

HINT: *contestants* is in the nominative case because it is the subject of *were disqualified*.

QUESTION 12: The judges disqualified two contestants, Martha and (she, *her*).

ANSWER EXPLAINED: The pronoun *her* must be in the objective case because it is in apposition with the noun *contestants*, which is in the objective case.

HINT: *contestants* is now in the objective case because it is the object of *disqualified*.

Rule 5: A pronoun that expresses ownership is in the possessive case.

*QUESTION 13: The girl refused to admit that the note was (her's, hers).

ANSWER EXPLAINED: *hers* is the correct spelling of the possessive case, which is needed here to express ownership (*belonging to her*).

HINT: Pronouns that express ownership (*yours, his, hers, its, ours,* etc.) never require an apostrophe.

*QUESTION 14: He became an authority on the theater and (*its, it's*) great personalities.

ANSWER EXPLAINED: *its* is the correct spelling of the possessive case, which is needed here to express ownership (*belonging to it*).

HINT: Don't confuse possessive pronouns with contractions.

POSSESSIVE PRONOUNS	CONTRACTIONS
its (belonging to it)	*it's* (it is)
your (belonging to you)	*you're* (you are)
their (belonging to them)	*they're* (they are)
whose (belonging to whom)	*who's* (who is)

QUESTION 15: Father disapproves of (me, *my*) staying up late before examinations.

ANSWER EXPLAINED: *my* (possessive case) is required by the meaning.

HINT: Of what does Father disapprove? *Me?* Certainly not. He disapproves of *my* (*belonging to me*) *staying up late.*

EXERCISE ON PRONOUNS

Write the correct choice and state the reason for your choice:

1. I'm not certain that (your's, yours) is the best solution.
2. Our club sent two delegates, Ruth and (I, me), to Oswego.
3. In the first row of the orchestra sat Robert and (he, him).
4. Did you know that Frank knows his Latin better than (she, her)?
5. Are you willing to allow (we, us) boys to form a cooking class?
6. Between you and (I, me), I think Henry is wrong.
7. (Us, We) two boys have been very close friends for a long time.
8. The committee consisted of John, Henry, Tom, and (I, me).
9. The audience gave our opponents and (we, us) a rousing ovation.
10. It was (they, them) who objected to the decision.
11. The candidate pleaded with (we, us) voters to go to the polls.
12. Divide the responsibilities between Jane and (her, she).
13. This is John (who, whom), I am sure, will be glad to serve you.
14. Few student officers have served as conscientiously as (she, her).
15. (Whom, Who) shall we invite to the Arista installation?
16. Father would not permit Tom and (I, me) to go swimming today.
17. May Geraldine and (me, I) support your motion?

18. The money found on the stairs proved to be neither John's nor (our's, ours).
19. (Who, Whom) do you think will be designated "most likely to succeed"?
20. I don't know what I would do if I were (him, he).
21. "(It's, Its) victory for them or (I, me)," he shouts.
22. Father criticized (me, my) playing the radio when I do my homework.
23. (We, Us) upperclassmen always have a greater share of responsibility.
24. When the dance was held, all came except (she, her).
25. Is this term paper (your's, yours) or Helen's?
26. We have no room in the car for suitcases as large as (your's, yours).
27. Gerald and (he, him) are always dependable in emergencies.
28. Mary and John wish to go because (their, they're, there) anxious to visit the museum.
29. Send Harvey and (I, me) the directions, as we have never been to your house.
30. I shall ask my father to let Louis and (he, him) come with us to the beach.
31. When that program is over, the children know (it's, its) time for bed.
32. Between you and (I, me) there have never been any serious misunderstandings.
33. Such a comment about anyone (who, whom) we know to be thoughtful is unfair.
34. The co-captains, Nick and (he, him), will sit on the platform.
35. It was (they, them) who first suggested that I should apply for membership.
36. The chairman appointed two alternates, John and (I, me).
37. I have always been able to read a map better than (she, her).
38. It must have been (they, them) who purchased the class gift.
39. Call on (whoever, whomever) raises his hand, provided he has not yet spoken.
40. (It's, Its) too bad that the dog hurt (it's, its) foot.
41. The principal recommended Peter and (I, me) as commencement speakers.
42. Tom, (who, whom) the captain that morning had assigned to the post, lay on the ground.
43. Father does not approve of (you, your) studying so late.

44. Tom knew he would have to start action before there was a chance of (them, their) planning an attack.
45. (Whom, Who) is taking you to the senior dance, Alice?
46. This is the story of a girl (who's, whose) father was a doctor.
47. I am as good in trigonometry as (she, her).
48. I find that an essential item for (we, us) beginners is missing.
49. The fault is unquestionably (our's, ours), not John's.
50. If you will describe (it's, its) color, perhaps we can find it.

B. VERBS

Irregular Verbs:

You must know the principal parts of important irregular verbs to be able to speak and write good English. Many questions on past usage tests have dealt with irregular verbs.

The principal parts of a verb are:

1. the present tense: *break*
2. the past tense: *broke*
3. the past participle: *broken* (used with a helping verb such as *am, is, was, were, has, have, will be,* etc.)

One of the most common verb errors is the use of the past tense instead of the past participle, as in this actual Regents question:

When I first saw the car, its steering wheel was *broke.*

To correct this sentence, you must change *broke* (past tense) to *broken* (past participle). Obviously you should know your principal parts. The following list is well worth reviewing:

PRESENT TENSE	PAST TENSE	PAST PARTICIPLE
arise	arose	arisen
bear	bore	borne, or born
beat	beat	beaten
become	became	become
begin	began	begun
bend	bent	bent
bite	bit	bitten
blow	blew	blown
break	broke	broken

PRESENT TENSE	PAST TENSE	PAST PARTICIPLE
bring	brought	brought
burst	burst	burst
catch	caught	caught
choose	chose	chosen
come	came	come
creep	crept	crept
dig	dug	dug
dive	dived	dived
do	did	done
draw	drew	drawn
drink	drank	drunk
drive	drove	driven
drown	drowned	drowned
eat	ate	eaten
fall	fell	fallen
fight	fought	fought
flee	fled	fled
fly	flew	flown
forget	forgot	forgotten
forgive	forgave	forgiven
freeze	froze	frozen
get	got	got, or gotten
give	gave	given
go	went	gone
grow	grew	grown
hang (suspend a thing)	hung	hung
hang (execute a person)	hanged	hanged
hide	hid	hidden
hold	held	held
hurt	hurt	hurt
kneel	knelt	knelt
know	knew	known
lay (to put)	laid	laid
lead	led	led
lend	lent	lent
lie (to recline)	lay	lain
lie (to tell a lie)	lied	lied

PRESENT TENSE	PAST TENSE	PAST PARTICIPLE
lose	lost	lost
mistake	mistook	mistaken
pay	paid	paid
prove	proved	proved, or proven
rid	rid	rid
ride	rode	ridden
ring	rang	rung
rise	rose	risen
run	ran	run
say	said	said
see	saw	seen
set	set	set
sew	sewed	sewed, or sewn
shake	shook	shaken
show	showed	showed, or shown
shrink	shrank	shrunk
sing	sang	sung
sink	sank	sunk
sit	sat	sat
slay	slew	slain
slide	slid	slid
speak	spoke	spoken
spend	spent	spent
spring	sprang	sprung
steal	stole	stolen
strike	struck	struck
swear	swore	sworn
sweep	swept	swept
swim	swam	swum
take	took	taken
teach	taught	taught
tear	tore	torn
throw	threw	thrown
wake	waked, or woke	waked, or woken
wear	wore	worn
weep	wept	wept
wind	wound	wound
wring	wrung	wrung
write	wrote	written

TYPICAL QUESTIONS ON IRREGULAR VERBS

Rule: After a helping verb, use the past participle (third principal part), rather than the past tense (second principal part).

> *QUESTION 1: If you had been more patient, you might not have (*tore, torn*) it.
>
> ANSWER EXPLAINED: The helping verb *might have* requires the third principal part (tear, tore, *torn*).
>
> HINT: Review the list of principal parts on pages 90-92.

> *QUESTION 2: There were fewer candidates than we had been (*led, lead*) to expect.
>
> ANSWER EXPLAINED: The helping verb *had been* requires the third principal part (lead, led, *led*).
>
> HINT: Don't confuse *led* with an altogether different word that happens to sound the same—*lead* (a metal).

EXERCISE ON IRREGULAR VERBS

Write the correct choice and state the reason for your choice:

1. I could not do the assignment because the pages were (tore, torn) from my book.
2. The general (lead, led) his troops into battle.
3. After George had (ran, run) the mile, he was breathless.
4. In all the confusion, nobody took the trouble to find out who had (rung, rang) the bell.
5. I can assure you that he has always (spoke, spoken) well of you.
6. When was the last time your picture was (took, taken)?
7. After she had (sang, sung) the national anthem, the game started.
8. I had (rode, ridden) over the same course many times before.
9. Tom (lay, laid) on the ground.
10. Mary, aren't you (suppose, supposed) to take part in the assembly program?
11. As a result, he has (become, became) a skilled worker.
12. My dog has never (bit, bitten) anyone, except when provoked.
13. How can you be so sure that he (did, done) it?
14. We were not allowed to skate on the pond until the ice had (froze, frozen) to a depth of ten inches.
15. Richard concluded that his pen must have (fell, fallen) from his pocket as he was running for the bus.

16. By four o'clock the water had (rose, risen) dangerously close to the top of the barrier.
17. The snow had (began, begun) to fall before we arrived home.
18. Mary was so thirsty that she (drank, drunk) several glasses of water.
19. My cousin framed the photographs and (hung, hanged) them on the wall of his den.
20. A lawyer is (suppose, supposed) to protect the interests of his client.

Verbs Often Confused:

To *accept,* to receive, agree to
   He *accepted* my apology.
To *except,* to leave out
   In granting raises, he *excepted* the newest employees.

To *affect,* to influence
   His dog's death *affected* him deeply.
To *effect,* to bring about
   The enemy *effected* a quick retreat.

To *borrow,* to take with the expressed intention of returning
   May I *borrow* your pen?
To *lend,* to give with the expressed intention of getting back
   I shall gladly *lend* you my pen.

To *bring,* to carry toward the speaker
   Bring the newspaper when you return from shopping.
To *take,* to carry from the speaker
   Take these shirts to the laundry.

Can, a helping verb expressing ability
   Can you (Are you able to) swim across the pool?
May, a helping verb expressing permission or possibility
   May I (not *Can* I) have another chance?
   It *may* rain tomorrow.

To *learn,* to receive knowledge
   I *learned* safe driving from Dad.
To *teach,* to impart knowledge
   Dad *taught* me safe driving.

To *leave*, to depart, let remain
When you *leave*, please shut the door.
Leave the key under the mat.

To *let*, to permit, allow
Let (not *Leave*) them do their work without interruption.

To *lie*, to recline

Present:	The dog *lies* (*is lying*) on the ground.
Future:	The dog *will lie* on the ground.
Past:	The dog *lay* on the ground.
Perfect Tenses:	The dog *has lain* (*had lain, will have lain*) on the ground.

To *lay*, to put

Present:	The player *lays* (*is laying*) his cards on the table.
Future:	The player *will lay* his cards on the table.
Past:	The player *laid* his cards on the table.
Perfect Tenses:	The player *has laid* (*had laid, will have laid*) his cards on the table.

To *precede*, to go before in rank or time
Evening *precedes* night.

To *proceed*, to move forward, advance
Proceed to the main entrance.

To *raise*, to lift, elevate
How can I *raise* my marks?

To *rise*, to go up, get up
Will the cost of living *rise?*
To ask a question, please *rise* and face the class.

TYPICAL QUESTIONS ON VERBS OFTEN CONFUSED

*QUESTION 1:	Overnight the river had (raised, *risen*) another foot.
ANSWER EXPLAINED:	The meaning of the sentence requires *risen*, which is the third principal part of *to rise*, meaning "to go up"; *raised* is the third principal part of another verb, *to raise*, meaning "to lift."
HINT:	Review "Verbs Often Confused."

*QUESTION 2: Where have you (lain, *laid*) the book I was reading?

ANSWER EXPLAINED: The meaning of the sentence requires *laid,* the third principal part of *to lay,* meaning "to put"; *lain* is the third principal part of another verb, *to lie,* meaning "to recline."

EXERCISE ON VERBS OFTEN CONFUSED

Write the correct choice and state the reason for your choice:

1. Have you ever tried to (learn, teach) a boy to tie knots?
2. Although he had (accepted, excepted) a deposit on the new automobile, he refused to deliver it for the agreed price.
3. May I (borrow, lend) your French dictionary over the weekend?
4. I had (lain, laid) awake all night, worrying about the final test.
5. The cost of living is (raising, rising) again.
6. (Bring, Take) these books to the library, as they will soon be overdue.
7. Where did you (lay, lie) the magazine I was reading?
8. When operas are performed on radio or television, they (effect, affect) the listener in that after hearing them he wants to buy recordings of the music.
9. My father didn't (leave, let) me go to the last dance because I had failed two subjects.
10. Weekly dances have become a popularly (accepted, excepted) feature of the summer schedule.
11. (Can, May) I have another helping of ice cream?
12. If anyone wants the book, tell him that it (lays, lies) on the table.
13. The news of his narrow escape (affected, effected) her visibly.
14. In these ways we are (preceding, proceeding) toward the goal of an educated and informed public.
15. At first, passengers were forbidden to enter the lifeboats, women and children (accepted, excepted).
16. Please (bring, take) this suit to the dry cleaner.
17. If you won't (let, leave) her solve the problem by herself, she will never learn.
18. With the new advances in medicine, doctors have been able to (affect, effect) some remarkable recoveries.
19. I could not recall where I had (lain, laid) my glasses.
20. When the fire alarm sounds, (precede, proceed) calmly to the nearest exit.

Typical Questions on Tenses of Verbs

Rule 1: Do not shift unnecessarily from one tense to another.

QUESTION 1: Whenever I asked him to explain, he (says, *said*), "Later, not now."

ANSWER EXPLAINED: *said* (past tense) is required because the sentence begins in the past tense (*asked*).

HINT: *says* (present tense) would be correct only if the sentence were to begin in the present tense (*ask*): Whenever I *ask* him to explain, he *says*, "Later, not now."

Exception to Rule 1: Use the present tense to express a universal truth (something that is true regardless of time).

QUESTION 2: He said that health (was, *is*) better than riches.

ANSWER EXPLAINED: *is* (present tense) is required to express a universal truth.

HINT: It has been, is, and always will be true that "health *is* better than riches."

Rule 2: In describing two past actions in the same sentence, use the past perfect tense for the earlier action.

QUESTION 3: In the bus I realized that I (took, *had taken*) my brother's notebook by mistake.

ANSWER EXPLAINED: *had taken* (past perfect tense) is needed to describe an action earlier than that of *realized* (past tense).

HINT: To form the past perfect tense, use *had* plus the past participle. (See pages 90-92.)

Rule 3: After *if*, do not use the helping verb *would have*; use *had*.

*QUESTION 4: If he (would have, *had*) studied harder, he would have received a passing grade.

ANSWER EXPLAINED: *had* (not *would have*) is required after *if*.

HINT: *would have* may be used in a main clause (he *would have* received a passing grade) but never in an *if* clause, which is a dependent clause.

Rule 4: Use the present infinitive to express action not completed at the time of the preceding verb.

Verbs have a present infinitive (*to do, to tell,* etc.) and a past infinitive (*to have done, to have told,* etc.).

°QUESTION 5: We intended (*to go,* to have gone) before Tuesday.

ANSWER EXPLAINED: *to go* (the present infinitive) is required because the action of "going" had not yet happened at the time of the preceding verb *intended.*

HINT: Ask yourself: At the time of the preceding verb (*intended*), had the "going" already taken place? Obviously not. Therefore, use *to go,* the present infinitive.

Note the correct use of the past infinitive: I am sorry *to have scolded* you yesterday. *to have scolded* (the past infinitive) is required because the action of "scolding" had already happened at the time of the preceding verb *am.*

EXERCISE ON TENSES OF VERBS

Write the correct choice and state the reason for your choice:

1. They expected to (meet, have met) us at the bus terminal.
2. If you (would have, had) called me earlier, I would unquestionably have gone with you.
3. Suddenly he yelled "George!" and (dashes, dashed) up the stairs.
4. The doctor suspected that I (sprained, had sprained) my ankle.
5. From that experience I learned that a friend in need (is, was) a friend indeed.
6. My father had promised to (increase, have increased) my weekly allowance.
7. If I (would have, had) been there, he would certainly have behaved differently.
8. Our teacher explained that the Grand Canyon (was, is) in Arizona.
9. I am sorry to (cause, have caused) so much trouble yesterday.
10. She could not recall the title of any one-act play that she (read, had read) in previous terms.
11. Mother would gladly have set an extra place for dinner if she (had, would have) known you were coming.
12. We were stunned to (learn, have learned) that you are moving.

13. If it (had not, would not have) rained, the mishap would never have occurred.
14. Susan's parents would have liked to (see, have seen) you.
15. If he (had, would have) shouted to me, I would not have run into that ditch.
16. As soon as Mother learned of my plan, she (begins, began) to worry.
17. I would have taken Latin if it (had, would have) been offered.
18. We should have preferred to (start, have started) immediately.
19. I would have liked to (see, have seen) that movie.
20. Jim is ashamed to (be, have been) so rude to your guests last Saturday.

C. TYPICAL QUESTIONS ON TROUBLESOME WORD PAIRS

Several word pairs that sound alike, or nearly alike, frequently cause errors in writing. Learn to distinguish the one from the other.

advise, advice

*QUESTION 1: In schools, teachers (*advise,* advice) their students to listen to or to view certain programs.

ANSWER EXPLAINED: the verb *advise* is required by the sentence.

OTHER WORD: *advice* is used only as a noun. (The teacher gave us good *advice.*)

altogether, all together

*QUESTION 2: I am not (*altogether,* all together) in agreement with the author's point of view.

ANSWER EXPLAINED: *altogether,* meaning "completely," is required by the sentence.

OTHER WORD: *all together,* written as two words, means "all at one time." (We recited the pledge of allegiance *all together.*)

effect, affect

*QUESTION 3: We expect the (affects, *effects*) of the trip will be beneficial.

ANSWER EXPLAINED: *effects,* meaning "results," is required by the sentence.

OTHER WORD: *affect* is used mostly as a verb meaning "to influence." (Alcohol *affects* the brain.)

have, of

*QUESTION 4: If people had helped Burns, instead of talking about him, he might (of, *have*) become a greater poet.

ANSWER EXPLAINED: *have*, a verb, is required by the sentence.

OTHER WORD: *of* is a preposition. (The rest *of* us protested.)

its, it's

*QUESTION 5: When that program is over, the children know (its, *it's*) time for bed.

ANSWER EXPLAINED: *it's* (contraction for "it is") is required by the sentence.

OTHER WORD: *its* means "belonging to it." (The dog injured *its* leg.)

lead, led

*QUESTION 6: The general (lead, *led*) his troops into battle.

ANSWER EXPLAINED: *led*, the past tense of *to lead*, is required by the sentence.

OTHER WORD: *lead*, as a noun, is a metal. (These boots are as heavy as *lead*.)

loose, lose

QUESTION 7: How did you (loose, *lose*) your wallet?

ANSWER EXPLAINED: *lose*, a verb meaning "part with accidentally," is required by the sentence.

OTHER WORD: *loose* is an adjective meaning "free, not fastened." (Who turned the dog *loose?*)

passed, past

QUESTION 8: We (*passed*, past) the bus stop.

ANSWER EXPLAINED: *passed*, the past tense of "to pass," a verb meaning "to go by," is required by the sentence.

OTHER WORD: *past* may be
a. an adjective. (He presided at *past* meetings.)
b. a noun. (Forget the *past*.)
c. a preposition. (We went *past* the bus stop.)

principal, principle

*QUESTION 9: The teacher explained the (principal, *principle*) of refrigeration.

ANSWER EXPLAINED: *principle,* meaning "underlying rule" or "general truth," is required by the sentence. Notice that the last two letters of princi*ple* and ru*le* are the same.

OTHER WORD: *principal,* as a noun, means "main teacher." (Our school has a new *principal.*)

principal, as an adjective, means "main." (Broadway is our city's *principal* street.)

quiet, quite

*QUESTION 10: When the teacher spoke, the room became (quite, *quiet*).

ANSWER EXPLAINED: *quiet,* meaning "silent," is required by the sentence.

OTHER WORD: *quite* means "completely." (By bedtime the children were *quite* exhausted.)

respectfully, respectively

*QUESTION 11: The blue, red, and yellow sweaters belong to Jean, Marie, and Alice (respectfully, *respectively*).

ANSWER EXPLAINED: *respectively,* meaning "in the order stated," is required by the sentence.

OTHER WORD: *respectfully* means "with proper respect." (The audience applauded *respectfully* as the principal rose to speak.)

than, then

*QUESTION 12: Try to find one that is shorter (*than,* then) this one.

ANSWER EXPLAINED: *than,* a conjunction used in comparisons, is required by the sentence.

OTHER WORD: *then* means "at that time." (He was *then* a lad of twelve.)

their, they're, there

*QUESTION 13: The enemy fled in many directions, leaving (*their,* they're, there) weapons on the battlefield.

ANSWER EXPLAINED: *their* (*belonging to them*) is required to show ownership.

OTHER WORDS: *they're* is a contraction for "they are." (*They're* altogether right.)

there means "in that place." (Have you ever been *there?*)

to, too, two

*QUESTION 14: He felt that he had paid (to, *too*, two) high a price for one mistake.

ANSWER EXPLAINED: *too*, meaning "excessively," is required by the sentence. (Sometimes *too* means "also": Donald is ill and his brother *too*.)

OTHER WORDS: *to* is a preposition. (Give it *to* me.)

two is a number. (One and one are *two*.)

who's, whose

*QUESTION 15: (Who's, *Whose*) money is on this desk?

ANSWER EXPLAINED: *Whose* (*belonging to whom*) is required to show ownership.

OTHER WORD: *Who's* is a contraction for "Who is." (*Who's* there?)

your, you're

*QUESTION 16: Do not hand in the report until (your, *you're*) certain that it is complete.

ANSWER EXPLAINED: *you're*, a contraction for "you are," is required by the sentence.

OTHER WORD: *your* means "belonging to you." (What is *your* principal worry?)

EXERCISE ON TROUBLESOME WORD PAIRS

Write the correct choice and state the reason for your choice:
1. John and Mary wish to go because (their, there, they're) eager to visit the museum.
2. Is that (your, you're) jacket on the floor?
3. Have you successfully (passed, past) all your final examinations?
4. The article describes the (principal, principle) (affects, effects) of the new drug.
5. (Who's, Whose) at the door?
6. In the violent storm, the boat broke (loose, lose) from its moorings.
7. We did not realize that the boys' father had forbidden them to keep (there, their, they're) puppy.
8. We want to go to the movies (to, too, two).
9. In the (passed, past) we have always held our commencement exercises in the evening.

10. He is taller (then, than) his brother by several inches.
11. He is the boy (who's, whose) poster was chosen for the contest.
12. I was advised to review the (principals, principles) of correct usage.
13. Howard, Richard, and Henry scored ninety, eighty, and seventy-five (respectfully, respectively).
14. She was (quite, quiet) breathless from running upstairs.
15. Macbeth was afraid he would (loose, lose) his crown to one of Banquo's descendants.
16. There were fewer candidates (then, than) we had been (led, lead) to expect.
17. Your interpretation of the results of the test is (all together, altogether) inaccurate.
18. Did you see that truck speed (passed, past) the red light?
19. How will the new tax (affect, effect) your business?
20. The (principle, principal) cause of failure is excessive absence.
21. The reward must (of, have) pleased them very much.
22. The pages in my old dictionary are (loose, lose) and dog-eared.
23. The horse lifted (its, it's) head and snorted.
24. My English teacher gave me ample opportunity to make up for (passed, past) mistakes.
25. You have been (led, lead) astray by your own carelessness.
26. (You're, Your) coming to visit me in the hospital certainly cheered me up.
27. (Who's, Whose) car is that?
28. Doing a task promptly is better (than, then) worrying about it.
29. It's (your, you're) turn to drive now, if you're ready.
30. The alumni have announced that (their, there, they're) sending a representative to our graduation.
31. You should (of, have) been in the assembly yesterday.
32. (Who's, Whose) going to make the arrangements for the dance?
33. What is the (affect, effect) of sunlight on plants?
34. (It's, Its) advisable to apply to at least three colleges early in your senior year.
35. (They're, There, Their) altogether overjoyed with the results.
36. Let them try to do it (there, their, they're) own way.
37. Tell me (who's, whose) on third base; I don't recognize him.
38. On his doctor's (advice, advise) he resumed a full program of physical activities.
39. The dog wagged (its, it's) tail and barked happily.
40. The merchant promised to refund my money if I were not (all together, altogether) satisfied.

D. TYPICAL QUESTIONS ON AGREEMENT

Rule 1: A singular subject requires a singular verb. A plural subject requires a plural verb.

*QUESTION 1: Too many commas in a passage often (*cause, causes*) confusion in the reader's mind.

ANSWER EXPLAINED: The plural subject *commas* requires the plural verb *cause*.

HINT: *causes* is singular—don't be misled by the final *s*.

Notice how we conjugate a verb in the present tense:

SINGULAR	PLURAL
I cause	we cause
you cause	you cause
he (she, it) causes	they cause

QUESTION 2: There ('s, are*) several ways to solve that problem.

ANSWER EXPLAINED: The plural subject *ways* requires the plural verb *are*.

HINT: When an expression such as *there is* (*there are*), *here is* (*here are*), or *it is* begins a sentence, look for the real subject to appear later in the sentence. In the sentence above, for example, the real subject is not *There* but *ways*.

*QUESTION 3: A box of materials (*is,* are) in the cabinet.

ANSWER EXPLAINED: The singular subject *box* requires the singular verb *is*.

HINT: Disregard *of*-phrases that come between subject and verb (example: *of materials* in the sentence above). They do not affect agreement.

*QUESTION 4: The leader of the flock, as well as most of his followers, (*has,* have) jumped the fence.

ANSWER EXPLAINED: The singular subject *leader* requires the singular helping verb *has*.

HINT: Interrupting expressions beginning with *as well as, together with, in addition to, rather than,* etc., do not affect agreement between subject and verb.

Rule 2: Subjects that are singular in meaning but plural in form (*news, economics, measles,* etc.) **require a singular verb.**

QUESTION 5: Mathematics (*is,* are) extremely important in today's world.

ANSWER EXPLAINED: The singular subject *Mathematics* requires the singular verb *is.*

ADDITIONAL EXAMPLE: The United States *has* (not *have*) many beautiful national parks.

Rule 3: Singular subjects connected by *or, nor, either . . . or,* or *neither . . . nor* **require a singular verb.**

QUESTION 6: Either the witness or the defendant (*is,* are) lying.

ANSWER EXPLAINED: The singular subjects *witness* and *defendant* are connected by *either . . . or* and require the singular verb *is.*

ADDITIONAL EXAMPLE: Neither the sergeant nor the corporal *was* (not *were*) off duty.

Rule 4: A compound subject connected by *and* **requires a plural verb.**

QUESTION 7: The arrival and departure (was, *were*) on schedule.

ANSWER EXPLAINED: The compound subject *arrival and departure* requires the plural verb *were.*

ADDITIONAL EXAMPLE: His study and preparation for the test *were* (not *was*) thorough.

Exception to Rule 4: A compound subject regarded as a single entity requires a singular verb.

QUESTION 8: Spaghetti and meatballs (*is,* are) a popular dish.

ANSWER EXPLAINED: *Spaghetti and meatballs,* regarded as a single entity, requires the singular verb *is.*

ADDITIONAL EXAMPLE: The long and short of the matter *is* (not *are*) that we won the game.

Rule 5: If a subject consists of two or more nouns or pronouns connected by *or* or *nor*, the verb agrees with the nearer noun or pronoun.

QUESTION 9: Neither my cousins nor Marie (*is*, are) leaving for the summer.

ANSWER EXPLAINED: The verb *is* agrees in number with the nearer noun *Marie*.

ALSO CORRECT: "Neither Marie nor my cousins *are* (not *is*) leaving for the summer." In this case the verb *are* agrees in number with the nearer noun *cousins*.

QUESTION 10: Either she or you (is, *are*) to blame.

ANSWER EXPLAINED: The verb *are* agrees in person with the nearer pronoun *you*.

ALSO CORRECT: "Either you or she *is* to blame." In this case the verb *is* agrees in person with the nearer pronoun *she*.

Rule 6: Make a pronoun agree with its antecedent.

(An antecedent is the previous word to which a pronoun refers.)

*QUESTION 11: If anyone has any doubt about the value of this tour, refer (*him*, them) to me.

ANSWER EXPLAINED: The singular antecedent *anyone* requires the singular pronoun *him*.

HINT: Remember that the following words are singular: *anyone, everyone, someone, no one, one, each, each one, either, neither, anybody, everybody, nobody, somebody, every* (person, etc.), *many a* (person, etc.).

*QUESTION 12: I believe that *Hamlet* is the greatest of all the plays that (has, *have*) ever been written.

ANSWER EXPLAINED: The plural subject *that* requires the plural helping verb *have*. We know *that* is plural because its antecedent is *plays*.

HINT: To determine whether *that, which,* or *who* is singular or plural, look at the antecedent.

°QUESTION 13: He is one of those persons (which, *who*) deserve great credit for perseverance.

ANSWER EXPLAINED: The antecedent *persons* requires the pronoun *who; which* cannot refer to people.

HINT: Use *who* to refer to people, *which* to refer to things, and *that* to refer to people or things.

EXERCISE ON AGREEMENT

Write the correct choice and state the reason for your choice:

1. There, crouching in the grass, (was, were) four enemies.
2. There (was, were) a dog and a cat in the chair.
3. Calisthenics (is, are) a part of Bob's morning routine.
4. The books they read (show, shows) their taste in literature.
5. He (don't, doesn't) speak very well on formal occasions.
6. Children's health (is, are) a serious concern of all parents.
7. Each of the girls (observe, observes) all the restrictions.
8. Neither he nor we (was, were) fully aware of the serious nature of your illness.
9. The number of foursomes on the course today (was, were) very few.
10. Macbeth himself, rather than the witches, (was, were) responsible for his downfall.
11. Everybody (was, were) asked to remain seated.
12. There, Alice, (is, are) some of my classmates.
13. Burns is one of the poets (which, that) we studied last term.
14. Corned beef and cabbage (is, are) on tonight's menu.
15. The present series of discussions on current events (was, were) started in January.
16. One of the girls lost (their, her) books as a result of the confusion.
17. (Are, Is) each of the pies the same size?
18. An important ingredient of high school life (is, are) intramural athletics.
19. Either your mother or your father (is, are) supposed to sign the report card.
20. (Doesn't, Don't) either of you girls want this?
21. The dog together with its puppies (has, have) come into the parlor again.
22. He is one of the juniors who (was, were) nominated for the G.O. presidency.
23. Each of the men did (his, their) duty with exemplary courage.
24. Interesting news (is, are) what sells our paper.

25. The doctor rather than the nurses (was, were) to blame for his being neglected.
26. If anyone wants the book, tell (him, them) that it lies on the table.
27. A bushel of peaches (cost, costs) five dollars.
28. Many a person had to earn (his, their) way through college.
29. The combination of the three colors (give, gives) a pleasing effect.
30. Your approach and delivery (is, are) faulty and in need of improvement.
31. Being both observant and curious about things (promote, promotes) learning.
32. A box of cigars (was, were) found on the porch, unopened.
33. Radio and television programs, along with other media of communication, (helps, help) us to appreciate the arts and to keep informed.
34. A magazine and a book (was, were) lying in disorder on the floor.
35. Neither of you (seem, seems) to be paying the slightest attention.
36. When operas are performed on radio or television, they affect the listener in that after hearing them (he wants, they want) to buy recordings of the music.
37. Will everyone please open (their, his) book to the preface.
38. The captain as well six of his men (was, were) wounded in the skirmish.
39. The students' ingenuity (was, were) particularly challenged by the third question on the physics test.
40. Such a rapid succession of unfortunate events (is, are) enough to discourage anybody.

E. TYPICAL QUESTIONS ON ADJECTIVES AND ADVERBS

Rule 1: Use an adverb to modify a verb.

*QUESTION 1: The magician waved his hands so (skillful, *skillfully*) that the audience was completely mystified.

ANSWER EXPLAINED: The adverb *skillfully* is required to modify the verb *waved*.

HINT: If the test word answers the question "How?" "To what extent?" "Where?" or "When?"—it is most likely an adverb. The adverb *skillfully* tells "how" the magician waved his hands. The adverb *completely* tells "to what extent" the audience was mystified.

Rule 2: Use an adverb to modify an adjective.

*QUESTION 2: He had an (unbelievable, *unbelievably*) large capacity for food.

ANSWER EXPLAINED: The adverb *unbelievably* is needed to modify the adjective *large*.

HINT: Note that *unbelievably* tells "how" large the capacity for food is.

Rule 3: Use an adjective after a linking verb.

[A linking verb is a verb that "links" or connects the subject with a modifier. The following are linking verbs: *be* (*is, am, was, were*, etc.), *seem, appear, look, feel, smell, sound, taste, become, grow, remain, stay, turn.*]

*QUESTION 3: Food prepared in this manner tastes more (*delicious*, deliciously).

ANSWER EXPLAINED: The adjective *delicious* is required after the linking verb *tastes*.

HINT: Study these further examples of the same rule:
The flowers smell *sweet*. (not sweetly)
This sounds *strange*. (not strangely)
The food looks *good*. (not well)

Rule 4: Use the comparative degree (the *-er* or *more* form) for comparing two persons or things; use the superlative degree (the *-est* or *most* form) for comparing more than two.

Adjectives and adverbs have three degrees, as follows:

POSITIVE	COMPARATIVE	SUPERLATIVE
(adj.) wide	wider	widest
(adv.) widely	more widely	most widely
(adj.) faithful	more faithful	most faithful
(adv.) faithfully	more faithfully	most faithfully

Good and *bad* have irregular forms:

POSITIVE	COMPARATIVE	SUPERLATIVE
(adj.) good	better	best
(adv.) well	better	best
(adj.) bad	worse	worst
(adv.) badly	worse	worst

*QUESTION 4: It was the (worse, *worst*) storm that the inhabitants of the island could remember.

ANSWER EXPLAINED: The superlative *worst* is needed because the sentence compares more than two storms.

HINT: The comparative *worse* can be used when only
two persons or things are compared, as in the following: This storm was *worse* than the last one.

**Rule 5: Use the word *other* when you compare a person (or thing)
with the rest of his (or its) group.**

*QUESTION 5: Peter is younger than any of (the, *the other*) boys.

ANSWER EXPLAINED: *other* must be included because the sentence compares Peter with the rest of his group (*boys*).
Peter is a boy too.

HINT: Note that *other* is not required in the following:
Pauline is younger than any of the boys. Pauline
is not a member of the group *boys*.

EXERCISE ON ADJECTIVES AND ADVERBS

Write the correct choice and state the reason for your choice:
1. It was a (real, really) comfortable seat; consequently, she felt no
inclination to move.
2. She spoke very (good, well) of her former classmates.
3. The food looks (delicious, deliciously) and is quite reasonable.
4. Our old television set works just as (good, well) as our new one.
5. Did you notice how (beautiful, beautifully) the sky looked?
6. The birds' morning song sounded (sweet, sweetly) to our ears.
7. A person who works as (efficient, efficiently) as John deserves high
praise.
8. My, how (sourly, sour) this buttermilk tastes!
9. Da Vinci was more brilliant than (any, any other) person in his
century.
10. Yes, my brother can do this work as (good, well) as I.
11. How (strange, strangely) the noise sounded in the quiet, abandoned house!
12. I am (real, really) sorry to have disturbed you, Mr. Jones.
13. Clara's piano playing seems no (worse, worst) than yours.

14. You are not likely to encounter another pupil who studies as (diligent, diligently) as Anne.
15. He has always done his work (well, good) and cheerfully.
16. This material feels so (soft, softly) that it reminds me of fur.
17. He was voted the most (handsome, handsomely) dressed boy in the senior class.
18. He (sure, surely) appeared glad to see me receive the award.
19. Notice how (rapid, rapidly) that chemical solution is dissolving the salt.
20. Sam should have received a trophy too, for he played just as (good, well).
21. I felt (bad, badly) when Mother scolded me about my failing history.
22. He could throw a fast ball and field a bunt as (good, well) as any pitcher I have ever seen.
23. If you try a slice, you'll see how (delicious, deliciously) the melon tastes.
24. When Paul first joined the team, he was no better than any of (the, the other) players.
25. The musicians (sure, surely) played that number well.
26. New cars ride (smoothly, smooth) on their low-pressure tires.
27. Herman Melville is one of the (real, really) distinguished authors in American literature.
28. Your conduct during this period has been the (worse, worst) in the class.
29. Our teacher (sure, surely) knows how to recite a poem to the class.
30. Florence listened (attentively, attentive) to the music.
31. The sun made us feel (warm, warmly) and glad to be alive.
32. You must admit, Dorothy, that you behaved very (rude, rudely).
33. Nothing tastes as (tempting, temptingly) as Mother's homemade pie.
34. Ben was brighter than (any, any other) pupil in the class.
35. No other character behaved more (faithful, faithfully) than Diggory Venn.
36. Mathematics problems must be done (accurately, accurate).
37. To the terrified wedding guest, the ancient mariner looked very (strange, strangely).
38. Jack does not swim so (good, well) as Fred.
39. Please turn down the radio; it sounds altogether too (loud, loudly).
40. For a (true, truly) enjoyable experience, read Sinclair Lewis' *Arrowsmith.*

F. TYPICAL QUESTIONS ON DOUBLE NEGATIVES

Rule: Use only one negative word to express a negative idea.

*QUESTION 1: He (*has*, hasn't) hardly a friend.

ANSWER EXPLAINED: *has* is correct because the sentence already has one negative (*hardly*).

HINT: Do not use an additional negative with *hardly* or *scarcely*. These words are considered negatives, in addition to *no, not* (*-n't*), *never, nobody, nowhere, no one, none, nothing, neither, barely, only, but* (meaning *only*), etc.

QUESTION 2: You haven't (no one, *anyone*) to blame but yourself for your low grades.

ANSWER EXPLAINED: Since *haven't* is a negative word, do not use *no one*, which is also a negative expression. Use *anyone*.

EXERCISE ON DOUBLE NEGATIVES

Write the correct choice and state the reason for your choice:
1. I (could, couldn't) hardly believe that he would desert the cause.
2. With their best player disqualified, Lincoln High (can, can't) barely hope to tie us in Saturday's game.
3. Johnson has scarcely (an, no) equal as a quarterback.
4. Jody (had, hadn't) no reason to doubt his father's judgment.
5. After paying our senior dues, we didn't have (anything, nothing) left in our savings account.
6. They stayed home and didn't go (nowhere, anywhere) all summer.
7. Jack looked everywhere for earthworms but he didn't see (none, any).
8. Her older brother scarcely (ever, never) works harder than necessary.
9. Where are Joe and Alec? I haven't seen (either, neither) one all week.
10. The term (had, hadn't) hardly begun when we got our first full-period test.
11. When we got to the dance, there wasn't (anybody, nobody) there yet from our club.
12. If you haven't (anything, nothing) better to do, why not join us at the beach?

13. There (is, isn't) barely an hour left before the train leaves.
14. Margaret's illness hadn't (nothing, anything) to do with this problem.
15. Our high-jump star had hardly (a, no) rival in the whole season.
16. How can you plan to go bowling if you (have, haven't) but two days to study?
17. I looked at all the passengers on the train but I didn't recognize (no one, anyone).
18. Alice gets the highest grades, yet she scarcely (ever, never) studies.
19. When my grandfather arrived in this country, he (had, hadn't) only ten dollars in his pocket.
20. I don't know why the dean questioned me because I didn't have (nothing, anything) to do with it.

G. TYPICAL QUESTIONS ON PARALLEL STRUCTURE

Rule: Put ideas of the same rank into the same grammatical structure.

*QUESTION 1: Mailing a letter a few days early is better than (to run, *running*) the risk of its arriving late.
ANSWER EXPLAINED: The verbal noun *running* is required for parallel structure with the verbal noun *mailing*.
HINT: If the sentence had begun with the infinitive *to mail*, the correct answer would have been the infinitive *to run: To mail* a letter a few days early is better than *to run* the risk of its arriving late.

QUESTION 2: You should select foods that are nourishing and (*tasty*, taste good).
ANSWER EXPLAINED: The predicate adjective *tasty* is required for parallel structure with the predicate adjective *nourishing*.

EXERCISE ON PARALLEL STRUCTURE

Write the correct choice and state the reason for your choice:
1. I enjoy playing basketball and then (to eat, eating).
2. The modern automobile has the advantages of strength and (being speedy, speed, moving swiftly).

3. To do a task promptly is better than (worrying, to worry) about doing it.
4. He likes dancing, skating, and (to go swimming, swimming).
5. Nylon dresses wash easily, drip dry readily, and (you can wear them a long time, wear durably).
6. He appeared tired and (disappointed, a disappointed man).
7. As a freshman George was unruly, inattentive, and (had no patience, impatient).
8. Mr. Smith promised me a good position and (to pay me a fair salary, a fair salary).
9. Last-minute studying is not so effective as (keeping up, to keep up) with the daily assignments.
10. My ambition is to be a doctor and (specializing, to specialize) in surgery.
11. Our neighbor is helpful, friendly, and (he talks a great deal, talkative).
12. To be completely outclassed is not so annoying as (losing, to lose) by one point.
13. We plan to go to college to study, to prepare for a career, and (for the purpose of making, to make) new friends.
14. The pioneers were industrious, ambitious, and (courageous, they had a great deal of courage).
15. A calculating machine offers the benefits of speed and (you can get accurate results, accuracy).
16. In the summer we enjoy picnicking, outdoor camping, and (to go sightseeing, sightseeing).
17. Paperback books are handy, inexpensive, and (you can get them anywhere, easily available).
18. She couldn't decide whether she should repeat the subject or (to drop, drop) it entirely.
19. To climb the mountain is much more fun than (to go, going) up by the scenic railway.
20. Charles has the qualities of intelligence, friendliness, and (you can depend on him, dependability).

H. TYPICAL QUESTIONS ON DANGLING CONSTRUCTIONS

Rule: Be sure to include the noun or pronoun to which a phrase or a clause refers. Otherwise, you will have a *dangling* or unattached phrase or clause.

(A *phrase* is an expression of two or more words having neither a subject nor a predicate. A *clause* is a group of words containing both a subject and a predicate.)

°QUESTION 1: (After preparing, After having prepared, *After I had prepared*) all day for Jane's visit, my desire to see her increased.

ANSWER EXPLAINED: Because *After I had prepared* has the pronoun *I*, it tells who did the preparing. The other choices do not.

HINT: Remember this amusing sample to help you detect the dangling-construction error: Coming up the stairs, the clock struck twelve.

QUESTION 2: While driving along the highway, (a fatal head-on collision was seen, *we saw a fatal head-on collision*).

ANSWER EXPLAINED: The italicized clause is correct because it includes the pronoun *we*, telling who saw the collision.

EXERCISE ON DANGLING CONSTRUCTIONS

Write the correct choice and state the reason for your choice:

1. All the next week, (driving, while driving, as I drove) back and forth to work, the scene remained vivid in my mind.
2. Though (troubled, we were troubled) by many fears, the results were altogether satisfactory.
3. The tomb of an Egyptian pharaoh commanded attention (as we came, coming) into the museum.
4. (Hurrying, As she hurried) down the stairs, her shoe fell off.
5. It started to snow (while we were going, going) to the stadium.
6. While (shopping, they were shopping) in the supermarket, their parking lights remained on.
7. (Buying, Since we had bought) tickets in advance, our worries about having good seats were lessened.
8. (After failing, Since they had failed) the examination, the teacher advised them to study regularly.
9. Sailing up the harbor, (the Statue of Liberty was seen, we saw the Statue of Liberty).
10. The five-o'clock whistle blew (coming, as we came) down the avenue.

I. INCORRECT EXPRESSIONS

Replace incorrect expressions with good English. Examples:

INCORRECT	CORRECT
1. Stop *aggravating* me.	Stop *annoying* me.
2. Try *and* do better.	Try *to* do better.
3. The reason is *because*	The reason is *that*
4. *Being that*	*Since*
5. He (she, it) *don't*	He (she, it) *doesn't*
6. *Due to* illness, etc.	*Because of* illness, etc.
7. Six *foot* tall	Six *feet* tall
8. He (she) dances *good.*	He (she) dances *well.*
9. We *had ought* to	We *ought* to
10. My *father, he says*	My *father says*
11. This *here* book	*This* book
12. *Hisself, theirselves*	*Himself, themselves*
13. *In* "Trees" *it* tells about	"Trees" *tells* about
14. *Irregardless*	*Regardless*
15. ·Kind of *a*	*Kind of*
16. *Like* I told you	*As* I told you
17. *Me and my friend* went.	*My friend and I* went.
18. *Most* always	*Almost* always
19. Off *of*	*Off*
20. A *real* good book	A *really* good book
21. He was *sure* alert.	He was *surely* alert.
22. Different *than*	Different *from*
23. *That there* boy	*That* boy
24. Hand me *them* tools.	Hand me *those* tools.
25. *This here* place	*This* place

TYPICAL QUESTIONS ON INCORRECT EXPRESSIONS

*QUESTION 1: (Irregardless, *Regardless*) of what you believe, your answer is correct.

ANSWER EXPLAINED: *Regardless* is good English. *Irregardless* is not acceptable.

HINT: *Regardless* means "without regard." *Irregardless* is poor English because it says "without" twice: (1) in the prefix *ir-* (meaning *not*), and (2) in the suffix *-less.*

QUESTION 2: Will you please tell me what (*kind of,* kind of a) book you would like to read.

ANSWER EXPLAINED: The article *a* in "kind of *a* book" is useless. Say "kind of book."

HINT: Similarly, say *sort of,* instead of *sort of a.*

EXERCISE ON INCORRECT EXPRESSIONS

Write the correct choice and state the reason for your choice:

1. (Being that, Since) he was the best qualified person, he received the appointment.
2. You (had ought, ought) to return this book before it's overdue.
3. Music, for example, (most, almost) always has listening and viewing audiences numbering in the hundreds of thousands.
4. What (kind of, kind of an) ending does *Moby Dick* have?
5. (Due to, Because of) a bookkeeping error, the customer has not yet received a refund.
6. The reason for my refusal is (that, because) you're undependable.
7. He hurriedly took the luggage (off, off of) the bus rack.
8. Would you please lend me (them, those) notes for tonight?
9. What (kind of, kind of a) gown did she buy?
10. Jesse James was six (feet, foot) tall.
11. My teacher (, he said, said) we should memorize that table.
12. Give me (that, that there) book lying on the desk.
13. William Shakespeare (sure, surely) was a master of words.
14. (Almost, Most) everyone there wore an election button.
15. Her style of penmanship is noticeably different (from, than) yours.
16. Try (and, to) call me up before ten-thirty.
17. We always get a friendly welcome in (that, that there) place.
18. I'm going to the party, (irregardless, regardless) of what you say.
19. (Being that, Since) he broke the watch, he should pay for the repairs.
20. They went to bed early, (like, as) little children should.
21. It (don't, doesn't) make the slightest difference to us.
22. Don't (aggravate, annoy) Father when he is having his dinner.
23. They did it (themselves, theirselves) in less than an hour.
24. She was five (foot, feet) two inches and had blue eyes.
25. (*The,* In *The*) *Return of the Native* (, it tells, tells) about a beautiful girl named Eustacia.
26. (Me and my brother, My brother and I) have always attended the same schools.

27. Can you recommend a (real, really) good short story?
28. The second problem was hardly different (than, from) the first.
29. Henry took all the old magazines (off, off of) the shelf.
30. Mr. Adams recites Shakespearean soliloquies very (good, well).
31. (This here, This) apparatus is certainly quite complicated.
32. (Regardless, Irregardless) of who wins, I hope we shall continue to be friends.
33. (Most, Almost) always we have a dance before the final examinations.
34. (Due to, Because of) unforeseen circumstances, the play had to be canceled.
35. My parents were (sure, surely) delighted to read about my citation.
36. The reason is (because, that) we were unavoidably delayed in leaving the house.
37. The club members prepared the stage setting all by (theirselves, themselves).
38. I checked all my answers, (like, as) my teacher had suggested.
39. After the first marking period, Helen resolved that she would try (to, and) do better.
40. My uncle (, he says, says) that fishing is the most relaxing sport.

J. TYPICAL QUESTIONS ON UNNEEDED WORDS

Rule: Do not repeat words or ideas already expressed.

*QUESTION 1: This is a club with which I wouldn't want to be (*associated,* associated with).

ANSWER EXPLAINED: *associated* ends the sentence correctly. The preposition *with* appears earlier in the clause and should not be repeated.

HINT: Do not begin and end a clause with the same preposition.

QUESTION 2: He refused (to accept my invitation, *my invitation*) to our club party.

ANSWER EXPLAINED: *to accept* are unneeded words that add nothing to the meaning of the sentence.

HINT: Unneeded words, sometimes called "deadwood," slow up reading and should be pruned from all sentences.

EXERCISE ON UNNEEDED WORDS

Rewrite the following sentences, omitting unneeded words:
1. Dennis, where will the game be held at?
2. She feels better, now that the operation is over with.
3. They didn't know to whom to give the supplies to.
4. After each stanza, repeat the chorus again.
5. Tell me for whom you are now working for.
6. I cannot remember where I met him at.
7. In my opinion, I think you are wrong.
8. The end result was that I was given a new test.
9. The secretary declined to accept my offer to type the report.
10. Richard, why are you so upset for?

REVIEW EXERCISE IN CORRECT USAGE

Each of the following sentences contains an underlined expression. Below each sentence are four suggested answers. Decide which answer is correct.

(1) I don't know who could possibly <u>of broken it.</u>

    1. Correct as is   3. have broke it.
    2. of broke it.   4. have broken it.

(2) Everyone knows that Sam can draw as <u>good as me.</u>

    1. Correct as is   3. well as I.
    2. good as I.   4. well as me.

(3) A collection of paintings <u>are on display</u> in the lobby.

    1. Correct as is   3. is on display
    2. are being displayed   4. are displayed

(4) Are you familiar with the <u>principal effects</u> of the Salk vaccine?

    1. Correct as is   3. principal affects
    2. principle effects   4. principle affects

(5) Walking to school is much more healthful <u>then to ride.</u>

    1. Correct as is   3. then riding.
    2. than riding.   4. than to ride.

(6) The two students who have been assigned to this project are <u>you and me.</u>

    1. Correct as is   3. I and you.
    2. you and I.   4. me and you.

(7) <u>Though I barely passed Biology,</u> I earned 90% in English.

    1. Correct as is
    2. Though I scarcely passed Biology,
    3. Though I barely past Biology,
    4. Though I barely passed biology,

(8) <u>Girls' and women's</u> shoes frequently change in style.

    1. Correct as is   3. Girl's and women's
    2. Girls' and womens'   4. Girl's and womens'

(9) If we <u>would have beat</u> Jefferson High School, we would have won the championship.

    1. Correct as is   3. had beaten
    2. would have beaten   4. had beat

(10) Marjorie's study habits are quite <u>different than your's.</u>

    1. Correct as is   3. than yours.
    2. then yours.   4. from yours.

(11) <u>Frank being</u> an only child has helped him in some ways and hurt him in others.

    1. Correct as is   3. Being that Frank is
    2. Frank's being   4. Frank having been

(12) My parents will <u>attend; they're</u> interested in seeing the performance.

    1. Correct as is   3. attend; their
    2. attend; there   4. attend, they're

(13) You were <u>suppose to learn</u> me how to do the backstroke.

    1. Correct as is   3. supposed to teach
    2. suppose to teach   4. supposed to learn

(14) <u>Can I lend</u> another quarter from you until tomorrow?

    1. Correct as is   3. May I lend
    2. Can I borrow   4. May I borrow

(15) Mother asked me to purchase the <u>following; stationery,</u> postage stamps, a pen, and rubber bands.

    1. Correct as is   3. following; stationary,
    2. following: stationery,   4. following: stationary,

(16) Our baseball coach is a person with <u>whom we are glad to be acquainted with.</u>

   1. Correct as is
   2. which we are glad to be acquainted with.
   3. whom we are glad to be acquainted.
   4. which we are glad to be acquainted.

(17) The sailor said that there is hardly <u>nothing worse than</u> a hurricane.

   1. Correct as is
   2. anything worst than
   3. anything worse then
   4. anything worse than

(18) If everyone does <u>their</u> share, we shall certainly finish on time.

   1. Correct as is
   2. his
   3. there
   4. they're

(19) <u>Approaching</u> the intersection, the light turned red.

   1. Correct as is
   2. While approaching
   3. In approaching
   4. As we approached

(20) <u>Like I explained, it doesn't</u> make any difference to me.

   1. Correct as is
   2. Like I explained, it don't
   3. As I explained, it doesn't
   4. As I explained, it don't

(21) The grocer allowed my brother and <u>I to bring</u> the wooden box home.

   1. Correct as is
   2. me to bring
   3. me to take
   4. I to take

(22) How did you happen to <u>lose the children's</u> tickets?

   1. Correct as is
   2. loose the children's
   3. loose the childrens'
   4. lose the childrens'

(23) I'm sure you'll enjoy the <u>film; it's real</u> good.

   1. Correct as is
   2. film, it's real
   3. film; its really
   4. film; it's really

(24) Patience and effort <u>has in the past led</u> many students to ultimate success.

   1. Correct as is
   2. have in the past lead
   3. has in the passed led
   4. have in the past led

(25) <u>Harvey, weren't you supposed to</u> nominate Paul?

   1. Correct as is
   2. Harvey, weren't you suppose to
   3. Harvey weren't you supposed to
   4. Harvey. Weren't you suppose to

(26) The usher <u>preceded to conduct Jane and I</u> to our seats.

    1. Correct as is
    2. preceded to conduct Jane and me
    3. proceeded to conduct Jane and I
    4. proceeded to conduct Jane and me

(27) If you <u>would have took my advice,</u> you would easily have passed.

    1. Correct as is   3. had taken my advise,
    2. had taken my advice,   4. would have took my advise,

(28) Politics <u>is most always</u> the topic that enlivens our meetings.

    1. Correct as is   3. is almost always
    2. are most always   4. are almost always

(29) Rereading the entire chapter takes much more time than <u>to review the principal</u> ideas.

    1. Correct as is   3. reviewing the principle
    2. to review the principle   4. reviewing the principal

(30) Your visit to the hospital, together with your thoughtful cards, <u>has made me feel more cheerful.</u>

    1. Correct as is
    2. have made me feel more cheerfully.
    3. have made me feel more cheerful.
    4. has made me feel more cheerfully.

(31) <u>Its already too</u> late to cancel the order.

    1. Correct as is   3. It's all ready too
    2. It's already too   4. Its all ready too

(32) All <u>students, who are absent,</u> must submit a note of explanation signed by the parent.

    1. Correct as is   3. students who are absent;
    2. students who are absent   4. students, who are absent

(33) They shouldn't <u>have told us</u> girls to come early.

    1. Correct as is   3. have told we
    2. of told us   4. of told we

(34) <u>Whom do you suppose</u> is our new chemistry teacher?

    1. Correct as is   3. Who do you suppose
    2. Whom, do you suppose,   4. Who do you suppose,

(35) The first presents opened were the <u>childrens, not ours.</u>

    1. Correct as is   3. childrens', not our's.
    2. children's, not ours.   4. children's, not ours'.

(36) <u>Being that I passed</u> all my tests, Father has increased my allowance.

    1. Correct as is   3. Since I passed
    2. Due to my passing   4. Because of me passing

(37) Since Marie had baked the cake, she was pleased at <u>its tasting so delicious.</u>

    1. Correct as is   3. its' tasting so delicious.
    2. it's tasting so deliciously.   4. it's tasting so delicious.

(38) If you had been there, you <u>might of</u> been elected president.

    1. Correct as is   3. could of
    2. might have   4. would of

(39) <u>Your being</u> the best student has earned you the honor of making the valedictory address.

    1. Correct as is   3. Being that you're
    2. You're being   4. Since your

(40) This <u>spring has been all together too</u> rainy.

    1. Correct as is
    2. Spring has been all together too
    3. spring has been altogether too
    4. spring has been altogether to

(41) Neither my notebook nor <u>your's is</u> as complete as Sarah's.

    1. Correct as is   3. yours is
    2. your's are   4. yours are

(42) <u>There's too</u> many officers in our club.

    1. Correct as is   3. There are to
    2. There are too   4. There's to

(43) <u>In The Tell-Tale Heart it tells</u> about an insane man.

    1. Correct as is   3. In "The Tell-Tale Heart" it tells
    2. The Tell-Tale Heart tells   4. "The Tell-Tale Heart" tells

(44) My father wants my brother and <u>I to attend college.</u>

    1. Correct as is   3. I to attend College.
    2. me to attend college.   4. me to attend College.

(45) <u>May I give a refund to whoever</u> asks for it?

    1. Correct as is
    2. May I give a refund to whomever
    3. Can I give a refund to whomever
    4. Can I give a refund to whoever

FORMER REGENTS QUESTIONS

Some of the following sentences contain errors. After each sentence that is *correct,* write the letter *C.* In each sentence that is *incorrect,* underline the word or expression that is incorrectly used and write the correct form. Do not change any correct part of a sentence.

1. Mother would not let Mary and I attend the hockey game.
2. They're not the only ones to be blamed for the incident.
3. It was easy to see that the coat had been laying on the ground for a long time.
4. The little boy refused to enter the Dentist's office when he was told to do so.
5. Mary and Joan waited breathlessly, each girl hoping she had won the award for outstanding scholarship.
6. People's efficiency are seriously affected by illness and worry.
7. One novel in which I have always taken great pleasure in is *Kidnapped.*
8. Whom did you say had recently moved to Washington, D.C.?
9. My clothes are correct to the occasion.
10. John, where is the party at?
11. In the morning, the enemy attackted our positions.
12. Everyone has a right to their opinion.
13. He pleaded with his mother to let John and he pitch a tent in the yard.
14. The number of votes cast in the election was very small.
15. She knows that there has been many changes made since that time.
16. If we cast aside our fears, the affect will prove encouraging.
17. The new office building has cost we taxpayers more then three million dollars.
18. "Don't you think that the old building, the one that was tore down would have served just as good?" Mr. Smithers asked.
19. The letters were intended for we two only.
20. There is sometimes only one course possible.
21. Its plan is similar to the plan of our house.
22. The books were laying on the davenport, just where Jack and she had left them.
23. Who's book is this one with the torn cover?
24. After the vocalist had sang his final number, he spoke briefly to the group.
25. Do you mind my borrowing a book from John?
26. Although he had excepted the invitation, John failed to appear at the party.
27. Here, Mr. Chairman, is all the reports of the executive committee.
28. At the school picnic the childrens lunches disappeared.
29. What have been the principal affects of the serum?
30. I was surprised to learn that he has not always spoke English fluently.
31. The most important feature of the series of swimming lessons were the large number of strokes taught.
32. That the prize proved to be beyond her reach did not surprise him.
33. If only we had began before it was too late!
34. Lets evaluate our semester's work.
35. I hoped that John could effect a compromise between the opposing forces.
36. He felt that he had paid to high a price for one mistake.
37. The combination of the three colors give a pleasing effect.
38. Who's money is this on the desk?
39. Being both observant and curious about things promote learning.
40. Neither my brother nor I was invited to the party.

Chapter 5

THE CORRECT USAGE TEST: PUNCTUATION (QUESTION 4)

If you know the rules of correct punctuation, you will be both a better writer and a better reader. In your writing you will be unlikely to commit such blunders as "After eating grandmother washed the dishes." When you encounter a colon [:] in your reading, you will immediately sense the author's next move: he will either present a series or explain more fully an idea he has just stated. To improve your punctuation skill, review the rules and do the exercises on the following pages.

REVIEW OF PUNCTUATION RULES

1. USE THE PERIOD [.]

   a. After a statement.
   Our school has a new physics laboratory.

   b. After a command.
   Put your pens down.

   c. After most abbreviations.
   Mr.   etc.   p.m.   op. cit.

   WITH CLOSING QUOTATION MARKS: The period precedes.
   Mother said, "Dinner is ready."

2. USE THE QUESTION MARK [?] after a question.

   When will you hand in your report?

   EXCEPTION: After a request phrased as a question for the sake of politeness, you may use a period.
   Will you please detach the stub and return it with your payment.

   WITH CLOSING QUOTATION MARKS: The question mark precedes if it belongs to the quotation only.
   Mr. Rossi asked, "Who would like to volunteer?"

The question mark follows if it belongs to the sentence as a whole.
> Do you know who wrote "The Death of the Hired Man"?

3. USE THE EXCLAMATION POINT [!] after an exclamation.

> What a fine throw Sam made!

WITH CLOSING QUOTATION MARKS: The exclamation point precedes if it belongs to the quotation only.
> She exclaimed, "What a delightful surprise!"

The exclamation point follows if it belongs to the sentence as a whole.
> How thrilling it was to hear the band play "Stars and Stripes Forever"!

4. USE THE COMMA [,]

a. To set off words of direct address (words that tell to whom a remark is addressed).
> *Mr. Jones,* that is the reason for my absence. (one comma)
> That is the reason for my absence, *Mr. Jones.* (one comma)
> That, *Mr. Jones,* is the reason for my absence. (Use two commas to set off a word or expression that neither begins nor ends a sentence.)

b. To set off words in apposition (words that give additional information about the preceding or following word or expression).
> A *light sleeper,* my father is the first to awake. (one comma)
> The first to awake is my father, *a light sleeper.* (one comma)
> My father, *a light sleeper,* is the first to awake. (two commas)

c. To set off a direct quotation.
> The chairman said, *"The meeting is adjourned."*
> *"The meeting is adjourned,"* said the chairman.
> *"The meeting,"* said the chairman, *"is adjourned."* (Use two commas to set off a divided quotation.)

d. To set off an interrupting expression.
> My sister, *Heaven help her,* has three finals on Friday.

e. Before the conjunction (*and, but, or, for,* etc.) in a compound sentence.

Geraldine was the first to leave the examination room, *and* I followed about five minutes later.

NOTE: The comma is unnecessary in a short compound sentence: Sarah washed the dishes and I dried them.

EXCEPTION: Use the comma before the conjunction *for* to prevent misreading.
Dad stopped the car, *for* Emma was ill.

f. After each item in a series, except the last.
The fruit bowl contained *peaches, pears, nectarines, plums, grapes,* and *bananas.* (The comma before *and* may be omitted.)

g. To set off a contrasting expression.
The girls did most of the work, *not the boys.*
The girls, *not the boys,* did most of the work.

h. After an introductory prepositional phrase.
Along the route from the airport to City Hall, the hero was wildly acclaimed.

NOTE: The comma may be omitted if the phrase is short:
Along the route the hero was wildly acclaimed.

i. After an introductory subordinate clause.
When I got the raise, Dad was surprised.

j. After an introductory participial phrase.
Frightened by our approach, the burglar fled.

k. To set off a nonessential clause (a clause that *can be omitted* without making the sentence illogical or changing its basic meaning).
Franklin D. Roosevelt, *who was elected President four times,* was an avid stamp collector.

CAUTION: Do not set off an essential clause (a clause that *cannot be omitted*).
Franklin D. Roosevelt is the only American *who was elected President four times.* (no comma before *who*)

l. To set off a nonessential participial phrase.
The patient, *weakened by loss of blood,* lapsed into unconsciousness.

CAUTION: Do not set off an essential participial phrase.

All people *weakened by loss of blood* need transfusions. (no commas)

m. After such words as *yes, no, ah, oh, well,* etc., at the beginning of a sentence.

Oh, I'm sorry to hear it.

n. After the salutation in a friendly letter.

Dear Joe,   Dear Agnes,   Dear Dad,

o. After the complimentary close in a friendly or business letter.

Your friend,   Sincerely yours,   Yours truly,

p. Between the day of the month and the year.

December 7, 1941   October 12, 1492

q. Before the state in an address.

Brooklyn 25, New York   Chicago 7, Illinois
Holdrege, Nebraska

r. To set off transitional expressions such as *however, moreover, furthermore, nevertheless, on the other hand, incidentally, of course,* etc.

The results, *nevertheless,* were quite satisfactory.

WITH CLOSING QUOTATION MARKS: The comma precedes.

"Remember to revise your paper," Mr. Brown concluded.

5. USE THE SEMICOLON [;]

a. To separate items in a series when the items contain commas.

The following officers were elected: *Marvin Bloch, president; Eleanor Swenson, vice president;* and *Mildred White, secretary.*

b. Between main clauses that contain commas.

Sydney Carton, the hero, resembles Charles Darnay, Lucie's husband; and he uses this resemblance to save Darnay's life.

c. Between main clauses when the conjunction *and, but, for, or,* etc., has been left out.

We have made many suggestions to your committee; not a single one has been accepted.

d. Between main clauses connected by *however, moreover, nevertheless, for example, consequently,* etc.

It was really a comfortable seat; *consequently,* she felt no inclination to move.

WITH CLOSING QUOTATION MARKS: The semicolon follows.

Edna St. Vincent Millay was only nineteen when she wrote "Renascence"; nevertheless, it is an outstanding poem.

6. USE THE COLON [:]

a. After the word *following* and similar expressions that introduce a list or series.

The dinner menu offered a choice of the *following:* broiled chicken, roast beef, liver and bacon, or baked mackerel.

b. Before a lengthy quotation.

On November 19, 1863, Abraham Lincoln uttered these memorable words: "Four score and seven years ago, . . ."

c. Before a part of a sentence that merely restates, explains, or gives an example of what has just been stated.

Our firm has a fixed policy: we will not be undersold.

A Shakespearean sonnet consists of four parts: three quatrains and a couplet.

d. After the salutation of a business letter.

Dear Sir: Gentlemen: Dear Mr. O'Brien:

WITH CLOSING QUOTATION MARKS: The colon follows.

There are three characters in "The Death of the Hired Man": Mary, Warren, and Silas.

7. USE THE DASH [—]

a. To show a sudden change in thought.

We have a democratic student government—*of course, we don't make all the rules*—that gives us a voice in school affairs.

b. Before a summary of what has just been stated in the sentence.

Staying on the team, graduation, going to college, the increased allowance Dad had promised—*everything depended on my getting better marks.*

8. USE PARENTHESES ( )

a. To enclose information added to the sentence to guide the reader.
"A Guide to Personal Reading" (*see pages* 251-284) offers helpful comments about more than three hundred worthwhile literary works.

b. To enclose numbers or letters used to list items in a sentence.
A book owned by a library is usually represented in the card catalog by (1) a title card, (2) an author card, and (3) a subject card.

9. USE BRACKETS [ ] to enclose a writer's comment that interrupts a direct quotation.

She said, "I helped Tom occasionally with his Latin [*in fact, she saved him from failing*] when he had Mrs. Brown."

10. USE QUOTATION MARKS [" "]

a. To set off titles of short works: poems, essays, short stories, one-act plays, songs, magazine articles, etc.
"The Rime of the Ancient Mariner" (poem)
"On Doors" (essay)
"The Gift of the Magi" (short story)
"The Star-Spangled Banner" (song)

NOTE: In handwritten or typewritten matter, underline titles of full-length works (novels, biographies, full-length plays, anthologies, nonfiction books, etc.) and titles of newspapers, magazines, operas, and motion pictures.
Macbeth (full-length play)
Modern American and British Poetry (anthology)
Giants in the Earth (novel)
Newsweek (magazine)

b. To set off a definition. (The word or expression being defined should be underlined.)
The expression to aggravate means "to make worse."

c. To set off a direct quotation (a speaker's exact words).

The principal said, *"We have been informed that our cafeteria will be renovated."* (Capitalize the first word of a direct quotation: use *We*, not *we*.)

"We have been informed that our cafeteria will be renovated," the principal said.

"We have been informed," the principal said, *"that our cafeteria will be renovated."* (Two sets of quotation marks are needed when a direct quotation is divided.)

CAUTION: Do not use quotation marks with an indirect quotation.

The principal said that we had been informed that our cafeteria would be renovated. (no quotation marks)

NOTE: To set off a quotation within a direct quotation, use single quotation marks.

"Please explain," the prosecutor asked, "what you mean by *'I don't remember exactly.'*"

11. USE THE APOSTROPHE [']

a. To indicate possession.

To make a singular noun possessive, add an *apostrophe* and *s* [*'s*].

    boy's tie   a year's delay   policeman's badge

To form the possessive of a plural noun ending in *s*, merely add an *apostrophe* [*'*].

    boys' ties   two years' delay   students' diplomas

To form the possessive of a plural noun not ending in *s*, add an *apostrophe* and *s* [*'s*].

    women's gloves   children's toys   policemen's badges

CAUTION: Add the apostrophe to the possessor, never to the thing possessed.

REMINDER: The following pronouns are already possessive and therefore do *not* require an apostrophe to indicate possession: *his, hers, its, ours, yours, theirs,* and *whose*.

Whose fault is it that the dog hurt *its* paw? Is it *his* or *hers?* Is it *ours,* or *yours,* or *theirs?* (no apostrophes needed)

b. To indicate the omission of one or more letters in a contraction.
   it's (it is)   who's (who is)   you're (you are)   we'll (we will)

c. To indicate the plural of a number, a letter, or a word considered as a word.
   There are three 4's in my telephone number.
   Mississippi has four i's and four s's.
   Reduce the number of and's and so's in your composition.

ANALYSIS OF TYPICAL PUNCTUATION QUESTIONS

Each of the following sentences contains an underlined expression. Below each sentence are four suggested answers. The correct answer has been inserted in the space at the right.

*QUESTION 1: In his locker we found the <u>following;</u> an old textbook, a banner, and an overcoat.

   1. Correct as is   3. following.
   2. following: 4. following,   ...2...

ANSWER EXPLAINED: A colon [:] is needed after *following* to introduce the series "an old textbook, a banner, and an overcoat."
RULE INVOLVED: 6a (page 129)

*QUESTION 2: That, <u>my friend</u> is not the correct answer.

   1. Correct as is   3. , my friend,
   2. my friend,   4. my friend   ...3...

ANSWER EXPLAINED: The words *my friend* are in direct address and must be set off from the rest of the sentence by two commas.
RULE INVOLVED: 4a (page 126)

*QUESTION 3: The store specializes in <u>infants' and childrens'</u> clothing.

1. Correct as is
2. infants' and children's
3. infant's and children's
4. infant's and childrens'

2
....

ANSWER EXPLAINED: To form the possessive plural of a noun ending in *s*, merely add an apostrophe.

infants + ['] = infants'

To form the possessive plural of a noun not ending in *s*, add an apostrophe and *s*.

children + ['s] = children's

The correct answer therefore is number 2: infants' and children's.

RULE INVOLVED: 11a (page 131)

*QUESTION 4: <u>Every man, who breaks the law, should be pun-</u>ished.

1. Correct as is
2. man who breaks the law; should
3. man who breaks the law should
4. man, who breaks the law should

3
....

ANSWER EXPLAINED: The clause *who breaks the law* is essential to the sentence and must not be set off by any punctuation. If we temporarily remove this clause, we are left with the illogical statement "Every man should be punished." This proves that the clause *who breaks the law* is essential to the sentence. Essential clauses must not be set off by any punctuation from the rest of the sentence.

RULE INVOLVED: 4k (page 127)

QUESTION 5: Have you read "The Murders in the Rue Morgue?"

1. Correct as is
2. <u>The Murders in the Rue Morgue?</u>
3. <u>The Murders in the Rue Morgue.</u>
4. <u>"The Murders in the Rue Morgue"?</u>

4
....

ANSWER EXPLAINED: The work mentioned in this sentence is a short story and should be enclosed by quotation marks. The question mark should follow the quotation marks, for it belongs to the sentence as a whole.

RULES INVOLVED: 10*a* (page 130) and 2 (pages 125-126)

EXERCISES IN PUNCTUATION SKILLS

A. Each of the following sentences contains an underlined expression. Below each sentence are four suggested answers. Decide which answer is correct. Be prepared to give the reasons for your choice.

(1) The proctor announced, "the examination has begun."

1. Correct as is
2. announced; "The

3. announced, "The
4. announced; "the

(2) Has the mail arrived, Mother? Is there anything for me?

1. Correct as is
2. arrived Mother? Is

3. arrived, Mother, is
4. arrived Mother; is

(3) The painting, a mass of colors, does'nt appeal to me.

1. Correct as is
2. a mass of colors, doesn't

3. a mass of colors does'nt
4. a mass of colors, don't

(4) All the students, whose reports were not handed in, failed.

1. Correct as is
2. students who's reports were not handed in failed.
3. students, who's reports were not handed in, failed.
4. students whose reports were not handed in failed.

(5) We saw three Shakespearean plays on television: "Macbeth," "Hamlet," and "Richard III."

1. Correct as is
2. television: "Macbeth," "Hamlet," and "Richard III".
3. television: Macbeth, Hamlet, and Richard III.
4. television; Macbeth, Hamlet, and Richard III.

(6) Mrs. Freund, our adviser, spoke about scholarship, service, and character.

1. Correct as is
2. spoke about:

3. spoke about,
4. spoke about;

(7) When asked how he liked the party, Bill replied, "Its wonderful."

    1. Correct as is   3. "Its wonderful".
    2. "It's wonderful."   4. "It's wonderful".

(8) You may not like spinach, however, it's good for you.

    1. Correct as is   3. spinach, however, its
    2. spinach; however, its   4. spinach; however, it's

(9) "Before starting to write your composition plan what you are going to say,"
Miss Wright advised.

    1. Correct as is
    2. composition plan what you are going to say",
    3. composition, plan what you are going to say,"
    4. composition, plan what you are going to say",

(10) Oh its a long, sad tale.

    1. Correct as is   3. Oh, its'
    2. Oh, its   4. Oh, it's

(11) On my first ride in our new car I thought, "How good to know that it's all
ours!"

    1. Correct as is   3. all our's!"
    2. all ours"!   4. all our's"!

(12) The contest winners are as follows; Mary, first; Agnes, second; and John,
third.

    1. Correct as is
    2. follows: Mary, first; Agnes, second; and John, third.
    3. follows: Mary, first, Agnes, second, and John, third.
    4. follows; Mary first; Agnes second; and John third.

(13) "When you come to the stop sign", Dad repeated, "make a full stop."

    1. Correct as is   3. sign," Dad repeated
    2. sign" Dad repeated,   4. sign," Dad repeated,

(14) My friends warned me, "Mrs. Ott doesn't like students, who chew gum in
class."

    1. Correct as is
    2. students who chew gum in class".
    3. students who chew gum in class."
    4. students, who chew gum in class".

(15) I have always liked "Sea Fever"; in fact, I know the first stanza by heart.

    1. Correct as is   3. Sea Fever; in fact,
    2. "Sea Fever;" in fact,   4. "Sea Fever"; In fact,

(16) Bill suggested, "Lets not wait, for the lines are too long."

    1. Correct as is   3. "Let's not wait, for
    2. "Lets not wait for   4. "Let's not wait for

(17) Every motorist, who is caught speeding, should lose his license.

    1. Correct as is
    2. motorist who is caught speeding should
    3. motorist who is caught speeding; should
    4. motorist, who is caught speeding should

(18) Your answer, not her's, caused all the excitement.

    1. Correct as is   3. , not hers,
    2. not hers   4. not her's

(19) Mabel asked, "To which colleges has Joan applied."

    1. Correct as is   3. applied".
    2. applied"?   4. applied?"

(20) Have you read the poem by Robert Frost entitled "Mending Wall?"

    1. Correct as is   3. Mending Wall?
    2. "Mending Wall"?   4. Mending Wall?

    B. Rewrite the following sentences, inserting the necessary punctuation. In a few sentences you may have to change a small letter to a capital. Make no other changes.

    1. Please add the following items to your shopping list onions salt tea and aluminum foil
    2. As my little brother came in he smilingly asserted I have two 80s and three 90s on my report card
    3. Anthony Gallo a student in my chemistry class is a good pianist
    4. You can usually buy mens womens and childrens hosiery in a department store
    5. The results I am happy to say took us by surprise
    6. Are Nancys grades better than yours
    7. We missed our train consequently we arrived after the performance had started
    8. Your trust in me my fellow students will not be betrayed
    9. These books are someone elses not yours explained Paul
    10. Linens draperies ladies hats and childrens shoes are on the next floor said the elevator operator

11. He asked how many 7s are there in your telephone number
12. Bens failure to stop at the patrolmans signal resulted in a ten-dollar fine
13. Fatigued after the first half hour Henry complained what a wet and miserable day we picked for a hike
14. Jackson High is the only school that beat us last year said Coach Shaw
15. Several attempts were made to refloat the capsized ship every one of them failed
16. Gerald who read the play last week thinks its difficult to understand
17. Television programs that have nothing worthwhile to offer should not be on the air
18. Hoping for better weather by morning we left Chicago at midnight
19. Next week I have to read The World Is Too Much With Us and four chapters in The Return of the Native
20. Have you ever considered Mr Jones began how exciting it must be to operate an electronic computer

Chapter 6

THE CORRECT USAGE TEST: CAPITALIZATION
(QUESTION 4)

Review your capitalization rules. They are essential for good composition technique. Don't feel that the only important use for a capital letter is to begin a new sentence. You should know too when to use and when not to use capitals with quotations, titles used with persons' names, titles of books and periodicals, etc.

Should you, for example, write *the Reader's Digest* or *The Reader's Digest?* Which is correct—*my Uncle John* or *my uncle John?* Are the names of the seasons capitalized (*spring* or *Spring*)? Is it *Seventy-second Street* or *Seventy-Second Street?*

The answers to these and other capitalization problems appear in the next few pages. Study the examples in the brief review of capitalization. Then do the exercises.

REVIEW OF CAPITALIZATION RULES

1. CAPITALIZE the opening word

   a. Of a sentence.
   > It is a pleasure to go hiking in spring.

   b. Of a direct quotation.
   > The officer explained, "If you go two blocks north, you will see the main entrance."

   DO NOT CAPITALIZE the opening word of the second half of a divided quotation, unless it begins a new sentence.
   > "If you go two blocks north," the officer explained, "you (*no capital*) will see the main entrance."
   > "Go two blocks north," the officer explained. "There (*a capital is used to begin the new sentence*) you will see the main entrance."

   c. Of a line of poetry.
   > "Tomorrow, and tomorrow, and tomorrow
   > Creeps in this petty pace from day to day."
   > > —*William Shakespeare*

DO NOT CAPITALIZE the opening word of a line if the poet himself did not do so.

> "The fog comes
> on (*no capital*) little cat feet."
> —*Carl Sandburg*

d. Of the salutation in a letter. In addition, capitalize *all nouns* in the salutation.

Dear Pat,   My dear Mr. Blum:
Dear Uncle Mike,   Dear Sirs:

e. Of the complimentary close of a letter. (Capitalize the opening word only.)

Your friend,   Sincerely yours,
Your best pal,   Very truly yours,
Your former pupil,   Yours very truly,

2. CAPITALIZE proper nouns (names of particular persons, places, things, etc.) and proper adjectives (adjectives formed from proper nouns).

A *common noun* refers to no particular person, place, or thing and is not capitalized. Examples: man, country, building.

A *proper noun* refers to a particular person, place, or thing and is always capitalized. Examples: Shakespeare (a particular man), Mexico (a particular country), Empire State Building (a particular building).

An adjective derived from a proper noun is also capitalized. Examples: a Shakespearean play, a Mexican village.

Learn to CAPITALIZE the proper nouns and proper adjectives in these important categories:

a. Names of persons.
   Stan Musial, Marian Anderson, William Faulkner

b. Names of geographical places.
   Europe, Pacific Ocean, United States, Hudson River, Bear Mountain, Albany, Broadway, Fifth Avenue, Central Park

DO NOT CAPITALIZE the second part of a hyphenated number. Example: Forty-second Street.

c. Names of sections of countries (especially of the United States) and their people.

New England, the South, the West, New Englander, Southerner

DO NOT CAPITALIZE north, south, east, and west when used to indicate direction.

Go one mile south and then turn east.

d. Names of buildings, museums, churches, etc.

Municipal Building, National Gallery of Art, Saint Patrick's Cathedral, Waldorf-Astoria Hotel

e. Names of institutions and organizations.

George Washington High School, American Automobile Association, General Motors Corporation, Boy Scouts of America

f. Names of governmental subdivisions.

House of Representatives, Department of Agriculture, Bureau of Motor Vehicles, New York Police Department

g. Names of days, months, and holidays.

Monday, December, Labor Day

DO NOT CAPITALIZE the seasons: spring, summer, autumn (fall), winter.

h. Names of historical events, eras, and documents.

Battle of the Coral Sea, the Renaissance, the Declaration of Independence

i. Names of languages.

English, French, Russian, Spanish, Hebrew

j. Names of nationalities.

American, Japanese, Egyptian, Israeli

k. Names of races.

Caucasian, Negro, Mongolian

l. Names of religions.

Christian, Roman Catholic, Protestant, Jewish, Mohammedan, Hindu

m. References to the Supreme Being.

God, the Creator, the Almighty, the Lord, Heaven, Jehovah, Jesus Christ, Savior, His name

"I will fear no evil: for Thou art with me."
—Twenty-third Psalm

DO NOT CAPITALIZE references to pagan divinities—only their names.

Zeus was the chief of the ancient Greek gods, and Jupiter was his Roman counterpart.

n. Titles preceding persons' names.

Dr. Berg, Professor Holmes, General Lee, President Lincoln, Uncle Jack, Cousin Ruth

DO NOT CAPITALIZE titles used alone, except for the highest officials.

The doctor came.

Who is the president of your club?

The President returned to the White House.

o. Titles of parents and relatives not preceded by a possessive word (e.g., my, your, Frank's, etc.).

I saw Father with Uncle George.

I saw my father with my uncle George.

p. Titles of books, plays, articles, poems, short stories, etc.

DO NOT CAPITALIZE the following words unless they stand first in the title: (1) *a, an, the;* (2) conjunctions (*and, or,* etc.); (3) short prepositions (*to, of, for,* etc.).

The Old Man and the Sea, An Enemy of the People, "A Night at an Inn," "To a Mouse"

q. Titles of newspapers and magazines.

DO NOT CAPITALIZE the word *the* before the title of a newspaper or magazine.

I read the *New York Times, Newsweek,* and the *Scientific American.*

r. Titles of courses.

This term I am taking English 8, Economics 1, Math 12, Physics 2, and French 6.

DO NOT CAPITALIZE school subjects, except languages.

This term I am taking English, economics, math, physics, and French.

s. Titles of holy writings and their subdivisions.

the Bible, the Old Testament, the New Testament, the Book of Ruth, the Gospel of St. Matthew

3. CAPITALIZE the words *I* and *O*.

> Jane and **I** hope you will come.
> "Exult **O** shores, and ring **O** bells!"
> —*Walt Whitman*

DO NOT CAPITALIZE the word *oh*, except at the beginning of a sentence.

> "Destroyer and preserver; hear, **oh**, hear!"
> —*Percy Bysshe Shelley*

4. CAPITALIZE personifications (ideas or abstract objects treated as persons).

> "O Liberty! Liberty! what crimes are committed in thy name!"
> —*Madame Roland*

ANALYSIS OF TYPICAL CAPITALIZATION QUESTION

The sentence below contains an underlined expression. Below the sentence are four suggested answers. The correct answer has been inserted in the space at the right.

> *QUESTION: After I had finished High School, I went on to college.
> 1. Correct as is
> 2. High School having been finished,
> 3. After finishing High School,
> 4. After I had finished high school,   4 . . . . . .

ANSWER EXPLAINED: Since they do not refer to a particular high school, the words *high school* should not be capitalized.

RULE INVOLVED: A common noun (a noun referring to no particular person, place, or thing) is not capitalized. (page 139)

EXERCISES IN CAPITALIZATION

A. Each of the following sentences contains an underlined expression. Below each sentence are four suggested answers. Decide which answer is correct. Be prepared to explain the reasons for your answers.

(1) I showed my <u>father your copy of the</u> *Reader's Digest*.

1. Correct as is	3. father your copy of The
2. Father your copy of the	4. Father your copy of The

(2) At what time did the President summon his Doctor to the White House?

   1. Correct as is
   2. The President summon his Doctor
   3. the president summon his doctor
   4. the President summon his doctor

(3) "My Cousin Arthur," he said, "has just left for Annapolis."

   1. Correct as is
   2. cousin Arthur," he said, "has
   3. cousin Arthur," he said, "Has
   4. Cousin Arthur," he said, "Has

(4) Is there a crosstown bus on Thirty-Fourth Street?

   1. Correct as is   3. Thirty-fourth Street?
   2. Thirty-Fourth street?   4. thirty-fourth street?

(5) The letter concluded with the words "Yours very truly, Salvatore De Vito."

   1. Correct as is   3. yours very truly,
   2. Yours Very Truly,   4. yours very Truly,

(6) Mr. Berson teaches us economics and American History.

   1. Correct as is
   2. Economics and American History.
   3. economics and American history.
   4. economics and american history.

(7) "Until three years ago," explained Bob, "My family lived in the South."

   1. Correct as is
   2. "my family lived in the south."
   3. "my family lived in the South."
   4. "My family lived in the south."

(8) Before coming here, she had attended High School in the city of Denver.

   1. Correct as is   3. High School in the City
   2. high school in the city   4. high school in the City

(9) You can see wonderful botanical displays in Prospect Park in the Spring.

   1. Correct as is   3. park in the Spring.
   2. park in the spring.   4. Park in the spring.

(10) I earned my best marks in chemistry 2 and Spanish 4.

   1. Correct as is
   2. Chemistry 2 and Spanish 4.
   3. chemistry 2 and spanish 4.
   4. Chemistry 2 and spanish 4.

(11) "There are several fine national parks in the <u>west," said Uncle Ben.</u>

    1. Correct as is   3. West," said uncle Ben.
    2. west," said uncle Ben.   4. West," said Uncle Ben.

(12) Didn't you know that <u>Grandfather and Aunt Isabel</u> were coming for dinner?

    1. Correct as is
    2. grandfather and Aunt Isabel
    3. Grandfather and aunt Isabel
    4. grandfather and aunt Isabel

(13) We shall read *The Call of the Wild* <u>in Literature</u> next term.

    1. Correct as is
    2. the *Call of the Wild* in literature
    3. *The Call of the Wild* in literature
    4. *The Call Of The Wild* in Literature

(14) "My speech teacher is a <u>Westerner," said Emily, "he</u> was raised in California."

    1. Correct as is
    2. Westerner," said Emily, "He
    3. westerner," said Emily. "He
    4. Westerner," said Emily. "He

(15) The turning point in the Civil <u>War was the battle</u> of Gettysburg.

    1. Correct as is   3. war was the battle
    2. War was the Battle   4. War was The Battle

(16) At Friday's assembly, Janet read the <u>Twenty-Third Psalm from the Bible.</u>

    1. Correct as is
    2. the Twenty-third Psalm from the Bible.
    3. The Twenty-Third Psalm from The Bible.
    4. the Twenty-third Psalm from The Bible.

(17) "A tree that looks at God all day,
      And lifts <u>Her</u> leafy arms to pray."

    1. Correct as is   3. and lifts Her
    2. and lifts her   4. And lifts her

(18) He expects to enter the <u>College of the City of New York next autumn.</u>

    1. Correct as is
    2. the College of the city of New York next autumn.
    3. the College of the City of New York next Autumn.
    4. the College of the city of New York next Autumn.

(19) Shall we learn about the <u>middle ages in European History I</u>?

    1. Correct as is
    2. Middle Ages in European history I?
    3. Middle Ages in European History I?
    4. middle ages in european history I?

(20) "Dear old Pete," began the letter <u>from my Cousin Harvey, "You'll probably be surprised to get this letter."</u>

    1. Correct as is
    2. "Dear Old Pete," began the letter from my cousin
    3. "Dear old Pete," began the letter from my cousin
    4. "Dear Old Pete," began the letter from my Cousin

B. Rewrite each of the following sentences, correcting all errors in capitalization:

1. Drive east about a mile and a half to the Sixty-Ninth Road exit.
2. In Junior High School I had excellent teachers in English, French, and Art.
3. "When you telephone mother," said Dad, "Tell her when you expect to be home."
4. The Lieutenant was asked to describe his experiences in The Korean War.
5. Tell us, o mathematical genius, how you solved the second Physics problem.
6. I expect to specialize in American Literature at College next Fall.
7. My Aunt Rose works in The New York Public Library at Fifth Avenue and Forty-Second Street.
8. Wordsworth's Poem "Daffodils" ends as follows:

> "And then my heart with pleasure fills,
> and dances with the daffodils."

9. As we traveled through the South last March, we saw many Spring shrubs already in bloom.
10. "Visitors to New York City," advises the travel book, "Should make sure to visit the metropolitan Museum of Art and The Museum of Natural history."

Chapter 7

THE CORRECT USAGE TEST: ABBREVIATIONS (QUESTION 4)

You should be familiar with abbreviations used in dictionaries and reference works and those commonly encountered in general reading. Many abbreviations have been the basis of questions on past Regents examinations.

TYPICAL REGENTS ABBREVIATIONS TEST

Do the following test in your notebook. Then consult the list below to verify your answers.

JUNE 1956

Give the common English meaning of each of *ten* of the following abbreviations: [5]

vol.	atty.	acct.	i.e.
pl.	enc.	vs.	ibid.
pp.	C.O.D.	E.S.T.	viz.

COMMON ABBREVIATIONS

(Check the ones you do not know and memorize them.)

acct., account, accountant
A.D., in the year of our Lord
adj., adjective
ad lib. or **ad libit.**, at one's pleasure, to the amount desired
adv., adverb
AFL-CIO, American Federation of Labor and Congress of Industrial Organizations
a.m., before noon
amt., amount
anon., anonymous
ant., antonym

Apr., April
asst., assistant
atty., attorney
Aug., August
A.W.O.L., absent without official leave

B.A., Bachelor of Arts
bal., balance
bbl., barrel(s)
B.C., before Christ
bibliog., bibliography
B/L, bill of lading

B.S., Bachelor of Science
bu., bushel(s)

cap., capital
cat., catalog
cc., cubic centimeter(s)
cf., compare
chm., chairman
circ., about
cm., centimeter(s)
C.O., Commanding Officer
c/o, care of
C.O.D., cash on delivery
Col., Colonel
colloq., colloquial
conj., conjunction
cont., continued
contr., contraction
corp., corporation
C.P.A., Certified Public Accountant
cu., cubic
cwt., hundredweight

D.A., District Attorney
D.D., Doctor of Divinity
D.D.S., Doctor of Dental Surgery
Dec., December
Dem., Democrat
dept., department
do., ditto (the same)
doz., dozen
D.S.T., Daylight Saving Time

ea., each
ed., edited, edition, editor
e.g., for example
enc., encl., enclosure
esp., especially
E.S.T., Eastern Standard Time
et al., and others

etc., et cetera (and so forth)
et seq., and the following
ex lib., from the books (of)

Feb., February
fem., feminine
ff., and what follows
FM, frequency modulation
f.o.b., free on board
Fri., Friday
ft., foot or feet

gal., gallon(s)
Gen., General
Gov., Governor
govt., government

H.M.S., His (Her) Majesty's Service or Ship
Hon., Honorable
H.Q., headquarters
hr., hour
ht., height

ibid., in the same place
id., the same
i.e., that is
in., inch(es)
incl., inclosure, inclusive
inst., of the current month
interj., interjection
I.Q., intelligence quotient
ital., italic (type)

Jan., January
Jr., Junior
Jul., July
Jun., June

kc., kilocycle(s)
kt., carat(s)

£, pound (money)
lat., latitude
lb., pound(s)
l.c., lower case
lit., literally
log., logarithm
long., longitude
Lt., Lieutenant

M, thousand
M.A., Master of Arts
Maj., Major
Mar., March
masc., masculine
max., maximum
M.D., Doctor of Medicine
mdse., merchandise
Messrs., plural of Mr.
mfg., manufacturing
mgr., manager
min., minimum
misc., miscellaneous
Mlle., Mademoiselle
mm., millimeter(s)
Mme., Madame
mo., month
Mon., Monday
m.p.h., miles per hour
ms., manuscript
M.S., Master of Science
mtg., mortgage

n., noun, neuter
N.B., Note well.
no., number
nos., numbers
Nov., November
nr., near
nt. wt., net weight

obs., obsolete

Oct., October
op. cit., in the work cited
opp., opposite
oz., ounce(s)

p., page
pat., patent, patented
payt., payment
pd., paid
pfd., preferred
Ph.D., Doctor of Philosophy
pkg., package
pl., plural
p.m., after noon
pop., population
pp., pages
prep., preposition
pron., pronoun, pronunciation
pro tem., for the time being
P.S., postscript
pseud., pseudonym
Pvt., Private

Q.E.D., which was to be demonstrated
qt., quart(s)
q.v., which see

Rep., Republican
Rev., Reverend
R.F.D., Rural Free Delivery
R.I.P., May he (she) rest in peace.
R.N., Registered Nurse, Royal Navy
r.p.m., revolutions per minute
R.S.V.P., Please reply.

Sat., Saturday
secy., secretary
Sept., September
Sgt., Sergeant

sing., singular

sq., square

Sr., Senior

S.R.O., standing room only

S.S., steamship

St., Saint

Sun., Sunday

supt., superintendent

syn., synonym

U.S.S.R., Union of Soviet Socialist
Republics

v., verb

Va., Virginia

v.i., intransitive verb

viz., namely

vol., volume

vs., versus (against)

v.t., transitive verb

Tues., Tuesday

Thurs., Thursday

Wed., Wednesday

wt., weight

yd., yard(s)

U.N., United Nations

yr., year

EXERCISES ON ABBREVIATIONS

1. Give the meaning of each of the following abbreviations commonly used in the dictionary:

1. syn.	6. obs.	11. pron.	16. ant.
2. adj.	7. v.i.	12. fem.	17. adv.
3. viz.	8. n.	13. id.	18. interj.
4. ff.	9. i.e.	14. v.	19. cf.
5. pl.	10. masc.	15. pp.	20. v.t.

2. Give the common English meaning of each of the following abbreviations:

1. vs.	11. atty.	21. enc.
2. vol.	12. Sat.	22. anon.
3. e.g.	13. no.	23. D.S.T.
4. C.O.D.	14. N.B.	24. etc.
5. op. cit.	15. ibid.	25. mm.
6. Hon.	16. Pvt.	26. B.C.
7. acct.	17. A.D.	27. Va.
8. R.S.V.P.	18. Apr.	28. m.p.h.
9. r.p.m.	19. cc.	29. prep.
10. viz.	20. E.S.T.	30. U.S.S.R.

Chapter 8

THE NEWSPAPER TEST (QUESTION 4)

READING A NEWSPAPER INTELLIGENTLY

One of the lifelong habits you are expected to develop in high school is reading a good daily newspaper intelligently. This means being able quickly to locate the important news of the day, editorials, special columns, sports news, reviews (of books, movies, television programs), letters to the editor, weather reports, and other newspaper features. It means being able to get a maximum of news in a minimum of time. Above all, it means being able to distinguish fact from opinion. Intelligent reading of a good daily newspaper will enrich your social, cultural, and business life and help you to make the decisions required of an American citizen.

TYPICAL REGENTS NEWSPAPER TEST

In the test of six questions below, note that you are asked to choose *five* only. If you fill in six, only the first five will be marked.

JANUARY 1958

Each of the following statements or questions concerns the newspaper. Choose *five* only, and in each case, in the space provided write the *number* of the expression that best completes the statement or answers the question.   [5]

(1) In most newspapers, the second most important story of the day appears   (1) on page 2   (2) at the bottom of page 1   (3) on the first page of the second section   (4) at the extreme left of page 1   (1) ...4...

(2) In newspapers, syndicated material is   (1) published in member newspapers   (2) a recopy of favorite news stories   (3) always on the editorial page   (4) purely fictional   (2) ...1...

150

(3) Much of the display advertising of a large newspaper is prepared by (1) the editor (2)
the newspaper staff (3) the news service (4)
advertising agencies

(3) .....4.....

(4) Which statement is an example of "editorializing"?
(1) The Giants won the pennant. (2) The proposed new highway will be very useful. (3)
The grand jury will reconvene tomorrow. (4)
Allen Williams heads the newly formed Chamber
of Commerce.

(4) .....2.....

(5) In most large newspapers, a detailed weather report and map appear (1) on page 1 (2)
on one of the inside pages (3) in the masthead
(4) in a byline

(5) .....2.....

(6) Information about important personalities in the
news is kept on file in the newspaper's (1)
editorial room (2) composing room (3)
morgue (4) copy room

(6) .....3.....

EXPLANATION OF ANSWERS

QUESTION 1: In most newspapers, the second most important story of
the day appears . . .
ANSWER: (4) at the extreme left of page 1.
HINT: The news story of *first* importance would appear in the
extreme *right*-hand column of page 1.

QUESTION 2: In newspapers, syndicated material is . . .
ANSWER: (1) published in member newspapers.
HINT: A syndicate is an association that centrally prepares news
stories, human-interest stories, cartoons, etc., for simultaneous publication in its member newspapers.

QUESTION 3: Much of the display advertising of a large newspaper is
prepared by . . .
ANSWER: (4) advertising agencies.
HINT: A display ad "shows off" a product through choice and
arrangement of words, type, illustrations, and photographs. Large-scale advertisers usually contract to have
their display ads composed and placed in publications by
advertising agencies.

QUESTION 4: Which statement is an example of "editorializing"?

ANSWER: (2) The proposed new highway will be very useful.

HINT: "Editorializing" is the bad practice of giving an opinion in a news article. News articles should report facts only. The statement "The proposed new highway will be very useful" is appropriate for an editorial, not a news article, since it expresses the writer's *opinion*.

QUESTION 5: In most large newspapers, a detailed weather report and map appear . . .

ANSWER: (2) on one of the inside pages.

HINT: Only a brief weather forecast appears on page 1. A detailed weather report and map are usually on one of the inside pages.

QUESTION 6: Information about important personalities in the news is kept on file in the newspaper's . . .

ANSWER: (3) morgue.

HINT: A morgue is the reference library of biographical information in a newspaper office.

REVIEWING FOR THE NEWSPAPER TEST

Past Regents questions on the newspaper have dealt with three main topics:

    A. Reporting the news
    B. Influencing reader opinion
    C. Understanding newspaper terms

A. REPORTING THE NEWS

A news story is written in such a way as to give the reader the most important facts first. Thus, the first sentence, known as the *lead* (rhymes with *feed*), sums up the news by answering most of the following questions: what? who? how? why? where? when?

Good journalism requires the writer of a news story to give an impartial, factual account of events, rigidly excluding his own opinions. The bad practice of injecting opinions into a news story is known as *editorializing,* or *slanting the news.*

The front page is reserved for the most important news of the day. Newspapers usually increase the amount of space for important news on page 1 by continuing page 1 stories on inside pages. The most important news story is to be found in the extreme right-hand column of page 1. In the extreme left-hand column of the front page appears the second most important news story.

Few local newspapers can afford their own reporters on all news fronts. For news of nonlocal events, most newspapers must rely upon reports by news service agencies. Two such agencies are A.P. (Associated Press) and U.P.I. (United Press International). Formerly the U.P.I. was two separate agencies: U.P. (United Press) and I.N.S. (International News Service).

Newspaper syndicates help newspapers reduce the cost of expensive features. Organizations like King Features, United Feature Syndicate, and Bell Syndicate purchase columns on a variety of subjects, as well as comic strips, dress patterns, puzzles, etc., for simultaneous publication in subscribing newspapers.

B. INFLUENCING READER OPINION

An *editorial* is an essay in which an editor or publisher may properly express his opinion about a current news event. Usually an editorial begins by stating the facts of a news item. It then interprets these facts. It ends with the point or conclusion that the editorial writer has reached from his interpretation of the facts.

Editorials are intended to enlighten readers and to influence their views. Columns, too, serve this purpose. A *column* is a regularly featured, signed article in which the columnist is expected to express his personal views on his particular specialty—politics, books, motion pictures, sports, television, etc. A columnist's views are not necessarily the views of his newspaper. *Political cartoons* are another way by which a newspaper can effectively interpret the news and influence the thinking of its readers. Incidentally, some newspapers exert a further influence on public opinion by their ownership of radio stations.

C. UNDERSTANDING NEWSPAPER TERMS

A *beat* is (1) a reporter's regular route of news sources, or (2) the publishing of a news story ahead of rival newspapers (known also as a *scoop*).

A *by-line* is the line at the head of an article telling by whom it was written. Example: By Harrison Salisbury.

A *caption* is (1) a title or explanatory note accompanying a picture, or (2) the headline of an item in a newspaper.

A *classified ad* is one of a group of advertisements arranged according to subject, usually appearing under specific headings (Help Wanted —Male, Apartments Wanted—Unfurnished, etc.) in a definite section of a newspaper.

Copy is manuscript prepared for publication.

A *dateline* is a line at the beginning of a news story giving the source and date of the story. Example: Leopoldville, the Congo, Feb. 23.

A *display ad* is an ad that "shows off" a product by choice and arrangement of words, type, illustrations, and photographs. It is usually composed by an advertising agency.

Editorializing is the bad practice of slanting the news by injecting opinions into a news story.

A *feature story*. See *human-interest story*.

A *galley* or *galley proof* is an impression (a copy) of the first setting of type. It is used for (1) proofreading, and (2) makeup into pages.

A *headline* is a line (or lines) of large type at the top (head) of an article, summarizing its contents.

A *human-interest story* is a story differing from the typical news story in appealing primarily to the emotions of the reader. Examples: a story on the daily rounds of a veterinarian at the zoo, the closing of a famous business establishment, etc. Also known as a *feature story*.

A *lead* (rhymes with *feed*) is the first sentence of a news story. It gives a summary of the story by answering most of these questions: what? who? how? why? when? where?

Magazine section is a supplement, usually included on Sunday, containing articles of general interest.

Makeup is the general arrangement of headlines, stories, and pictures on a newspaper page.

The *masthead* is the statement of the newspaper's title and ownership. It appears on the editorial page.

The *morgue* is the reference library in a newspaper office. It keeps on file information about important personalities in the news.

A *news service agency* is an organization that supplies subscribing newspapers with reports of nonlocal events. Examples: United Press International (U.P.I.) and Associated Press (A.P.).

An *obituary* is a notice of death, often with a brief account of the person's life.

A *scoop*. See item (2) under *beat*.

A *syndicate* is an association that purchases columns, comic strips, dress patterns, etc., for simultaneous publication in member newspapers.

A *tabloid* is a newspaper having half the ordinary size newspaper page, numerous pictures, and compressed news stories.

A *want ad* is a short classified advertisement, usually found in the last pages of an issue, stating that something is wanted. Example: Sales Help Wanted—Male.

A *weather report* is a brief statement about the weather usually appearing on page 1. In most large newspapers a detailed weather report and map appear on one of the inside pages.

FORMER REGENTS QUESTIONS

Each of the following statements concerns the newspaper. In each case, write the *number* of the expression that best completes the statement.

1. Most serious newspaper cartoonists are nearest in point of view to (1) comic strip artists (2) drama critics (3) editorial writers (4) "roving reporters."
2. The first paragraph in a news story (1) gives a detailed account of the event that occurred (2) gives a summarized statement of the event (3) seeks to entertain the reader (4) receives little attention from most readers.
3. A *beat* is (1) a kind of teletype (2) an explanatory note in a news story (3) a reporter's regular route of news sources (4) a file of old news stories.
4. In a Sunday newspaper, articles of general interest are included in the (1) magazine section (2) book review section (3) monthly news summary (4) financial section.
5. The point of view of the publishers of our best newspapers is usually set forth (1) on the first pages of an issue (2) on the editorial page (3) in the financial section (4) in feature stories.
6. Most daily newspapers obtain news of nonlocal events by relying upon (1) "tips" telephoned in by long distance (2) local reporters (3) the newspaper "grapevine" (4) reports by news service agencies.
7. From the standpoint of high-grade journalism, the most important factor in a news story is its (1) location in the paper (2) length (3) headline (4) impartial reporting.
8. Several newspaper syndicates provide member papers with (1) feature stories (2) weather reports (3) classified advertisements (4) society news.
9. The *masthead* of a newspaper is (1) a summary of the day's news (2) a heading over a picture (3) the statement of the newspaper's title and ownership (4) the chief editorial of each issue.
10. The most important purpose of political cartoons is to (1) make readers laugh (2) help readers keep up-to-date (3) meet reader demand for "escape" reading (4) influence readers' views.

11. The *date line* of a news story indicates the date that   (1) the story was written or filed   (2) the event happened   (3) the story was sent out by the news service   (4) the story was due on the editor's desk.
12. Newspaper want ads are usually found   (1) in the last pages of an issue   (2) throughout an issue   (3) at the foot of each page   (4) at the end of the first section.
13. Newspapers increase the amount of space for important news on the front page by   (1) using double headlines   (2) continuing stories on inside pages   (3) placing all local news on inside pages   (4) printing action pictures of the news.
14. Some newspapers influence public opinion by their ownership of   (1) radio stations   (2) book publishing companies   (3) motion picture studios   (4) varied public utilities.
15. A good news story always   (1) deals with sensational information   (2) is written by an experienced reporter   (3) presents the most important facts first   (4) closes with an emphasis upon the main item.
16. It is a function of the newspaper columnist to   (1) assign pages for advertisements   (2) divide the news into columns   (3) write the headlines for the front page   (4) express his personal opinions.
17. *Slanting the news* in reporting an event is known as   (1) editorializing   (2) covering   (3) revising   (4) proofreading.
18. The Associated Press and the United Press International distribute stories to   (1) movie critics   (2) member papers   (3) syndicates   (4) book companies.
19. The first requirement of a good newspaper story is   (1) accuracy   (2) brevity   (3) completeness   (4) partiality.
20. Which of the following statements about the newspaper is *not* true?
    (1) The chief source of income for most newspapers is advertising.
    (2) The Associated Press is a news service agency.
    (3) A headline helps to "slant" the news.
    (4) The size of a newspaper's circulation proves its worth.

Chapter 9

THE MAGAZINE TEST (QUESTION 4)

THE IMPORTANCE OF MAGAZINES

Magazines today are a popular source of information and recreation. In our country alone nearly four billion copies of more than seven thousand magazines are sold each year. Magazines frequently contain more up-to-date information than books. You will surely have many occasions to use magazines for research and entertainment.

TYPICAL REGENTS QUESTIONS ON MAGAZINES

JUNE 1959

QUESTION: To locate a magazine article on educational television, a person should first consult the (1) card catalog (2) *Encyclopedia Americana* (3) *Readers' Guide to Periodical Literature* (4) *Reader's Digest.* ....3....

ANSWER EXPLAINED: (3) *Readers' Guide to Periodical Literature* indexes current magazine articles alphabetically by author and subject.

WRONG CHOICES: (1) The card catalog indexes books, not magazine articles.

(2) *Encyclopedia Americana* is a general reference work, not a guide to magazine articles.

(4) *Reader's Digest*, a monthly magazine, offers condensed versions of about thirty articles originally printed in other magazines. It is not a tool for locating magazine articles.

JANUARY 1962

QUESTION: An essay of literary criticism would be most likely to appear in (1) *Harper's* (2) *Holiday* (3) *McCall's* (4) *Fortune.* ....1....

ANSWER EXPLAINED: (1) *Harper's* features articles on literary topics (as well as politics and current problems).

WRONG CHOICES: (2) *Holiday* is a travel magazine.

(3) *McCall's* advises the American woman on fashions, housekeeping, interior decorating, etc.

(4) *Fortune* is a business magazine.

REVIEWING FOR THE MAGAZINE TEST

Past Regents questions on magazines show that you are expected to be familiar with:

A. The *Readers' Guide to Periodical Literature*
B. Several worthwhile magazines

A. READERS' GUIDE TO PERIODICAL LITERATURE

To locate a magazine article, first consult this valuable research tool published twice monthly from September through June and monthly in July and August. It is a directory to articles appearing in more than 125 leading magazines. Entries in the *Readers' Guide* are for the most part arranged alphabetically by (*a*) subject, and (*b*) author.

a. Sample Entry by Subject:

PYRENEES

> **Guideless in the Pyrenees. V. S. Pritchett**
> **il Holiday 31:60-5+ Ja '62**

EXPLANATION:

Line 1

PYRENEES—the subject of the article

Line 2

Guideless in the Pyrenees—the title of the article
V. S. Pritchett—the author's name

Line 3

il—the article is illustrated (accompanied by pictures)

Holiday—the title of the magazine

31—the volume number of the issue

60-5+—the article appears on pages 60-65 and is continued on later pages

Ja '62—January 1962 (the date of this issue)

b. Sample Entry by Author:

PRITCHETT, Victor Sawdon

Guideless in the Pyrenees. Holiday 31:60-5+
Ja '62

B. SOME WORTHWHILE MAGAZINES

The magazines described below have been referred to at one time or another in past Regents questions. Investigate five or six that appeal to you. You will be well compensated in information and enjoyment.

The American Home specializes in articles on the purchase, maintenance, and improvement of homes and offers advice on interior decorating, gardening, and meal planning. It is published monthly, except for bimonthly issues for January-February and July-August.

The American Observer, published weekly during the school year, presents "current news and issues—with pros and cons."

The Atlantic Monthly presents essays of literary criticism as well as original fiction and poetry, book reviews, articles on current issues, and "The Atlantic Report on the World Today." Among its contributors are some of the most distinguished living writers.

Boys' Life, published monthly by the Boy Scouts of America, offers true adventure tales about the achievements of youth, scout news, scout lore, and short stories.

Fortune, a business monthly, reports developments in big corporations, presents biographical sketches of key business figures, and advises on business problems. Typical departments are "Business around the Globe" and "Businessmen in the News."

Good Housekeeping, published monthly, contains articles on family living, food, beauty, fashions, needlework, textiles, medicine, and child care, as well as short stories, poetry, and a book condensation.

Harper's Magazine, published monthly, offers articles by outstanding writers on literary criticism, politics, and current issues, as well as short stories, poetry, and reviews of books and recordings. Its department of editorial comment is entitled "The Easy Chair."

Holiday, a monthly travel magazine, describes trips and places of interest both at home and abroad through well-written articles and fine photography.

Ladies' Home Journal presents articles on family living, short stories, poems, condensations of novels, and biographies of successful women. There are also several short articles on "Fashion and Beauty," "Food and Homemaking," and "Interior Decorating." It is published monthly, except for bimonthly issues for January-February and July-August.

Life, published weekly, reports the news with extravagant use of pictures. Often a whole issue or series of issues is dedicated to a cultural topic: the history of man, the great religions, full-color reproductions of painting masterpieces, the Civil War, etc. *Life* devotes a page exclusively to editorials.

Look, published biweekly, relies heavily on pictures. *Look's* articles deal mainly with important news and entertainment personalities. Also offered are articles on food and fashions and a "photoquiz."

Mademoiselle, published monthly, is intended mainly for the college girl. It offers hints on fashion, beauty, and shopping; articles on travel, college, and careers; essays on the arts; poetry; and short stories. Through its "College Fiction Contest," *Mademoiselle* encourages young writers.

McCall's, published monthly, is intended for the American woman and her family. It contains articles on fashions, housekeeping, child-rearing, interior decorating, health, and beauty. In addition to short stories and poems, it frequently offers a complete novel.

National Geographic is published monthly for members of the National Geographic Society, sponsor of dozens of scientific expeditions. The articles, maps, and abundant color photographs provide reliable facts about places, peoples, customs, animal and plant life, and undersea phenomena.

Newsweek, published weekly, reports the news under more than twenty categories: "The Americas," "National Affairs," "Sports," "Business Trends," etc. "The Periscope" is a column of "inside" news that tries to stay "ahead" of the news.

Popular Mechanics, published monthly, appeals to both the science-minded and the gadget-minded. The articles, some of them serialized, offer suggestions for the homecraftsman, the "do-it-yourselfer," and the motorist, with the aid of pictures and diagrams.

Popular Science, published monthly, makes a similar appeal. It offers more than forty complete articles, including numerous pictures and diagrams, under such headings as "Cars and Driving," "Discoveries and Inventions," "Consumer News," "Home and Shop," and "Short Cuts and Tips."

Reader's Digest, issued monthly, condenses "articles of lasting interest" originally published in other magazines. It also contains a few uncut articles written to order for the *Reader's Digest.* The contents generally present a constructive picture of our nation or of human nature; deal with health, science, or current problems; or discuss entertaining, little-known facts on various subjects. Each issue contains a book condensation, a biographical sketch called "My Most Unforgettable Character," and a department of reader-contributed anecdotes entitled "Life in These United States."

The Saturday Evening Post publishes stories on personalities in the news, articles on national problems, short stories, and serialized fiction. "People on the Way Up" is a department of photographs and short biographies of the newly successful. It is published weekly, forty-five times a year.

The Saturday Review (formerly *The Saturday Review of Literature*), published weekly, features reviews of newly published books. It includes articles on topics of current interest, as well as reviews of recordings, movies, and plays.

Scientific American, published monthly, offers articles by outstanding scientists on the newest developments in the different sciences. Departments include "Science and the Citizen," "Mathematical Games," and "The Amateur Scientist."

Senior Scholastic, published weekly during the school year, reviews national and world affairs. Its "Forum Topic of the Week" discusses the pro and con sides of a controversial issue. Also offered are reviews of movies and recordings, previews of suggested television fare, and information on etiquette.

Seventeen, a monthly magazine for the teenage girl, offers short picture articles under such headings as "What You Wear," "How You Look and Feel," "Home and Food," and "Having Fun." There are some short stories too.

Time, "the weekly newsmagazine," reports the news in story form under about twenty sections: "Art," "Medicine," "The Nation," "Science," etc. The "Time Listings" section reviews current movies, plays, and books; lists fiction and nonfiction best sellers; and recommends TV fare for the week. (Formerly *Time* regularly offered reviews of radio and television programs.)

U.S. News and World Report, published weekly, emphasizes economic and political developments in its news coverage. Several telegram-style "newsletters" sum up domestic and foreign business trends. An editorial appears on the last page.

FORMER REGENTS QUESTIONS

1. A South American wants to learn more about the United States and our way of life through subscribing to five of our magazines. List *five* good magazines that represent varied interests of American life and, in a sentence or two for each, give specific reasons for your choice.   [10]

2. There are some magazines and some radio programs that may properly be called "molders of public opinion." Show briefly why in your opinion one magazine *or* one radio program merits this designation. If you choose a magazine, give the title in full; if you choose a radio program, give the station and the name of the person or persons who broadcast the program.   [5]

3. Of the following magazines, choose *five* and indicate in one or two sentences for *each* its special values to the reader. [Where alternates are given, choose only one.]   [5]

> *Newsweek* (or *Time*)
> *The National Geographic Magazine*
> *The Atlantic Monthly* (or *Harper's Magazine*)
> *The Saturday Evening Post*
> *Seventeen* (or *Mademoiselle*)
> *Boys' Life*
> *Popular Science* (or *Popular Mechanics*)
> *Life*
> *Good Housekeeping* (or *Ladies' Home Journal*)

4. Each of the following statements concerns magazines. Choose *five* only, and write the *number* of the expression that best completes the statement.   [5]

A. Magazine articles are indexed in   (1) *The Reader's Handbook*   (2) Ayer's *Index to Newspapers and Periodicals*   (3) the card catalog   (4) *Readers' Guide to Periodical Literature.*

B. "Life in These United States" (or "Life in This Wide World") appears in   (1) *Saturday Review*   (2) *Harper's Magazine*   (3) *The Reader's Digest*   (4) *U.S. News and World Report.*

C. A magazine that regularly features articles on business enterprise is   (1) *Fortune*   (2) *Scholastic*   (3) *Variety*   (4) *Popular Science.*

D. A magazine that usually contains information on etiquette is   (1) *Holiday*   (2) *Life*   (3) *The Atlantic*   (4) *Scholastic.*

E. A magazine that contains a page devoted exclusively to editorials is   (1) *The National Geographic Magazine*   (2) *Scientific American*   (3) *Life*   (4) *The American Home.*

F. Informal essays regularly appear in a special section of   (1) *The Atlantic*   (2) *Time*   (3) *Look*   (4) *The American Observer.*

G. Book reviews regularly appear in   (1) *Harper's Magazine*   (2) *Encyclopedia Americana*   (3) *Look*   (4) *The Reader's Digest.*

Chapter 10

THE PARLIAMENTARY PROCEDURE TEST (QUESTION 4)

Parliamentary procedure is a widely accepted set of rules for conducting a meeting democratically and efficiently. Not only clubs, but deliberative bodies like Congress and the United Nations, observe parliamentary procedure.

TYPICAL REGENTS QUESTIONS ON PARLIAMENTARY PROCEDURE

JANUARY 1961

QUESTION: In a meeting, according to parliamentary procedure, "new business" immediately follows   (1) reading of the minutes   (2) roll call   (3) call to order   (4) "old business."   4

ANSWER EXPLAINED: The order of business in conducting a meeting requires that "new business" should immediately follow "old business." (See page 165, ORDER OF BUSINESS IN CONDUCTING MEETINGS.)

JUNE 1952

QUESTION: A duty that is *not* the usual responsibility of the chairman is to   (1) adjourn a meeting   (2) conduct elections   (3) state the purpose of the meeting   (4) keep the official copy of the constitution.   4

ANSWER EXPLAINED: All the responsibilities mentioned belong to the chairman except to keep the official copy of the constitution, which is a responsibility of the secretary. (See pages 165-166, DUTIES OF OFFICERS.)

REVIEWING PARLIAMENTARY PROCEDURE

Past Regents questions indicate that you are expected to know:
  A. The procedure for organizing a club
  B. The order of business in conducting meetings
  C. The duties of officers
  D. Parliamentary motions
  E. Common parliamentary terms

A. PROCEDURE FOR ORGANIZING A CLUB

Suppose you decide, after conferring with a few interested individuals, that it would be a good idea to form a debating club. To make sure that you are going about it in the right way, you will want to consult an authoritative book on parliamentary procedure such as Robert's *Rules of Order*. Here are the basic steps required to complete the organization of a club:

BEFORE THE FIRST MEETING

1. You and your associates announce the time, place, and object of the meeting.

AT THE FIRST MEETING

2. The assembly (those who have come) elects a temporary chairman.
3. The assembly elects a temporary secretary.
4. The temporary chairman states the object of the meeting: to organize the club.
5. The assembly adopts a resolution formally organizing the club.
6. The temporary chairman, on a motion of the assembly, appoints a committee to draft a constitution and bylaws (laws of secondary importance).
7. The temporary chairman, on a motion of the assembly, adjourns (closes) the meeting.

AT THE SECOND MEETING

8. The committee reports the constitution and the bylaws.
9. The assembly discusses the constitution and the bylaws, making necessary amendments. If a majority votes in favor, the constitution and the bylaws are adopted. At this time all who wish to become members sign the constitution.
10. The members elect the permanent officers.

B. ORDER OF BUSINESS IN CONDUCTING MEETINGS

Now that your club has been established, it can proceed to hold regular meetings. Parliamentary procedure requires meetings to be conducted in the following order, known as the *order of business:*

1. Call to order.
2. Reading, correction, and adoption of the minutes.
3. Officers' reports and reports of standing (permanent) committees.
4. Reports of special committees.
5. Old business (also called unfinished business).
6. New business.
7. Program for the day (a guest speaker, a debate, etc.).
8. Adjournment.

Note: If the members wish to take up an item of business out of its parliamentary order, they must adopt a motion to *suspend the rules,* which requires a two-thirds vote.

C. DUTIES OF OFFICERS

The *president* or *chairman* (referred to as "the chair")
  Calls the meeting to order.
  Announces the business before the organization.
  Recognizes speakers entitled to the floor.
  States the question when a vote is to be taken.
  Announces the results of voting.
  Conducts elections.
  Determines points of order.
  Adjourns the meeting.

The president is an *ex officio* member of certain committees, which means that he is a member of these committees because of the office he holds. He may not vote on a motion except in cases where his vote would change the result; for example, to break a tie vote.

The *secretary*
  Records the minutes.
  Reads the minutes of the previous meeting.
  Calls the roll when necessary.
  Keeps the official copy of the constitution and bylaws.
  Conducts correspondence.

The *treasurer*
Keeps the financial records.
Collects dues.
Deposits funds.
Makes authorized payments.
Makes a periodic treasurer's report.

The *parliamentarian* is appointed by the president to advise him on matters of parliamentary procedure.

The *sergeant-at-arms* maintains order and rounds up absent members (for example, in Congress) when less than a quorum is present.

D. PARLIAMENTARY MOTIONS

The following commonly used motions have been arranged in order of rank from 1 (highest rank) to 13 (lowest rank).

1. *To fix the time of the next meeting* (not debatable)
2. *To adjourn* (not debatable)
3. *To take a recess* (not debatable)
4. *To raise a question of privilege*—as when a member wishes to reply to an attack on his character, or to request that the heating, lighting, or ventilation be adjusted, etc. (no seconding required and not debatable)
5. *To call for the orders of the day*—to insist that the group return to the agenda of the meeting (no seconding required and not debatable)
6. *To lay on the table*—to put aside a pending motion so that the group may take up more pressing business (not debatable)
7. *To move the previous question* (or *to call for the question*)—to stop debate and to take an immediate vote on the question before the group (two-thirds vote required and not debatable)
8. *To limit or extend debate* (two-thirds vote required and not debatable)
9. *To postpone a question to a certain time* (debatable)
10. *To refer a question to a committee*—as when a motion requires extensive rewording or more careful investigation (debatable)
11. *To amend*—to change the wording of a pending motion (debatable). Note: An amendment to a motion must be voted on *before* the motion itself.
12. *To postpone indefinitely* (debatable)
13. *Main motion*—a motion to bring up any topic for consideration by the group (debatable). Note: It is the motion of lowest rank.

Whenever more than one motion is on the floor, the one of highest rank must be taken up at once; motions ranking below it are declared out of order.

PROBLEM: Suppose that a *main motion* (rank #13) is on the floor: "Resolved that our club accept the invitation of the Forum Club to participate in a joint debate next September 20." Suppose further that one. member has moved *to postpone* this matter/ *indefinitely* (rank #12), and a second member has moved the *previous question* (rank #7). What happens?

ANSWER: Further discussion on the *main motion* (rank #13) is out of order. So, too, is the motion *to postpone indefinitely* (rank #12). The *previous question* (rank #7) takes precedence. This motion, if seconded and adopted by a two-thirds vote, has the effect of shutting off further debate on the main motion and putting it to an immediate vote.

E. COMMON PARLIAMENTARY TERMS

Adjournment. Closing of a meeting.

Agenda. List of the items of business to be taken up at a meeting.

Bylaws. Rules of secondary importance governing the time and place of meetings, methods of voting, etc. The more important rules are stated in the constitution.

Division of the house. A rising vote. When a member questions the outcome of a voice (*viva voce*) vote, he may call for a division of the house. This requires first the affirmative and then the negative to stand and be counted.

Ex officio. Because of one's office. The bylaws usually state that the president shall be an ex officio member of certain committees.

Majority vote. A vote of more than half of the votes cast. If 100 votes are cast, 51 or more constitute a *majority*.

Plurality vote. A larger vote than that received by any other, but less than a majority. If, out of 100 votes cast, A receives 40, B 35, and C 25, A is said to have a *plurality*.

Point of information. When a member desires information about a matter on the floor, he may interrupt (without waiting to be recognized) by stating: "Mr. Chairman, I rise to a point of information."

Point of order. When a member notices a violation of parliamentary procedure, he may interrupt (without waiting to be recognized) by stating: "Mr. Chairman, I rise to a point of order."

Quorum. The minimum number of members that must be present before a meeting can legally be held. The number constituting a quorum is usually stated in the constitution.

Roll call. A vote taken by calling the roll. As a member's name is called, he rises and declares his vote. The secretary records each vote and gives the tally to the chairman, who announces the results.

Seconding. Endorsement of a motion by a member other than its maker.

Note: *No seconding* is required for the following:

questions of privilege	points of order
nominations	calls for division of the house
points of information	calls for orders of the day

Standing committee. A permanent committee (not to be confused with other committees appointed, as the need arises, for special purposes).

Suspend the rules. When the group wants to take an action in conflict with its rules (consider an item not on the agenda, vote on a motion without debate, etc.), it must adopt a motion to suspend the rules. This requires a two-thirds vote.

Table. Put off discussion of a motion. Same as *to lay on the table* (see page 166).

Teller. A member appointed by the chairman to count the votes.

FORMER REGENTS QUESTIONS

1

Complete correctly, in accordance with parliamentary practice, each of the *five* statements, (1) to (5), by choosing from among the following expressions the one that best applies: [Use no expression twice.]   [5]

amend	limit debate	amend the amendment
adjourn	take a recess	rise to a point of order
nominate	lay on the table	

   (1) Of the motions listed above, highest privilege is given to the motion to
   . . . .
   (2) It requires a two-thirds vote to . . . .
   (3) A correct procedure for interrupting one who has the floor is to . . . .
   (4) No seconding statement is required to . . . .
   (5) A proposal is defeated indirectly by a vote to . . . .

2

A small group of high school students, talking informally, agree that an athletic association with membership open to all students in the school is desirable. Beginning at this point, give in order *five* distinct steps *required by parliamentary procedure* to complete the organization of such an association. [10]

3

State briefly, but clearly and in correct order, the procedure that should be followed, according to the rules of parliamentary practice, in beginning, conducting, and closing the business of a regular meeting of a club or school organization. (Your answer may be in outline form and should include at least five major steps.) [5]

4

Each of the following, A, B, C, D and E, concerns parliamentary procedure. In each case, write the *number* of the best answer. [5]

A. In the order of business of a club meeting, which one of the following precedes the others? (1) the treasurer's report (2) new business (3) reports of standing committees (4) the secretary's report.

B. A motion that has as its purpose to change the wording of a previous motion is a motion to (1) limit debate (2) amend (3) move the previous question (4) withdraw the motion.

C. The number of persons who must be present before business can be conducted is called a (1) quorum (2) majority (3) plurality (4) division.

D. If there has been a violation of parliamentary procedure, a member may (1) rise to a point of order (2) propose an amendment (3) call for the previous question (4) move to table the motion.

E. A member who calls for the orders of the day wishes to (1) present a resolution (2) hear the secretary's report (3) return the group to the agenda of the meeting (4) hear a report by the committee.

5

Each of the following statements concerns parliamentary procedure. In *each* case, write the *number* of the expression that best completes the statement. [5]

A. The person responsible for stating the question when a vote is to be taken by the group is the (1) secretary (2) sergeant-at-arms (3) parliamentarian (4) chairman.

B. If a motion requires extensive rewording, the usual procedure is to (1) refer it to a committee (2) table it indefinitely (3) reconsider it (4) debate it indefinitely.

C. An authoritative book on parliamentary procedure is (1) *The Statesman's Year-Book* (2) *It's More Fun When You Know the Rules* (3) *This Way, Please* (4) Robert's *Rules of Order.*

D. A motion to suspend the rules usually requires, to pass, (1) a two-thirds affirmative vote (2) a majority vote (3) a roll call (4) a division of the house.

E. After several persons have spoken on a motion, a member may (1) call for a division of the house (2) call for the question (3) make a new motion (4) move to reconsider the question.

Chapter 11

THE LIBRARY AND REFERENCE SKILLS TEST
(QUESTION 4)

THE IMPORTANCE OF LIBRARY AND REFERENCE SKILLS

A vital part of English instruction deals with library and reference skills. Without these skills you may spend so much time locating materials that you will have little time left for actual reading. With these skills you will be better able to find and use information needed for completing school assignments and—much more important—solving problems throughout life.

TYPICAL REGENTS QUESTIONS ON LIBRARY AND REFERENCE SKILLS

JUNE 1961

QUESTION: A biography of Edgar Allan Poe can be found in (1) *Who's Who* (2) *Current Biography* (3) *Twentieth Century Authors* (4) *Encyclopedia Americana.*   4
....

ANSWER EXPLAINED: Poe was a nineteenth-century author. Of the reference works mentioned in this question, only the *Encyclopedia Americana* includes nineteenth-century material.

JANUARY 1962

QUESTION: To locate the book *The Last of the Mohicans* in a library, one should first look in the card catalog under the word (1) The (2) Mohicans (3) Last (4) Indians.   3
....

ANSWER EXPLAINED: A title beginning with *The, A,* or *An* is alphabetized in the card catalog according to its second word. Therefore, look under *Last.*

REVIEWING LIBRARY AND REFERENCE SKILLS

Past Regents questions indicate that you are expected to know how to do research with the aid of the parts of a book, the card catalog, the dictionary, and other reference works. You are also expected to be familiar with library and reference terms.

A. THE PARTS OF A BOOK

To locate and make good use of the information in a book, you should know these basic parts of a book and their functions:

Title page—the page at the very beginning of the book that officially states (1) the complete title, (2) the author's full name, (3) the publisher's name, (4) the place of publication, and (5) occasionally, the publisher's date of actual printing (not to be confused with copyright date).

Copyright page—the reverse side of the title page. It contains the all-important *copyright date,* which is a clue to the up-to-dateness of the material in the book.

Preface (also known as *introduction* or *foreword*)—a statement of the author's purpose.

Table of contents—an outline of the subjects treated in the book. It lists chapter titles in the order in which they appear, telling on which page each chapter begins. By glancing at the table of contents you can obtain an overview of the material in a book.

List of maps or illustrations—a summary of the maps or illustrations and their page locations.

Footnote—an explanatory note at the bottom (foot) of a page.

Bibliography—a list of (1) the books consulted by the author, or (2) books containing further information on the subject under discussion. A bibliography may appear at the end of the book or the end of each chapter.

Appendix—a section added at the end of the book to supplement the main text. An appendix may include notes, tables, lists, past examination questions, etc.

Glossary—an alphabetical list of unfamiliar terms used in the book, together with their definitions.

Index—a complete alphabetical list (at the very end of the book) of the topics dealt with in the book. It gives the exact pages on which each topic is discussed. The fastest way to locate information in a book is to consult its index.

B. THE CARD CATALOG

A library's *card catalog* is the index of all the books owned by that library. It consists of small cards filed alphabetically in a cabinet of drawers. For each book the library owns you will normally find three cards in the card catalog: (1) an *author card,* (2) a *title card,* and (3) a *subject card.* The first is useful for locating a book when you know only its *author's name;* the second, when you know only its *title;* the third, when you know only the *subject* of the book. Below are three cards for the same book:

1. Author card (so called because the *author's name*[1] is on the first line).

943.086   **Shirer, William L.**
S
        The rise and fall of the Third Reich; a history of Nazi Germany. Simon & Schuster 1960
        1245 p.

Author Card Explained

UPPER LEFT-HAND CORNER: the *call number* $\left(\dfrac{943.086}{S}\right)$ is made up of the class number for the subject of this book (943.086) and the initial of the author's last name (S). The call number indicates where you will find the book on the shelves.

FIRST LINE: the *author's full name* (Shirer, William L.)

SECOND AND THIRD LINES:

    the *title* and *subtitle* (The rise and fall of the Third Reich; a history of Nazi Germany)
    the *publisher* (Simon & Schuster)
    the *copyright date* (1960)

FOURTH LINE: the *number of pages* (1245)

---

[1] Sometimes the author may be an institution, as the Smithsonian Institution, or a Government department, as the U.S. Department of Agriculture.

2. Title card (so called because the *title* is on the first line).

943.086   **The rise and fall of the Third Reich**
 S
 	
 Shirer, William L.
      The rise and fall of the Third Reich; a history of
 Nazi Germany. Simon & Schuster 1960
      1245 p.

3. Subject card (so called because the *subject*[1] of the book is on the first line in black capitals or red letters).

GERMANY—HISTORY—1918-1945
 943.086   **Shirer, William L.**
 S
 	
      The rise and fall of the Third Reich; a history of
 Nazi Germany. Simon & Schuster 1960
      1245 p.

Cross reference cards are cards containing the words "See" or "See also." They tell you under what other subject headings to look for the information you are seeking. Examples:

CAPITAL AND LABOR   SEE   INDUSTRIAL RELATIONS

POLIOMYELITIS   SEE ALSO   INFANTILE PARALYSIS

---

[1] Sometimes the subject of a book may be a person, as in a biography.

C. CALL NUMBERS: THE DEWEY DECIMAL SYSTEM

The *call number* is the number by which you look for a book on the shelves. Examples:

$$583 \qquad 821 \qquad 943.086$$
$$M \qquad K \qquad S$$

The call number appears on the back binding of a book and also on each of the cards for that book in the card catalog. The lower part of a call number is the initial of the author's last name. The upper part, known as the *class number*, identifies the subject of the book.

The widely used *Dewey Decimal System* groups books by subject into ten large classes. Each class has numerous subdivisions. Below are the ten classes plus a typical subdivision in each class:

CLASS	TYPICAL SUBDIVISION
000-099 General Works	030 Encyclopedias
100-199 Philosophy	150 Psychology
200-299 Religion	220 The Bible
300-399 Sociology	330 Economics
400-499 Languages	423 English Dictionaries
500-599 Science	570 Biology
600-699 Useful Arts	641 Cook Books
700-799 Fine Arts	770 Photography
800-899 Literature	822.3 Shakespeare
900-999 History	973 United States History

Collective biography (any book containing several short biographies) is grouped under 920.

Individual biography (any book devoted entirely to one person's life) is commonly assigned the letter B instead of a class number. It is shelved alphabetically by the last name of the subject (the person written about).

Fiction (novels and short stories) written in English has no call number. It is shelved alphabetically by the author's last name.

D. THE DICTIONARY

To make the fullest use of the dictionary, you should be able to understand everything that the dictionary says about a word. Much of this information is conveyed with the aid of symbols and abbreviations fully explained for you in the introduction of the dictionary.

Below is a dictionary paragraph for the word *affable*, reproduced from *Webster's New Collegiate Dictionary*, copyright 1959. On a sheet of paper jot down all the information you can extract from the numbered items. Then compare with the full explanation given below.

$$\overset{1}{\downarrow} \quad \overset{2}{\downarrow} \quad \overset{3}{\downarrow} \qquad \overset{4}{\downarrow}$$

af'fa·ble (ăf'*à*·b'l), *adj.* [F., fr. L. *affabilis*, fr. *affari* to speak to,

fr. *ad-* + *fari* to speak.] **1.** Easy to speak to; courteous and amiable

5 ─────────────────────────────────↑

in response to another's address; sociable. **2.** Mild and gracious;—

5 ──────────────────────────────────────↑

of mien.—**Syn.** See GRACIOUS.—**af'fa·bil'i·ty** (-bĭl'ĭ·tĭ), **af'fa·ble-**

6 ─────↑   ↑   ↑   ↑
                                            7   2   7

ness, *n.*—**af'fa·bly,** *adv.*

↑   ↑   ↑
3   7   3

Dictionary Paragraph Explained

1. The word being defined, known as the **main entry** or **vocabulary entry,** tells us:

a. how to spell **affable.**

b. that the syllable **af'** is stressed. A heavy accent mark (') comes immediately after the stressed syllable.

c. that **affable** has three syllables: af'fa·ble.

2. The **pronunciation,** written in parentheses, tells us how to say the word. The ă in the first syllable sounds like ă in ădd, whereas *à* in the second syllable sounds like *à* in sof*à*. The apostrophe shows there is practically no vowel sound between b and l in the last syllable. The heavy accent mark (') immediately after af tells us again that the first syllable is stressed.

Notice that **affability** has a light accent mark (') after the first syllable and a heavy one (') after the third. This indicates that the third syllable gets the main stress; the first receives a lighter stress.

3. The **part of speech,** abbreviated in italics, tells us how the word is used. Thus we learn that **affable** is used as an adjective (*adj.*), **affability** and **affableness** as nouns (*n.*), and **affably** as an adverb (*adv.*).

4. The **derivation,** written in brackets, explains how the word came into our language and what it meant originally. Thus we learn that **affable** comes from French (F.) through the Latin (L.) *affabilis,* which is derived from *affari* meaning "to speak to." Furthermore, *affari* comes from *ad* (a prefix meaning "to") and *fari* (a word root meaning "to speak").

5. The **definitions** tell us the meanings of a word. These are numbered. You should find out the order in which your dictionary lists definitions. For this information consult the preface. *Webster's New Collegiate Dictionary* lists definitions in historical order as far as possible.

Of the two definitions for **affable,** number 1 (Easy to speak to) is closer to the word's derivation. It is clearly the earlier definition. Number 2 (Mild and gracious) developed later. The words "of mien" indicate that the number 2 definition is used to describe a person's *mien* (demeanor or bearing).

6. The **synonyms** (—Syn.). The cross reference "See GRACIOUS" tells us that a full explanation of the synonyms for **affable** will be found under the entry for **gracious.** If you turn to that entry in *Webster's New Collegiate Dictionary,* you will find these synonyms explained and differentiated: **gracious, cordial, affable, genial, sociable.**

7. The **derivatives** or **run-on entries** (**affability, affableness, affably**) are words derived from the main entry (**affable**). They have not been defined because you can tell their meaning from the definition of **affable.**

E. OTHER REFERENCE WORKS

1. General Encyclopedias

(When you use a general encyclopedia, consult the index volume first to save time in locating the specific information you want. For leads to additional information, see the bibliography that often follows the encyclopedia article.)

Encyclopaedia Britannica
Encyclopedia Americana
Collier's Encyclopedia
World Book Encyclopedia
Compton's Pictured Encyclopedia

2. One-Volume Encyclopedias

Columbia Encyclopedia
Lincoln Library of Essential Information

3. Encyclopedia Supplements

(Encyclopedia publishers supply their subscribers with up-to-date information by issuing an annual supplement or yearbook that sums up the events and discoveries of the preceding year.)

Britannica Book of the Year
Americana Annual
Collier's Encyclopedia Yearbook
World Book Encyclopedia Annual Supplement
Compton Yearbook

4. Almanacs and Yearbooks

(Consult an almanac or yearbook for statistical information about a specific year. Since the contents are not arranged alphabetically, consult the index first.)

World Almanac and Book of Facts (News summaries, world facts, major events in medicine and science, Academy Award films, sports champions, etc. Index at beginning.)
Information Please Almanac, Atlas and Yearbook (News chronology, map section, reviews of the year in theater, books, television, opera, etc.)
Statesman's Year-book (Population, exports, constitutions, government officials, etc., of all countries of the world.)

5. Biographical Reference Works

FOR NOTABLE PERSONS OF OUR TIMES:

Who's Who (Prominent living Englishmen.)
Who's Who in America (Prominent living Americans.)
Current Biography (Prominent persons of many countries. Portraits. Published monthly and in annual cumulated volumes.)
Twentieth Century Authors (Informal treatment. Portraits. Supersedes *Living Authors.*)
Official Congressional Directory (Sketches of important government officials in Washington, D.C.)

FOR NOTABLE PERSONS OF THE PAST:

Dictionary of National Biography (Prominent Englishmen no longer living.)

Dictionary of American Biography (Prominent Americans no longer living.)

Webster's Biographical Dictionary (Prominent persons of all countries, including some living persons.)

6. Unabridged Dictionaries

Funk and Wagnalls New Standard Dictionary
Oxford English Dictionary
Webster's New International Dictionary

7. Readers' Handbooks

Benét— *Reader's Encyclopedia*
Brewer—*Dictionary of Phrase and Fable*
Hart—*Oxford Companion to American Literature*
Harvey—*Oxford Companion to English Literature*

8. Indexes

ESSAYS AND MISCELLANEOUS ARTICLES:

Sears and Shaw—*Essay and General Literature Index*

MAGAZINE ARTICLES FROM 1900 TO PRESENT:

Readers' Guide to Periodical Literature (See pages 158-159.)

MAGAZINE ARTICLES FROM 1802-1907:

Poole's Index to Periodical Literature

NEWSPAPER ARTICLES PUBLISHED IN THE "NEW YORK TIMES":

New York Times Index

ONE-ACT PLAYS:

Logasa and Ver Nooy—*An Index to One-Act Plays*

PLAYS:

Firkins—*Index to Plays*, 1800-1926. Supplement, 1927-34.
West and Peake—*Play Index*, 1949-1952

POEMS:

Granger's Index to Poetry

SHORT STORIES:

Firkins—*Index to Short Stories*
Cook and Fidell—*Short Story Index*, 1950-1954
Fidell and Flory—*Short Story Index*, 1955-1958

9. Reference Works for a Particular Subject

CONGRESS—DAILY PROCEEDINGS IN BOTH HOUSES:

Congressional Record

ETIQUETTE:

Emily Post—*Etiquette*

GEOGRAPHY:

Goode's World Atlas: Physical, Political and Economic
Rand McNally Cosmopolitan World Atlas
Webster's Geographical Dictionary
Columbia Lippincott Gazetteer of the World

LANGUAGE:

Crabb—*English Synonyms*
Evans and Evans—*Dictionary of Contemporary American Usage*
Fernald—*English Synonyms and Antonyms*
Fowler—*Dictionary of Modern English Usage*
Mencken—*The American Language*
Nicholson—*Dictionary of American-English Usage*
Roget's International Thesaurus of English Words and Phrases
Webster's Dictionary of Synonyms

LITERATURE:

Becker—*Adventures in Reading*
Bennett—*Much Loved Books*
Boas and Hahn—*Social Backgrounds of English Literature*
Cambridge History of American Literature
Cambridge History of English Literature
Keller—*Reader's Digest of Books*
Manly and Rickert—*Contemporary British Literature*
Spiller and others—*Literary History of the United States*

MYTHOLOGY:

Bulfinch's Mythology

PARLIAMENTARY PROCEDURE:

Robert's *Rules of Order*
Wines and Card—*Come to Order!*

QUOTATIONS:

Bartlett's Familiar Quotations
Hoyt's New Cyclopedia of Practical Quotations
Stevenson's Home Book of Quotations

REVIEWS OF IMPORTANT BOOKS (1905-PRESENT):

Book Review Digest

F. MISCELLANEOUS LIBRARY AND REFERENCE TERMS

Most of the terms below have been mentioned in past Regents questions but have not yet been discussed in this chapter.

Abridged dictionary—a shortened dictionary condensed from an unabridged (complete) work, but still adequate for normal reference purposes. Example: *Webster's New Collegiate Dictionary* is an abridgement of *Webster's New International Dictionary.*

Annotation—a short note of explanation. For example, the comments next to each biographical reference work on pages 177-178 are annotations.

Anthology—a collection. Examples: *Modern American and British Poetry,* an anthology of poems edited by Louis Untermeyer; *Essays Old and New,* an anthology of essays edited by Robert U. Jameson.

Archaic—a dictionary term describing a definition no longer used except in a special phrase. For example, in the expression "the quick and the dead," the meaning of *quick* is *living.* This meaning, though, is archaic.

Atlas—a book of maps. Example: *Goode's World Atlas.*

Autobiography—a book about a person's life written by the person himself. Example: *An American Doctor's Odyssey* by Victor Heiser.

Biography—a book about a person's life written by someone else. Example: *George Washington Carver* by Rackham Holt.

Book-jacket "blurb"—a high commendation inscribed on the paper cover (book jacket) of a book. Example: "Here is the greatest novel ever written."

Book review—an article about a book, evaluating its strengths and weaknesses. Example: Clifton Fadiman's review of *Madame Curie* by Eve Curie.

Colloq.—abbreviation for *colloquial* meaning "correct for everyday informal writing or conversation, but not for formal occasions." Example: *dad* is colloquial for *father*.

Fiction—prose works dealing with imaginary people and events. Examples: novels and short stories.

Gazetteer—a dictionary of geographical names. Examples: *Webster's Geographical Dictionary, Columbia Lippincott Gazetteer of the World.*

Nonfiction—prose works dealing with real people and events. Examples: biographies and history books.

Obs.—abbreviation for *obsolete* meaning "no longer used." Example: In Shakespeare's time, *to owe* meant *to own* or *possess*, but this meaning is now obsolete.

Thesaurus—a book that is a storehouse or treasury of information about words. Examples: *Roget's International Thesaurus of English Words and Phrases*, or any dictionary.

Unabridged dictionary—a full and complete dictionary of all the words in a language. Examples: *Funk and Wagnalls New Standard Dictionary, Webster's New International Dictionary.*

Vertical File—a cabinet of large drawers containing pamphlets, newspaper clippings, and pictures about current topics. This material is usually filed alphabetically by subjects.

FORMER REGENTS QUESTIONS

1

Name *five* standard reference works, each of a different type, not including the dictionary, the card catalog, textbooks and anthologies. Give their complete titles and state briefly the kind or kinds of material found in each *or* the purpose for which it is used.   [5]

2

The names of the authors of special reference books are frequently used to suggest the titles of their books or the kind of information to be found in their books. Name the reference book or the special reference field with which each of *five* of the following is associated: [5]

J. Paul Goode	Hoyt	Fowler	Granger
Thomas Bulfinch	Brewer	Fernald	Keller
Boas and Hahn	Bartlett	Roget	Robert
Wines and Card	Firkins	Crabb	Emily Post
Manly and Rickert	Becker	Poole	Bennett

3

Assume that you are preparing an informative article entiled *How to Use the Library Card Catalog*. Write the notes that you would make for the article, showing that you have a good knowledge of how to use the card catalog.   [5]

4

Below are two lists: first, names of the parts of a book; second, brief definitions. In the parentheses after any *five* of the names, enter the *numbers* of the correct definitions.   [10]

table of contents	( )	preface	( )
glossary	( )	footnote	( )
bibliography	( )	index	( )

Definitions:

1. Dates of copyright and publication
2. A statement of the author's purpose
3. Subtitle
4. An alphabetical list of topics dealt with
5. The publisher's headquarters
6. A list of definitions of unfamiliar terms
7. Added information placed in the book proper to supplement the main text
8. A list of the books consulted by the author
9. An outline of the subjects treated
10. A discussion of a special topic following the book proper

5

In each of *five* of the following, (*a*) to (*h*), clearly state the meaning of *each* of the *two* terms in such a manner as to make plain the difference between them: [10]

a. Book review and book-jacket "blurb"
b. Subject card and title card in the card catalog
c. Copyright date and publisher's date
d. Table of contents and index
e. Word root and suffix
f. *Who's Who* and *Who's Who in America*
g. Gazetteer and anthology
h. Footnote and appendix

6

Excluding title page, copyright date, and illustrations, name *five* important parts of the contents usually found in nonfiction books and explain the use of each.   [5]

7

Explain *each* of the following items, with reference to the card below, copied from a card catalog: (1) 920,   (2) p.312-326,   (3) C,   (4) Twenty Modern Americans,   (5) White, William Allen.   [5]

920	White, William Allen.
C	Cooper, A. C. and Palmer, C. A.
	Twenty modern Americans. N. Y. Harcourt.
1942. p. 312-326	

8

State briefly and clearly the nature of the information given by each of *five* of the underlined items in the following entry from a dictionary: [5]

tru'ant (trōō'ănt), *n.* [OF., a vagrant, beggar, of Celt. origin.]
One who stays away from business or any duty, esp. from school, without leave. —*adj.* 1. Idle, and shirking duty; esp. absent from school without leave. 2. Like or characteristic of a truant; as a *truant* mood. —tru'an·cy (–ăn·sĭ), *n.*

9

Each of the following statements concerns the use of the dictionary or the library. Write the *number* of the expression which best completes the statement.

1. Which one of the following is published monthly as well as annually?   (1) *Congressional Record*   (2) *The World Almanac*   (3) *Information Please Almanac*   (4) *Current Biography.*
2. The vertical file in a library is most often used to hold   (1) pamphlets or clippings   (2) card-catalog cards   (3) book reviews   (4) reference books.
3. Which one of the following is *least* likely to contain detailed information about, or reference to sources of information on, Sinclair Lewis?   (1) *Who's Who in America*   (2) an encyclopedia   (3) *Readers' Guide to Periodical Literature*   (4) an unabridged dictionary.
4. Part of an entry in the *Readers' Guide to Periodical Literature* reads "720:46-7." The "46-7" refers to   (1) the pages on which the article appears   (2) the number of words in the article   (3) the author's code number   (4) the volume number of the magazine.
5. An article in an encyclopedia is often followed immediately by   (1) a list of unfamiliar terms used in the article   (2) a biography of the author   (3) the date of writing of the article   (4) a bibliography.
6. Which one of the following is *not* usually found on the title page of a book?   (1) place of publication   (2) author   (3) date of printing of that copy of the book   (4) copyright date.
7. The source that treats informally the life of a person discussed is   (1) *Who's Who in America*   (2) the *Encyclopaedia Britannica*   (3) *Twentieth Century Authors*   (4) *Who's Who.*

8. The meaning of "Sch Rev" in a *Readers' Guide to Periodical Literature* entry can be determined by consulting the list of abbreviations which appears (1) in the back of each issue (2) in the front of each issue (3) at the foot of each page (4) in the yearly edition only.

9. An author famous for his book on mythology is (1) Stuart Chase (2) Clifton Fadiman (3) Dallas Lore Sharp (4) Thomas Bulfinch.

10. Pictures of famous persons appear in (1) *Current Biography* (2) Brewer's *Reader's Handbook* (3) *The Statesman's Year-book* (4) *Congressional Record.*

11. For detailed, current information about a subject, one should consult (1) the card catalog (2) the vertical file (3) an atlas (4) an abridged dictionary.

12. The chief purpose of a bibliography is to (1) refer the reader to additional sources (2) describe the author's background (3) explain special terms used in the book (4) include additional material, such as statistics, tables, etc.

13. Movie reviews are indexed in (1) *Readers' Guide to Periodical Literature* (2) the card catalog (3) *Book Review Digest* (4) the *Yale Review.*

14. The Dewey Decimal System arranges books on the shelves by (1) size (2) author (3) subject (4) publication date.

15. Reference books usually are distinguished from other library books in that they (1) may not be borrowed for home use (2) are never revised (3) are published only annually (4) are not listed in the card catalog.

16. To find in what state President Lincoln was born, one should first consult (1) *Who's Who in America* (2) *Who's Who* (3) the card catalog (4) an encyclopedia.

17. In a dictionary, the abbreviations "colloq." and "Obs." refer to a word's (1) usage (2) pronunciation (3) syllabication (4) part of speech.

18. A reference book whose content is *not* arranged alphabetically is (1) *Current Biography* (2) *Britannica Book of the Year* (3) *The World Almanac* (4) *Twentieth Century Authors.*

19. A newspaper which periodically publishes an index of its contents is the (1) *St. Louis Post-Dispatch* (2) *Christian Science Monitor* (3) *New York Post* (4) *New York Times.*

20. To obtain an overview of the material in a book, one should first consult the (1) preface (2) table of contents (3) glossary (4) index.

21. To find the names of outstanding motion pictures of a particular year, one should first consult (1) an encyclopedia (2) the card catalog (3) *The World Almanac* (4) *Readers' Guide to Periodical Literature.*

22. A book of synonyms and antonyms has been compiled by (1) Firkins (2) Fowler (3) Hoyt (4) Roget.

23. Which source gives the most complete information about the history of a word? (1) an abridged dictionary (2) an unabridged dictionary (3) a thesaurus (4) a glossary.

24. Entries in the *Readers' Guide to Periodical Literature* are for the most part arranged (1) alphabetically by title (2) alphabetically by author and subject (3) alphabetically by the countries in which the authors lived (4) chronologically by the periods in which the authors wrote.

25. Which of these sources should be consulted first to find the area and population of Brazil? (1) the card catalog (2) an anthology (3) a gazetteer (4) a thesaurus.

Chapter 12

THE LITERATURE TEST (QUESTIONS 5a AND 5b)

MAIN PURPOSE OF THE LITERATURE TEST

The main purpose of this twenty-credit test is to evaluate how well you have understood and appreciated literature that you have read as a secondary-school student. This includes:

1. the works you have read in class in the principal literary types—novels, short stories, plays, biographies, essays, poetry—and

2. the personal supplementary reading you have done in these literary types.

(At this point you should make your first acquaintance with "A Guide to Personal Reading," which begins on page 251. This guide will suggest interesting and worthwhile works for future reading. It may also refresh your memory about works that you have already read.)

CHOICES OFFERED IN THE LITERATURE TEST

The literature test requires you to answer *one* of three questions: 5a, 5b, or 5c. Each is worth twenty credits.

If you choose 5a or 5b, you must write an answer to a question about literary works. Usually one of these questions (either 5a or 5b) asks you to discuss four short works. The other asks you to discuss two full-length works.

For a description of 5c, see pages 211-234.

TYPICAL REGENTS LITERATURE TEST: 5a AND 5b

JUNE 1959

a A reader may be satisfied with the ending of a story because it seems to be the natural result of the events in the story. On the other hand, the reader may be dissatisfied because the ending does not seem logical or believable in view of what has happened in the story or because it leaves questions unanswered in his mind. From the short stories and narrative poems you have read, choose a total of any *four,* and in *each* case show by definite references that you found the ending satisfying or unsatisfying for one of the reasons mentioned. Give titles and authors.   [20]

b People make adjustments with varying degrees of success to certain factors in their environment. These factors may be their physical surroundings, other people, or the customs and traditions of the society in which they live. From the novels and full-length plays you have read, choose a total of any *two* books. In *each* case show by definite references to what extent a person in the book was successful in adjusting to one or more of the above factors. Give titles and authors.   [20]

Later in this chapter you will find eight pupil answers to 5*a* and seven to 5*b*. About half of these answers have been analyzed (for strengths and weaknesses) and rated. You will be asked (and helped) to analyze and rate the rest.

THE RATING OF 5a AND 5b

To learn what is expected in your answer to 5*a* or 5*b*, study these instructions to teachers on the rating of such answers:

> "Judge literature answers primarily on content, but expect adequate technique of composition.
> "In general, require that a pupil in his answer (1) meet the requirements of the question, (2) show familiarity with the piece of literature he is discussing, (3) demonstrate his power to judge and to generalize with clearness and forcefulness of expression, (4) use specific references in support of statements made, and (5) show adequate technique of composition."

The above excerpt is from *Suggestions on the Rating of Regents Examination Papers in English,* New York State Education Department.

CAREFUL READING OF THE QUESTION

Never begin your answer without carefully reading and analyzing the literature question to find out what it requires you to write about. Here are four guiding questions to help you with your analysis of

5*a* or 5*b*. Memorize them. At the examination, jot down the answers to these guiding questions on a sheet of scrap paper before beginning to write your answer.

FOUR GUIDING QUESTIONS

1. What does the question ask me to do?
2. How many works must I discuss, and of what literary types (novels, full-length plays, poems, etc.) must they be?
3. What are the titles and authors of two works (or four, if the question so specifies) suitable for answering the question?
4. What definite references (specific incidents, characters, ideas) can I remember that will help me to do what the question asks me to do? (Jot these down.)

PENALTY FOR PLOT SUMMARIES

Some pupils, either because they fail to understand the question or do not bother to find out what it calls for, make the mistake of retelling the whole plot. If you do this, the maximum credit you will receive for your answer is only half the number of points allotted to the question.

A REVIEW OF LITERARY TERMS

Prose is the language we ordinarily speak and write.
Verse is the rhythmical, measured language of poetry.
Fiction is prose writing dealing with *imaginary* people and events.
Nonfiction is prose writing dealing with *real* people and events.

A REVIEW OF LITERARY TYPES

1. The Novel—a full-length work of prose fiction that involves several characters in a series of incidents or plot. Examples: Sinclair Lewis' *Arrowsmith*, Thomas Hardy's *The Return of the Native*.

Caution: Fictionalized biographies are classified as *novels*. Example: Irving Stone's *Love Is Eternal* (a fictionalized portrayal of Abraham Lincoln's wife).

2. The Short Story—a short work of prose fiction, more concentrated than the novel, with fewer characters and only one main incident. Examples: Edgar Allan Poe's "The Cask of Amontillado," William Faulkner's "Two Soldiers."

3. The Full-Length Play—a work written for stage performance and divided into acts, the plot unfolding through the conversations and actions of the characters. It may be in prose or in verse. Examples:

> PROSE DRAMA: Eugene O'Neill's *Beyond the Horizon*
> VERSE DRAMA: William Shakespeare's *As You Like It*

4. The One-Act Play—a short prose drama, more concentrated than the full-length play because it consists of only one act. Examples: Lord Dunsany's "The Lost Silk Hat," John M. Synge's "Riders to the Sea."

5. The Biography—a prose nonfiction work about a person's life written by another person. When a person writes a work about his own life, we call it an *autobiography*. Examples:

> FULL-LENGTH BIOGRAPHY: James Boswell's *Life of Samuel Johnson*, Carl Sandburg's *Abraham Lincoln*
> FULL-LENGTH AUTOBIOGRAPHY: Lincoln Steffens' *The Autobiography of Lincoln Steffens*, Helen Keller's *The Story of My Life*
> COLLECTIONS OF SHORT BIOGRAPHIES: Paul de Kruif's *Microbe Hunters*, John F. Kennedy's *Profiles in Courage*

(Reminder: Fictionalized biographies are considered *novels*, not biographies.)

6. The Essay—a short prose nonfiction work in which an author discusses from his personal point of view a topic that interests him, no matter how serious or trivial it may be. Examples: William Faulkner's "Nobel Prize Acceptance Speech," James Thurber's "The Night the Bed Fell."

7. Books of Travel, History, Current Events, Art, Science, etc. These prose nonfiction works present factual information. Examples: William L. Shirer's *The Rise and Fall of the Third Reich*, John Gunther's *Inside Europe Today*, Thor Heyerdahl's *Kon-Tiki*.

8. The Poem—a literary composition in verse. Each line of a poem usually has a fixed number of syllables. Poetry compresses more thought, feeling, and beauty into its carefully chosen words than any other type of literature. Two principal kinds of poetry are:

a. A *narrative poem* is a poem that tells a story. Example: Robert Frost's "The Death of the Hired Man."

b. A *lyric poem* is one that expresses personal emotion. Example: Christina Rossetti's "My Heart Is Like a Singing Bird."

ANALYZING A QUESTION ABOUT SHORT WORKS

Let us now analyze 5*a* (a typical question about short works) reprinted from pages 185-186.

A reader may be satisfied with the ending of a story because it seems to be the natural result of the events in the story. On the other hand, the reader may be dissatisfied because the ending does not seem logical or believable in view of what has happened in the story or because it leaves questions unanswered in his mind. From the short stories and narrative poems you have read, choose a total of any *four,* and in *each* case show by definite references that you found the ending satisfying or unsatisfying for one of the reasons mentioned. Give titles and authors.

GUIDING QUESTION 1

What does the question ask you to do?

ANSWER

You have to show why each of four endings was either "satisfying or unsatisfying" to you, but you must be careful to discuss only the kinds of endings specified in the question. There are three kinds:

1. An ending that is satisfying "because it seems to be the natural result of events in the story."

2. An ending that is unsatisfying because it "does not seem logical or believable in view of what has happened in the story."

3. An ending that is unsatisfying "because it leaves questions unanswered in your mind."

You may *not* discuss endings that are satisfying or unsatisfying for a reason other than the three given above.

GUIDING QUESTION 2

How many works must you discuss, and of what literary types must they be?

ANSWER

You may discuss any four works from the category "short stories and narrative poems."

QUESTION: What is a narrative poem?
ANSWER: It is a poem that tells a story.

GUIDING QUESTION 3

What are the titles and authors of four works suitable for answering the question?

ANSWER

"The Gift of the Magi" by O. Henry (short story)
"The Tell-Tale Heart" by Edgar Allan Poe (short story)
"The Highwayman" by Alfred Noyes (narrative poem)
"Richard Cory" by Edwin Arlington Robinson (narrative poem)

GUIDING QUESTION 4

What definite references (specific incidents, characters, ideas) can you remember that will help you to do what the question asks you to do?

ANSWER

FIRST WORK: "The Gift of the Magi"

Story ends as Della and Jim exchange Christmas gifts. Della had sold her long hair to buy Jim a watch chain, but he had sold his watch to buy a set of combs for her beautiful hair. Ending is nevertheless satisfying, as it is the natural result of the love they have for each other.

QUESTION: Suppose I can't remember the exact names of the characters. Should I use another short story?
ANSWER: The exact names are not important as long as you identify the characters properly. For example, instead of "Della and Jim," you may write "a young wife and her husband."

SECOND WORK: "The Tell-Tale Heart"

Murderer buries victim under floorboards. Detectives arrive. Murderer confesses when he can no longer endure ticking of victim's watch, which he thinks is the dead man's heart—still beating. Ending is satisfying because it is natural result of murderer's bad conscience.

THIRD WORK: "The Highwayman"

Bess, landlord's daughter, shoots herself so that noise may warn highwayman of trap set for him. When he hears of her death, highwayman deliberately rides into redcoats' gunfire. Ending is satisfying because highwayman, naturally, did not care to live after his sweetheart's death.

FOURTH WORK: "Richard Cory"

Richard Cory seemed to have everything—money, good looks, clothes, jewelry. One day he went home and put a bullet through his head. Ending is unsatisfying because it leaves unanswered the question of why he committed suicide.

ANALYZING PUPIL ANSWERS

One valuable way of improving your ability to write answers to discussion-type literature questions is to study the weaknesses and strengths of other pupils. The following four pupil essays are answers to the typical 5a question on page 189. Notice that each sentence in the answer has been numbered. This will enable you to locate quickly the weaknesses and strengths discussed in the evaluation.

Pupil A

¹The main character in "The Highwayman," a narrative poem by Alfred Noyes, risked his life many times to see his beloved Bess. ²Bess gave her life so that he would not be captured by the British. ³A stablehand, also in love with Bess, informed the Redcoats that the highwayman was coming on this particular night. ⁴As the soldiers lay in waiting, with Bess bound so as not to give a warning, the hoofbeats of the highwayman's horse were heard approaching. ⁵Bess managed somehow to grab hold of a rifle. ⁶The shot that killed her warned the highwayman of the impending danger. ⁷He could not stay away very long, however, and as he returned to find out what had happened, he was shot and killed.

⁸This ending, though it is sad, is satisfying because it seems natural. ⁹Since these two characters loved each other so much, it is evident that neither would have been happy living if the other were dead.

EVALUATION: PUPIL A

1. *Content:* The choice of "The Highwayman" is excellent, as it is a narrative poem with an ending that fits the requirements of the question. The generalizations in S8 and 9 are clearly superior and richly supported by the definite references in the previous sentences.

2. *Composition Technique:* Pupil A's writing is on the whole excellent, except for his somewhat faulty organization. We get the impression that Pupil A is disregarding the question and merely retelling the plot, until we get to S8. The essence of S8 should have been stated at the beginning of the answer.

Rating: 4½ (out of 5) or 90%

Pupil B

¹A story that I liked was "Disertation about Roast Pig" by Lamb. ²He tells how a Chinese boy, Bobo, discovered roast pig long ago. ³By accident when his house burned down with a young pig in it. ⁴The roast pig was so delicious that people use to burn down houses with pigs in them. ⁵Until they learned you don't have to burn up a house to roast a pig. ⁶I enjoyed the ending because it was very funny.

EVALUATION: PUPIL B

1. *Content:* Since Pupil B made an incorrect choice ("A Dissertation Upon Roast Pig" is neither a short story nor a narrative poem, but an essay), the maximum credit he may receive for this part of his answer is 2½ (out of 5) or 50%. Furthermore, his answer fails to meet the requirements of the question. He states that he is satisfied with the ending "because it was very funny," whereas he is supposed to show that it was satisfying "because it seems to be the natural result of the events in the story." Pupil B does show familiarity with the work he discusses.

2. *Composition Technique:* Pupil B gave the title incorrectly and omitted an "s" in his spelling of "Dissertation." In S4 "use" should be "used." There are two sentence fragments: S3 and 5.

S3 should be joined to S2 as follows: He tells how a Chinese boy, Bobo, discovered roast pig long ago by accident, when his house burned down with a young pig in it.

S5 should be joined to S4: The roast pig was so delicious that people used to burn down houses with pigs in them, until they learned you don't have to burn up a house to roast a pig.

(For additional help in correcting sentence fragments, see page 296.)

Rating: 1½ (out of 5) or 30%

Pupil C

[1]In the short story, "The Gift of the Magi" by O. Henry, I was satisfied with the ending. [2]Della and her husband did not have much money. [3]It was Christmas and Della decided to sell her most prized possession, her beautiful long hair, to buy her husband a present. [4]With the money she bought an expensive chain for her husband's watch. [5]But as fate would have it, Jim had sold his watch to buy Della some beautiful ivory combs for her long hair. [6]Even though it was sad when they gave each other the presents, I think it was perfectly natural for them to make such sacrifices for each other. [7]It only brought them more love and happiness.

Evaluation: Pupil C

1. *Content:* The short story Pupil C chose meets the requirements of the question excellently. Her statement in S6 shows that she has the ability to generalize intelligently. The definite references in S2, 3, 4, and 5 present the necessary supporting details briefly and effectively.
2. *Composition Technique:* Very good.

Rating: 5 (out of 5) or 100%

Pupil D

[1]In the poem "Richard Cory" I found the ending dissatisfying because it does not seem logical. [2]I do not believe a man with all the money Richard Cory had would kill himself just because he had no friends. [3]Richard Cory could have made many friend from the people in the town but he thought he was to good for them. [4]This is where the poem loses logic, if he wanted friends bad enought he would have gotten many from the town, but he kills him self instead.

EVALUATION: PUPIL D

1. *Content:* Pupil D is to be commended for his choice of "Richard Cory" and for his statement in S1 about the ending. However, he goes too far in declaring that Richard Cory killed himself "because he had no friends (S2)" and "thought he was to(o) good" for the townspeople (S3). The author (Edwin A. Robinson, whom the pupil did not name) does not make these statements. He leaves the reasons for Richard Cory's suicide to our imagination. Pupil D's statements in S2 and S3 are his own (they are plausible explanations), and he should have labeled them as such by stating, "*I think* that Richard Cory killed himself because."

2. *Composition Technique:* In S4 "bad" should be "badly" and "kills" should be "killed."

    A serious error is the structure of S4, which is a long run-on sentence. It should be rewritten as three separate sentences: "This is where the poem loses logic. If he wanted friends badly enough, he would have gotten many from the town. But he killed himself instead."

    (For help in correcting run-on sentences, see page 295.)
    Note also the spelling errors:

SENTENCE	ERROR	CORRECT SPELLING
3	"friend"	**friends**
3	"to"	**too**
4	"enought"	**enough**
4	"him self"	**himself**

Rating: 3 (out of 5) or 60%

EXERCISE

See how well you can evaluate the following four students' answers to the typical question on page 189. Before rating an answer, carefully consider its main strengths and weaknesses with the help of the evaluation aids. (The teachers who graded these answers rated them 60%, 70%, 90%, and 100%. Can you tell which is which?)

Pupil E

[1]I found the ending of "Richard Cory" by E. A. Robinson both natural and satisfying. [2]For me it left no unanswered questions. [3]It confirmed a belief that I, and perhaps many others, have held for quite a while: it is impossible to know the workings of a person's mind simply from his outward appearance.

[4]Richard Cory was the man everyone else hoped to be. [5]While the poorer men and women worked constantly just so they might eat, Richard Cory had everything without lifting a finger. [6]His looks were admired; his possessions coveted.

[7]Yet no one really knew Richard Cory. [8]If someone had, perhaps he could have told us why he went home one night and put a bullet through his head.

EVALUATION AIDS: PUPIL E

1. Compare E's answer with D's. Who impresses you as having a better understanding of "Richard Cory"? Why?
2. What admirable generalization does E make in S3? With what definite references does E support it?
3. Find a sentence in paragraph 2 that conveys meaning effectively with a minimum of words. Find another in paragraph 3.

Rating: 60%, 70%, 90%, or 100%?

Pupil F

[1]The Gift of the Magi by O. Henry also had a natural ending. [2]In this household there were two things that were cherished. [3]The wifes long beautiful hair and her husbands gold watch.

[4]In order to buy each other a Christmas present each sold his most cherished possession. [5]There was much love between these two that it was only natural that they do what they did for one another.

EVALUATION AIDS: PUPIL F

1. Pupils F and C both discussed O. Henry's "The Gift of the Magi." Whose answer meets the requirements of the question better? Why?
2. Which "sentence" is really a sentence fragment? Find two additional errors in that sentence. Find an error in S1.

Rating: 60%, 70%, 90%, or 100%?

Pupil G

[1]Poe's short story, "The Tell-Tale Heart," expresses once again the moral that "crime does not pay." [2]Somehow the lawbreaker is always found out. [3]The events of the story, which included the murderer's strange fear of his victim's one eye, the dismembering of the victim's body, and the supposed beating of the victim's heart, led to the natural result of being found out. [4]As the detectives were questioning him, the murderer's guilty conscience showed itself when he imagined he heard the continued beating of his victim's heart from under the floor-boards, louder and louder. [5]The murderer's natural nervousness led me to believe that he would be found out. [6]The ending was very satisfying since I believe criminals should not go unpunished.

EVALUATION AIDS: PUPIL G

1. Compare G's S1 with C's. Which meets the requirements of the question better? Why? In what sentence does G really begin to answer the question? Why?
2. To make S3 clearer, what word or words should be inserted before "being found out"?
3. How do the words "supposed" (S3) and "imagined" (S4) prove that G has understood the story well?

Rating: 60%, 70%, 90%, or 100%?

Pupil H

[1]In the poem "The Highwayman" by Alfred Noyes the reader could easily be dissatisfied because there was so much love between the Highwayman and the landlords daughter. [2]Because of their love each one died. [3]The daughter trying to save her lover and he because she was gone.

EVALUATION AIDS: PUPIL H

1. Before rating H's answer, reread A's, as it too deals with "The Highwayman." Why are H's supporting references inferior to A's?
2. Why might H's S1 puzzle a reader who is not familiar with the poem?
3. What is wrong with S3? Suggest a way of eliminating the error.
4. Find an error in S1 that appears also in S3 of F's answer.

Rating: 60%, 70%, 90%, or 100%?

ANALYZING A QUESTION ABOUT FULL-LENGTH WORKS

Let us now analyze 5*b* (a typical question about full-length works) reprinted from page 186:

People make adjustments with varying degrees of success to certain factors in their environment. These factors may be their physical surroundings, other people, or the customs and traditions of the society in which they live. From the novels and full-length plays you have read, choose a total of any *two* books. In *each* case show by definite references to what extent a person in the book was successful in adjusting to one or more of the above factors. Give titles and authors.

Here is how to analyze this typical question by using the suggested "four guiding questions":

GUIDING QUESTION 1

What does the question ask you to do?

ANSWER

You have to show how successful two persons were in adjusting to their environment. Each person must be taken from a different book.

Here are some related questions that may occur to you. In each case you can arrive at the answer by carefully reading the test question.

QUESTION: What does "environment" mean?
ANSWER: The question defines it as the "physical surroundings, other people, or the customs and traditions of the society in which they (the persons you are to write about) live."

QUESTION: Is it necessary to write about all three of these environmental factors?
ANSWER: Obviously not, for the question asks you to discuss "one or more of the above factors" for "each case."

QUESTION: Is it permissible to write about a person who was *not* successful in adjusting?
ANSWER: Of course. The question asks you to show "to what extent" each person was successful in adjusting to his environment. This permits you to discuss *any* character, from an outstanding success to a complete failure.

QUESTION: If I write about adjustment to "physical surroundings" for person 1, will any deduction be made if I write about adjustment to "physical surroundings" for person 2 also?
ANSWER: None whatsoever. The wording of the question clearly allows you to write about the same environmental factor for each character, if you wish.

GUIDING QUESTION 2

How many works must you discuss, and of what literary types must they be?

ANSWER

You may discuss any two works from the category "novels and full-length plays." This means you may write about: (*a*) two novels, or (*b*) two full-length plays, or (*c*) one novel and one full-length play.

Caution: If, through carelessness, you should write about a character from a literary type not permitted by the test question (for example, a one-act play or a biography), you would immediately lose half credit for that part of the answer.

GUIDING QUESTION 3

What are the titles and authors of two works suitable for answering the question?

ANSWER

O. E. Rölvaag's *Giants in the Earth* (a novel) and Eugene O'Neill's *Beyond the Horizon* (a full-length play).

QUESTION: Suppose I don't remember too much about *Beyond the Horizon*. On the other hand, I am very familiar with a novel that I feel is excellently suited for answering the question, *The Return of the Native*, but I can't remember the author's name. Which work should I write about—*Beyond the Horizon* or *The Return of the Native*?

ANSWER: Write about *The Return of the Native*, since you are better acquainted with it. The most you may lose for omitting the author's name (Thomas Hardy) is a half point or a point.

GUIDING QUESTION 4

What definite references (specific incidents, characters, ideas) can you remember that will help you to do what the question asks you to do?

ANSWER

FIRST WORK: *Giants in the Earth*

Per Hansa made a very good adjustment to his physical surroundings, as proved by his:

—building a comfortable house and barn under one roof
—planting crops
—whitewashing the sod walls
—introducing landscaping
—learning to love the vast prairie

and to other people, too, as proved by his:

—winning the Indians' friendship by healing their chief
—carrying on a profitable trade with neighboring settlements, the Indians, and the Irish
—persuading the Solum boys to stay in the community and become schoolteachers

SECOND WORK: *The Return of the Native*

Eustacia Vye made a poor adjustment to her physical surroundings (Egdon Heath) as proved by her:

—regarding Egdon as a prison
—inability to appreciate Egdon's beauties
—yearning to go to Paris

and to other people, as proved by her:

—keeping aloof from Egdon's residents
—quarrels with Wildeve
—feud with Mrs. Yeobright
—failure to adjust to her husband's way of life

ANALYZING PUPIL ANSWERS

Here is a detailed analysis of four pupil answers to the typical question (page 197) we have just analyzed:

Pupil I

[1]In the novel *Giants in the Earth* by O. E. Rölvaag, Beret, Per Hansa's wife, did not adjust too well to the Dakota plains. [2]Brought up in decent surroundings in Norway, Beret found it depressing to live in a sod hut with the earth for a floor and a barn and animals under the same roof. [3]The vast, treeless prairie frightened her. [4]She imagined it was an ominous demon closing in on her with its long tentacles. [5]This, she felt, was God's punishment for her sins. [6]She had broken her parents' hearts by marrying the reckless Per Hansa against their wishes and emigrating to America.

[7]Gradually Beret became depressed almost to the point of losing her mind. [8]Instead of encouraging her husband or appreciating everything he did to make life pleasanter for her, she brooded and said little. [9]When he was gone for supplies, she would cover up the windows with pieces of material to keep out the prairie. [10]She was short-tempered with the children and beat them for almost no reason.

[11]During the locust plague Per Hansa found her and the two youngest children shut up in a large wooden chest, where Beret had sought to hide from an evil demon. [12]Because of his wife's strange behavior, Per Hansa was in constant fear that she might harm herself or the little ones.

[13]With the aid of a kind minister who visited the settlement, Beret was finally able to tolerate her physical surroundings. [14]However, she became so stubbornly pious and virtuous that she drove her husband to his death by sending him on an impossible mission to get a minister for a dying neighbor.

EVALUATION: PUPIL I

1. *Content:* Pupil I is to be commended for selecting Beret as one of the two characters to be discussed. His generalizations about Beret in S1, 7, and 13 show a fine insight into her character and are very well supported by definite references. His understanding of the novel is clearly superior.
2. *Composition Technique:* Excellent.

   Rating: 10 (out of 10) or 100%

Pupil J

[1]People make adjustments with varying degrees of success to certain factors in their environment. [2]These factors may be their physical surroundings, other people, or the customs and traditions of the society in which they live. [3]In *Giants in the Earth* by O. Rölvaag, Beret found it almost too difficult to adjust herself to her new environment.

[4]All Beret's life had been spent in the mountains of Norway surrounded by trees, lakes and streams. [5]The change from this environment to one of flat prairie and open country was a drastic one. [6]Her terrible fear of the western part of the United States, where she felt no one could hide, caused her slowly to lose control of her senses. [7]She spoke very little and was constantly seeing monsterous figures in the sky. [8]Her husband, Per Hansa, once came back at night and found her locked in the hope chest, where she had tried to escape from the evils of the surrounding country. [9]Later on she began talking to her dead mother and insisting that she was being called away.

[10]The only success she was able to obtain in adjusting to her new life came at the end of the novel. [11]Here she became completely en-

veloped within herself and confided only in God, to whom she had intrusted all her faith.

EVALUATION: PUPIL J

1. *Content:* Pupil J deserves the same commendation as Pupil I for choosing to discuss Beret. His statements about Beret in S3, 5, and 10 are correct and adequately supported by specific references. Pupil J has proved that he is well acquainted with the novel and knows how to make intelligent judgments about it.

2. *Composition Technique:* Pupil J's ability to write is commendable but not perfect. S1 and 2 should have been omitted altogether, as they are merely a word-by-word repetition of the first two sentences of the question; S3 by itself can serve as an adequate introduction for Pupil J's essay. S7 contains a misspelling—"monsterous," instead of "monstrous." Aside from these minor faults, Pupil J shows good ability to organize his ideas in correct, clear, and forceful sentences.

Rating: 9 (out of 10) or 90%

Pupil K

[1]People make adjustments with varying degrees of success to certain factors in their environment. [2]These factors may be their physical surroundings, other people, or the customs and traditions of the society in which they live. [3]In *Giants in the Earth* by Rölvaak, a character who was able to adjust to his physical surroundings was Per Hansa. [4]He was among the many settlers who came to the West to start a new life. [5]Per Hansa's surroundings was one in which contained many miles of prairie and open grasslands. [6]From every direction of the small settlement all that one could see was the many miles of wilderness. [7]It wasn't easy for Per Hansa to adjust himself to this kind of environment. [8]During the long cold winters he would try to keep himself busy and occupied at all times. [9]He thought of ways of improving his home to make it feel and look more comfortable for himself and his family. [10]During the winters the people had no choice but to stay in their houses because of the heavy snowstorms that lasted sometimes for a week or more. [11]Per Hansa helped create a school for the people.

¹²In the summer months he also tried new methods of farming and building. ¹³The people listened to many of his ideas, which many times proved effective. ¹⁴Per Hansa was not only able to adjust to this wilderness and barren way of life, but he also tried to help the others overcome the effects of the environment.

EVALUATION: PUPIL K

1. *Content:* Pupil K's choice of Per Hansa, it must be conceded, is a very good one for answering the question. However, he makes several general statements that he fails to support with definite references. For example, he writes in S13 that "the people listened to many of his (Per Hansa's) ideas, which many times proved effective," but he neglects to mention any of these ideas or times. Again, in S12, Pupil K states that Per Hansa "tried new methods of farming and building," but he does not explain a single one of these methods. Pupil K makes no untrue statement about the novel. It is nevertheless clear that his ability to generalize about the novel is inferior to that of Pupil I or Pupil J, and his supporting references are comparatively few and weak.

2. *Composition Technique:* Though Pupil K knows how to write grammatically complete sentences, many of them are not too effective because of such faults as the following:

   a. *Repetition:* "*many* settlers (S4)," "*many miles* of prairie (S5)," "*many miles* of wilderness (S6)," "*many* of his ideas, which *many* times proved effective (S13)."

   As in the case of Pupil J, Pupil K receives no credit at all for S1 and S2, since they are verbatim repetitions of part of the question.

   b. *Lack of agreement:* In S5, "Per Hansa's surroundings was one" should be revised to "Per Hansa's environment was one."

   c. *Awkward expressions:* The word "in" in S5 should be removed. Likewise, omitting "feel and look" in S9 will improve that sentence.

   d. *Spelling:* Except for the misspelling of the author's name in S3, Pupil K's spelling is excellent.

   Rating: 7½ (out of 10) or 75%

Pupil L

[1]People make adjustments with varying degrees of success to certain factors in their environment. [2]Roovalg points out in Giants in the Earth one character that adjusted himself with degrees of success to certain factors in their environment. [3]This character is Per Hansa.

[4]Per Hansa, his wife Beret, and a group of other people started out for the West. [5]They wanted to start a new settlement. [6]It was hard to adjust themselves to this kind of life. [7]Beret didn't want to come out West, but she went anyway because she loved her husband. [8]Per Hansa had to build there new house and plant crops so they can eat. [9]It took them along time to get started and before you knew it most of it was done.

[10]Per Hansa had to take alot from his wife Beret. [11]She never wanted to go out there and she kept on nagging Per. [12]Per Hansa kept on telling her not to worry everything would turn out okay. [13]The reason why she was worrying so much is that she was expecting a baby. [14]There were no doctors there and she was afraid of having a baby without a doctor. [15]One night Indians came, everyone in the settlement was afraid. [16]Per Hansa was too but he went to them. [17]There chief was badly injurged, he was ready to die. [18]Per Hansa helped him get well. [19]When the Indians left, they gave Per Hansa a pony for saving there chief.

[20]Per Hansa had to get adjusted to that kind of life if he wanted to stay there. [21]He also had to get adjusted to his wife.

EVALUATION: PUPIL L

1. *Content:* Pupil L indicates in his first paragraph that he is going to discuss how Per Hansa adjusted to his environment. Unfortunately, he hardly discusses this; instead he devotes the bulk of his essay to retelling the plot. Pupil L obviously knows many of the facts about the novel, but he does not give evidence of being able to select and organize the specific facts necessary for a good answer. The weak and uncertain language of S20 and 21 suggests that Pupil L is not too confident about his understanding of Per Hansa or of the question he was supposed to answer.

2. *Composition Technique:* Pupil L is seriously deficient in composition skills. There is an error in agreement in S2: "their" should be changed to "his." Also, the title in S2 should have been underlined. S10 and S12 contain slangy expressions that

should be avoided in written composition ("*had to take alot from his wife,*" and "*okay*"). There is a tense error in S8 ("*can*" should be "*would be able to*") and another in S11 ("*wanted*" should be "*had wanted*").

In addition, Pupil L has three run-on sentences: S12, 15, and 17. These sentences should be corrected as follows:

S12: Per Hansa kept on telling her not to worry because everything would turn out all right.

S15: One night Indians came. Everyone in the settlement was afraid.

S17: Their chief was badly injured. He was ready to die.

(For additional help in correcting run-on sentences, see page 295.)

There are numerous spelling errors:

SENTENCE	ERROR	CORRECT SPELLING
2	"Roovalg"	Rölvaag
8, 17, 19	"there"	their
9	"along"	a long
10	"alot"	a lot
17	"injurged"	injured

Rating: 5½ (out of 10) or 55%

EXERCISE

Test yourself by rating the following three pupil answers to the typical question on page 197. They are all based on a novel usually studied in high school: Thomas Hardy's *The Return of the Native.* Evaluation aids have been provided after each answer to guide you to some of the strengths and weaknesses and to help you arrive at a sound rating. (The teachers who marked these essays rated one 100%, another 80%, and the third 60%. Which is which?)

Pupil M

[1]People make adjustments with varying degrees of success to certain factors in their environment. [2]One of these factors may be their physical surroundings. [3]In *Return of the Native,* a novel by Thomas Hardy,

Eustacia was unsuccessful in adjusting to her environment. [4]Unlike Beret in *Giants in the Earth,* Eustasia couldn't adjust because she didn't want to. [5]She thought herself above the others on the heath and all she wanted was escape. [6]She was a beautiful and intelligent woman and could have had a good life on the heath if she had tried. [7]Instead of that she attempted to escape but failed each time. [8]Her first attempt to escape occurred when she married Clym. [9]She though he would take her away from the heath. [10]This attempt failed and soon she became desperate. [11]In her second attempt, she tried to kill herself but was stopped by a servant. [12]In Wildeve, she saw another means of escape. [13]Eustasia and Wildeve tried to run away. [14]Finally she would be rid of this horrible place. [15]In her efforts, she ended everything by falling and drowning. [16]Because of her unwillingness to adjust to her environment, she lost her life.

EVALUATION AIDS: PUPIL M

1. Would M's answer be weakened or improved if S1 and 2 were omitted? Why?
2. How many definite references does M offer in support of his statement in S7?
3. In which sentence is the heroine's name spelled correctly, S3 or 4? Find a spelling error in S9 and another in S13.

Rating: 100%, 80%, or 60%?

Pupil N

[1]Another book was *The Return of the Native* by Thomas Hardy. [2]Clym Yeobright first lived and worked in London. [3]He had a very good life and he was also very well educated. [4]He wanted to live in Egdon Heath so he can help the people by opening a school house. [5]His mother disapproved of this very much. [6]She wanted him to stay in London where he was doing much better. [7]His mother Mrs. Yeobright could not get adjusted to this. [8]She also had to adjust herself when he married Eustacia. [9]Mrs. Yeobright didn't like Eustacia because she thought she was evil a witch. [10]She also thought that Eustacia married Clym because she wanted to get out of Egdon Heath and go to London. [11]Mrs. Yeobright had to adjust herself with other people. [12]To get along with them better.

EVALUATION AIDS: PUPIL N

1. State two reasons why N's S1 is not as good as M's S3.
2. S2 contains an error of fact which is repeated in S6 and 10. What is the error?
3. Why does the statement in S11 fail to meet the requirements of the question?
4. Which "sentence" is really a sentence fragment?
5. Locate an error of tense in S4 and another in S10.

Rating: 100%, 80%, or 60%?

Pupil O

[1]In *The Return of the Native,* a novel by Thomas Hardy, Eustacia was not very successful in adjusting to her environment. [2]Eustacia had been brought up in the gay seacoast town of Budmouth and had moved to the Heath when she was still a young woman. [3]She considered the Heath a lonely, dreary place to live, and she was not content there. [4]Eustacia thought of ways that she could get away from the Heath, and, when she married Clym, she was sure that it would be a short matter of time before her desire would be fulfilled. [5]However, her marriage did not result in her leaving the Heath.

[6]Eustacia never really adjusted to the people in the Heath. [7]She was very different from them in a number of ways. [8]Because she had more education than the Heath folk, Eustacia was not happy with the dull life led by them. [9]She never went out of her way to be friendly. [10]One evidence of her relationship with the people was shown by the fact that she wasn't invited to Clym's party when he came home for Christmas. [11]Almost everybody else was.

[12]One custom of the Heath folk was the lighting of bonfires on Guy Fawkes Day, November 5th. [13]The people would gather around the fires and have a good time singing and dancing. [14]Eustacia never joined in these affairs.

[15]Eustacia was not very successful in adjusting to her surroundings in any respect.

EVALUATION AIDS: PUPIL O

1. Compare O's opening sentence with M's and N's. Which is the best of the three? Why?
2. With what environmental factor does O deal in paragraph 1? in paragraph 2? in paragraph 3? What does this suggest about O's knowledge of the novel? about O's ability to organize a composition?
3. What evidence of good reasoning does O offer in paragraph 2? in paragraph 3?

Rating: 100%, 80%, or 60%?

FORMER REGENTS QUESTIONS

Answer *a* or *b*:   [20]

1

a. The enjoyment or appreciation of literature often depends on the mood of the reader. From the poems and essays you have read, choose *four* selections (using at least one poem and one essay). In each case show by definite references how the selection chosen would appeal to a person in one of the following moods: gay, questioning, sad, discouraged, serious, sentimental. Give titles and authors.

b. We can better understand the world of today through reading books of true experience, such as books of travel, eye-witness accounts of great historical events, or biographies of persons who took part in important happenings. Select *two* full-length books of the types mentioned and show by definite references how each book contributes to this understanding. Give titles and authors.

2

a. Many stories present the experiences of young people. By references to a novel *and* a play (or to a novel and two short stories), show to what degree the authors have presented young people as they really are. Give titles and authors.

b. Some people are made unhappy by circumstances or events that appear to be beyond their control. Others make misfortunes a means to future success or happiness. Use a novel to show the truth of *one* of the above statements, and a biography (or book of true experience) to show the truth of the other. Give titles and authors.

3

a. Many recent books are considered "escape" reading; that is, they provide relaxation and entertainment through presenting an unusual person, a humorous situation, a fantastic event, or a faraway place. Select *two* well-written, full-length books published since 1900, and show by definite references how *each* would appeal to a reader in any of the ways mentioned. Give titles and authors.

b. A person's life may be influenced by the time in which he lives, his love of country, his personal ambition, or his love of others. Show by definite references how a person in a novel or a full-length biography was influenced by *one* of the forces mentioned, and how a person in a different novel or full-length biography was influenced by another of the forces mentioned. Give titles and authors.

4

a. In writing a short story, a narrative poem or a one-act play, an author may present a basic theme or idea concerning human conduct or human relations. From short stories, narrative poems and one-act plays, choose a total of *four* selections, using at least *two* of the types mentioned above. For *each* selection chosen, indicate what theme or idea is presented, and by means of specific references show how the action brings out this theme or idea. Give titles and authors.

b. In their youth, people are influenced not only by their parents but also by other adults: relatives, friends, neighbors, teachers, religious leaders. Choose *one* novel and *one* full-length biography, and show by definite references how a young person in *each* selection was helped or hindered by an adult. Give titles and authors.

5

a. A poet or an essayist frequently describes a personal experience involving a place, a person (or persons), an event or a mood. From the poems and essays you have read, choose a total of *four* selections, and in *each* case indicate by definite references the nature of the experience and the author's reaction to it. Give titles and authors.

b. Some agencies in the United States are sending to libraries and schools abroad books which help to give to people in foreign countries a better understanding of the American way of life. Choose *one* novel and *one* book of nonfiction, and in *each* case show by definite references how the book presents a true picture of American life. Give titles and authors.

6

a. In literature, as in life, a person may have an experience within his family which brings him happiness or sorrow. From the short stories and one-act plays you have read, choose a total of *four* selections, and in *each* case show by definite references how a person in the selection was made happy or sorrowful by such an experience. Give titles and authors.

b. From the novels and full-length biographies you have read, choose *two* books in each of which a person is confronted with unfavorable circumstances arising from economic conditions, cultural differences or home background. By definite references in each case, indicate the nature of the circumstances and whether or not the person was successful in overcoming them. Give titles and authors.

7

a. Often a scene in a novel or play is so dramatic that it might be effective if presented on radio or television. The scene may involve an exciting episode, a conflict between two persons, a surprise, or a happy or tragic incident. Choose *two* such scenes, one from a novel and one from a *full-length* play, and in *each* case show by specific references that the scene chosen would be effective on radio or television. Give titles and authors.

b. In a world torn by crises and tension, literature can be a source of reassurance by presenting a positive or optimistic view of life. From the poems and essays you have read choose a total of *four* selections, and in *each* case show by specific references that the selection presents such an outlook. Give titles and authors.

8

a. In reading, as in life, we may meet some people who are very wise and other people who are very unwise. From your reading of novels and full-length plays, choose a total of *two* books. For one book, show by definite references why you consider a person in the book to be very wise; for the other book, show by definite references why you consider a person to be very unwise. Give titles and authors.

b. The sea has been a popular subject for writers. Some have written books of fiction with the sea as the setting; other writers have given their personal reaction to the sea or have presented new facts about it. In either case, the reader can learn much about the sea. Choose *two* full-length books (novels, books of non-fiction) *or four* shorter selections (poems, essays, one-act plays) *or one* such full-length book and *two* such shorter selections. In each case, show by definite references how you have become better acquainted with the sea through reading. Give titles and authors.

9

a. A writer sometimes achieves humor by exaggerating the details of a situation or the characteristics and actions of a person. Choose a total of any *four* selections from among the essays, poems, short stories, and one-act plays that you have read. In *each* case show by specific references how exaggeration has made a situation or a character humorous. Give titles and authors.

b. Many books deal with the problems faced by men and women in achieving success in a job or profession. Choose a total of any *two* books from among the novels, *full-length* biographies, and books of true experience you have read. In *each* case describe a problem that a person met in attaining his goal in his life's work, and show by specific references how he solved this problem. Give titles and authors.

10

a. In books, as in life, an incident that seems unimportant at the time of happening may lead to momentous results. From the novels and full-length plays you have read, choose any *two* selections. In *each* case show by definite references how a seemingly unimportant event led to either a happy or a tragic result. Give titles and authors.

b. The very nature of man makes it impossible for him to live "by bread alone"; he must live by faith—faith in an ideal or a principle, faith in his country, faith in mankind. From the poems and essays you have read, choose any *four* selections. In *each* case show by definite references that the author expresses one of the kinds of faith mentioned. Give titles and authors.

Chapter 13

THE LITERATURE TEST (QUESTION 5c)

PURPOSE OF THE MULTIPLE-CHOICE LITERATURE TEST

The purpose of the multiple-choice literature test (question 5c) is to evaluate your knowledge of a broad range of literary works and related topics. It is a challenging test, as you will see below, since it requires accurate knowledge of many more works than questions 5a or 5b. You will do better to choose 5a or 5b (as the vast majority of students have done in the past), unless you have read more widely in good literature than the average student.

TYPICAL MULTIPLE-CHOICE LITERATURE TEST: 5c

One way of deciding whether you should seriously consider 5c is to try several tests like the typical one below. Cover up the correct answers in the right-hand column and jot down your own. Then compare.

JUNE 1959

c Each of the statements below involves a reference to literature. Choose 20 only and on the line at the right of each of the 20 statements write the *number* of the word or phrase that correctly completes the statement. [20]

1 When Tom Sawyer was told to whitewash the fence, he got the job done by (1) hiring his pal to help him (2) pretending he was an artist (3) using a brush in each hand (4) talking his friends into doing it .... 1...4...

2 In *Julius Caesar,* a fatal mistake of the conspirators proved to be (1) failing to kill Cicero (2) concealing their plans from Portia (3) allowing Antony to speak at Caesar's funeral (4) allowing the Soothsayer to live .... 2...3...

3 The name of the first atomic-powered submarine is the same as that of a craft in (1) *The Sea Around Us* (2) *Moby Dick* (3) *Twenty Thousand Leagues Under the Sea* (4) *The Caine Mutiny* .... 3...3...

211

4 In *Our Town,* the dead told Emily that reliving part of her life would   (1) be impossible   (2) bring added grief to her family   (3) condemn her soul to haunt the earth forever   (4) bring her only unhappiness .... 4 ...4...

5 In *The Keys of the Kingdom,* Father Chisholm's first task upon arriving in China was to   (1) found a mission   (2) placate the British   (3) arrange for a visa to Tibet   (4) ask for a large force of servants .... 5 ...1...

6 *Idylls of the King* is about the court of   (1) King Henry VIII   (2) King Richard III   (3) King Arthur   (4) King George V .... 6 ...3...

7 *Beyond the Horizon* by Eugene O'Neill is chiefly concerned with   (1) the thrills of travel   (2) unrealized dreams   (3) a happy marriage   (4) the opening of new frontiers .... 7 ...2...

8 "The Devil and Tom Walker" has a theme similar to that of a story by   (1) Lewis   (2) Benét   (3) Mansfield   (4) Parker .... 8 ...2...

9 In her sleep-walking scene, Lady Macbeth reveals her   (1) distrust of Banquo   (2) suspicion of Macduff   (3) pride in her husband   (4) suffering for her crimes .... 9 ...4...

10 Pegasus was   (1) a fire bringer   (2) a winged horse   (3) a serpent   (4) the north wind .... 10 ...2...

11 According to Norse mythology, the only persons admitted to Valhalla were   (1) women   (2) small children   (3) brave warriors killed in battle   (4) those recommended by Odin .... 11 ...3...

12 Molly Farren was the mother of   (1) Eppie   (2) Heathcliff   (3) Pip   (4) the Artful Dodger 12 ...1...

13 In *Treasure Island,* Jim and his mother found the map among the possessions of   (1) John Silver   (2) Captain Bones   (3) Black Dog   (4) Pew ..... 13 ...2...

14 Sam McGee was cremated in a   (1) desert   (2) boiler   (3) cemetery   (4) hotel fire .... 14 ...2...

15 In *A Man Called Peter,* Catherine Marshall tells of her husband, who was a   (1) victim of amnesia   (2) missionary to China   (3) founder of a religious sect   (4) chaplain of the United States Senate .... 15 ...4...

16 *Wind, Sand and Stars* describes the experiences of a well-known   (1) statesman   (2) astronomer   (3) aviator   (4) mountain climber ....   16 ...3...

17 "The world stands out on either side
No wider than the heart is wide"
are lines written by   (1) William Cullen Bryant   (2) Emily Dickinson   (3) Vachel Lindsay   (4) Edna St. Vincent Millay ....   17 ...4...

18 A novel whose setting is a South American jungle is   (1) *The Wild Place*   (2) *Green Mansions*   (3) *The Green Years*   (4) *Wilderness Trail* ....   18 ...2...

19 *Captains Courageous* tells of life on   (1) a submarine   (2) an island   (3) a fishing boat   (4) a steamboat on the Mississippi ....   19 ...3...

20 Mrs. Malaprop is an important figure in   (1) *The Rivals*   (2) *Pygmalion*   (3) *Quality Street*   (4) *She Stoops to Conquer* ....   20 ...1...

21 Captain Andy Hawks was the master of   (1) a pirate ship   (2) a private yacht   (3) an ocean-going tug   (4) a showboat ....   21 ...4...

22 The commander of H.M.S. *Lydia* was Captain   (1) Bligh   (2) Slocum   (3) Smollett   (4) Hornblower ....   22 ...4...

23 A short-story character famous for his skill as a gambler was   (1) Roderick Usher   (2) Jabez Stone   (3) John Oakhurst   (4) Penrod Schofield ......   23 ...3...

24 A man was hired to copy the *Encyclopaedia Britannica* in   (1) "The Stockbroker's Clerk"   (2) "The Adventure of the Bruce-Partington Plans"   (3) "The Red-headed League"   (4) "The Adventure of the Six Napoleons" ....   24 ...3...

25 In which essay did the prospective customer know the value of the product better than the salesman?   (1) "The Wounded Oyster"   (2) "I Entertain an Agent Unawares"   (3) "Quality"   (4) "What Men Live By" ....   25 ...2...

26 The words "Then conquer we must, when our cause it is just,—" come from   (1) "O Captain! My Captain!"   (2) "In Flanders Fields"   (3) "The Star-Spangled Banner"   (4) "America the Beautiful" ..   26 ...3...

27 A recent book by Kenneth Roberts concerns   (1) a shipwreck   (2) a plague   (3) interplanetary

travel   (4) New York City .... 27 .. 1 ...

28 The guest in "The Fall of the House of Usher" helped
entomb the body of Usher's   (1) stepfather
(2) son   (3) doctor   (4) sister .... 28 ... 4 ...

29 A "crime" of the duke's wife in "My Last Duchess"
was that she   (1) brought no dowry   (2) bore
no sons   (3) gave the same smile to everyone
(4) prevented her husband's promotion .... 29 ... 3 ...

30 The attempt of a young girl to live above her station in
life is recounted in   (1) *Cress Delahanty*   (2)
Alice Adams   (3) *Renown*   (4) *Seventeenth
Summer* .... 30 ... 2 ...

31 *The Man Who Never Was* takes place during   (1)
World War I   (2) World War II   (3) the
French Revolution   (4) the Civil War .... 31 ... 2 ...

32 Tennyson's "In Memoriam" describes his grief at the
death of his   (1) bride   (2) eldest son   (3)
father   (4) college friend .... 32 ... 4 ...

33 In *Flush* by Virginia Woolf, a cocker spaniel describes
the romance between his owner and   (1) Mark
Twain   (2) Alfred Tennyson   (3) Robert Browning   (4) Prince Edward .... 33 ... 3 ...

34 Sir Roger de Coverley's behavior in church revealed
that he was   (1) extremely devout   (2) doubtful of the pastor's sincerity   (3) ill at ease in Sunday clothing   (4) critical of his tenants' behavior 34 ... 4 ...

35 In Shelley's poem, Ozymandias is   (1) a king
(2) a shepherd lad   (3) a caliph of Baghdad
(4) Aladdin's genie .... 35 ... 1 ...

36 "Little we see in Nature that is ours" is a line from a
poem by   (1) Herrick   (2) Kipling   (3) Coleridge   (4) Wordsworth .... 36 ... 4 ...

37 In Chekhov's "The Bet," the subject of controversy was
(1) religion   (2) government subsidies   (3)
military conscription   (4) capital punishment .... 37 ... 4 ...

38 Dr. Jekyll and Mr. Hyde are   (1) a divided personality   (2) aliases of a famous faker   (3) part-
ners in a criminal enterprise   (4) rival suitors for
the hand of an American socialite .... 38 ... 1 ...

39 Ivan T. Sanderson has written widely about   (1)
   sports   (2) music   (3) the Civil War   (4) wild
   animals ....   39 ... 4 ...

40 "We are such stuff
   As dreams are made on,"
   is a quotation from   (1) Lamb   (2) Milton
   (3) Shakespeare   (4) Byron ....   40 ... 3 ...

ANALYSIS OF 5c

The test consists of forty incomplete statements about literature, each followed by four suggested endings. You are asked to recognize the correct way of ending *only twenty* of the incomplete statements. The total value of 5c is twenty credits (the same as for 5a or 5b).

Among the matters you are asked to recognize are the following:

1. A Detail About a Character, the Setting, or the Theme of a Work. This type of question is fair because the detail called for is not usually an obscure one; anyone who has really read and understood the work should easily be able to recognize the detail. More than three-fourths of the entire test consists of questions of this type.

CHARACTER DETAIL:

1 When Tom Sawyer was told to whitewash the fence, he
   got the job done by   (1) hiring his pal to help him
   (2) pretending he was an artist   (3) using a brush in
   each hand   (4) talking his friends into doing it .... 4 ...

SETTING DETAIL:

18 A novel whose setting is a South American jungle is
   (1) *The Wild Place*   (2) *Green Mansions*   (3)
   The Green Years   (4) *Wilderness Trail* .... 2 ...

THEME DETAIL:

8 "The Devil and Tom Walker" has a theme similar to that
   of a story by   (1) Lewis   (2) Benét   (3) Mansfield   (4) Parker .... 2 ...

2. A Quotation

17 "The world stands out on either side
   No wider than the heart is wide"

are lines written by (1) William Cullen Bryant
(2) Emily Dickinson (3) Vachel Lindsay (4)
Edna St. Vincent Millay ....4...

3. An Author's Specialty

39 Ivan T. Sanderson has written widely about (1) sports
(2) music (3) the Civil War (4) wild animals ...4...

4. A Reference to Mythology

11 According to Norse mythology, the only persons admitted to Valhalla were (1) women (2) small
children (3) brave warriors killed in battle (4)
those recommended by Odin ....3...

Additional types of 5c questions, not represented in the test above
but frequently used in past examinations, are in these areas:

5. Literary Associations

The river Avon is associated with (1) Robert Burns
(2) Sidney Lanier (3) William Wordsworth (4)
William Shakespeare ....4...

6. Poetic Devices and Verse Forms

"The furrow followed free" is an example of (1) simile
(2) synecdoche (3) onomatopoeia (4) alliteration ...4...

Blank verse and free verse are similar in (1) complete
lack of rhythm (2) lack of rhyme (3) length of line
(4) length of stanza ....2...

7. Related Areas of English (library skills, newspapers, periodicals, parliamentary procedure, films)

LIBRARY SKILLS:

For detailed current information about a subject, one should
consult (1) the card catalog (2) the vertical file
(3) an atlas (4) an abridged dictionary ....2...

NEWSPAPERS:

The date line of a news story indicates the date that (1)
the story was written or filed (2) the event happened

(3) the story was sent out by the news service   (4) the story was due on the editor's desk. . . . . 1 . . .

PERIODICALS:

Which one of the following is published monthly as well as annually?   (1) *Congressional Record*   (2) *The World Almanac*   (3) *Information Please Almanac*   (4) *Current Biography* . . . . 4 . . .

PARLIAMENTARY PROCEDURE:

A motion that requires a second is one to   (1) nominate (2) withdraw a motion   (3) rise to a point of order (4) table a motion . . . . 4 . . .

FILMS:

In motion pictures, Louis de Rochemont has won fame as a producer of   (1) comedies   (2) westerns   (3) documentaries   (4) psychological thrillers . . . . 3 . . .

RECOGNIZING LITERARY CHARACTERS

Don't waste time memorizing the names of characters in books you haven't read. You would do much better to spend the time reading another worthwhile work. Regents questions that ask you to identify a character usually also require familiarity with the plot, setting, or theme. For example, if you had memorized that Elizabeth Bennet is the principal character in *Pride and Prejudice,* without having read that novel, you would have insufficient information to answer this question:

Elizabeth Bennet married   (1) Mr. Rochester   (2) George Osborne   (3) Mr. Collins   (4) Mr. Darcy

Here is an alphabetical listing of characters who have been the basis of 5c questions in the past.

CHARACTER	TITLE AND AUTHOR
Captain Ahab	*Moby Dick*, Herman Melville
Mrs. Alving	*Ghosts*, Henrik Ibsen
Sir Andrew Aguecheek	*Twelfth Night*, William Shakespeare
Antonia Shimerda	*My Ántonia*, Willa Cather
Barkis	*David Copperfield*, Charles Dickens
Willie Baxter	*Seventeen*, Booth Tarkington

CHARACTER	TITLE AND AUTHOR
Sir Toby Belch	*Twelfth Night,* William Shakespeare
Elizabeth Bennet	*Pride and Prejudice,* Jane Austen
Harvey Birch	*The Spy,* James Fenimore Cooper
Bottom the Weaver	*A Midsummer Night's Dream,* William Shakespeare
Alan Breck	*Kidnapped,* Robert Louis Stevenson
Colonel Jim Brewton	*The Sea of Grass,* Conrad Richter
Natty Bumppo	*The Pioneers,* James Fenimore Cooper
Jim Burden	*My Ántonia,* Willa Cather
Caliban	*The Tempest,* William Shakespeare
Sydney Carton	*A Tale of Two Cities,* Charles Dickens
Godfrey Cass	*Silas Marner,* George Eliot
Cassius	*Julius Caesar,* William Shakespeare
Cedric the Saxon	*Ivanhoe,* Sir Walter Scott
Roger Chillingworth	*The Scarlet Letter,* Nathaniel Hawthorne
Chingachgook	*The Last of the Mohicans,* James Fenimore Cooper
Father Chisholm	*The Keys of the Kingdom,* A. J. Cronin
Angel Clare	*Tess of the d'Urbervilles,* Thomas Hardy
Long Tom Coffin	*The Pilot,* James Fenimore Cooper
Hugh Conway	*Lost Horizon,* James Hilton
Cordelia	*King Lear,* William Shakespeare
Sir Roger de Coverley	*The Spectator,* Joseph Addison and Richard Steele
Ichabod Crane	*The Legend of Sleepy Hollow,* Washington Irving
Bob Cratchit	*A Christmas Carol,* Charles Dickens
William Crichton	*The Admirable Crichton,* James M. Barrie
Jerry Cruncher	*A Tale of Two Cities,* Charles Dickens
Edmond Dantes	*The Count of Monte Cristo,* Alexander Dumas
Charles Darnay	*A Tale of Two Cities,* Charles Dickens
Madame Defarge	*A Tale of Two Cities,* Charles Dickens
Arthur Dimmesdale	*The Scarlet Letter,* Nathaniel Hawthorne
Eliza Doolittle	*Pygmalion,* George Bernard Shaw
Ellen Douglas	*The Lady of the Lake,* Sir Walter Scott
C. Auguste Dupin	"The Purloined Letter," Edgar Allan Poe
Tess Durbeyfield	*Tess of the d'Urbervilles,* Thomas Hardy
Morgan Evans	*The Corn Is Green,* Emlyn Williams
Fagin	*Oliver Twist,* Charles Dickens
Rosemary Fell	"A Cup of Tea," Katharine Mansfield

CHARACTER	TITLE AND AUTHOR
Fortunato	"The Cask of Amontillado," Edgar Allan Poe
Man Friday	*Robinson Crusoe*, Daniel Defoe
Fuzzy-Wuzzy	*Barrack-Room Ballads*, Rudyard Kipling
Sarah Gamp	*Martin Chuzzlewit*, Charles Dickens
Launcelot Gobbo	*The Merchant of Venice*, William Shakespeare
Guinevere	*Idylls of the King*, Alfred Lord Tennyson
Prince Hal	*Henry IV*, William Shakespeare
Richard Hannay	*The Thirty-nine Steps*, John Buchan
Miss Havisham	*Great Expectations*, Charles Dickens
Jim Hawkins	*Treasure Island*, Robert Louis Stevenson
Heathcliff	*Wuthering Heights*, Emily Brontë
Uriah Heep	*David Copperfield*, Charles Dickens
Professor Higgins	*Pygmalion*, George Bernard Shaw
Iago	*Othello*, William Shakespeare
Major Joppolo	*A Bell for Adano*, John Hersey
Katharina	*The Taming of the Shrew*, William Shakespeare
Carol Kennicott	*Main Street*, Sinclair Lewis
Hazen Kinch	"They Grind Exceeding Small," Ben Ames Williams
Nancy Lammeter	*Silas Marner*, George Eliot
Launcelot of the Lake	*Idylls of the King*, Alfred Lord Tennyson
Leatherstocking	*The Pathfinder*, James Fenimore Cooper
Simon Legree	*Uncle Tom's Cabin*, Harriet Beecher Stowe
Tony Lumpkin	*She Stoops to Conquer*, Oliver Goldsmith
Madeline	"The Eve of St. Agnes," John Keats
Magwitch	*Great Expectations*, Charles Dickens
Mrs. Malaprop	*The Rivals*, Richard B. Sheridan
Malvolio	*Twelfth Night*, William Shakespeare
Dr. Manette	*A Tale of Two Cities*, Charles Dickens
Mattie Silver	*Ethan Frome*, Edith Wharton
Wilkins Micawber	*David Copperfield*, Charles Dickens
Montresor	"The Cask of Amontillado," Edgar Allan Poe
Captain Nemo	*Twenty Thousand Leagues Under the Sea*, Jules Verne
Philip Nolan	"The Man Without a Country," Edward Everett Hale
John Oakhurst	"The Luck of Roaring Camp," Bret Harte
Ophelia	*Hamlet*, William Shakespeare

CHARACTER	TITLE AND AUTHOR
Sancho Panza	*Don Quixote*, Cervantes
Pecksniff	*Martin Chuzzlewit*, Charles Dickens
Clara Peggotty	*David Copperfield*, Charles Dickens
Samuel Pickwick	*The Pickwick Papers*, Charles Dickens
Pip	*Great Expectations*, Charles Dickens
Polonius	*Hamlet*, William Shakespeare
Pompilia	*The Ring and the Book*, Robert Browning
Porphyro	"The Eve of St. Agnes," John Keats
Portia	*The Merchant of Venice*, William Shakespeare
Dr. Primrose	*The Vicar of Wakefield*, Oliver Goldsmith
Miss Pross	*A Tale of Two Cities*, Charles Dickens
Hester Prynne	*The Scarlet Letter*, Nathaniel Hawthorne
Rebecca	*Ivanhoe*, Sir Walter Scott
John Ridd	*Lorna Doone*, R. D. Blackmore
Rikki-Tikki-Tavi	*The Jungle Book*, Rudyard Kipling
Edward Rochester	*Jane Eyre*, Charlotte Brontë
Robert Rogers	*Northwest Passage*, Kenneth Roberts
Rosalind	*As You Like It*, William Shakespeare
Roxane	*Cyrano de Bergerac*, Edmond Rostand
Santiago	*The Old Man and the Sea*, Ernest Hemingway
Ebenezer Scrooge	*A Christmas Carol*, Charles Dickens
John Shand	*What Every Woman Knows*, James M. Barrie
Becky Sharp	*Vanity Fair*, William Makepeace Thackeray
Shylock	*The Merchant of Venice*, William Shakespeare
Long John Silver	*Treasure Island*, Robert Louis Stevenson
Augustus Snodgrass	*The Pickwick Papers*, Charles Dickens
Dr. Stockmann	*An Enemy of the People*, Henrik Ibsen
Jabez Stone	"The Devil and Daniel Webster," Stephen Vincent Benét
Touchstone	*As You Like It*, William Shakespeare
Leora Tozer	*Arrowsmith*, Sinclair Lewis
Squire Trelawney	*Treasure Island*, Robert Louis Stevenson
Jean Valjean	*Les Misérables*, Victor Hugo
Eustacia Vye	*The Return of the Native*, Thomas Hardy
Emily Webb	*Our Town*, Thornton Wilder
Sam Weller	*The Pickwick Papers*, Charles Dickens
Dolly Winthrop	*Silas Marner*, George Eliot
Mrs. Yeobright	*The Return of the Native*, Thomas Hardy
Zeena	*Ethan Frome*, Edith Wharton

RECOGNIZING QUOTATIONS

The following quotations have been the basis of questions in past examinations.

Quotations From Plays

Julius Caesar by William Shakespeare

"Why, man, he doth bestride the narrow world
  Like a Colossus."
                                        (spoken by Cassius)

"Yond Cassius has a lean and hungry look;
  He thinks too much; such men are dangerous."
                                        (spoken by Caesar)

"Cowards die many times before their deaths;
  The valiant never taste of death but once."
                                        (spoken by Caesar)

"But 'tis a common proof
  That lowliness is young ambition's ladder."
                                        (spoken by Brutus)

"The fault, dear Brutus, is not in our stars,
  But in ourselves, that we are underlings."
                                        (spoken by Cassius)

"The evil that men do lives after them;
  The good is oft interred with their bones."
                                        (spoken by Antony)

Hamlet by William Shakespeare

"The time is out of joint; O cursed spite,
  That ever I was born to set it right!"
                                        (spoken by Hamlet)

"The play's the thing
  Wherein I'll catch the conscience of the king."
                                        (spoken by Hamlet)

"Good night, sweet prince."
                                        (spoken by Horatio)

"For the apparel oft proclaims the man."
                                        (spoken by Polonius)

"Alas, poor Yorick! I knew him, Horatio."
(spoken by Hamlet)

Macbeth by William Shakespeare
"Is this a dagger which I see before me?"
(spoken by Macbeth)

"Tomorrow and tomorrow and tomorrow
Creeps in this petty pace from day to day."
(spoken by Macbeth)

"Infirm of purpose!
Give me the daggers."
(spoken by Lady Macbeth)

"Methought I heard a voice cry 'Sleep no more!
Macbeth does murder sleep.'"
(spoken by Macbeth)

Romeo and Juliet by William Shakespeare
"Parting is such sweet sorrow."
(spoken by Juliet)

"A plague on both your houses!"
(spoken by Mercutio)

A Midsummer Night's Dream by William Shakespeare
"Lord, what fools these mortals be!"
(spoken by Puck)

Richard III by William Shakespeare
"A horse! a horse! my kingdom for a horse!"
(spoken by Richard III)

The Tempest by William Shakespeare
"We are such stuff
As dreams are made on."
(spoken by Prospero)

Our Town by Thornton Wilder
"A man looks pretty small at a wedding, George. All those good women standing shoulder to shoulder making sure that the knot's tied in a mighty public way."
(spoken by Mr. Webb)

Quotations From Novels

Alice in Wonderland by Lewis Carroll
"Off with their heads!"
(a common expression of the queen)

David Copperfield by Charles Dickens
"Something will turn up."
(a common expression of Micawber)

"Barkis is willin'."
(Barkis' proposal to Peggotty)

A Tale of Two Cities by Charles Dickens
"It is a far, far better thing that I do, than I have ever done."
(Carton's reflection on his way to the guillotine)

Quotations From Poems

Elizabeth Barrett Browning
"And, if God choose,
I shall but love thee better after death."
(*Sonnets from the Portuguese*)

Robert Browning
"If I can rid your town of rats,
Will you give me a thousand guilders?"
("The Pied Piper")

William Cullen Bryant
"The groves were God's first temples."
("A Forest Hymn")

"To him who in the love of Nature holds
Communion with her visible forms"
("Thanatopsis")

Robert Burns
"Wee, sleekit, cow'rin, tim'rous beastie"
("To a Mouse")

"Still thou art blessed, compared wi' me!"
("To a Mouse")

"O wad some Pow'r the giftie gie us
  To see oursels as ithers see us!"
                    ("To a Louse")

"And I will luve thee still, my dear,
  Till a' the seas gang dry."
                    ("A Red, Red Rose")

Samuel Taylor Coleridge
  "As idle as a painted ship
  Upon a painted ocean"
                    ("The Rime of the Ancient Mariner")

Emily Dickinson
  "I like to see it lap the miles."
                    (from the poem of the same name)

"I never spoke with God,
  Nor visited in heaven."
                    ("Chartless")

Ralph Waldo Emerson
  "Tell them, dear, that if eyes were made for seeing,
  Then Beauty is its own excuse for being."
                    ("The Rhodora")

Robert Frost
  "When I see birches bend to left and right"
                    ("Birches")

"One could do worse than be a swinger of birches."
                    ("Birches")

"Whose woods these are I think I know."
                    ("Stopping by Woods on a Snowy Evening")

"But I have promises to keep,
  And miles to go before I sleep."
                    ("Stopping by Woods on a Snowy Evening")

"Home is the place where, when you have to go there,
  They have to take you in."
                    ("The Death of the Hired Man")

" 'Dead,' was all he answered."
                    ("The Death of the Hired Man")

Oliver Goldsmith

"And still they gazed, and still the wonder grew
That one small head could carry all he knew."
("The Deserted Village")

Thomas Gray

"Far from the madding crowd's ignoble strife"
("Elegy Written in a Country Churchyard")

Oliver Wendell Holmes

"Ay, tear her tattered ensign down!"
("Old Ironsides")

Ben Jonson

"Drink to me only with thine eyes."
("To Celia")

John Keats

"Heard melodies are sweet, but those unheard
Are sweeter."
("Ode on a Grecian Urn")

"Beauty is truth, truth beauty."
("Ode on a Grecian Urn")

"When I have fears that I may cease to be"
(from the sonnet of the same name)

"Much have I traveled in the realms of gold."
("On First Looking Into Chapman's
Homer")

Francis Scott Key

"The war's desolation"
("The Star-Spangled Banner")

"Then conquer we must, when our cause it is just."
("The Star-Spangled Banner")

Rudyard Kipling

"Lest we forget!"
(refrain from "Recessional")

Vachel Lindsay

"Beat an empty barrel with the handle of a broom."
("The Congo")

Henry Wadsworth Longfellow

"Over the wide and rushing rivers
In his arms he bore the maiden."
("Song of Hiawatha")

"A boy's will is the wind's will."
("My Lost Youth")

"I heard the trailing garments of the Night
Sweep through her marble halls."
("Hymn to Night")

James Russell Lowell

"And what is so rare as a day in June?
Then, if ever, come perfect days."
("The Vision of Sir Launfal")

Edwin Markham

"Bowed by the weight of centuries"
("The Man With the Hoe")

Edgar Lee Masters

"Degenerate sons and daughters,
Life is too strong for you."
("Lucinda Matlock")

John McCrea

"We shall not sleep, though poppies grow"
("In Flanders Fields")

Edna St. Vincent Millay

"The world stands out on either side
No wider than the heart is wide."
("Renascence")

John Milton

"When I consider how my light is spent"
("On His Blindness")

"They also serve who only stand and wait."
("On His Blindness")

Alfred Noyes

"Come down to Kew in lilac time."
> (refrain from "The Barrel-Organ")

"The moon was a ghostly galleon."
> ("The Highwayman")

Edgar Allan Poe

"I was a child and she was a child,
In this kingdom by the sea."
> ("Annabel Lee")

"Hear the mellow wedding bells, golden bells."
> ("The Bells")

Edwin Arlington Robinson

"And he glittered when he walked."
> ("Richard Cory")

Carl Sandburg

"Come and show me another city with head lifted and singing so proud to be alive."
> ("Chicago")

William Shakespeare

"But if the while I think on thee, dear friend,
All losses are restored and sorrows end."
> ("When to the Sessions of Sweet Silent Thought")

Percy Bysshe Shelley

"Music, when soft voices die,
Vibrates in the memory."
> ("To—: Music, When Soft Voices Die")

"Hail to thee, blithe spirit!
Bird thou never wert."
> ("To a Skylark")

"Destroyer and preserver; hear, oh hear!"
> ("Ode to the West Wind")

Robert Southey

"It was a famous victory."
> (refrain from "The Battle of Blenheim")

Samuel F. Smith

"From every mountain-side
Let freedom ring."

("America")

Alfred, Lord Tennyson

"Theirs not to reason why."

("The Charge of the Light Brigade")

"Follow Christ, the King.
Live pure, speak true, right wrong, follow the King."

("Gareth and Lynette")

Louis Untermeyer

"Fling us a handful of stars."

("Caliban in the Coal Mines")

William Wordsworth

"Our birth is but a sleep and a forgetting."

("Ode on the Intimations of Immortality")

"Little we see in Nature that is ours."

("The World Is Too Much With Us")

Quotations From Essays

Francis Bacon

"Some books are to be chewed and digested."

("Of Studies")

"Reading maketh a full man."

("Of Studies")

"Read not to contradict and confute; nor to believe and take for granted; nor to find talk and discourse; but to weigh and consider."

("Of Studies")

Winston Churchill

"Never . . . was so much owed by so many to so few."

(Speech on the Battle of Britain)

Thomas Jefferson

"When in the course of human events"

("The Declaration of Independence")

"We hold these truths to be self-evident."

("The Declaration of Independence")

Abraham Lincoln

"Government of the people, by the people and for the people"
("The Gettysburg Address")

"With malice toward none, with charity for all."
("Second Inaugural Address")

Christopher Morley

"There are degrees of sadness in the closing of doors."
("On Doors")

Thomas Paine

"These are the times that try men's souls."
("The American Crisis")

Quotations From Short Stories

Stephen Vincent Benét

"But even the damned may salute the eloquence of Mr. Webster."
(spoken by Walter Butler in "The Devil
and Daniel Webster")

Edward Everett Hale

"He loved his country as no man loved her; but no man deserved less at her hands."
(said of Philip Nolan in
"The Man Without a Country")

Edgar Allan Poe

"During the whole of a dull, dark and soundless day in the autumn of the year, when the clouds hung oppressively low in the heavens"
("The Fall of the House of Usher")

Quotations From the Bible

Old Testament

"He leadeth me beside the still waters."
(Twenty-third Psalm)

"The valley of the shadow of death"
(Twenty-third Psalm)

"Thy people shall be my people, and thy God my God."
(Book of Ruth)

New Testament

"Blessed are the poor in spirit, for theirs is the kingdom of heaven."
(Sermon on the Mount)

RECOGNIZING AN AUTHOR'S SPECIALTY

These writers and their specialties have been the subject of questions in past examinations:

Louis Agassiz—a great naturalist
William Beebe—famous naturalist and well-known writer
Homer Bigart—foreign correspondent
Elizabeth Barrett Browning—author of famous sonnet sequence
Bruce Catton—books about the Civil War
Betty Cavanna—books about high school girls
Winston Churchill—well-known statesman, author, and painter
Esther Forbes—specialist on Paul Revere
Frank Graham—books about sports
Robert Heinlein—science-fiction writer
Gilbert Highet—writer of literary criticism
Paul de Kruif—written accounts of the work of scientists
Sinclair Lewis—novels about middle-class Americans
John Lomax—American folklore
Anne O'Hare McCormick—foreign correspondent
Ruth McKenney—contemporary humorist
Tom Meany—books about sports
Ogden Nash—contemporary humorist, unusual rhymes
Howard Pyle—reteller of Robin Hood stories
Lew Sarett—a poet of the American Indian
Dorothy Sayers—writer of mystery stories
Robert E. Sherwood—American playwright
Edwin Way Teale—books about nature
James Thurber—humorous essays about his family
John R. Tunis—stories about sports
H. G. Wells—several works of science fiction
E. B. White—American essayist
Emlyn Williams—oral rendition of Dickens

RECOGNIZING MYTHOLOGICAL ALLUSIONS

The following mythological references have been the subject of previous Regents questions:

Achilles—Greek hero vulnerable only in his heel
The Argonauts—sailors who sought the golden fleece
Athene—Athens was named after her because she gave it the olive tree.
Atlas—Greek god sentenced to bear the weight of the heavens
Camelot—legendary court of King Arthur
Cupid—loved Psyche

Excalibur—King Arthur's sword

Guinevere—King Arthur's queen. She spent her last years in a convent.

Hercules—Greek hero of superhuman strength

Mercury—messenger of the gods, equipped with winged sandals

Odysseus—Greek hero who misled Polyphemus by calling himself Noman

Pegasus—winged horse of the Muses

Prometheus—bringer of fire to man

Scylla and Charybdis—treacherous rocks (personified as sea monsters) in the Straits of Messina. To be "between Scylla and Charybdis" means to be in a predicament.

Sherwood Forest—home of Robin Hood, Friar Tuck, and Little John

Valhalla—Norse paradise for brave warriors killed in battle

The Valkyries—twelve maidens of Scandinavian legend who conducted slain heroes to Valhalla

RECOGNIZING LITERARY ASSOCIATIONS

American Nobel Prize Winners: Sinclair Lewis, Eugene O'Neill, Pearl S. Buck, William Faulkner, Ernest Hemingway, John Steinbeck

British Nobel Prize Winners: Rudyard Kipling, William Butler Yeats (Irish), George Bernard Shaw (Irish), John Galsworthy

Present poet-laureate of England—John Masefield

The river Avon—William Shakespeare

The river Afton—Robert Burns

The river Chattahoochee—Sidney Lanier

Elia—pen name of Charles Lamb

Lambarene—Albert Schweitzer

The "blind poet"—Homer or John Milton

"Marlowe's mighty line"—blank verse

Tabard Inn—Geoffrey Chaucer (*Canterbury Tales*)

PRINCIPAL POETIC DEVICES

To achieve its special effects, poetry makes use of a number of special devices. Let us review some of the principal ones:

1. **Rhythm** is the regular repetition of stressed and unstressed syllables.

> "But if the while I think on thee, dear friend,
> All losses are restored and sorrows end."
> *—William Shakespeare*

Notice that the pattern of unstressed syllable followed by stressed syllable is maintained regularly throughout these two lines. This kind of rhythm (unstressed syllable followed by stressed syllable) is the most frequently encountered rhythm in English and American poetry. It is called *iambic*. An unstressed syllable followed by a stressed syllable constitutes an *iamb*.

2. **Rhyme** is the repetition of similar sounds at the ends of lines of poetry. Example: "friend" and "end" in the lines just quoted.

3. **Alliteration** is the repetition of initial consonant sounds. Example: the repetition of the hard "c" ("k") in this line by Alfred Noyes:

"Over the *c*obbles he *c*lattered and *c*lashed in the dark inn yard."

4. **Onomatopoeia** is the use of words whose sound suggests their meaning.

"The *m*oan of doves in immemorial elms
And the *m*urmuring of innumerable bees."
—*Alfred, Lord Tennyson*

These lines, when read aloud, sound like the humming of bees because of the repetition of the "m" sound ("*m*oan," "im*m*emorial," "elms," "*m*urmuring," "innu*m*erable") and the "z" sound ("dove*s*," "elm*s*," "bee*s*").

5. **Simile** is a comparison that makes use of "like" or "as."

"How like a winter hath my absence been
From thee."
—*William Shakespeare*

6. **Metaphor** is a more condensed comparison, without "like" or "as."

"The winds that will be howling at all hours."
—*William Wordsworth*

The poet likens the sound of the winds to the cries of wolves or dogs.

7. **Personification** is the giving of human characteristics to objects, ideas, animals, or plants.

"The mountain sat upon the plain
In his eternal chair."
—*Emily Dickinson*

PRINCIPAL VERSE FORMS

1. **Free verse** consists of unrhymed lines and has no definite rhythm. Example:

"As toilsome I wandered Virginia's woods,
    To the music of rustling leaves kicked by my feet (for 'twas autumn)
I marked at the foot of a tree the grave of a soldier."
        —Walt Whitman

2. **Blank verse** consists of unrhymed lines of iambic pentameter. (A line of iambic pentameter is made up of five iambs.)

"O pardon me, thou bleeding piece of earth,
That I am meek and gentle with these butchers!
Thou art the ruins of the noblest man
That ever lived in the tide of times."
                (from *Julius Caesar*
                        by William Shakespeare)

3. The **ballad stanza** consists of four lines, of which only the second and fourth rhyme. The first and third lines consist of four iambs each. The second and fourth lines have three iambs each.

"I fear thee, ancient Mariner!
I fear thy skinny hand!
And thou art long, and lank, and brown
As is the ribbed sea sand."
        —Samuel Taylor Coleridge

4. The **sonnet** consists of fourteen lines of iambic pentameter (lines having five iambs each). There are two main sonnet types:

a. The *Shakespearean sonnet* has the following rhyme scheme: abab, cdcd, efef, gg.

"When in disgrace with fortune and men's eyes,
I all alone beweep my outcast state,
And trouble deaf heaven with my bootless cries,
And look upon myself, and curse my fate,
Wishing me like to one more rich in hope,
Featured like him, like him with friends possessed,
Desiring this man's art, and that man's scope,
With what I most enjoy contented least;

Yet in these thoughts myself almost despising,
Haply I think on thee—and then my state
(Like to the lark at break of day arising
From sullen earth) sings hymns at heaven's gate;
For thy sweet love remembered such wealth brings
That then I scorn to change my state with kings."
                                        —*William Shakespeare*

b. The *Italian sonnet* has the following rhyme scheme for the first eight lines: abba, abba. The last six lines may follow any of a variety of rhyme schemes except that the last two lines may not rhyme.

"Earth has not anything to show more fair:
Dull would he be of soul who could pass by
A sight so touching in its majesty:
This City now doth like a garment wear
The beauty of the morning: silent, bare,
Ships, towers, domes, theatres and temples lie
Open unto the fields, and to the sky—
All bright and glittering in the smokeless air.
Never did sun more beautifully steep
In his first splendor valley, rock, or hill;
Ne'er saw I, never felt, a calm so deep!
The river glideth at his own sweet will:
Dear God! the very houses seem asleep;
And all that mighty heart is lying still!"
                                        —*William Wordsworth*

FORMER REGENTS QUESTIONS

Each of the statements below involves a literary reference. Choose 20 only and write the *number* of the word or phrase that correctly completes the statement.   [20]

1

1. Johnny Tremain was forced to give up his apprenticeship because of   (1) his master's death   (2) an accident   (3) his master's financial ruin   (4) the jealousy of the other apprentices
2. The subject of Rachel L. Carson's best seller is   (1) astronomy   (2) the sea   (3) mountain climbing   (4) birds
3. Clarence Day's father finally agrees to   (1) buy an airplane   (2) buy a new car   (3) run for mayor   (4) be baptized
4. At the end of *My Cousin Rachel,* the hero   (1) marries Rachel   (2) indirectly causes her death   (3) is convinced of her true nature   (4) leaves her to go to Italy

5. Indiana is the setting for many of the novels of   (1) J. P. Marquand (2) James Street   (3) Booth Tarkington   (4) Kenneth Roberts

6. The Pulitzer Prizes are named after   (1) an actor   (2) a publisher (3) a historian   (4) a poet laureate

7. A teacher is the main character of   (1) *Goodbye, Mr. Chips*   (2) *The Uninvited*   (3) *Far Away and Long Ago*   (4) *As the Earth Turns*

8. Montresor was able to get Fortunato into the catacombs by   (1) having him kidnapped   (2) appealing to his vanity   (3) offering him money (4) threatening him

9. In *The Silver Box,* Jones declared that he should be acquitted because   (1) he was no more guilty than young Barthwick   (2) his children were homeless   (3) his wife was really guilty   (4) he could not afford a lawyer

10. Wouter Van Twiller earned a reputation for wisdom by   (1) praising scholars   (2) studying at night   (3) speaking little   (4) consulting books

11. *The Kid from Tompkinsville* describes the experiences of   (1) a tennis champion   (2) a baseball player   (3) a football star   (4) the owner of a racing car

12. *Annapurna* tells of an expedition in the   (1) Andes   (2) Alps   (3) Himalayas   (4) Rockies

13. Sinclair Lewis's novels are often concerned with   (1) immigrants   (2) inventors   (3) teen-agers   (4) middle-class Americans

14. "The Cotter's Saturday Night" is a poem about a   (1) midnight escapade (2) proud New England fisherman   (3) servant's ball   (4) poor but honest family

15. A tragedy occurs at the end of   (1) "Mia Carlotta"   (2) "Richard Cory"   (3) "King Robert of Sicily"   (4) "Renascence"

16. In *Silas Marner,* Dunstan Cass's eventual fate is to   (1) fall into a stone pit   (2) die as the result of a fall from his horse   (3) be sent away by his father   (4) die in a duel with Godfrey Cass

17. In "Fog," Carl Sandburg compares the fog to   (1) a wolf   (2) a bear (3) a cat   (4) an owl

18. *Young Hickory* is a biography of   (1) Ulysses S. Grant   (2) Andrew Johnson   (3) Thomas Jefferson   (4) Andrew Jackson

19. Rebecca's defender against the charge of witchcraft was   (1) Ivanhoe (2) the Black Knight   (3) Bois Guilbert   (4) Athelstane

20. The deacon's "masterpiece" was a   (1) carriage   (2) patriotic speech (3) flying machine   (4) portrait of his aunt

21. Huck Finn feared that his share of the fortune he and Tom had found would be claimed by   (1) his father   (2) the Widow Douglas   (3) its rightful owners   (4) the Duke and the King

22. At one point in *Gone With the Wind,* Scarlett O'Hara vowed that she would (1) report Rhett for smuggling   (2) never be hungry again   (3) never trust Rhett again   (4) never speak to a Yankee

23. Odysseus misled Polyphemus by   (1) calling himself Noman   (2) reversing his shield   (3) pretending to be insane   (4) having his men walk backward

24. *Yankee from Olympus* is a biography of   (1) Theodore Roosevelt   (2) James Fenimore Cooper   (3) Douglas MacArthur   (4) Justice Holmes

25. In *Wuthering Heights,* Heathcliff married Isabella because   (1) he wanted to spite Cathy   (2) he felt sorry for her   (3) she was an heiress (4) he felt remorse for his treatment of Cathy

26. Leiningen defeated the ants by (1) destroying their nests (2) poisoning their food (3) flooding the plantation (4) importing starlings
27. *This I Believe* was edited by (1) Albert Schweitzer (2) Fulton J. Sheen (3) Edward R. Murrow (4) Harry Emerson Fosdick
28. A grave robber works in (1) *Adam Bede* (2) *A Tale of Two Cities* (3) *Ramona* (4) *The Bridge of San Luis Rey*
29. Phil Fuller's two enthusiasms are baseball and (1) girls (2) horses (3) books (4) cows
30. "The play's the thing" is quoted from (1) *Macbeth* (2) *Joan of Lorraine* (3) *Hamlet* (4) *Henry V*
31. The "ile" in O'Neill's play is (1) whale oil (2) a gusher in Texas (3) an oil made from cotton seed (4) gasoline
32. Stanhope did not wish to have Raleigh in his company because Raleigh (1) was an inexperienced officer (2) was the nephew of a general (3) might try to assume command (4) might write home about Stanhope's demoralization
33. *John Brown's Body* was written by (1) Carl Sandburg (2) Stephen Vincent Benét (3) Walt Whitman (4) Archibald MacLeish
34. At the explosion of the first atomic bomb, William L. Laurence felt as if he were viewing (1) doomsday (2) the moment of creation (3) the gates of hell (4) a magician's performance
35. The chief character in "Plain Language from Truthful James" is (1) a card "shark" (2) a steamboat engineer (3) an infantryman (4) a small boy
36. Acres and O'Trigger are characters created by (1) Oliver Goldsmith (2) Richard B. Sheridan (3) George Bernard Shaw (4) Eugene O'Neill
37. In *So Big*, Selina was disappointed in Dirk because he (1) did not know the value of money (2) forsook architecture for bond selling (3) refused to go to college (4) refused to carry on her business
38. Jimmy Valentine is the central character in (1) "The Whirligig of Life" (2) "The Last Leaf" (3) "A Retrieved Reformation" (4) "The Ransom of Red Chief"
39. A motion that can not be debated is one to (1) limit debate (2) table a motion (3) adjourn (4) amend a motion
40. No second is required to (1) lay a motion on the table (2) adjourn (3) nominate (4) amend a motion

2

1. Hercules is associated with (1) swiftness (2) strength (3) wisdom (4) music
2. The tragedy in *Romeo and Juliet* results from (1) a case of mistaken identity (2) Juliet's distrust of her maid (3) the delay of a message (4) Romeo's jealousy of Paris
3. The bell of Atri was made famous for all time by a (1) famous knight (2) saintly king (3) starving horse (4) pious monk
4. The Admirable Crichton was (1) cowardly (2) resourceful (3) disloyal (4) careless
5. In "The Listeners" the Traveler came back to the house (1) on horseback (2) on foot (3) by boat (4) by stagecoach

6. The person referred to by "Good night, sweet prince" is (1) Hamlet (2) Henry V (3) Tom Canty (4) Bonnie Prince Charlie

7. Ogden Nash is noted for his (1) brief epitaphs (2) rondels (3) eulogies (4) unusual rhymes

8. Lucie Manette first met Charles Darnay (1) at his trial (2) at an inn at Dover (3) on board a packet-ship (4) at Defarge's wineshop

9. The Jo in *Little Women* was in real life (1) Harriet Beecher Stowe (2) Mary Lincoln (3) Louisa May Alcott (4) Julia Ward Howe

10. "I'd simply adore to go on waltzing" concludes a story by (1) Dorothy Parker (2) Ring Lardner (3) Maureen Daly (4) Ruth McKenney

11. "The valiant never taste of death but once" was spoken by (1) Dickens' Sydney Carton (2) Fitch's Nathan Hale (3) Shakespeare's Julius Caesar (4) Drinkwater's Abraham Lincoln

12. The theme of *The Bent Twig* is the (1) problems of the physically handicapped (2) value of good home training (3) evils of financial insecurity (4) dangers of wasting natural resources

13. Cooper's *Leatherstocking Tales* are (1) stories reported to have been written by a New York Dutchman (2) pioneer tales of life with Daniel Boone (3) tales of Indians and white men in the early days of America (4) stories of Western ranch life

14. The setting of "Windwagon Smith" is (1) an army camp (2) a prairie town (3) a jungle outpost (4) a naval base

15. P. T. Barnum used an elephant to (1) carry Tom Thumb across the Alps (2) advertise the first moving pictures (3) plow a field in Connecticut (4) travel from Boston to New York

16. *The Sojourner* is by the author of (1) *The Black Rose* (2) *The Yearling* (3) *The Citadel* (4) *The Black Stallion*

17. In *The Caine Mutiny* the mutiny takes place in the (1) South Seas (2) Arctic (3) North Atlantic (4) Gulf of Mexico

18. An author of a famous sonnet sequence is (1) Elizabeth Barrett Browning (2) Amy Lowell (3) John Masefield (4) Robert Frost

19. *Abe Lincoln in Illinois* was written by (1) Carl Sandburg (2) John Drinkwater (3) Robert Sherwood (4) Honoré Morrow

20. The heroine of *My Ántonia* was born in (1) Italy (2) Spain (3) Russia (4) Bohemia

21. A book concerned with an attempt to prove a theory of migration is (1) *West with the Night* (2) *Wind, Sand, and Stars* (3) *Kon-Tiki* (4) *The Sea Around Us*

22. The magic ring described by Kenneth Grahame is a (1) wedding ring (2) good-luck charm (3) circus ring (4) child's game

23. The vessel *not* associated with the correct book is (1) the *Pequod—Moby Dick* (2) the *Bounty—Pitcairn's Island* (3) the *Hispaniola—Two Years Before the Mast* (4) the *We're Here—Captains Courageous*

24. Lady Macbeth assisted her husband in the killing of Duncan by (1) "discovering" the crime so as to divert suspicion from Macbeth (2) returning the daggers to the scene of the crime (3) inviting Duncan to come to Macbeth's castle (4) casting suspicion upon Macduff

25. In *The Turmoil*, when Sheridan of the Sheridan Trust Company gets into trouble, he is helped by (1) his wife (2) Mary Vertrees (3) Bibbs (4) Jim

26. Rivalry between doctors is important in   (1) *The Doctor's Dilemma*
    (2) *Treasure Island*   (3) *Arrowsmith*   (4) *The Thirty-nine Steps*
27. *Snips and Snails* relates the experiences of a   (1) scientist   (2) dress
    designer   (3) teacher   (4) radio announcer
28. The words "Whoever has made a voyage up the Hudson" begin a story about
    (1) Ichabod Crane   (2) a black fisherman   (3) a ghostly bridegroom
    (4) Rip Van Winkle
29. The recognition of courage is the theme of   (1) "Requiem"   (2) "High-
    land Mary"   (3) "The Ballad of East and West"   (4) "Richard Cory"
30. *Room for One More* concerns   (1) a group of men who are cast adrift in
    the Pacific   (2) a family which adopts two children   (3) a high school
    club   (4) a group of scientists who make a voyage into space
31. "Everybody knows that *something* is eternal" is said by a character in   (1)
    Our Town   (2) *Othello*   (3) *Dear Brutus*   (4) *The Emperor Jones*
32. The "antiseptic baby" and the "prophylactic pup" were disturbed in their
    play by   (1) the baby's nurse   (2) the doctor   (3) a larger dog
    (4) a rabbit
33. Priscilla refused to marry Miles Standish because   (1) she was anxious to
    return to England   (2) Standish had not proposed in person   (3) she
    could not leave her father   (4) she loved another
34. Before moving to Raveloe, Silas had lived in   (1) London   (2) Lan-
    tern Yard   (3) Casterbridge   (4) Canterbury
35. A man is saved by an eclipse in   (1) *Julius Caesar*   (2) *A Connecticut
    Yankee in King Arthur's Court*   (3) *Around the World in Eighty Days*
    (4) *Scaramouche*
36. A person who sighed for the days of old was   (1) Bewick Finzer   (2)
    Giuseppe, the barber   (3) Miniver Cheevy   (4) Jim Bludso
37. A play that might be considered a fantasy is   (1) *Peter Pan*   (2) *Alice
    Sit-by-the-Fire*   (3) *Quality Street*   (4) *What Every Woman Knows*
38. The chief character in *Seventeen* is   (1) Sam   (2) Penrod   (3) Wil-
    lie Baxter   (4) Henry Aldrich
39. "Pogo" is the creation of   (1) Walt Kelly   (2) George Price   (3)
    L. J. Clark   (4) Ted Key
40. The names Goldman and Paul LaValle are associated with radio   (1) quiz
    programs   (2) band music   (3) forums   (4) documentaries

3

1. "Sleep no more" is associated with   (1) *Hamlet*   (2) *Coriolanus*   (3)
   Macbeth   (4) *Julius Caesar*
2. Gallegher won the promotion he sought through being the first to   (1)
   arrive at a fire   (2) interview the President   (3) identify a criminal
   (4) travel inside the Iron Curtain
3. *The Great Escape* by Brickhill is a record of the mass escape of   (1) prisoners of war   (2) hardened criminals   (3) political refugees   (4)
   the British at Dunkirk
4. A person who had an understanding parent was   (1) Oliver Twist   (2)
   Dunstan Cass   (3) Jody Baxter   (4) Johnny Tremain
5. " 'Dead,' was all he answered" is the last line of (1) "The Dead" by Rupert
   Brooke   (2) "The Death of the Hired Man" by Robert Frost   (3)
   "Cool Tombs" by Carl Sandburg   (4) "Tears" by Lizette W. Reese

6. The author of *Lady with a Spear* searches for (1) rare fish (2) polar bears (3) rare African animals (4) American game of all kinds
7. Sherlock Holmes owed his success primarily to (1) his wide knowledge (2) tips from informants (3) assistance from Dr. Watson (4) the simplicity of the crimes
8. *The White Continent* is a story of (1) Asia (2) the Alps (3) Antarctica (4) the Arctic regions
9. The term "Jolly Roger" is usually associated with (1) piracy (2) whaling (3) lumbering (4) radio broadcasting
10. Homer Macauley surprised his history class by his extemporaneous speech on (1) mice (2) noses (3) fountain pens (4) Fort Ticonderoga
11. At the end of *Treasure Island* the fate of Long John Silver is (1) murder by Black Dog (2) hanging from the yardarm (3) death in a duel with Squire Trelawney (4) escape through the efforts of Ben Gunn
12. A crucial scene in *The Good Earth* occurs when O-Lan pleads with her husband not to (1) go south (2) leave her (3) sell the land (4) punish his sons
13. A poet of the American Indian is (1) Lew Sarett (2) Karl Shapiro (3) John Greenleaf Whittier (4) James Whitcomb Riley
14. In "Gulliver the Great" a central figure overcame (1) fear (2) greed (3) ambition (4) jealousy
15. *The Bounty Trilogy* tells the story of (1) the crew of an English ship (2) a ransom for a king (3) slave trade (4) whaling in the Atlantic
16. "Don't Die on Third" first appeared as a (1) poem (2) short story (3) biographical sketch (4) newspaper editorial
17. *Our Animal Neighbors* is a book about animals (1) in Brazil (2) in Australia (3) on a Berkshire farm (4) on an American game preserve
18. Which was on the side of the Loyalists during the American Revolution? (1) Harvey Birch (2) Oliver Wiswell (3) Richard Carvel (4) Gilbert Martin
19. *Prince of Players* is the biography of (1) Edwin Booth (2) John Gielgud (3) Maurice Evans (4) Laurence Olivier
20. "'Tis common proof that lowliness is young ambition's ladder" is quoted from (1) *Othello* (2) *Macbeth* (3) *King Lear* (4) *Julius Caesar*
21. Eugene Field's "Little Boy Blue" concerns (1) an orphan (2) a painting (3) a child's prayer (4) the death of a child
22. Frank Graham and Tom Meany write books about (1) sports (2) aviation (3) mountain climbing (4) radio broadcasting
23. Most of Poe's short stories involve (1) many characters (2) much unnecessary description (3) a character who tells the story (4) at least two problems confronting the main character
24. Wells' Martian invaders succumbed to the earth's (1) bacteria (2) guided missiles (3) atomic radiation (4) low temperatures
25. "When I have fears that I may cease to be" begins a poem by (1) Milton (2) Byron (3) Tennyson (4) Keats
26. Chanteys were sung by (1) voodoos (2) sailors (3) revival groups (4) railroad workers
27. France at the time of the French Revolution is the background of (1) *Quentin Durward* (2) *War and Peace* (3) *Les Misérables* (4) *The Scarlet Pimpernel*

28. Jean Valjean is   (1) a banker   (2) a guardsman   (3) an ex-convict   (4) a hunchback
29. Captain Nemo appears in   (1) *Ile*   (2) *Moby Dick*   (3) *Two Years Before the Mast*   (4) *Twenty Thousand Leagues Under the Sea*
30. Mary Hallam's physical handicap prevented her having a career as a   (1) painter   (2) ballet dancer   (3) fashion designer   (4) concert pianist
31. "Dead thoughts . . . . like withered leaves" is an example of   (1) metaphor   (2) simile   (3) personification   (4) onomatopoeia
32. The eventual fate of Jane Eyre was   (1) widowhood   (2) death in a plague   (3) marriage to a blind man   (4) marriage to a wealthy scientist
33. Clarence Day's father was convinced that   (1) he knew best   (2) servants were unnecessary   (3) his children usually misbehaved   (4) his wife was a careful manager of household finances
34. Galahad saw the Holy Grail because of all the knights he was the   (1) wisest   (2) purest   (3) bravest   (4) humblest
35. *The Great Iron Ship* is the story of   (1) a submarine   (2) an interspatial plane   (3) a trans-Atlantic steamer   (4) the largest "show boat" on the Mississippi
36. Mrs. Malaprop is remembered for her   (1) dishonesty   (2) mis-use of words   (3) cruelty to servants   (4) poor taste
37. The person who turned men into loathsome creatures was   (1) Circe   (2) Calpurnia   (3) Helen of Troy   (4) Old Mother Hubbard
38. *The Man Who Never Was* describes the ingenious plans of   (1) an F.B.I. agent   (2) a Canadian airman   (3) a Los Angeles police officer   (4) a British Intelligence officer
39. The good news brought from Ghent to Aix was taken by   (1) carrier pigeon   (2) canoe   (3) horseback   (4) runners
40. Newspapers, radio and television are alike in that *all*   (1) receive reports from news-service agencies   (2) are censored by the United States Censor   (3) are regulated by the FCC   (4) contain no copyrighted material

4

1. "We hold these truths to be self-evident" is quoted from   (1) the Constitution   (2) the Gettysburg Address   (3) Washington's Farewell Address   (4) the Declaration of Independence
2. The bridge of San Luis Rey in Wilder's novel is located in   (1) Spain   (2) Mexico   (3) Peru   (4) California
3. In Lindsay's poem, Lincoln "walks at midnight" because   (1) he fears for his life   (2) he pities the wounded   (3) the South despises him   (4) the nation is again at war
4. The movie *Lili* concerns the life of a   (1) carnival troupe   (2) team of acrobats   (3) stranger in New York   (4) girl in a Paris perfume shop
5. *Meet the Press* is a television and radio presentation in which   (1) a leader in public life is interviewed   (2) the workings of a newspaper are explained   (3) a reporter solves crimes   (4) two experts formally debate a controversial issue
6. The Shimerda family in *My Ántonia* lived in   (1) an old fort   (2) a houseboat   (3) a log cabin   (4) a sod dugout

7. John Lomax was chiefly noted as a   (1) poet   (2) news reporter   (3) opera singer   (4) folklorist
8. The setting of *The Teahouse of the August Moon* is   (1) Japan   (2) Korea   (3) Okinawa   (4) Formosa
9. *Fire in the Ashes* concerns the problems of   (1) college life   (2) modern Europe   (3) juvenile delinquency   (4) South America's economy
10. "The Postmistress of Laurel Run" is a story of   (1) the West   (2) the South   (3) the Southeast   (4) the Far North
11. Bulldog Drummond is a   (1) jewel thief   (2) detective   (3) Secret Service agent   (4) sea captain
12. Ingo in Morley's essay is a   (1) monkey   (2) lake   (3) boy   (4) game
13. The line "The fault, dear Brutus, is not in our stars," was spoken by   (1) Portia   (2) Caesar   (3) Cassius   (4) Marc Antony
14. In *The Caine Mutiny* the person chiefly responsible for the downfall of Captain Queeg was   (1) Keefer   (2) Maryk   (3) Keith   (4) the admiral
15. It is probable that Dr. Manette was released from his 18-year stay in the Bastille through the influence of   (1) Lucie Manette   (2) the Marquis   (3) the Jacquerie   (4) Charles Darnay
16. In "The Ransom of Red Chief" the criminals were surprised at   (1) the vigilance of the police   (2) the ease with which they managed Red Chief   (3) the anger of the townspeople   (4) the unpredictable behavior of Red Chief
17. The narrator in "The Road to Mandalay" is   (1) a British Tommy   (2) a Buddhist priest   (3) a homesick Indian   (4) an American jurist
18. Brookfield School is associated with   (1) *Tom Brown's School Days*   (2) *Jane Eyre*   (3) *David Copperfield*   (4) *Goodbye, Mr. Chips*
19. The line "Alas, poor Yorick! I knew him, Horatio!" was spoken by   (1) Hamlet   (2) Othello   (3) Henry V   (4) King Lear
20. "Incident of the French Camp" describes an episode of the days of   (1) Roland   (2) Napoleon   (3) Joan of Arc   (4) Charlemagne
21. In "My Financial Career" the narrator   (1) becomes a banker   (2) inherits a large fortune   (3) gains control of millions   (4) loses his poise at the bank
22. *The Living Desert* is a movie produced by   (1) John Ford   (2) Walt Disney   (3) Cecil B. De Mille   (4) Darryl F. Zanuck
23. Injun Joe was a grave robber in   (1) *Roughing It*   (2) *A Tale of Two Cities*   (3) *The Adventures of Tom Sawyer*   (4) *Boots and Saddles*
24. Sabra Cravat earned her living   (1) modeling   (2) editing a newspaper   (3) doing missionary work   (4) managing a store
25. In the quotation "I was a child and *she* was a child In this kingdom by the sea," *she* refers to   (1) Elaine   (2) Celia   (3) Lucy Gray   (4) Annabel Lee
26. Which was *not* a warning of the witches to Macbeth?   (1) to beware of Banquo   (2) to beware of Macduff   (3) not to fear man born of woman   (4) not to fear until Birnam Wood comes to Dunsinane
27. Pip's great expectations actually arose from the generosity of   (1) a convict   (2) an old lady   (3) a lawyer   (4) a distant relative
28. *Romeo and Juliet* takes place in   (1) Rome   (2) Padua   (3) Verona   (4) Venice

29. Martin Arrowsmith first met Leora   (1) in a hospital   (2) at Madeline's house   (3) on the college campus   (4) at a fraternity dance
30. *The Doctors Jacobi* describes the medical career of   (1) two brothers   (2) a father and a son   (3) a husband and a wife   (4) an uncle and a nephew
31. In *The Education of Hyman Kaplan,* the title character has considerable difficulty in   (1) learning English   (2) meeting strangers   (3) entering an eastern university   (4) teaching himself algebra and geometry
32. *The Lady of Arlington* tells the story of the wife of   (1) William Byrd   (2) Andrew Jackson   (3) Jefferson Davis   (4) Robert E. Lee
33. E. B. White has won fame chiefly in the field of   (1) biography   (2) the novel   (3) the drama   (4) the essay
34. Guinevere spent her last years in a   (1) castle   (2) prison   (3) convent   (4) hospital
35. Sherlock Holmes solved most of his cases by using   (1) intuition   (2) deduction   (3) mental telepathy   (4) séances
36. "The furrow followed free" is an example of   (1) simile   (2) synecdoche   (3) onomatopoeia   (4) alliteration
37. Evangeline's childhood home was in   (1) Astolat   (2) Arcady   (3) Avalon   (4) Acadia
38. Robert Heinlein writes chiefly   (1) poetry   (2) travel stories   (3) science fiction   (4) historical novels
39. *How Do I Love Thee* is a biography of   (1) a brother and sister   (2) three sisters   (3) two poets   (4) an engineer and his wife
40. The river Avon is associated with   (1) Robert Burns   (2) Sidney Lanier   (3) William Wordsworth   (4) William Shakespeare

5

1. Moti Guj is   (1) a wolf   (2) a tiger   (3) an elephant   (4) a cobra
2. The most exciting episode of *The Pharmacist's Mate* is   (1) an encounter with an enemy submarine   (2) an emergency operation   (3) a false surrender   (4) a collision with an iceberg
3. *Fourteen Men* is the story of   (1) an Antarctic expedition   (2) an undersea exploration   (3) an African safari   (4) pioneers in chemistry
4. A game which Rip Van Winkle enjoyed was   (1) curling   (2) bowling   (3) cribbage   (4) quoits
5. Decius persuaded Caesar to go to the Capitol by appealing to Caesar's   (1) jealousy   (2) suspicions of his wife   (3) pride   (4) love for Brutus
6. In *The Bridge of San Luis Rey* Brother Juniper shows that   (1) the accident was fate   (2) the accident was caused by sabotage   (3) each character was worthless   (4) the Comtessa was generous to all
7. A leprechaun is an important character in   (1) "The Rising of the Moon"   (2) "O'Halloran's Luck"   (3) "The Monkey's Paw"   (4) "O'Meara, the *Mayflower*—and Mrs. MacLirr"
8. Madame Defarge's purpose in knitting was to   (1) warn the Revolutionists of danger   (2) pass the time away   (3) satisfy her husband's liking for color designs   (4) record the names of those marked for death
9. "This Is Going to Hurt Just a Little Bit" concerns   (1) a hospital operation   (2) a trip to the dentist   (3) a vaccination   (4) a haircut

10. In *The Old Man and the Sea* the old fisherman   (1) loses his life   (2) fails to find a fish   (3) catches a fish quickly   (4) after weeks of fishing makes a catch
11. John Tunis is best known for stories about   (1) the sea   (2) sports   (3) early American history   (4) science
12. Onomatopoeia is   (1) the treatment of a past event as if it were in the present   (2) exaggeration for effect   (3) the use of words in which sound suggests the sense   (4) the repetition of the first sounds of words
13. Captain Ahab was a captain of a   (1) clipper ship   (2) whaling vessel   (3) British man-of-war   (4) pirate ship
14. The days referred to in "Then, if ever, come perfect days" occur in   (1) April   (2) June   (3) August   (4) October
15. Mr. Rochester concealed from Jane Eyre his   (1) sagging fortune   (2) previous marriage   (3) love for Miss Ingram   (4) contempt for her upbringing
16. In "My Last Duchess" the Duke expresses   (1) sorrow for his wife's death   (2) admiration for a painting   (3) a desire for learning   (4) sympathy for the common man
17. After Duncan's murder, Lady Macbeth   (1) plays an increasingly important role in Macbeth's decisions   (2) has little influence on Macbeth   (3) ignores Macbeth   (4) plots against Macbeth
18. Louis Agassiz was a great   (1) naturalist   (2) lawyer   (3) engineer   (4) explorer
19. A tea party is the opening scene of   (1) "Sham"   (2) "The Old Lady Shows Her Medals"   (3) "Trifles"   (4) "Two Crooks and a Lady"
20. Mr. Gilbreth taught his children the Morse Code by   (1) singing them to sleep by it   (2) speaking to them in it   (3) painting it on the ceiling   (4) hiring a telegraph operator
21. Squire Trelawney is an important character in   (1) *Silas Marner*   (2) *The Spy*   (3) *Kidnapped*   (4) *Treasure Island*
22. *Dance to the Piper* describes the career of a   (1) musician   (2) movie star   (3) politician   (4) dancer
23. Elizabeth Bennet married   (1) Mr. Rochester   (2) George Osborne   (3) Mr. Collins   (4) Mr. Darcy
24. Sam McGee supposedly met his death by   (1) hanging   (2) drowning   (3) shooting   (4) freezing
25. The author of *Windows for the Crown Prince* was   (1) the wife of a diplomat   (2) a war correspondent   (3) an architect   (4) a teacher
26. *Man of the Family* is a sequel to   (1) *Little Britches*   (2) *Belles on Their Toes*   (3) *So Dear to My Heart*   (4) *My Friend Flicka*
27. The War of 1812 forms the background of   (1) *Captain Caution*   (2) *Marching On*   (3) *The Citadel*   (4) *Dawn's Early Light*
28. The lovers in "John Anderson, My Jo" are   (1) elderly   (2) misunderstood   (3) unfaithful   (4) impetuous
29. In "The Night the Ghost Got In," the ghost was   (1) seen only by Grandfather   (2) heard running around the dining room table   (3) shot at by the police   (4) found in the attic
30. Dorothy Sayers is known chiefly as a writer of   (1) historical novels   (2) mystery stories   (3) humorous poetry   (4) dramas of controversial issues

31. Agnes Wickfield exercised a strong influence on the life of   (1) Pip (2) Peter Ibbetson   (3) David Copperfield   (4) Renny Whiteoak
32. Frost's "The Runaway" describes a   (1) small boy   (2) hired man (3) colt   (4) puppy
33. By the drawing of lots, Silas Marner was found guilty of   (1) murdering his landlord   (2) slander   (3) robbing the deacon   (4) cheating
34. Penelope was the wife of   (1) Odysseus   (2) Hercules   (3) Prometheus   (4) Oedipus
35. Alice, Allegra and Edith appear in   (1) "The Children's Hour" (2) "Dream Children"   (3) "The Old Familiar Faces"   (4) "The Magic Ring"
36. Which book is *not* fictional?   (1) *The Cruel Sea*   (2) *The Sea Around Us*   (3) *Men Against the Sea*   (4) *The Old Man and the Sea*
37. Which was an Indian water carrier?   (1) Kim   (2) Mowgli (3) Gunga Din   (4) Scheherazade
38. In "An Argument with a Millionaire," the millionaire helped David Grayson (1) celebrate Thanksgiving   (2) grease an axle   (3) buy a farm (4) get in hay
39. Bennett Cerf is best known for his   (1) humor   (2) novels   (3) historical plays   (4) literary criticism
40. "My head is bloody, but unbowed" is from   (1) "The World Is Too Much with Us"   (2) "Thanatopsis"   (3) "Crossing the Bar"   (4) "Invictus"

6

1. In real life Johnny Appleseed was   (1) a Florida cattleman   (2) a Montana rancher   (3) a pioneer   (4) an actor
2. Queen Guinevere was the wife of   (1) King Richard I   (2) King Arthur   (3) King Louis XIV   (4) Charlemagne
3. A song usually associated with the Civil War is   (1) *America the Beautiful*   (2) *The Star-Spangled Banner*   (3) *The Battle Hymn of the Republic*   (4) *God Bless America*
4. A person who committed a crime believing it was for the good of the state appears in   (1) *King Lear*   (2) *King Henry V*   (3) *Macbeth* (4) *Julius Caesar*
5. In "The Road Not Taken," Robert Frost chose the road that was (1) straighter   (2) less traveled   (3) more level   (4) less dangerous
6. The four people in "Dr. Heidegger's Experiment" had the opportunity to (1) relive their lives   (2) take a trip to the moon   (3) possess a fortune   (4) become eternally happy
7. In *Arrowsmith,* the ideal of pure scientific research is personified by (1) Dr. Gottlieb   (2) Cliff Clawson   (3) Almus Pickerbaugh   (4) Gustave Sondelius
8. The heroes of Shakespeare's tragedies have in common   (1) a cynical attitude toward life   (2) a fatal flaw in their characters   (3) a happy home life   (4) an optimistic view of the future
9. *Out of My Life and Thought* is a book about   (1) President Eisenhower (2) Sir Winston Churchill   (3) Albert Schweitzer   (4) Mortimer Adler

10. Gentle fun is poked at procrastination in   (1) "On Doors"   (2) "On Unanswering Letters"   (3) "What Will Power Did For Me"   (4) "I Entertain an Agent Unawares"

11. In *Ivanhoe,* Isaac was torn between love for   (1) King John and King Richard   (2) Rebecca and Ivanhoe   (3) Rebecca and Bois-Guilbert   (4) Rebecca and his gold

12. A reform movement seriously affects the lives of characters in   (1) "Fame's Little Day"   (2) "The Ransom of Red Chief"   (3) "The Outcasts of Poker Flat"   (4) "The Man Who Would Be King"

13. At the end of "When I Was One and Twenty" the poet is more   (1) wise   (2) sociable   (3) optimistic   (4) suspicious

14. *Those Devils in Baggy Pants* concerns a group of   (1) paratroopers   (2) ballplayers   (3) Chinese peasants   (4) Dutch farmers

15. According to Lamb's essay, the custom of roasting meat had its origin in   (1) Brittany   (2) England   (3) Abyssinia   (4) China

16. Miss Pross is a character in   (1) *A Tale of Two Cities*   (2) *Vanity Fair*   (3) *Seventeen*   (4) *David Copperfield*

17. *The Second Tree from the Corner* is a collection of   (1) light poems   (2) short stories   (3) informal essays   (4) biographical sketches

18. Zekle and Huldy are characters in   (1) "The Courtin'"   (2) "Skipper Ireson's Ride"   (3) "The Death of the Hired Man"   (4) "Snow-Bound"

19. Hamlet confided in   (1) Claudius   (2) Polonius   (3) Fortinbras   (4) Horatio

20. In *High Tor,* Van Dorn is most influenced by   (1) his aversion to work   (2) his love for a mountain   (3) his desire for money   (4) the spirits of the Dutch sailors

21. A. J. Cronin's *Beyond This Place* deals with the relationship of   (1) two brothers   (2) brother and sister   (3) mother and daughter   (4) father and son

22. The sonnet beginning "When in disgrace with fortune and men's eyes" pays a tribute to   (1) nature   (2) patriotism   (3) friendship   (4) married love

23. An actress-writer whose father was a famous actor is   (1) Helen Hayes   (2) Cornelia Otis Skinner   (3) Emily Kimbrough   (4) Katharine Cornell

24. *Rogue Male* tells the story of   (1) a pirate's career   (2) a man hunt   (3) a big-game expedition   (4) an unsolved murder

25. A heroine whose romantic ideas were derived from reading sentimental novels is   (1) Elizabeth Bennet   (2) Lydia Languish   (3) Maggie Shand   (4) Kate Hardcastle

26. The Biblical character plagued by a serious disease was   (1) Job   (2) David   (3) Isaiah   (4) Ezekiel

27. In *Moby Dick,* the sole survivor of the wreck was   (1) Ahab   (2) Ishmael   (3) Starbuck   (4) Queequeg

28. The sons of the Wife of Usher's Well   (1) plot a murder   (2) marry heiresses   (3) return as ghosts   (4) rescue a famous knight

29. *Always the Young Strangers* is an autobiography of the author of   (1) "The Man with the Hoe"   (2) "The Fall of the City"   (3) "Birches"   (4) "Chicago"

30. In Lindsay's poem, the bronco could not be broken of   (1) running away
(2) whinnying   (3) dancing   (4) kicking
31. Simon Legree was a   (1) slave dealer in the South   (2) renegade
British officer   (3) servant in *Little Women*   (4) French pirate in the
War of 1812
32. *Bears in the Caviar* relates the author's experiences as a   (1) refugee
(2) diplomat   (3) chef   (4) big-game hunter
33. *Sonnets from the Portuguese* concerns Elizabeth Barrett Browning's   (1)
love for Italy   (2) devotion to her husband   (3) sympathy for children
(4) travels in Portugal
34. *That Reminds Me* is an autobiography of   (1) Bing Crosby   (2) Harold Ickes   (3) Alben Barkley   (4) Bernard Baruch
35. The home of Odysseus was   (1) Troy   (2) Sparta   (3) Crete
(4) Ithaca
36. "Far from the madding crowd's ignoble strife" is quoted from   (1) "Elegy
Written in a Country Churchyard"   (2) "The Deserted Village"   (3)
"Snow-Bound"   (4) "Telling the Bees"
37. *The Vicious Circle* contains many anecdotes about   (1) the author's children   (2) the author's stage career   (3) noted literary figures
(4) the early days of radio
38. Tybalt killed   (1) Mercutio   (2) Romeo   (3) Bernardo   (4)
Friar Lawrence
39. "Come down to Kew in lilac time" is a refrain from   (1) "Patterns"
(2) "The Barrel Organ"   (3) "A Song of Sherwood"   (4) "A Vagabond Song"
40. *Marching On* by James Boyd takes place during the   (1) Colonial Period
(2) American Revolution   (3) Civil War   (4) Reconstruction Period

7

1. In *Giants in the Earth,* the author portrays   (1) a man succumbing to the
forces of nature   (2) a man easily conquering the land   (3) the collapse of a settlement   (4) a massacre by the Indians
2. Jody "grew up" when he realized that   (1) education at school is necessary   (2) books can be important in living   (3) one must face reality
(4) parents are always right
3. Walter Mitty engaged in daydreaming to escape from   (1) a nagging wife
(2) a lazy brother-in-law   (3) his spoiled children   (4) an overbear-
ing employer
4. The central character of *Amahl and the Night Visitors* is a   (1) doctor
(2) soldier   (3) boy   (4) ghost
5. *Love Is Eternal* tells the story of   (1) Elizabeth Barrett Browning
(2) Mary Todd Lincoln   (3) Rachel Jackson   (4) Rose Hawthorne
6. *Karen* is the story of a girl who   (1) goes abroad at an early age
(2) has an incurable disease   (3) becomes a schoolteacher   (4) wins
a Ford fellowship
7. The poet Le Gallienne in "I Meant To Do My Work Today" was distracted by
(1) his financial worries   (2) children's voices   (3) his neighbor's
radio   (4) a bird's song
8. Conscience reveals a murderer in   (1) "The Gold Bug"   (2) "The Tell-

Tale Heart"   (3) "The Cask of Amontillado"   (4) "The Masque of the Red Death"

9. In "The Arsenal at Springfield" the poet expresses   (1) admiration for warriors   (2) gratitude to his guide   (3) his fear of death   (4) a plea for peace

10. *Tiger of the Snows* tells the experiences of   (1) a war correspondent (2) a mountain climber   (3) a pioneer in atomic research   (4) an anti-Communist guerrilla

11. In *Peter Pan*, Mr. Darling later appears in the play as   (1) Smee (2) Captain Hook   (3) a dog   (4) one of Peter's friends

12. A father kills his son in   (1) "The Prisoner of Chillon"   (2) "Enoch Arden"   (3) "The Passing of Arthur"   (4) "Sohrab and Rustum"

13. "The moon is a ghostly galleon" is an example of a   (1) grammatical error   (2) colloquialism   (3) metaphor   (4) simile

14. A musical comedy based on Shaw's *Pygmalion* is   (1) *My Fair Lady* (2) *Carousel* · (3) *Kiss Me, Kate*   (4) *Of Thee I Sing*

15. *Atoms in the Family* was written by the central figure's   (1) brother (2) wife   (3) daughter   (4) pupil

16. *Me and Kit* describes the author's experiences as   (1) a stage director (2) a newspaper editor   (3) an archaeologist   (4) a gentleman-farmer

17. In Pearl Buck's "The Enemy" the central character is torn between his loyalty to his country and his   (1) fondness for Americans   (2) hatred of the general   (3) duty as a physician   (4) love for his wife

18. "I never spoke with God, Nor visited in heaven" was written by   (1) Amy Lowell   (2) Sara Teasdale   (3) Emily Dickinson   (4) Elinor Wylie

19. Ogden Nash and Ruth McKenney are contemporary   (1) humorists (2) novelists   (3) dramatists   (4) newspaper columnists

20. Javert suspected who Father Madeleine really was when he saw him (1) lift a heavy cart   (2) display his candlesticks   (3) visit Fantine in the hospital   (4) appear in court to help a friend

21. At the end of *My Ántonia*, Ántonia   (1) marries Jim   (2) goes to Canada   (3) returns to Bohemia   (4) enjoys a normal homelife

22. *Gift from the Sea* is a collection of   (1) poems   (2) philosophical essays   (3) stories of hidden treasure   (4) stories of deep-sea fishing

23. The evil genius in *The Silver Chalice* is   (1) Delilah   (2) Simon (3) Orestes   (4) Goliath

24. The Shangri-La of fiction was reached by   (1) plane   (2) rocket (3) ship   (4) submarine

25. "A plague on both your houses" is the curse of the dying   (1) Tybalt (2) Romeo   (3) Mercutio   (4) Laertes

26. Sir Richard Grenville is an important figure in   (1) "Lepanto"   (2) "The *Revenge*"   (3) "The Highwayman"   (4) "An Incident of the French Camp"

27. "Thy people shall be my people, and thy God my God" is quoted from the Book of   (1) Psalms   (2) Kings   (3) Genesis   (4) Ruth

28. The poet promises to be true until "a' the seas gang dry" in   (1) "The Cotter's Saturday Night"   (2) "Auld Lang Syne"   (3) "A Red, Red Rose"   (4) "Sweet Afton"

29. In "Mammon and the Archer" Anthony Rockwell proves that   (1) cab-drivers are unreliable   (2) bad manners are inexcusable   (3) crime does not pay   (4) money can accomplish miracles

30. Which character "glittered" when he walked? (1) George Gray (2) Miniver Cheevy (3) Bewick Finzer (4) Richard Cory
31. Which is associated with "The Moonstone"? (1) a curse (2) a hurricane (3) a trip through space (4) a difficult mining operation
32. A person whose ability to foretell evil had been given her by a god was (1) Diana (2) Europa (3) Cassandra (4) Juno
33. Hidden papers are used to develop the plot of (1) "The Lost Silk Hat" (2) "Two Crooks and a Lady" (3) "Trifles" (4) "The Patchwork Quilt"
34. *The Men of Colditz* describes the adventures of (1) jet pilots (2) prisoners of war (3) political refugees (4) Hungarian circus performers
35. Iago plays upon Othello's (1) ambition (2) jealousy (3) cowardice (4) superstition
36. In *Quality Street* the heroine, Phoebe, (1) spurns her lover (2) becomes a seamstress (3) poses as her own niece (4) goes abroad
37. "Our birth is but a sleep and a forgetting" is quoted from (1) "On His Blindness" (2) "When I Have Fears That I May Cease To Be" (3) "Renascence" (4) "Ode on the Intimations of Immortality"
38. Growing up in pleasant surroundings is portrayed in (1) *Jane Eyre* (2) *Oliver Twist* (3) *Cress Delahanty* (4) *Nicholas Nickleby*
39. Mr. Toad is a lighthearted character in (1) *Just So Stories* (2) *The Wind in the Willows* (3) *Through the Looking-Glass* (4) *Uncle Remus, His Songs and His Sayings*
40. *Margaret Ogilvy* is a biography of (1) Barrie's mother (2) Keats' sweetheart (3) a 19th-century actress (4) Stevenson's nurse

8

1. *A Night to Remember* is a recent account of (1) the bombing of Pearl Harbor (2) the sinking of the *Titanic* (3) a visit to Samoa (4) the war in Korea
2. The central figures of many of Betty Cavanna's books are (1) high school athletes (2) high school girls (3) exchange students (4) amateur detectives
3. In "The Country of the Blind," the central character must choose between his eyesight and (1) his life (2) disgrace (3) the power of speech (4) the girl he loves
4. In Galsworthy's "Quality," the Gessler brothers failed in business because they (1) tried to cheat their customers (2) overinvested their money (3) spent too much money on luxuries (4) refused to change their methods
5. "Ay, tear her tattered ensign down!" is a line from (1) "Barbara Frietchie" (2) "O Captain! My Captain!" (3) "Old Ironsides" (4) "Concord Hymn"
6. The signal to Macbeth that preparations for the murder of Duncan were complete was the (1) sending of a messenger (2) ringing of a bell (3) showing of a light (4) crying of a bird
7. "Mending Wall" is a poem which deals with repairing (1) a cellar (2) a fort (3) a feudal castle (4) farm fences
8. A bare stage with chairs in a row representing graves is the setting of the third act in a play by (1) Wilder (2) Shakespeare (3) Williams (4) O'Neill

9. In *The Corn Is Green* Morgan Evans resented the fact that Miss Moffat (1) did not treat him as an individual   (2) forced him to go back to the mines   (3) would not let him take the examination   (4) criticized him to the Squire

10. In *A Bell for Adano,* Major Joppolo shows   (1) an appreciation for music   (2) an unwillingness to accept responsibility   (3) an understanding of others' points of view   (4) cowardice under fire

11. Lambarene is the present home of   (1) Winston Churchill   (2) Albert Schweitzer   (3) Eleanor Roosevelt   (4) John Foster Dulles

12. "From every mountain-side, Let freedom ring" is found in   (1) "America"   (2) "America the Beautiful"   (3) "God Bless America"   (4) "The Star-Spangled Banner"

13. In *The Deerslayer,* Natty Bumppo   (1) captures Peyrol, an old sea bandit   (2) rescues Cora and Alice Munro   (3) fights against the Hurons   (4) kills Uncas

14. In *Good Morning, Miss Dove,* one of Miss Dove's important problems is   (1) caring for her invalid mother   (2) gaining an increase in salary   (3) teaching foreign students   (4) learning how to have fun

15. After Pandora had opened the magic box, all that remained within it was   (1) fear   (2) jealousy   (3) hope   (4) loyalty

16. Much of the story of *So Big* revolves about   (1) the emancipation of women   (2) a conflict between two sets of values   (3) the need for more social workers   (4) a conflict between father and daughter

17. Which best describes Brutus' wife?   (1) thoughtless   (2) greedy   (3) shrewish   (4) understanding

18. In "A Vagabond's Song," the poet sings of the glories of   (1) spring   (2) winter   (3) autumn   (4) summer

19. In "The Deserted Village," the lines "And still they gazed, and still the wonder grew That one small head could carry all he knew" describe a   (1) lawyer   (2) doctor   (3) minister   (4) schoolmaster

20. Ellen Douglas married   (1) Roderick Dhu   (2) James Fitz-James   (3) Allan-Bane   (4) Malcolm Graeme

21. The setting of *The Spoon River Anthology* is   (1) Illinois   (2) Nebraska   (3) California   (4) New York

22. In *Little Women,* Laurie *first* loved   (1) Amy   (2) Beth   (3) Jo   (4) Meg

23. In Amy Lowell's "Patterns," Lord Hartwell   (1) carried Elaine's favor into battle   (2) was killed in battle   (3) ran off with the Laird's daughter   (4) dreamed of fame in war

24. The stories of Robin Hood have been retold by   (1) Charles Dickens   (2) Arthur Conan Doyle   (3) Howard Pyle   (4) Joseph Conrad

25. The chief characters in Ibsen's *A Doll's House* are   (1) American   (2) British   (3) French   (4) Norwegian

26. *We Die Alone* is a story of   (1) a trained saboteur in World War II   (2) undersea exploration   (3) the poor in a large city   (4) the Korean War

27. In Anderson's *Elizabeth the Queen,* Elizabeth let Essex go to his death because she   (1) knew that he no longer loved her   (2) had to follow the advice of her cabinet   (3) had ceased to care for him   (4) feared that he would seize power from her

28. The setting of much of Robert P. Tristram Coffin's poetry is   (1) Maine
(2) Florida   (3) Alaska   (4) Kentucky
29. Which statement is probably true of *Hamlet?*   (1) Horatio betrayed Hamlet to the King.   (2) Claudius did not inform Polonius of his intention to
trap Hamlet.   (3) Gertrude knew nothing of Claudius' plan to kill her
husband.   (4) Ophelia had a lover other than Hamlet.
30. An episode in which a teacher is "spelled down" occurs in   (1) *And
Gladly Teach*   (2) *The Thread That Runs So True*   (3) *Goodbye, Mr.
Chips*   (4) *The Hoosier Schoolmaster*
31. *The President's Lady* tells of the life of   (1) Mary Lincoln   (2) Mamie
Eisenhower   (3) Rachel Jackson   (4) Eleanor Roosevelt
32. Examples of internal rhyme may be found in   (1) "Birches"   (2) "Annabel Lee"   (3) "Crossing the Bar"   (4) "How Do I Love Thee"
33. In *The Importance of Being Earnest,* Algy posed as Ernest to   (1) win a
girl   (2) escape his creditors   (3) locate the real Ernest   (4) get
material for a novel
34. *The Reason Why* deals with events of the   (1) Children's Crusade
(2) Crimean War   (3) Battle of Britain   (4) Korean War
35. *Francie* by Emily Hahn concerns   (1) Communist rule in China   (2)
life in an English school   (3) the troubles of an Army mule   (4) the
life of a student nurse
36. *The Last Hurrah* is a story of   (1) an Olympic athlete   (2) a politician
(3) a boxer   (4) a radio announcer
37. Which pair of lovers conversed through a hole in a wall?   (1) Romeo and
Juliet   (2) Antony and Cleopatra   (3) Cyrano and Roxane   (4)
Pyramus and Thisbe
38. The author of *Shakespeare of London* has recently published a biography
of   (1) Ben Jonson   (2) David Garrick   (3) Christopher Marlowe
(4) Beaumont and Fletcher
39. *The Human Comedy* by Saroyan shows life as viewed by   (1) a college
student   (2) an immigration officer   (3) a telegraph delivery boy
(4) a clown
40. Fagin would be most likely to find a friend in   (1) Miles Falworth
(2) David Copperfield   (3) Jim Hawkins   (4) Uriah Heep

Chapter 14

THE LITERATURE TEST (A GUIDE
TO PERSONAL READING)

Purpose of the Guide

The purpose of this guide is to help you to select interesting and worthwhile readings, both full-length books and shorter works. It will also help you to refresh your memory about works that you have already read.

Interest Centers

One helpful way to group literary works is by *centers of interest*. In this chapter you will find an annotated list of over three hundred works of all types (novels, plays, biographies and autobiographies, travel books, short stories, essays, poems) arranged under ten different centers of interest. For an enjoyable and profitable reading experience, turn to an interest center that appeals to you and, with the aid of the brief annotations provided for your guidance, choose one or more promising titles to look into on your next visit to the library or bookshop.

Interest Centers Used in This Guide:

1. Escape, Adventure, Mystery, Suspense
2. Occupations, Sports, Hobbies
3. Man vs. Environment
4. History Made Alive
5. The American Way and the American Scene
6. Other Ways, Other Peoples, Other Places
7. Progress—Curse or Blessing?
8. Ethics and Human Relations
9. The Lighter Side
10. Idealism

Note: There is hardly one literary work that cannot be grouped under more than one interest center. Herman Melville's *Moby Dick*, for example, may properly be listed under interest center 1, 2, 3, 4, 6, 8, or 10. In this chapter, however, a work will be listed under only *one* of its appropriate interest centers.

INTEREST CENTER 1: ESCAPE, ADVENTURE, MYSTERY, SUSPENSE

Captain Horatio Hornblower—C. S. Forester   NOVEL
Fighting pirates and outwitting the enemy fleets of the 1800's, this resourceful British officer sailed the seas with luck and skill that triumphed over all.

Scaramouche—Rafael Sabatini   NOVEL
Here are the ingredients of romance: the handsome hero of noble birth in disguise, the lovely lady, the duel, and all the mystery of cloak and dagger.

Ben Hur—Lew Wallace   NOVEL
You will never forget the famous chariot race in the ancient Roman arena as the former galley slave makes you stand and cheer with life and death as the stakes.

Kidnapped—Robert Louis Stevenson   NOVEL
Young David Balfour narrowly escapes a deathtrap set by his miserly uncle, who then has the lad kidnapped and sent abroad. But at the end David comes into his rightful inheritance.

Twenty Thousand Leagues Under the Sea—Jules Verne   NOVEL
The father of today's amazing science fiction invented a marvelous electric submarine which took Captain Nemo on adventure-packed cruises.

Air Raid—Archibald MacLeish   RADIO PLAY
This memorable radio play in free verse portrays the terror, suspense, and destruction of an air raid.

"A Night at an Inn"—Lord Dunsany   ONE-ACT PLAY
Some Cockney sailors and a gentleman adventurer who have stolen a precious stone from an idol in a temple are relentlessly pursued by native Hindu priests.

"In the Zone"—Eugene O'Neill   ONE-ACT PLAY
The lesson of this little drama of the sea is that wartime hysteria can lead normally decent people to strange actions.

The Emperor Jones—Eugene O'Neill   PLAY
The tom-tom beats in rhythm with the panic in the heart of Jones, as he flees the vengeance of some West Indian natives he has exploited.

"The Valiant"—Hall and Middlemass   ONE-ACT PLAY
Awaiting electrocution, a young man keeps up his courage by re-

minding himself through immortal lines from Shakespeare that honor is worth more than life itself.

There Shall Be No Night—Robert E. Sherwood   PLAY
This play pictured the invasion of Finland, that brave little nation caught in the crossfire of Germany and Russia in the Second World War.

The Lonely Sky—
W. B. Bridgeman and Jacqueline Hazard   BIOGRAPHY
Tension-packed and fascinating, this is the personal story of the test pilot chosen to fly the Douglas Skyrocket, a top-secret experimental plane.

Quest in the Desert—Roy Chapman Andrews   AUTOBIOGRAPHY
Sponsored by the American Museum of Natural History, this famous explorer traveled all over the world to collect specimens of ancient man.

Danger Is My Business—John Craig   AUTOBIOGRAPHY
In an intimate style, this captain describes his exciting adventures as a deep-sea diver and photographer who plans someday to salvage the sunken ship *Lusitania*.

Wind, Sand, and Stars—
Antoine de Saint-Exupéry   AUTOBIOGRAPHY
This famous French pilot discusses not only his flying experiences in North Africa and Europe, but also his hopes, dreams, and ideals.

I Married Adventure—Osa Johnson   AUTOBIOGRAPHY
When Osa Helen Leighty married Martin Johnson, famous explorer and photographer of wild animals, she started a partnership that survived unusual jungle hardships.

Assigned to Adventure—Irene Kuhn   AUTOBIOGRAPHY
A clever roving woman journalist records the romance and adventure of daily newspaper reporting.

"The Monkey's Paw"—W. W. Jacobs   SHORT STORY
Into a quiet home and happy family comes a visiting Major from India with a strange tale about the evil power of a bewitched monkey's paw.

"The Gold Bug"—Edgar Allan Poe   SHORT STORY
Can you solve a cryptogram? Here is a masterpiece of deductive reasoning by which a brilliant mind solves the mystery of a code and map to buried treasure.

"Noon Wine"—Katherine Anne Porter   SHORT STORY
A mysterious stranger appears at a Texas farm to seek work. He
serves well for many years, bringing prosperity to the farm, until an
ill-fated day when he is discovered to be an escaped maniac.

"The Innocence of Father Brown"—
     Gilbert K. Chesterton   SHORT STORY
Among the world's sleuths in fact or fiction, none is so modest and
surprisingly clever as this little, unobtrusive Catholic priest.

"The Speckled Band"—Arthur Conan Doyle   SHORT STORY
When Sherlock Holmes adds up all the clues, there is only one possible deduction to be made: the criminal will be caught in the act of
committing his own terrible deeds.

The Sea and the Jungle—H. M. Tomlinson   ESSAYS
The author writes informally of a voyage that began in Wales and
took him two thousand miles up the Amazon River into the luxuriant
Brazilian jungle.

"A Message to Garcia"—Elbert Hubbard   ESSAY
Lieutenant Rowan's fulfillment of a dangerous mission in the Span-
ish-American War is a memorable example of daring and perseverance.

"The Fifty-first Dragon"—Heywood Broun   ESSAY
Can a magic word like "rumplesnitz" give us courage to face all the
obstacles of life? Poor Gawaine failed only when he had to face reality with the lance of truth.

"Hell on Ice"—Edward Ellsberg   ESSAY
The same vigorous style with which he told of deep-sea diving and
salvage in the book *On the Bottom* makes an exciting yarn of this
expedition to the North Pole.

"On Running After One's Hat"—Gilbert K. Chesterton   ESSAY
Make an adventure out of an inconvenience is GKC's advice as he
proves in his paradoxical style that a man running after his hat is
not half so funny as a man running after a wife.

"The Highwayman"—Alfred Noyes   POEM
Bess, the landlord's daughter, gives up her life to save the highwayman, her lover, from the redcoat troops.

"The Raven"—Edgar Allan Poe   POEM
You will be enchanted by the sad music in this weird tale of the lost
Lenore, who haunted the thoughts of her lover.

"The Rime of the Ancient Mariner"—
Samuel Taylor Coleridge   POEM
The story of the ᛫wanton slaying of the albatross and of the spell
which cursed the killer until he prayed for forgiveness creates a picture of unearthly beauty and terror.

"Sea Fever"—John Masefield   POEM
The desire to return to the sea, "for the call of the running tide is
a wild call and a clear call that may not be denied," makes this a
perfect example of "escape."

"Renascence"—Edna St. Vincent Millay   POEM
Here is the passionate eagerness of youth to embrace nature and the
world with horizons forever expanding "as wide as the heart is wide."

INTEREST CENTER 2: OCCUPATIONS, SPORTS, HOBBIES

Moby Dick—Herman Melville   NOVEL
Captain Ahab and his hunt for the great white whale that cost him
a leg make a tale of revenge and adventure on the high seas.

The Moon and Sixpence—William Somerset Maugham   NOVEL
Charles Strickland, a painter, runs away from Europe to Tahiti. This
novel parallels the true story of the painter Gauguin.

Tono-Bungay—H. G. Wells   NOVEL
George Ponderevo is a kind of modern huckster who makes a fortune
by selling a worthless patent medicine called "tono-bungay."

Giants in the Earth—O. E. Rölvaag   NOVEL
Per Hansa and his wife Beret represent the kind of brave immigrant
farmers who helped to settle the lonely plains of the pioneer days in
the West.

Johnny Tremain—Esther Forbes   NOVEL
This young apprentice silversmith took part in the stirring events
that led to the Boston Tea Party and the Battle of Lexington.

The Admirable Crichton—James Barrie   PLAY
The perfect butler in the aristocratic home in England is trans-
formed into the natural leader when the family is shipwrecked on a
lonely island.

Beyond the Horizon—Eugene O'Neill   PLAY
The life of a New England farmer was the wrong occupation for
Robert Mayo; the consequences of this mistake are serious for the
three principal characters.

Pygmalion—George Bernard Shaw   PLAY
The speech expert tries to impose a pattern of Oxford diction on a
Cockney flower girl in order to prove his theories about social classes
and linguistics.

Clarence—Booth Tarkington   PLAY
Into an average American family with its involved relations, domestic
and marital, comes quite by accident a young entomologist named
Clarence who solves all problems.

Death of a Salesman—Arthur Miller   PLAY
Salesman Willy Loman ruins himself and his family by his blind
worship of false goals commonly accepted in today's world.

Lou Gehrig: A Quiet Hero—Frank Graham   BIOGRAPHY
This is the poignant life story of the "iron man of baseball," the immortal first baseman of the New York Yankees.

The Thread That Runs So True—Jesse Stuart   AUTOBIOGRAPHY
A successful writer who enjoys living and is not afraid of hard work
recalls his experiences as a teacher in Kentucky and Ohio.

Strikeout Story—Bob Feller   AUTOBIOGRAPHY
When he was just a youngster on the farm, Bob started training that
right arm, with the result that at seventeen he was pitching for the
Cleveland Indians.

We—Charles Lindbergh   AUTOBIOGRAPHY
This is the story of the first aviator to fly solo and nonstop across the
Atlantic. It follows his career from his early barnstorming days to his
epic flight to Paris.

I Like Diving—Thomas Eadie   AUTOBIOGRAPHY
Here is a professional's story of deep-sea diving with all the color
and excitement of raising such craft as the sunken S-4.

Lucky To Be a Yankee—Joe Di Maggio   AUTOBIOGRAPHY
Whenever there was a need for a hit or a run, "jolting Joe" could be
counted on to come through. Of course, the fans loved him.

Daniel Boone, Wilderness Scout—
    Stewart Edward White   BIOGRAPHY
This is the suspenseful account of the restless Daniel Boone, whose
pioneering gave impetus to westward expansion.

"*The Elephant Remembers*"—Edison Marshall   SHORT STORY
The love of man and animal and the last-minute rescue from a trap
in the jungle make this a memorable story.

"Meadow Lark"—Edna Ferber SHORT STORY
The farmer's son wanted wings so that his spirit could soar beyond the daily chores and rigid conventions that seemed to hem him in from his dreams.

"The Three Strangers"—Thomas Hardy SHORT STORY
A hangman, en route to perform his services, passes an hour in song and drinking with a companion who, ironically, is his intended victim.

"Quality"—John Galsworthy SHORT STORY
The Gessler brothers, who were skilled craftsmen in the art of shoe-making, could never hope to compete with the cheap products of mass-production methods.

"The Outcasts of Poker Flat"—Bret Harte SHORT STORY
A group of characters from the rough and tumble days of 1849 find themselves stranded by a blizzard which reveals the high courage and loyalty even professional gamblers may have.

Farewell to Sport—Paul Gallico ESSAYS
A sports reporter reminisces about some outstanding athletes and shows the reader both the ugliness and gallantry of the sports world.

"I Get a Colt To Break In"—Lincoln Steffens ESSAY
What youngster has not dreamed of someday having a colt of his own? Here is the straightforward account of one whose dreams came true. (This essay is a chapter from his *Autobiography*.)

"For a Fierce Game, There's Hockey"—Robert F. Kelley ESSAY
The author discusses the speed and smash of professional hockey and some of its great stars, like Les Patrick.

"The Great Sports Myth"—John R. Tunis ESSAY
Tunis attacks the exaggerated sentimental notions we have of sports and comes out for genuine amateur sports.

The Cabin—Stewart Edward White ESSAYS
Lovers of the outdoors will enjoy this volume, which tells of the construction of a cabin high in the Sierras and the beauties and mysteries of the forest.

"Gunga Din"—Rudyard Kipling POEM
The heroism of the native water carrier who remained faithful to his post has made the whole world remember: "You're a better man than I am, Gunga Din!"

"Song of the Open Road"—Walt Whitman   POEM
The wanderer who loves the freedom of the outdoors as surcease
from worldly cares will enjoy the gay and earthy mood of this song
in praise of vagabondage.

"The Barrel-Organ"—Alfred Noyes   POEM
When spring returns to the big city, the barrel organ playing in the
streets brings with it the recollection of lilac time.

"Dorlan's Home-Walk"—Arthur Guiterman   POEM
Baseball fans will surely love this strange episode from a major
league ball game when a squabble with the umpire allowed the bat-
ter to walk around the bases.

"The Death of the Hired Man"—Robert Frost   POEM
Everyone has seen the type of the old hired man who has outworn
his usefulness, yet holds strings on our hearts because of man's need
for human sympathy.

INTEREST CENTER 3: MAN VS. ENVIRONMENT

Ethan Frome—Edith Wharton   NOVEL
Here is the old triangle presented in the bleak New England environment: Ethan Frome, married to nagging Zeena, falls disastrously
in love with young Mattie Silver.

The Return of the Native—Thomas Hardy   NOVEL
A tragic tale involving Clym Yeobright and the beautiful Eustacia
Vye against the attraction of Damon Wildeve and the loneliness of
the surrounding heath.

David Copperfield—Charles Dickens   NOVEL
David grew up in an environment that included a harsh stepfather
(Mr. Murdstone) and a cruel schoolmaster (Mr. Creakle).

Let the Hurricane Roar—Rose W. Lane   NOVEL
Charles and Caroline, a young married couple, courageously face
the problems of pioneer living in the Dakotas in the 1870's.

The Late George Apley—John P. Marquand   NOVEL
An aristocratic family residing in Beacon Hill, district of the so-called
"proper Bostonians," is amusingly and satirically portrayed in all
its futile pretenses.

The Yearling—Marjorie K. Rawlings   NOVEL
A tender and eloquent story of a boy named Jody who loved his pet
fawn and grew toward maturity out of this experience.

Lord of the Flies—William Golding   NOVEL
In an atomic war, a group of English youngsters, aged six to twelve,
is stranded on a tropical island. What ensues is a frightening conflict between the children's civilized ways and their savage instincts.

The Glass Menagerie—Tennessee Williams   PLAY
The pathetic emptiness of Laura's life becomes understandable when
we realize that she is the product of an environment dominated by
a selfish, stupidly sentimental mother.

"Riders to the Sea"—John M. Synge   ONE-ACT PLAY
The heartrending series of drownings which leaves Maurya destitute
of her sons will make you long remember this one-act tragedy.

I Remember Mama—John Van Druten   PLAY
What a delightful family circle is presented here: so loyal and devoted to each other and to their parents that we mingle our smiles
with our tears as we watch them!

The Late Christopher Bean—Sidney Howard   PLAY
Nobody in his environment appreciated Christopher Bean's artistic
genius, except Abby, a servant girl. But with posthumous recognition, there was a mad scramble for his paintings.

"The Twelve-Pound Look"—James Barrie   ONE-ACT PLAY
Why should a woman bear the arrogance of her husband and lord
when she can easily win her independence by learning how to type-
write and become a secretary?

Death, Be Not Proud—John Gunther   BIOGRAPHY
The well-known author of the "inside" books (on Africa, the U.S.A.,
Latin America, Asia, and Europe) recounts his son's brave struggle
against death and the triumph of the human spirit against all odds.

This I Remember—Eleanor Roosevelt   AUTOBIOGRAPHY
An extraordinary woman tells her personal recollections of men and
events associated with a remarkable President of the United States.

My Sister Eileen—Ruth McKenney   BIOGRAPHY
A lively and amusing sketch of two girls who learned to face life
together and met its hardships and surprises with the spirit of gallantry and adventure.

Life with Father—Clarence Day   AUTOBIOGRAPHY
The old Victorian days are usually symbolized by a kindly tyrant
of a father; here is a clever and scheming mother who knows how
to subdue such a redheaded terror as "Father."

Labrador Doctor—Wilfred T. Grenfell   AUTOBIOGRAPHY
Way up in the cold and barren wastes of Labrador this kindly and
gentle doctor helped the sick and brought comfort to the fisherfolk.

"The Revolt of Mother"—Mary W. Freeman   SHORT STORY
The husband's plan for a new barn ran counter to the wife's plan
for a new home and the prospects for her marriageable daughter.
Can you guess who won?

"Paul's Case"—Willa Cather   SHORT STORY
When Paul stood before his high school principal to answer the
charges presented by his teachers, the gleam of defiance in his eye
foretold his last gesture in life.

"Sixteen"—Maureen Daly   SHORT STORY
This is one of those "different" stories because it gives a frank and
sensitive picture of an adolescent expressed in the image and language of today.

"The Apple Tree"—John Galsworthy   SHORT STORY
The Modern Library chose this as one of the twelve "great modern
short stories" because of its sympathetic presentation of love full of
memories and regrets.

"Moti Guj, Mutineer"—Rudyard Kipling   SHORT STORY
The characterizations of the elephant and its keeper make this humorous tale one of the most delightful animal stories.

"The Ambitious Guest"—Nathaniel Hawthorne   SHORT STORY
A young man stops at a house on a mountainside and falls in love
at first sight with the lovely daughter, but an accidental landslide
overtakes and destroys them.

"The Making of Americans"—Louis Adamic   ESSAY
With passionate pen and sincere heart, this naturalized citizen tries
to open the eyes of his fellow Americans to the diversity and merit
of all nationalities who live here.

"Personal Recollections of Joan of Arc"—Mark Twain   ESSAY
"The most extraordinary person the human race has ever produced,"
says the author of his heroine. Her genius triumphed despite obstacles of birth, sex, youth, illiteracy, military inexperience, and hostile
environment.

"Dream Children: A Reverie"—Charles Lamb   ESSAY
A man who devoted his life to taking care of his invalid sister here
tenderly talks of those children that inhabited his unfulfilled dreams.

"An Apology for Idlers"—Robert Louis Stevenson   ESSAY
This brilliant essay wittily attacks the error of "all work and no play"
and emphasizes one's "duty of being happy" in this world.

"Self-Reliance"—Ralph Waldo Emerson   ESSAY
Emerson advises us to be leaders, not followers. Rely on your own
powers; do not merely try to conform to whatever is generally accepted.

"The World Is Too Much With Us"—
    William Wordsworth   POEM
Are we so occupied with the business of making a living and spending our money on material things that we overlook the beauties of
nature?

"A Man's a Man for A' That"—Robert Burns   POEM
Nowadays, even more than in the century of Burns, we believe in
the dignity and worth of the individual regardless of birth, race,
creed, or color.

"Chicago"—Carl Sandburg   POEM
Sandburg gives a balanced picture of this huge metropolis. Freely
admitting its wickedness and crime, he nevertheless admires its
youth, power, and industrial activities.

"Invictus"—William E. Henley   POEM
The title is a Latin word meaning "unconquered," and the occasion
of the writing was a serious operation; yet the message of courage
and defiance rings true.

"Leisure"—William H. Davies   POEM
In contrast with the sonnet above by Wordsworth, this poem has a
quiet mood and reflective attitude toward the hurly-burly of contemporary life.

INTEREST CENTER 4: HISTORY MADE ALIVE

Northwest Passage—Kenneth Roberts   NOVEL
Major Rogers and his Rangers fought the Indians two hundred years
ago in the French and Indian War, but you can relive their experiences now in this vivid novel.

Gone With the Wind—Margaret Mitchell   NOVEL
If you are looking for a solid story about the South and the Civil War
with a beautiful heroine and a dashing hero, curl up on your sofa
with this stirring tale.

Ivanhoe—Walter Scott   NOVEL
This is a colorful tale of the days when knights were bold and ladies
sat in the grandstand to watch them fight for their honor. Guess who
was the Black Knight?

The Good Earth—Pearl Buck   NOVEL
Wang Lung married O-Lan and together they cultivated the soil, but
tragedy came when their sons forsook the good earth and sought
their livelihood elsewhere.

Death Comes for the Archbishop—Willa Cather   NOVEL
The heartwarming story of a Catholic priest who devotes his life to
doing good in a community of the American Southwest where legend
and reality blend.

The Guns of Navarone—Alistair MacLean   NOVEL
This suspenseful World War II adventure story deals with a British
sabotage team assigned to blow up a vital Nazi target in the eastern
Mediterranean.

What Price Glory?—Stallings and Anderson   PLAY
After the First World War, this study of soldiers in action had great
impact on the emotions of war-weary America. The language and
ideas of the common soldier are expressed vigorously.

Abraham Lincoln—John Drinkwater   PLAY
How did Lincoln treat the members of his war cabinet? Is it true
that he carried a joke book into the meetings? This play presents a
clear and vivid portrait of Lincoln.

Elizabeth the Queen—Maxwell Anderson   PLAY
The play reveals the jealousies and intrigues of a strong queen who
valued England and royal tradition more than personal happiness
and welfare.

Saint Joan—George Bernard Shaw   PLAY
This great play about the tender and moving life of a saint was written by one who called himself an "atheist."

Julius Caesar—William Shakespeare   PLAY
The tragedy of Brutus, "the noblest Roman of them all," begins when
he allows himself to be misled into taking part in the assassination of
Julius Caesar.

Paul Revere and the World He Lived In—
  Esther Forbes   BIOGRAPHY
This work won the Pulitzer Prize for biography and certainly de-

served it, for it not only portrays the man but also clarifies the times and the men of the Revolution.

The Raven—Marquis James   BIOGRAPHY
This biography of Sam Houston describes those stirring days in the early Southwest when a courageous scout made a reputation for himself as a leader of men and a brave fighter.

Queen Victoria—Lytton Strachey   BIOGRAPHY
The human, lovable qualities of the queen who skillfully manipulated prime ministers and artfully depended upon her royal consort, Prince Albert, will charm you.

Abraham Lincoln, the Prairie Years—
   Carl Sandburg   BIOGRAPHY
Sandburg's aim was to present Lincoln so realistically that young people would feel they had actually known him.

Christopher Columbus, Mariner—
   Samuel Eliot Morison   BIOGRAPHY
This scholarly biography of the great navigator makes exciting reading. The author is a recognized authority on Columbus, knows the sea, and writes well.

Diary of a Young Girl—Anne Frank   AUTOBIOGRAPHY
A girl of thirteen, hiding from the Nazis with her family in a secret portion of an Amsterdam attic, records her day-to-day thoughts.

"The Man Without a Country"—
   Edward Everett Hale   SHORT STORY
Philip Nolan, fictitious hero of this moving tale of patriotism, is so skillfully presented that almost everyone believes he actually existed.

"The Siege of Berlin"—Alphonse Daudet   SHORT STORY
An aged, dying French colonel lives some extra days because his granddaughter cleverly alters the bad battlefront reports of the Franco-Prussian War.

"For Esmé—With Love and Squalor"—
   J. D. Salinger   SHORT STORY
Six years later, an American ex-soldier reminisces about a child who had befriended him in wartime London just before the Normandy invasion.

"Two Soldiers"—William Faulkner   SHORT STORY
A nine-year-old tells how he tried to enlist in the U.S. Army to stay with his brother Pete just after Pearl Harbor.

"Hunger"—Anzia Yezierska   SHORT STORY
Though the heroine, a young Jewish immigrant girl, toiled in a factory on the lower East Side in New York City, she always dreamed
of better things because she had a "hunger" unsatisfied.

The Alhambra—Washington Irving   ESSAYS
This tourist and lover of the glories of ancient Moorish castles gives
his impressionistic views of the Spain of yesteryear.

The Plains of Patagonia—William H. Hudson   ESSAYS
This naturalist has given us the benefit of his firsthand travels and
experiences in the South American continent.

Flight to Arras—Antoine de Saint-Exupéry   ESSAYS
A gifted French writer and pilot describes a perilous flight over
the Nazi lines in World War II and records his reflections on the
crushing defeat of his nation.

"Sir Roger de Coverley in Church"—Joseph Addison   ESSAY
The amusing relationships of a country squire with his tenants and
chaplain recreate a bit of eighteenth-century England.

"A Modest Proposal"—Jonathan Swift   ESSAY
With savage satire the author attacks the problem of starvation in
Ireland by calmly "proposing" that little babies be eaten. He also
wrote *Gulliver's Travels*.

"John Brown's Body"—Stephen Vincent Benét   POEM
This long narrative poem describes the Civil War in terms of the
struggle for individual freedom and human worth.

"The Charge of the Light Brigade"—
    Alfred Lord Tennyson   POEM
You will thrill to the immortal but futile charge by the six hundred
men of the Light Brigade in the Crimean War battle of Balaclava.

"I Am an American"—Elias Lieberman   POEM
An immigrant speaks out with the passionate fire of a patriot whose
heart and soul tingle with love for America.

"Let America Be America Again"—
    Langston Hughes   POEM
Disillusioned but not despairing, the Negro poet laments the gulf
that exist between the dream of equality and the anguish of prejudice in America.

"As Toilsome I Wandered Virginia's Woods"—
Walt Whitman   POEM
The speaker will always remember the rude inscription he encoun-
tered one day on the grave of a Civil War soldier.

INTEREST CENTER 5: THE AMERICAN WAY AND THE AMERICAN SCENE

Red Badge of Courage—Stephen Crane   NOVEL
This story takes place during the Civil War. It describes the individual's reactions, fears, cowardice, and courage in the battle zone.

Intruder in the Dust—William Faulkner   NOVEL
A proud, elderly Negro, jailed on suspicion of murder, is cleared
through the heroic efforts of two whites—a boy of sixteen and a
woman of seventy.

My Ántonia—Willa Cather   NOVEL
The story of Ántonia Shimerda and her family in Nebraska's pioneer
days shows the hardihood which enabled these folk to endure all
things.

Main Street—Sinclair Lewis   NOVEL
Every small town in America has its Main Street with its typical
stores, peoples, ideas, and conventions—all of which may lead to
smugness and dullness.

The Turmoil—Booth Tarkington   NOVEL
The Sheridan family stood for big business and industry, whereas
the Vertrees typified the genteel and aristocratic tradition, but Bibbs
and Mary united the two happily.

The Virginian—Owen Wister   NOVEL
The hero of this novel about cowboy life has a fine character and
personality but lacks formal education. Eventually he marries a
young schoolteacher from the East.

Valley Forge—Maxwell Anderson   PLAY
The heroic sufferings of General Washington and his band of faithful
followers during that bitter winter before the Battle of Trenton never
dimmed the spirit of "freeborn men."

The Devil's Disciple—George Bernard Shaw   PLAY
This play about the American Revolution is appealing because of
witty lines and clever situations involving Gentleman Johnny Bur-
goyne of the British army.

Home of the Brave—Arthur Laurents   PLAY
A World War II soldier loses his ability to walk as a result of
psychological shock in combat. His cure provides a fascinating lesson
in the mysteries of the mind and the evils of prejudice.

Abe Lincoln in Illinois—Robert Sherwood   PLAY
This is a truly gripping account of Lincoln amid his own townsfolk
and of the pathos of his love for Anne Rutledge, who lights his
dreams of the future as President of the United States.

The Male Animal—Thurber and Nugent   PLAY
A professor's insistence on reading Vanzetti's letter to his class, as
an example of eloquent though broken English, creates a crisis at
at Midwestern University.

Crusade in Europe—Dwight D. Eisenhower   AUTOBIOGRAPHY
A national hero presents history in the making with his pungent
comments and well-documented account of those stirring events of
World War II.

Profiles in Courage—John F. Kennedy   BIOGRAPHIES
These sketches portray courageous American statesmen, especially
senators, who refused to yield to the pressures of the majority at
critical moments in our history.

Brave Men—Ernie Pyle   BIOGRAPHY
This is a different kind of war book, written not by the top brass,
but by a special kind of war correspondent who interviewed only the
G.I.'s—lovable and friendly Ernie Pyle.

Up From Slavery—Booker T. Washington   AUTOBIOGRAPHY
The title is significant because it depicts the life of the author who
was able to rise "up from slavery" to a position as an American
educator and leader.

Autobiography of Benjamin Franklin—
Benjamin Franklin   AUTOBIOGRAPHY
The work does not go beyond 1757, but by that time Franklin had
had an amazingly successful career as printer, publisher, philosopher,
inventor, scientist, legislator, and diplomat.

Life on the Mississippi—Mark Twain   AUTOBIOGRAPHY
One of America's greatest writers discusses his life as a Mississippi
River steamboat pilot and the charms and mysteries of that river.

"The Devil and Daniel Webster"—
Stephen Vincent Benét   SHORT STORY
Only a sharp and shrewd New Englander like Daniel Webster could

corner the devil in this highly amusing and utterly improbable battle over a man's immortal soul.

"The Luck of Roaring Camp"—Bret Harte   SHORT STORY
The birth of a child alters the manners, hygiene, and spiritual outlook of a rough-and-ready California mining town.

"Haircut"—Ring Lardner   SHORT STORY
As he gives the newcomer a haircut, the village barber recounts an exciting local episode of recent occurrence.

"The Whirligig of Life"—O. Henry   SHORT STORY
The Cumberland Mountains furnish the scene for this humorous tale of marital discord and reconciliation.

"The Killers"—Ernest Hemingway   SHORT STORY
You will cower with the occupants of Henry's lunchroom when two gunmen come in and wait for their intended victim.

"On Discovering the United States"—
    Alistair Cooke   ESSAY
From his experiences as a traveler in the United States, the author offers excellent suggestions about how to travel and what to see when you tour your country.

"A Lincoln Preface"—Carl Sandburg   ESSAY
If you read these few beautifully written pages about Lincoln's statesmanship and humanity, you will want to read Sandburg's excellent biography of Lincoln.

"How to Detect and Analyze Propaganda"—
    Clyde R. Miller   ESSAY
In a democracy there is critical thinking because of freedom to choose between different types of propaganda, but in a dictatorship there is a monopoly of propaganda or "thought control." Beware!

"A Garland of Ibids for Van Wyck Brooks"—
    Frank Sullivan   ESSAY
This is a cleverly humorous satire on the overuse of footnotes and, incidentally, on some distinguished New England personalities.

"I Hear America Singing"—Walt Whitman   POEM
With a kind of swaggering pride, the poet extols the various workers and the common folk who make the swelling chorus of the new continent into a hymn of brotherhood.

"Brass Spittoons"—Langston Hughes   POEM
This is a sympathetic picture of a Negro workman who performs menial tasks in order to earn a living for his family, yet sanctifies his drudgery by prayer.

"Mending Wall"—Robert Frost   POEM
The custom of replacing the fallen rocks from the stone wall dividing the land of two New England neighbors brings together two very different persons.

"Lucinda Matlock"—Edgar Lee Masters   POEM
Do we still have people like Lucinda in America today? She raised a houseful of children, tended the garden, nursed the sick, and had time to enjoy life abundantly.

"Jesse James"—William Rose Benét   POEM
You will enjoy this tall tale of the exploits of a daring, generous outlaw who has become an American folk hero.

INTEREST CENTER 6: OTHER WAYS, OTHER PEOPLES, OTHER PLACES

Sons—Pearl Buck   NOVEL
In this sequel to *The Good Earth*, the sons of Wang Lung sell their father's land and seek their fortunes in other fields of endeavor.

The Robe—Lloyd Douglas   NOVEL
Jerusalem and the Middle East at the time of Christ form the vivid historical background for this study of human faith and greed. No wonder it is one of the most popular novels!

The Song of Bernadette—Franz Werfel   NOVEL
When he fled from the Nazis, Franz Werfel sought refuge in France, and it was at the shrine at Lourdes that he was inspired to write this story.

Adam Bede—George Eliot   NOVEL
An intelligent young carpenter eventually recovers from his tragic love for a silly, vain young beauty. The novel gives an interesting picture of English farm life in the last century.

Mutiny on the Bounty—
    Charles Nordhoff and James Hall   NOVEL
This is the fictionalized treatment of a South Seas episode—the mutiny of a part of the crew, led by Fletcher Christian, against harsh Captain Bligh of H.M.S. *Bounty*.

Nectar in a Sieve—Kamala Taylor   NOVEL
Though they constantly face poverty and the threat of starvation, a devoted peasant couple in southern India confronts life with courage and dignity.

"Spreading the News"—Lady Gregory   ONE-ACT PLAY
The fine embroidery and exaggeration of a lie in the Irish manner provide the humorous situation of this one-act play by a well-known Irish dramatist.

The Corn Is Green—Emlyn Williams   PLAY
In this stirring drama, an idealistic schoolteacher discovers a talented young Welsh miner and coaches him into a scholastic genius.

The Cherry Orchard—Anton Chekhov   PLAY
In this Russian masterpiece a decadent upper-class family in financial straits rejects a sensible way out because it means cutting down their famous cherry trees.

An Enemy of the People—Henrik Ibsen   PLAY
Dr. Stockmann faces persecution because he tells the truth about the sewage that pollutes a seashore resort.

Cyrano de Bergerac—Edmond Rostand   PLAY
The poet and swordsman with the monstrously long nose sings his love songs beneath the balcony to fair Roxane, while another gathers the romantic rewards.

The Barretts of Wimpole Street—Rudolf Besier   PLAY
This comedy, based on the romance between the English poets Elizabeth Barrett and Robert Browning, shows how love triumphs over the tyranny of an unsympathetic Victorian father.

High Jungle—William Beebe   AUTOBIOGRAPHY
This is an account by a famous naturalist of his unusual laboratory, set up in the "high jungle" of Venezuela so that he could examine strange specimens in their own habitat.

The Exile—Pearl Buck   BIOGRAPHY
This is the story of an unusual person, the author's mother, who dedicated her life to service in China and at the same time raised a family.

Cradle of the Storms—Bernard Hubbard   AUTOBIOGRAPHY
A Catholic priest, Father Hubbard, won large audiences with his personal talks and pictures of his expedition to Alaska and the Aleutians.

My Life With the Eskimos—
Vilhjalmur Stefansson   AUTOBIOGRAPHY
This noted Arctic explorer spent many years actually living with the
Eskimos in the Polar regions.

Eminent Victorians—Lytton Strachey   BIOGRAPHIES
The author provides valuable insights into the Victorian Age by his
portraits of four of its outstanding personalities: Cardinal Manning,
Florence Nightingale, Dr. Arnold, and General Gordon.

Life of Johnson—James Boswell   BIOGRAPHY
This classic biography resulted from the close association of James
Boswell, a gifted observer, with Dr. Samuel Johnson, a leading in-
tellectual of eighteenth-century England.

Three Worlds of Peru—Frances Toor   TRAVEL BOOK
If you are interested in a refreshing book that not only gives an account of the author's experiences but also illuminates the life and
customs of the people, read this one.

"The Heart of Darkness"—Joseph Conrad   SHORT STORY
A fine psychological study of the experiences and reactions of a
white man confronted by the mystery and strangeness of "the heart
of darkness" in Africa.

"The Necklace"—Guy de Maupassant   SHORT STORY
The vanity of a pretty young Frenchwoman who borrows, loses, and
replaces a necklace which she believes to be of great value leads to
a life of drudgery for herself and her husband.

"The Murders in the Rue Morgue"—
Edgar Allan Poe   SHORT STORY
By his genius and narrative skill, Poe took an actual murder case
in New York City and transplanted it to Paris. There, by marvelous
deduction, his sleuth, C. Auguste Dupin, solved it before the police
did.

Japanese Fairy Tales—Lafcadio Hearn   SHORT STORIES
Hearn, who spent many years in Japan, was able to convey the true
folk atmosphere and exotic flavor of the Orient. You will enjoy this
volume.

"The Overcoat"—Nikolai Gogol   SHORT STORY
This sad tale about an obscure clerk whose overcoat was stolen is
an artful critique of Russian society in the nineteenth century.

Patterns of Culture—Ruth Benedict   ESSAYS
This slim volume contains the author's comments from the anthropologist's point of view on taboos and customs she found among many native tribes.

Heart of Asia—Roy Chapman Andrews   ESSAYS
A noted American explorer and scientist recounts twelve exciting true tales of the Far East.

Inside Europe Today—John Gunther   ESSAYS
A prominent reporter discusses the major contemporary problems and leading political personalities of European nations.

"Ingo"—Christopher Morley   ESSAY
This is a moving account of an American's wartime concern for a young friend in an enemy country.

Strange Lands and Friendly People—
   William O. Douglas   ESSAYS
A U.S. Supreme Court Justice, who is also a world traveler, reports on conditions he observed in a number of Eastern countries.

"My Last Duchess"—Robert Browning   POEM
A Renaissance duke, about to remarry, talks of his last duchess. In so doing, he reveals his own character and some of the characteristics of his era.

"Cargoes"—John Masefield   POEM
By depicting three ships, each of a different epoch, the author, Britain's poet-laureate, communicates the spirit of three different civilizations.

The Odyssey—Homer   POEM
This epic of ancient Greece narrates the wanderings and adventures of Odysseus in the ten years that it took him to return home from the Trojan War.

"On the Road to Mandalay"—Rudyard Kipling   POEM
A British soldier reminisces about the Burma girl waiting for him by the old Moulmein Pagoda. This lilting ballad has been set to music.

"Lepanto"—Gilbert K. Chesterton   POEM
Don John of Austria in 1571 defeated the Turks in the great naval battle of Lepanto. You will thrill to this rousing rendition of the last crusade with all its color and sound effects.

INTEREST CENTER 7: PROGRESS—CURSE OR BLESSING?

Arrowsmith—Sinclair Lewis   NOVEL
Martin's struggles from country doctor to bacteriologist and research
worker are entwined with the lives of Leora, his wife, and Max
Gottlieb, the pure scientist working for humanity.

The Pit—Frank Norris   NOVEL
This is the story of the Chicago wheat-pit where the speculators
gamble human welfare against their own greed in setting prices for
a basic commodity.

How Green Was My Valley—Richard Llewellyn   NOVEL
The title is the keynote to the mood of regret and nostalgia with
which the author views the departed glory of his youth before the
huge slag heaps had blotted out the countryside.

Nineteen Eighty-Four—George Orwell   NOVEL
This novel depicts the plausible horrors of future totalitarianism, in
which the state employs science (the telescreen, propaganda techniques, thought control) to deprive the individual of all freedom and
dignity.

Cimarron—Edna Ferber   NOVEL
Yancey Cravat and his wife Sabra are the contrasting main characters in this exciting novel about the Oklahoma land rush.

The Star-Wagon—Maxwell Anderson   PLAY
Suppose a man were to invent a rubber tire that would last for a
hundred thousand miles or the life of the car. Do you sincerely think
any manufacturer would produce it? Why?

R.U.R.—Karel Capek   PLAY
Rossum's Universal Robots represent the mechanical men that would
result if our machine-age civilization were allowed to run to its
extreme in making "the common man" extinct.

Strife—John Galsworthy   PLAY
The modern industrialist and the crusading labor leader cross swords
in a costly and prolonged strike that ends in tragedy for both sides.

Men in White—Sidney Kingsley   PLAY
Here are the unsung heroes who wage a constant battle for life
and health in hospitals and laboratories dedicated to service.

"The Lost Silk Hat"—Lord Dunsany   ONE-ACT PLAY
Dreading to be seen hatless in public, a fashionable twentieth-century Londoner amuses us with his odd sense of values.

Hiroshima—John Hersey   BIOGRAPHY
This is a firsthand report by an author who visited Hiroshima after
the terrible atomic attack and recorded the actual impact of the
disaster in the words of the victims he interviewed.

Half Mile Down—William Beebe   AUTOBIOGRAPHY
You have probably read of the diving bell called the "bathysphere"
in which Dr. Beebe descended a half mile to the ocean's floor in
quest of rare specimens.

Microbe Hunters—Paul de Kruif   BIOGRAPHIES
Here is a series of popular biographical sketches of those pioneers
like Pasteur, Leeuwenhoek, and Spallanzani who devoted their lives
and genius to bacteriological research.

Heroes of Civilization—
      Joseph Cottler and Haym Jaffe   BIOGRAPHIES
These sketches of scientists, explorers, and inventors include Lister,
the Wright Brothers, Darwin, Mendel, Newton, Koch, and many
others of interest to high school pupils.

Kon-Tiki—Thor Heyerdahl   TRAVEL BOOK
By a daring 4000-mile balsa-raft crossing of the Pacific from Peru
to Polynesia, the author and his companions demonstrate a fascinating relationship between these two widely separated areas.

"Locomotive 38, the Ojibway"—William Saroyan   SHORT STORY
You wouldn't believe it, but Locomotive 38 is an American Indian
with a million-dollar bank account from his Oklahoma oil wells.

"The Whoffing Gods"—Norma Patterson   SHORT STORY
This human-interest tale begins when the "whoffing gods" (road-
construction machines) arrive to repave the roadway in front of
Mrs. Battle's orphanage.

"Dr. Heidegger's Experiment"—
      Nathaniel Hawthorne   SHORT STORY
Not exactly a scientific experiment, this investigation nevertheless
tells us whether people would avoid the follies they have committed,
if given the chance to relive their lives.

"The Blood of the Martyrs"—
      Stephen Vincent Benét   SHORT STORY
Should a scientist sell his soul to a dictator? Professor Malzius, the
scientist, dared to take a stand for truth and therefore to face a firing
squad as the consequence.

"The Remarkable Wreck of the *Thomas Hyke*"—
  Frank Stockton   SHORT STORY
What was the unusual construction feature of the good ship *Thomas Hyke* that saved the lives of the three who did not abandon her? An ingenious scientific tale.

The Hidden Persuaders—Vance O. Packard   ESSAYS
The author shows how advertising uses psychological research to make us buy certain products and influence our voting for political candidates.

"The Rivalry of Nations"—Walter Lippmann   ESSAY
Why is it that we keep on losing the peace though we win the wars? The writer investigates this problem and suggests a remedy.

"Nobel Prize Acceptance Speech"—William Faulkner   ESSAY
What should be the role of a writer in this world endangered by imminent atomic destruction? William Faulkner addresses himself to this question eloquently and inspiringly.

"The First Citizens of the Atomic Age"—
  Norman Cousins   ESSAY
The citizens of Hiroshima have regained their faith in humanity. They hope that their suffering will avert thousands of future Hiroshimas.

The Sea Around Us—Rachel Carson   ESSAYS
In beautifully vivid and clear language, these essays present fascinating scientific knowledge about the oceans and the earth.

"The Express"—Stephen Spender   POEM
The modern steam locomotive moves with a music unmatched by nature as it passes through metropolis and countryside to its mysterious destination.

"When I Heard the Learn'd Astronomer"—
  Walt Whitman   POEM
The astronomer's complicated figures, diagrams, and charts bore the poet. Leaving the lecture hall, he gazes up at the night sky and drinks in the beauty of the stars.

"The Factories"—Margaret Widdemer   POEM
There is no picture more pathetic than that of a child chained to a factory job instead of enjoying the outdoors at play. This poem stirs our social conscience against child labor.

"The Song of the Shirt"—Thomas Hood   POEM
This is another poem of protest against inhuman work in the sweat-
shops. The monotonous whirring of the machine makes the worker's
soul cry out in anguish.

The People, Yes—Carl Sandburg   POEMS
This volume contains some fine free verse concerning the scientific
and artistic march of man through the ages, always hopeful and tri-
umphant over the forces that seek to enslave him.

INTEREST CENTER 8: ETHICS AND HUMAN RELATIONS

The Pearl—John Steinbeck   NOVEL
Human greed leads to misery and tragedy because of the rare pearl
which a poor native finds but which his envious neighbors and others
will not let him keep.

Beyond This Place—A. J. Cronin   NOVEL
An innocent man, victimized by an unethical, ambitious prosecutor,
rots in jail as a convicted murderer until his courageous son, grown
to manhood, secures his release. A moving tale of filial devotion.

Vanity Fair—William M. Thackeray   NOVEL
The problem of social classes and a vain woman's scheming to advance to dubious position make this an intriguing novel.

Oliver Twist—Charles Dickens   NOVEL
The problem of orphans and workhouses in England was so scandalous that Dickens wrote the sad tale of Oliver Twist to start reforms.
So moving was the story that it resulted in laws improving conditions.

Silas Marner—George Eliot   NOVEL
Wrongly accused of a crime his best friend had committed, Silas
becomes a social outcast.

"Trifles"—Susan Glaspell   ONE-ACT PLAY
A woman has murdered her husband. As the drama unfolds, we
learn of some highly extenuating circumstances.

Justice—John Galsworthy   PLAY
Is there special consideration before the law for people of wealth
and social position? Can an ex-convict readjust himself to a wholesome life in the community? Read this powerful tragedy.

Winterset—Maxwell Anderson   PLAY
The son seeks the crooked judge who allowed his father to die even

though he knew he was innocent. He meets a girl whose destiny is to love him and share sudden death by machine gun.

Man and Superman—George Bernard Shaw   PLAY
Jack Tanner is the man; Ann Whitfield is the "superman." Shaw believes that when a woman has made up her mind to marry a certain man, he hasn't the ghost of a chance to escape.

A Doll's House—Henrik Ibsen   PLAY
When a woman finds that her husband treats her like a doll, that is, with a certain affection but with no regard for her intelligence, should she slam the door and assert her independence?

Loyalties—John Galsworthy   PLAY
This social drama deals frankly with class consciousness and religious prejudice.

Adrift on an Ice-Pan—Wilfred T. Grenfell   AUTOBIOGRAPHY
Sir Grenfell became famous because of his work with the natives near the frozen Arctic wastes. This is the true account of his experiences when trapped on a floating section of ice.

Junípero Serra—Agnes Repplier   BIOGRAPHY
Father Serra was a pioneer colonist in California; he founded the Franciscan Missions in California and contributed much to the development of the Southwest.

The Making of an American—Jacob A. Riis   AUTOBIOGRAPHY
The making of an American can be an inspiration to all of us. Riis came here as a boy from Denmark and made a great success as reporter, writer, lecturer, reformer.

This Is My Story—Eleanor Roosevelt   AUTOBIOGRAPHY
The wife of the former President, famous in her own right as a columnist and diplomat, tells the inside story of some history-making events. Worth reading.

Out of My Life and Thought—
   Albert Schweitzer   AUTOBIOGRAPHY
This is the inspiring life story of a remarkably brilliant humanitarian who dedicated himself wholly to the service of the unfortunate.

"A Piece of String"—Guy de Maupassant   SHORT STORY
Vindictiveness on the part of a personal enemy results in a poor man's derangement, imprisonment, and tragic end "just for a piece of string."

"The Little Cask"—Guy de Maupassant   SHORT STORY
This masterful portrayal of greed pits a crafty French innkeeper against an old woman who rivals him in avarice.

"The Bet"—Anton Chekhov   SHORT STORY
Chekhov has made a clever situation teach us a lesson about life: it is possible for the human spirit to enjoy more freedom in a prison cell than in the world outside.

"They Grind Exceeding Small"—
    Ben Ames Williams   SHORT STORY
A man who is ruthless and coldblooded regarding other people and their troubles learns the terrible consequences of his meanness when the vengeful gods strike at his only son.

"Markheim"—Robert Louis Stevenson   SHORT STORY
This is a thrilling psychological study of how a guilty conscience affects a murderer, ultimately compelling him to confess his crime.

"A Warning to Labor and Management"—
    Eric Johnston   ESSAY
In the interests of a strong America, the author appeals to both management and labor to refrain from monopolistic practices.

"Tolerance"—Edward M. Forster   ESSAY
In masterful prose, a great twentieth-century writer tells how to rebuild a war-torn world.

"Holiday"—John Galsworthy   ESSAY
Perhaps you will regret how you have misspent holidays and vacations, once you have read this provocative essay.

"One of the Best"—Jan Struther   ESSAY
This is a stimulating account of the predicament we shall all be in if we are falsely generous in judging incompetent people.

"Where I Lived and What I Lived For"—
    Henry D. Thoreau   ESSAY
This essay comes from the well-known volume, *Walden,* which is the story of how Thoreau took to the woods and enjoyed life with nature remote from tax collectors and other woes of civilization.

"The Tuft of Flowers"—Robert Frost   POEM
The speaker, turning the grass that another worker had mown earlier, sees some flowers that the worker had spared, evidently for their beauty. The speaker, too, appreciates their beauty and feels a closer kinship with the absent worker.

"A Consecration"—John Masefield   POEM
The writer dedicates himself to telling the story of the nameless
ordinary people who do the world's work and fight its battles.

"Ulysses"—Alfred Lord Tennyson   POEM
When should a man retire from an active life? After many years
of toil and travels, Ulysses the wanderer finds that he cannot stay
home, for he still hungers for new knowledge.

"The Man With the Hoe"—Edwin Markham   POEM
Social indignation and prophetic fury make this poem a powerful
indictment of the exploitation of labor by "masters, lords, and rulers
in all lands."

"The Man He Killed"—Thomas Hardy   POEM
The speaker is haunted by the memory of a foe he killed in battle.
He feels that, had they met in a time of peace, they might have
been friends.

INTEREST CENTER 9: THE LIGHTER SIDE

Pickwick Papers—Charles Dickens   NOVEL
Literature affords few adventures as amusing as those that befall
Mr. Pickwick and his traveling companions. These include Mr. Tup-
man, Mr. Winkle, Mr. Snodgrass, and the immortal Sam Weller.

The Good Companions—John B. Priestley   NOVEL
This entertaining work has often been compared to Dickens' novels.
Jess Oakroyd leaves his nagging wife to travel about England and
becomes involved with an actors' troupe called "The Good Companions."

The Crock of Gold—James Stephens   NOVEL
Here is the Irish love of fantasy and humor blended with a slender
plot and lots of atmosphere. You will like the tang of subdued
laughter bordering on pathos and philosophy.

Seventeen—Booth Tarkington   NOVEL
Teenage problems involving the hero's "best girl" and his own
family become unnecessarily complicated by the presence of an
older sister and her beau. Are you a Willie Baxter?

Animal Farm—George Orwell   NOVEL
Through animal counterparts, the author portrays some of the leading figures in the Russian Revolution.

The Mikado—Gilbert and Sullivan   PLAY
This is one of those immortal musical comedies that everyone must love. Who can forget the Lord High Executioner, lovely Peep-Bo, the song of the "wandering minstrel," and the sheer fun?

As You Like It—William Shakespeare   PLAY
In the idyllic forest of Arden, we meet the clown Touchstone and the philosopher Jaques, the beautiful Rosalind and the dashing Orlando, and we hear that "all the world's a stage."

Playboy of the Western World—John M. Synge   PLAY
The fancy of the Irish and their lilting melody of speech permeate this play. The "playboy" struts his brief hour as he claims that he has cracked his father's head in two.

She Stoops to Conquer—Oliver Goldsmith   PLAY
You will enjoy the antics of the mischievous Tony Lumpkin, as well as the romance between Kate Hardcastle, disguised as a servant girl, and her shy lover, young Marlow.

Life With Father—Howard Lindsay and Russell Crouse   PLAY
Based on the autobiographical sketches, *Life With Father* by Clarence Day, Jr., this enjoyable comedy of American family life amused Broadway audiences for seven years.

P. T. Barnum—Morris R. Werner   BIOGRAPHY
You will enjoy the many anecdotes told about the greatest showman on earth: how an elephant "swam" from the Battery to Staten Island for publicity; how patrons paid cash to see the "Great Egress" (the exit).

Cheaper by the Dozen—Gilbreth and Carey   AUTOBIOGRAPHY
Father was a genius at organizing the lives and activities of his family so that each would develop to the fullest the potential that God gave him—or else!

I Never Left Home—Bob Hope   AUTOBIOGRAPHY
One of America's foremost comedians relates some of the experiences he had when he toured Army camps.

The Egg and I—Betty MacDonald   AUTOBIOGRAPHY
This is a variation on those books about people who take to the woods and lead a trouble-free, glorious life. The author tells the truth amid laughter and tears. It was rough going!

Horse and Buggy Doctor—Arthur E. Hertzler   AUTOBIOGRAPHY
This is the story of the general practitioner who served so well in

caring for his patients and spreading genial philosophy. Humor lights the picture of forty years of service.

"The Ransom of Red Chief"—O. Henry   SHORT STORY
When two tough desperadoes kidnaped the little redheaded boy, they thought his father would be glad to pay them money to get him back, but the tables were turned on them!

Tut, Tut, Mr. Tutt—Arthur Train   SHORT STORIES
A volume of stories about old Ephraim Tutt, shrewd Yankee lawyer, who outwits all kinds of schemers who seek to defraud his hapless clients. Entertaining and informative humorous tales.

"Zenobia's Infidelity"—Henry C. Bunner   SHORT STORY
When an elephant falls in love with a man who is already engaged to be married, only a dose of terrible medicine can make her stop chasing him through the streets of the town. Wonderful!

"That Brute Simmons"—Arthur Morrison   SHORT STORY
A wife nags her husband so much that he runs away from home. Many years later he returns to find her nagging someone else.

"The Jumping Frog of Calaveras County"—
   Samuel Clemens   SHORT STORY
This is a tall tale about the frontier. It has an unusual character in it, a frog that wins bets for its master by jumping tremendous distances, until someone loads it with buckshot!

"The Night the Bed Fell"—James Thurber   ESSAY
Thurber satirizes some of the unreasonable fears that people have. His delineation of Aunt Gracie Shoaf is especially entertaining.

"A, B, and C—The Human Element in Mathematics"—
   Stephen Leacock   ESSAY
In mathematics problems involving A, B, and C, it was a common practice to have A come off the best, with poor B and C faring much worse. Leacock pokes fun at this practice.

"A Dissertation Upon Roast Pig"—Charles Lamb   ESSAY
Meet Bo-bo, a lubberly shepherd boy of ancient China. His carelessness resulted in the discovery of a great delicacy—roast pig.

Chips Off the Old Benchley—Robert Benchley   ESSAYS
Take this volume with you whenever you need cheering up. The homeliest topics of his life and times made Benchley muse about the ways of men. The style is simply delightful.

"The Macbeth Murder Mystery"—James Thurber   ESSAY
When Shakespeare wrote the tragic story of Macbeth, did he make
clear who the third murderer was? Here is an amusing theory for
explaining the secret killer's identity.

The Face Is Familiar—Ogden Nash   POEMS
Modern in idiom and pace, these poems move along on an electric
charge of wit and sparkling tidbits of language. One title: "To a
small boy standing on my shoes while I am wearing them." See?

Lyric Laughter—Arthur Guiterman   POEMS
This is the poet who wrote that wonderful bit of nonsense about the
"antiseptic baby and the prophylactic pup." He makes us understand
people as well as smile at their foibles.

"The Ballad of the Oysterman"—Oliver W. Holmes   POEM
You will be amused to learn what happened when the fisherman discovered that a young oysterman was courting his daughter.

Enough Rope—Dorothy Parker   POEMS
A slim volume of the sophisticated verse that has made Dorothy
Parker a byword for cynicism. Read the short lyric called "One Per-
fect Rose" and you will understand why.

"The Yarn of the *Nancy Bell*"—William S. Gilbert   POEM
How is it possible for the cook to be also the captain, mate, bo'sun,
midshipmite, and the crew of the captain's gig? Read this amusing
tall tale of cannibalism.

INTEREST CENTER 10: IDEALISM

Lost Horizon—James Hilton   NOVEL
You will dream of Shangri-La and its ideally happy people high up
in the mountains of Tibet, and you will share the adventure of Con-
way, who was kidnaped by a pilot sent from the lamasery.

The Bridge of San Luis Rey—Thornton Wilder   NOVEL
It was either blind fate or the hand of God which caused the old
bridge in Peru to collapse when there were five travelers going
across it. Which was it? Their life stories offer a clue.

Lord Jim—Joseph Conrad   NOVEL
Jim devotes his life to atoning for one mistake: in a moment of
nervous excitement, he had abandoned a seemingly doomed ship.

A Tale of Two Cities—Charles Dickens   NOVEL
Sydney Carton's act of self-sacrifice to protect Lucie Manette and her

loved ones is one of the noblest instances of pure idealism in all literature.

Lust for Life—Irving Stone   NOVEL
This is the fictionalized biography of Vincent van Gogh, the Dutch painter of sunflowers and the bridge at Arles, who had such a burning intensity of spirit.

The Human Comedy—William Saroyan   NOVEL
The author makes us feel that Marcus Macauley, killed in World War II, lives again in the memories of his loving family and wartime buddy.

The Winslow Boy—Terence Rattigan   PLAY
A father believes in the innocence of his son, expelled from the Royal Naval College for stealing. The play, based on a famous lawsuit, involves individual liberty in conflict with government bureaucracy.

Our Town—Thornton Wilder   PLAY
Here are the ideals, joys, and sorrows of a typical New England town in the early part of this century. An unusual character is the talkative commentator who stands apart from the action and ties the incidents together.

Watch on the Rhine—Lillian Hellman   PLAY
The title recalls the phrase from the Second World War when America weighed the necessity of joining in the struggle against Nazism to preserve human freedom.

"*Porgy*"—Du Bose Heyward   PLAY
The tragic tale of love among the Negroes in Charleston is told through the medium of a cripple, Porgy (the name of one of the fish sold in Catfish Row), and his woman, Bess.

Outward Bound—Sutton Vane   PLAY
An ingenious setting is provided by having all the characters meet aboard a vessel which is "outward bound" from the world to the land of death. Philosophy in retrospect makes it interesting.

Hamlet—William Shakespeare   PLAY
This is the tragedy of the noble prince of Denmark whose mind struggled with the terrible burden of revenge. He sums up for all humanity the conflict between the forces of good and evil.

The Autobiography of Lincoln Steffens—
   Lincoln Steffens   AUTOBIOGRAPHY
Those who are sickened by today's municipal scandals will find an

equally depressing picture of political corruption in America's principal cities uncovered by this crusading reporter two generations ago.

Yankee From Olympus—Catherine D. Bowen   BIOGRAPHY
This is the prize-winning life story of Supreme Court Justice Oliver Wendell Holmes who was indeed a "Yankee" with the royal authority of the gods from "Olympus."

God Is My Co-Pilot—Robert L. Scott   AUTOBIOGRAPHY
During World War II, Colonel Scott made a reputation for himself as a distinguished air pilot, particularly in the China-Burma-India theater of war as one of the Flying Tigers.

The Seven Storey Mountain—Thomas Merton   AUTOBIOGRAPHY
Allowed to drift from childhood into a pagan kind of worldly life, this brilliant but disillusioned Columbia graduate became a Trappist monk to find true peace of soul.

Seven Came Through—Eddie Rickenbacker   BIOGRAPHY
When these men bailed out of their airplane and found themselves floating on a rubber raft in the vast Pacific, they had plenty of time to discover the consolation of prayer.

"The Gift of the Magi"—O. Henry   SHORT STORY
The ironic gifts that a financially embarrassed young couple exchange on Christmas morning reveal ideal marital devotion in this most famous of O. Henry's writings.

"Happiness"—Guy de Maupassant   SHORT STORY
An aged couple lived in seclusion on a small island. Once the wife had been a member of a rich family on the mainland, but she left everything to be with the man she loved. Did she find "happiness"?

"Young Man Axelbrod"—Sinclair Lewis   SHORT STORY
At the age of sixty-five, "Old Cottonwood" went to college to satisfy his repressed wish to reach a kind of intellectual beauty that life on the farm could never yield.

"A Christmas Carol"—Charles Dickens   SHORT STORY
This is the imperishable tale of that tightfisted old Ebenezer Scrooge and the ghost of his former partner, Jacob Marley, and the miracle of the true Christmas spirit.

"The Lost Phoebe"—Theodore Dreiser   SHORT STORY
Here is a poignant tale of the binding power of love told in a manner

at once restrained and subdued such as we would never expect from a realist like Dreiser.

"Three Days To See"—Helen Keller   ESSAY
If you had only three days to see, how would you spend them most profitably? Here is a brilliant and inspiring plan for living life to its fullest every day by one who conquered unusual handicaps.

"What Men Live By"—Christopher Morley   ESSAY
Are you a good listener in company? The art of conversation implies the removal of most of our pet prejudices and a willingness to face the truth. Morley gives sensible advice.

"A Piece of Chalk"—G. K. Chesterton   ESSAY
Only a mind as scintillating as Chesterton's could be inspired by such a common thing as a piece of chalk and give us so many thoughts on art, nature, life, religion, and the fine dreams of man.

"Character and Success"—Theodore Roosevelt   ESSAY
The philosophy of the strenuous life which Roosevelt always advised the young people of his day to heed still holds good. We must dare to live in order to build our character and success.

"Of Truth"—Francis Bacon   ESSAY
Bacon studded his short essays with Latin phrases and apt quotations such as this: "There is no vice that doth so cover a man with shame as to be found false and perfidious."

"Rabbi Ben Ezra"—Robert Browning   POEM
Life is based on optimism and faith: "Grow old along with me, the best is yet to be!" Here is a poem that deserves study for its inspiring philosophy of life.

"Elegy Written in a Country Churchyard"—
    Thomas Gray   POEM
One of the most famous poems in English literature, this work contains such quotable lines as the following:

> "Full many a flower is born to blush unseen,
>   And waste its sweetness on the desert air."

"The Hound of Heaven"—Francis Thompson   POEM
This spiritual autobiography conveys in magnificent style the flight of man from God and the unrelenting pursuit by "the Hound of Heaven," who is the Creator of all things.

Chapter 15

THE COMPOSITION TEST (QUESTION 6)

THE IMPORTANCE OF COMPOSITION ABILITY

Composition ability—the ability to think and express yourself effectively in writing—is a basic requirement for a high school diploma. Students who write well are eagerly sought by employers and college admissions officers because composition ability is urgently needed in the modern world. You can grow in composition ability through study and practice. The present chapter will help you to do so.

PURPOSE OF THE COMPOSITION TEST

Worth thirty credits, more than any other part of the examination, the composition test measures your ability to use most of the English skills tested in earlier parts of the examination: vocabulary, spelling, grammar, correct usage, punctuation, etc. But even more important— the composition test measures your ability to think. This means the ability to collect your thoughts on a topic and organize them under main headings into an effective plan. It means also the ability to introduce the topic interestingly, to connect your thoughts logically from sentence to sentence and paragraph to paragraph, and to come to an intelligent conclusion. The pages that follow will give you special assistance with the thinking and planning required for a good composition.

THE NEED FOR CAREFUL REVISION

Keep in mind the following statement printed in bold type in the heading of the examination: "**No paper seriously deficient in English composition will be accepted for Regents credit.**" This means that a paper passing in subject matter may nevertheless be rejected if it contains "several serious errors in composition, such as faulty sentence structure or gross illiteracy in grammatical expression or many minor errors." (Reprinted from *Suggestions on the Rating of Regents Examination Papers in English,* New York State Education Department.)

From experience we know that many careless errors can be detected and eliminated from a first draft by patient rereading. Therefore:

Carefully revise your composition—and literature-discussion essay, too—before handing in your paper.

TYPICAL REGENTS COMPOSITION TEST

JUNE 1961

Write a composition of 250 to 300 words on one of the topics below: [30]

Problems of the space age
A look at the new administration
The effects of new chemicals on our food
Adjusting to life in a new community
Are we "doers" or "viewers"?
The bowling boom
The farmer as a businessman
I express myself through music (*or* painting *or* writing *or* acting).
Courtesy on the waterways
The United States and world leadership today
The problems of new nations
International espionage
The art of saying no
Spending the weekend at home
Current humor

ANALYSIS OF TYPICAL COMPOSITION TOPICS

The fifteen topics in the above test may be grouped into two categories: *general topics* and *specific topics*.

1. **General topics** are those that fall within the experience of practically every person. Our typical composition test has four topics in this category:

Adjusting to life in a new community
Are we "doers" or "viewers"?
The art of saying no
Spending the weekend at home

You should be able to get sufficient material for a composition on a general topic by recalling personal experiences or by using your imagination.

2. **Specific topics** are those that require exact information about a particular subject. The eleven specific topics on our typical composition test are classified as follows:

SOCIAL STUDIES: Problems of the space age (May be listed also
as a science topic.)
A look at the new administration
The United States and world leadership today
The problems of new nations
International espionage
SPORTS: The bowling boom
Courtesy on the waterways
SCIENCE: The effects of new chemicals on our food
FARMING: The farmer as a businessman
ARTS AND HOBBIES: I express myself through music (*or* painting *or*
writing *or* acting).
ENTERTAINMENT: Current humor

Though social studies seems to be a favored area, there is a sufficient variety of topics to give you a fair choice. You should easily find at least one specific topic (if the general topics do not appeal to you) on which you have enough correct information for a composition.

Notice the emphasis on the present ("new," "today," "current," etc.) in specific topics. This suggests that if you keep up with the news, you will not lack composition material.

CHOOSING A TOPIC

People write best about the things they know. You cannot, for example, write a satisfactory composition about "Courtesy on the waterways" unless you know something about boating and the problems resulting from the rapid growth of this pastime. If you lack information on the specific topics, choose a general one that you can develop by using your imagination or by recalling past incidents. Example: "Spending the weekend at home."

Caution: If you select a topic on which you present inadequate material, you will be charged with *poor development of the topic*. This is a common reason for failure in the composition test.

PLANNING THE COMPOSITION

The following section is intended to help pupils who have had difficulty in organizing a composition. The discussion is based on a four-paragraph approach. In four paragraphs it should not be too difficult to meet the minimum length requirement of 250 words. Do not hastily conclude, though, that a Regents composition should be limited to four paragraphs. If you think and write well, you may (and should) write five or even six paragraphs.

1. Composition Length. Deductions will be made for compositions noticeably below 250 words. If you write only 200 words, the maximum your composition can earn is 24 points (instead of 30). If you write only 150, the maximum drops to 18. No deduction, on the other hand, will be made for length beyond 300 words if it is not excessive and helps to develop the composition.

2. Providing for Four Paragraphs. Naturally you will want one paragraph as an introduction and another as a conclusion. This means that in the body (paragraphs 2 and 3) of your 250- to 300-word composition you will in most cases have room to discuss *two* main ideas or phases of your topic.

3. General Plan.

PARAGRAPH 1. Introduce the topic in an interesting way.
PARAGRAPH 2. Discuss one main idea or phase of the topic.
PARAGRAPH 3. Discuss another main idea or phase of the topic.
PARAGRAPH 4. Arrive at a conclusion that stresses your chief point.

4. The Main Problem: Paragraphs 2 and 3. If you know what you will discuss in paragraphs 2 and 3, you should have no difficulty in writing a suitable introduction and conclusion. The main problem, however, is: "What are you going to discuss in paragraphs 2 and 3?"

5. Six Ways to Organize Paragraphs 2 and 3. The following are not the only ways to organize a composition. You will, however, find them very useful if you have had difficulty in planning.

1. By *advantages* and *disadvantages*. Discuss the advantages of your topic in paragraph 2 and the disadvantages in paragraph 3, or vice versa.

TOPIC	IN PARAGRAPH 2 DISCUSS:	IN PARAGRAPH 3 DISCUSS:
Spending the weekend at home	Advantages of spending the weekend at home	Disadvantages of spending the weekend at home
The effects of new chemicals on our food	Advantages of new chemicals in our food	Disadvantages of new chemicals in our food

2. By *typical examples*. Discuss one typical example of your topic in paragraph 2 and another in paragraph 3.

TOPIC	IN PARAGRAPH 2 DISCUSS:	IN PARAGRAPH 3 DISCUSS:
The art of saying no	One example of the right way to say no	Another such example
International espionage	A typical spy case	Another such case

3. By *comparisons*. Compare and contrast one phase of your topic with another.

TOPIC	IN PARAGRAPH 2 DISCUSS:	IN PARAGRAPH 3 DISCUSS:
Adjusting to life in a new community	Ways of life in your former community	Ways of life in your new community
A look at the new administration	The old administration's handling of problems	The new administration's handling of these problems
The art of saying no	The wrong way to say no	The right way to say no

4. By *time division*. Discuss one chronological phase of your topic in paragraph 2 and another in paragraph 3.

TOPIC	IN PARAGRAPH 2 DISCUSS:	IN PARAGRAPH 3 DISCUSS:
Spending the weekend at home	What you did (or would do) on Saturday	What you did (or would do) on Sunday

TOPIC	IN PARAGRAPH 2 DISCUSS:	IN PARAGRAPH 3 DISCUSS:
The problems of new nations	The immediate problems of new nations	The long-range problems of new nations
A look at the new administration	Its achievements up to now	Its plans for the future

5. By *social, political,* and *economic aspects* (also *educational, scientific, military,* and similar aspects suggested by your topic). Discuss one of these phases in paragraph 2 and another in paragraph 3.

TOPIC	IN PARAGRAPH 2 DISCUSS:	IN PARAGRAPH 3 DISCUSS:
A look at the new administration	Its economic program	Its program for social improvements
The problems of new nations	Their political problems	Their social or economic problems
Problems of the space age	Scientific problems of the space age	Political problems of the space age

6. By explaining *reasons* or *causes* (why things happened). Discuss one main cause of your topic in paragraph 2 and another in paragraph 3.

TOPIC	IN PARAGRAPH 2 DISCUSS:	IN PARAGRAPH 3 DISCUSS:
The bowling boom	One cause of the bowling boom	Another cause of the bowling boom
Are we "doers" or "viewers"?	One cause of our being "viewers" (for example, television)	A second cause (prosperity, laziness, lack of creativity, etc.)

ORGANIZING THE WHOLE COMPOSITION

Suppose that you have decided, after careful deliberation, that the best topic for you is: Are we "doers" or "viewers"? Here are some helpful suggestions about what to do next.

Step One: *List your thoughts about the topic on scrap paper exactly as they occur to you.* Example:

Are We "Doers" or "Viewers"?

1. We are "viewers."
2. What would we do if our TV sets broke down?
3. We are not "doers."
4. The pioneers were "doers."
5. They hunted.
6. They chopped wood.
7. They got water for their families.
8. They fought Indians.
9. The women sewed.
10. The women churned butter.
11. The women scrubbed.
12. They had quilting bees.
13. They had square dancing.
14. We have central heating.
15. We have running water.
16. We have washing machines.
17. We have dryers.
18. We have vacuum cleaners.
19. We sit in easy chairs.
20. We watch television.
21. Television is bad for children.
22. Children don't like educational programs.
23. We ought to become "doers."
24. We should participate in sports.
25. We should learn to play instruments.
26. We should take courses.

Step Two: *Cross out any thoughts that are off the topic or repeat an idea already stated.* Examples:

Items 21 and 22 are off the topic. They belong in a composition entitled "The Effects of Television on Children"—not in this one. Cross out items 21 and 22.

Item 3 should be crossed out because it is already implied in items 1, 19, and 20.

Step Three: *Find the main headings under which your thoughts can be grouped.* They will show you how to organize the body (paragraphs 2 and 3) and develop the whole composition. Example:

One possible main heading is *Why the pioneers were "doers."* Items 4-13 clearly belong under this heading.

Another possible main heading is *Why we may be called "viewers."* This heading is supported by items 1, 2, and 20, which state that we are "viewers," and items 14-19, which explain why we are not "doers."

Under these headings you will be able to organize the body of the composition by the method of *comparison* (see page 289): discuss the pioneers' way of life (paragraph 2) in comparison with ours (paragraph 3).

Another possible heading is *We should become "doers,"* supported by items 23-26. This is good material for your conclusion—paragraph 4. It makes a point that you should stress at the end.

Now all you need is an introduction. You remember that the topic asks: Are we "doers" or "viewers"? On the basis of the evidence you have jotted down, there can be but one answer: *We are definitely viewers.* This can be the main heading for paragraph 1.

WRITING THE OUTLINE

    I. We are definitely "viewers."
   II. Why were the pioneers "doers"? (items 4-13)
 III. Why may we be called "viewers"? (items 1, 2, and 14-20)
 IV. We should become "doers." (items 23-26)

Step Four: *Write the composition, following your writing outline.* Do not feel obliged to present the supporting items in strict numerical order. Change the order when necessary to achieve the best effect.

Let us now examine the composition that a student wrote from the outline just discussed. The student wisely left himself enough time to revise his first draft. As a result he was able to eliminate some obvious errors and make some minor improvements. This is the composition as finally submitted:

Are We "Doers" or "Viewers"?

The American people have become a nation of "viewers." They expect to be entertained and are lost when their television sets break down. How did they get this way?

The pioneers used to get things done by using their ingenuity. Instead of getting up at 7:30 in the morning and catching the 8:05 to work, they rose at or before dawn and waited many hours in the bushes for the right animal to appear. Then they had to skin it and prepare it for use. They also had to chop wood for the fire, scare away the Indians, get water for the family, and do many other backbreaking tasks. The women of those days sewed all the clothes, churned butter, made the fire, scrubbed floors on hands and knees, and cooked and washed for a large family. The pioneers made their own entertainment. There were quilting bees, or perhaps the settlement would get together for square dancing. On the whole, they had little time for entertainment. These people were the "doers."

We, today, live quite differently. We have running water, central heating, vacuum cleaners, washing machines, dryers—you name it; we have it. All these conveniences require just a push of the button and we can sit back and relax. Quite different from the old days, isn't it? Nowadays we have plenty of time to sit in easy chairs and watch the one-eyed monster called television. We are the "viewers."

Instead of watching television, we should learn to entertain ourselves. We should go in more for sports, learn to play musical instruments, or even take a few courses to improve our minds. What would happen if all the television entertainers should suddenly decide to become "viewers"?

SERIOUS ERRORS IN COMPOSITION TECHNIQUE

1. POOR INTRODUCTION

Your introduction may be considered poor if it fails to achieve two goals: (1) to start discussing the topic and (2) to arouse the reader's interest.

Study the following introductions from pupil compositions:

The Bowling Boom

Poor Introduction: Pupil A

There are many sports being played in the world today. The one I think will be the most liked and played in a few years is bowling. There is more than one reason why I say this. I am going to tell you the reasons for the boom of bowling.

Better Introduction: Pupil B

All of a sudden everyone seems to be heading for the nearest bowling alley. New bowling alleys are going up all over the country. Men, women, young and old, are going bowling. Bowling is now America's most popular indoor sport. Why is this sport so popular?

Pupils A and B Compared

Pupil A manages to introduce his topic, but bores the reader. His first sentence states something so obvious that it is not worth saying. His second sentence confuses the reader by suggesting that the bowling boom is some years off, whereas the title implies that it is with us now. His fourth sentence is essentially a repetition of the third and should be omitted altogether. Pupil A has made a slow, uninteresting start.

Pupil B, by contrast, builds to a climax of interest in four short declarative sentences on the popularity of bowling. They add up to a good start on the discussion of the topic. Pupil B then concludes with an interrogative sentence that arouses interest in the rest of the composition.

2. POOR THOUGHT COHERENCE

Your thought coherence is poor if your sentences and paragraphs do not follow logically one from the other. Study the thought coherence in these two excerpts from pupil compositions:

Adjusting to Life in a New Community

Poor Thought Coherence: Pupil C

Since there are homes being put up in many sections of our city, it is important that we know how to adjust. I think there is nothing nicer than making new friends, and joining new clubs.

Before moving to a new town you usually ride around, see if there is activity, recreation, churches, and schools. The few things that I have mentioned will more than likely supply a young person with things to do.

Better Thought Coherence: Pupil D

The first problem in adjusting to a new environment is that of getting to know the people of the vicinity and determining which of these you want to be friendly with. Once one has made friends the rest of the "adjusting process" is made easier, for these friends can now help the newcomers with the rest of the problems.

The second problem is that of finding adequate schooling and recreational facilities for one's children. Young children often become upset in going from a familiar school to a strange one. Frequently the burden of moving to a new community can be greatest for the children.

Pupils C and D Compared

Pupil C has some material on the topic but cannot express it coherently. The opening half of the first sentence would have been much more closely connected with the thought of the second half if Pupil C had written: "Since we shall all probably have to move to a new neighborhood some day, it is important that we know how to adjust." Notice also the gap in thought between the first sentence and the second, as well as between the first paragraph and the second one. In fact, some of C's sentences are off the topic. The third sentence, for example, deals with choosing a new community rather than adjusting to one. To sum up, C is floundering from sentence to sentence and paragraph to paragraph. He has poor thought coherence.

Pupil D, on the other hand, is a careful thinker. Notice how his thought flows logically from sentence to sentence and paragraph to paragraph. He has arranged his ideas in the order of importance. Pupil D has a definite overall plan for his composition.

3. POOR SENTENCE STRUCTURE

Your sentence structure must be considered poor if you write (1) run-on sentences or (2) sentence fragments. These errors entail heavy deductions. Learn to avoid them by studying the following:

1. **A run-on sentence** results from running together two or more sentences.

TYPICAL RUN-ON: Cooperatives take nothing for *granted, they* act only with the approval of the majority of the members.
RUN-ON CORRECTED: Cooperatives take nothing for *granted. They* act only with the approval of the majority of the members.
EXPLANATION: Since *granted* ends the first sentence, it must be followed by a period. Since the next word starts a new sentence, it should begin with a capital (*They*).

2. A **sentence fragment** results from writing a piece (fragment) of a sentence as if it were a whole sentence.

TYPICAL SENTENCE FRAGMENT (from the end of a sentence): There are many problems. *Which arise when you move into a new neighborhood.*

SENTENCE FRAGMENT CORRECTED: There are many problems *which* arise when you move into a new neighborhood.

EXPLANATION: "Which arise when you move into a new neighborhood" is merely a piece (fragment) of the previous sentence. Therefore (1) there must be no period before *which,* and (2) *which* must start with a small letter.

TYPICAL SENTENCE FRAGMENT (from the beginning of a sentence): *When they leave their old home.* They have the difficult task of saying goodby.

SENTENCE FRAGMENT CORRECTED: When they leave their old *home, they* have the difficult task of saying goodby.

EXPLANATION: "When they leave their old home" is merely a piece (fragment) of the next sentence. Therefore (1) the period after *home* must be replaced by a comma, and (2) the next word (*they*) must start with a small letter.

4. POOR PARAGRAPHING

Here are some reasons why paragraphing may be considered poor:

1. Including material that is irrelevant (off the topic of the paragraph).

2. Failing to support the general statement (topic sentence) of the paragraph by specific facts, details, examples, etc.

3. Failing to begin a new paragraph at the point where a new unit of thought begins.

Study the paragraphing in these two excerpts from pupil compositions:

Spending the Weekend at Home

Poor Paragraphing: Pupil E

The next day we all went shopping, and prepared the list for a going-away party on the next weekend. That evening Oscar, my brother, showed us his pictures from Japan again. They were beautiful, and one could never tire looking at them. My brother's fiancée came over then and we played cards for the rest of the evening. We laughed, kidded around, and had a wonderful time. On Sunday, my mother made a tremendous turkey with all the trimmings. My aunt and uncle, my brother's fiancée, and my best friend came for dinner. The dishes were piled high so we excused the men and they went downstairs and talked. We were stuck with the dishes. After the dishes, we went downstairs also, only to find my father sound asleep in his easy chair. We all laughed and he woke up. After chatting for an hour or so, we had coffee and cake. Soon after, everyone left, but although it ended early, we had a pleasant afternoon.

Better Paragraphing: Pupil F

Saturday started with the usual task of cleaning my room and doing the shopping. In the afternoon, when all my chores were done, my mother suggested that since I had the time, I could clean the attic. "Who wants to clean a dusty old attic?" I thought to myself, but having nothing better to do, I agreed to help. The enjoyment I had cannot be put into words. In the attic I found grandmother's old clothes, pictures of Mom and Dad when they were young (and do you know they really did wear those funny bathing suits) and even pictures of myself when I was younger. That was my first adventure of the weekend.

Sunday, too, started off in its usual manner. After church and dinner, Father felt that I needed a little exercise. He put me to work in the garden. This is one task I do not mind, for all those little creatures that you find there always seem to fascinate me. Sunday, however, must have been our lucky day. In the back of the old maple, we found an ant colony. Although I had heard much about one, I never had the opportunity to watch those little creatures at work. It is really an education in itself. We became so interested in them, we never really did finish weeding the garden.

Pupils E and F Compared

Pupil E has interesting material, but has crammed the events of *two* days into *one* lengthy paragraph. Her writing would have been clearer if she had used a separate paragraph for each day.

Pupil F has presented essentially the same material more effectively by organizing it into two paragraphs—one for Saturday, and one for Sunday.

5. LACK OF UNITY

Your composition should contain *only material directly related to the topic*. Otherwise it will be considered to lack unity.

Study the following excerpt from a pupil composition:

Adjusting to Life in a New Community

Lack of Unity: Pupil G

A business woman will almost never find it hard adjusting to life in a new community, but a mother with young children about two years old and some still in baby carriages will sometimes find it hard to adjust. She will try to find someone near her with children and related problems, such as finding a baby sitter.

Some sitters will sit for you if you have a television set and an icebox full of delicious things to eat. Of course one needs a telephone in the house to be convenient for the sitter. She most likely would call her boyfriend, stay on the phone for two hours and it'll be free of charge for her, but *you'll* have to pay for it.

Restoring Unity: Pupil G

Pupil G's second paragraph spoils the unity of her entire composition, for it is *not directly related* to the topic. It does not belong in this composition. (It would be appropriate in a composition entitled "Problems of Baby Sitters.") To restore unity, Pupil G must leave out the unrelated material, the entire second paragraph.

6. POOR CONCLUSION

Your conclusion may be judged poor for these reasons: (1) failure to sum up, briefly but interestingly, the main points you have made, or (2) failure to stress the main point that you wish to leave with your reader.

Study the following conclusions from pupil compositions:

The Art of Saying "No"

Poor Conclusion: Pupil H

No matter how the word "no" is used, there really is an art to saying it. As you can see, "no" is used many times, in many ways, by many people, for many reasons.

Better Conclusion: Pupil I

There remains only one trustworthy method of saying "no." It is very simple, involving only a slow, side-to-side motion of the head, from left to right. This is easy, irrefutable, and actually very effective. It seems to be the best method to rely upon.

Pupils H and I Compared

Pupil H is not thinking. He merely wants to end his composition and does so mechanically. The first sentence is a careless statement. He didn't stop to think that saying "no" sometimes may be the result of anger or thoughtlessness and therefore involves no art. The second sentence states an obvious truth that leaves no deep impression. Pupil H has not concluded his composition. To do so properly, he should have summed up his important ideas or stressed a single point to be impressed on the reader.

Pupil I's first sentence neatly sums up the ways of saying "no" discussed earlier in her composition. By stating that there is only one trustworthy way of saying "no," she implies that all the other ways are unreliable. Then she cleverly describes this way of saying "no" in her second sentence. Pupil I has both summed up her thoughts and stressed what she considers an important point.

7. OTHER SERIOUS FAULTS IN COMPOSITION TECHNIQUE

Faults in the following fundamentals of writing are also considered serious and entail the loss of valuable credit. Review:

> Incorrect Spelling: pages 20-39
> Incorrect Grammar: pages 82-124
> Errors in Punctuation: pages 125-137
> Errors in Capitalization: pages 138-145
> Errors in Abbreviation: pages 146-149

Again, you should be reminded that you will in most cases be able to eliminate errors and improve your composition if you take the pains to revise your paper. With the review suggested above, you will be better equipped to do this. Begin now to develop a lifelong habit of carefully rereading everything you write. It will pay dividends.

ANALYZING PUPIL COMPOSITIONS

One valuable way to improve your ability to write a composition is to analyze the compositions of other pupils. The following are all on the same topic: "Spending the weekend at home."

Notice that each sentence has been numbered. This will help you locate the writing strengths and weaknesses discussed in the evaluation that follows each composition.

Pupil J

Spending the Weekend at Home

¹In this hectic modern life spending a weekend at home can be a rare treat. ²Your home is your own intimate world and probably thoroughly permeated with you as an individual. ³A weekend at home offers you a chance to become reacquainted with yourself and to get all sorts of necessary things done.

⁴Let's see. ⁵It's a warm, sunny Saturday. ⁶Why not give the dog that bath that he and I have been putting off? ⁷So I fill the tub, grab the flea soap and Dad's good backbrush, only to discover the "mutt" has fled. ⁸This prompts me to crawl on my stomach in the dust under the bed (which reminds me I should clean under the bed, too), coaxing the ungrateful canine. ⁹Grasping the dog firmly by the scruff of the neck, I plunge him into the tub of, by now, cold water.

¹⁰The dust in my mouth from under the bed makes me decide to clean my room. ¹¹This task involves supreme concentration. ¹²I find so many personal things to sidetrack me. ¹³There is that needlepoint that I put away months ago. ¹⁴I think I'll just do a row or two of the background. ¹⁵And here are my old rock and roll records from grammar school. ¹⁶I think I'll play a few. ¹⁷There is my guitar gathering dust in the corner. ¹⁸The "g" string is missing, but I guess I'll tune it anyway. ¹⁹Back in the closet is one ballet slipper. ²⁰Now where is the other? ²¹Cleaning my room becomes a reacquaintance with parts of myself that have been left to stagnate.

²²Sunday morning I decide to surprise my parents by making breakfast for them. ²³Oh dear! ²⁴What are the ingredients for pancakes, and where is that griddle? ²⁵Griddle recovered, ingredients recalled, and breakfast on the table, it is pleasant to sit down to the old family tradition of Sunday breakfast together.

²⁶With a whole afternoon to myself, I think I'll finish reading that novel. ²⁷By now, people have noticed that I'm home for the weekend. ²⁸The doorbell begins to ring, and callers come. ²⁹Soon my room is filled with old friends and acquaintances. ³⁰"Why yes, Mary, I'd love to spend next weekend at your country place!"

EVALUATION: PUPIL J

1. *General Plan:* Very clear. The opening paragraph makes generalizations (S3) about spending a weekend at home. The rest of the composition supports these generalizations by retelling some incidents of a specific weekend. These have been arranged by time-division, or chronological order (page 289), for greater clarity. A natural remark to a friend (S30) effectively concludes the composition.
2. *Thought Coherence:* Excellent. The third paragraph is a fine example. The word *dust* (S10) is a clever link with the second paragraph, as well as an introduction to the topic of the third paragraph. S11 makes a generalization which is admirably supported by S12-20. Then S21 aptly sums up the paragraph (and also links up with the thought of S3).
3. *Sentence Variety:* Superior. There is skillful variety of sentence length, opening, and structure. There is effective use of interrogative sentences (S6, 20, 24) and exclamatory sentences (S23, 30).
4. *Vocabulary:* Above average. Pupil J knows how to achieve humor by choice of words and details, as in S7 and 8.
5. *Spelling:* Very good, except for one word in S13. It should be *needlepoint.*

Rating: 29 (out of 30) or 97%

Pupil K

Spending the Weekend at Home

¹Do you know the thing I dislike most? ²It is spending the weekend at home. ³Now don't get me wrong by thinking I dislike my home. ⁴I really love it, but sitting home on a Saturday and Sunday is not my idea of fun. ⁵This weekend, unfortunately, was an exception. ⁶With two little Regents tests coming up, I just had to stay home and study.

⁷Usually on a weekened you could find me bowling on a Friday night, or at a dance, or a party at a friend's house. ⁸Saturday morning I catch up on my sleep. ⁹In the afternoon, if the weather is nice, I'm usually at the beach, and Sunday too. ¹⁰Saturday night you'll find me at a dance, or a party, or a movie. ¹¹Sometimes I go into the city for a good movie or a play. ¹²Briefly, I am out somewhere having a good time.

[13]But this weekend found me locked in my little room studying, and boy did I study! [14]I must admit I fell asleep a few times because I don't particularly find the causes and results of the American Civil War very exciting. [15]Trying to study Sunday was quite a job. [16]Not only was the sun shining and it was beautiful beach weather, but because it was Father's day everyone was over. [17]My aunt and uncle came with their lovely children. [18]My restless cousins added to the excitement. [19]It was so noisy in the house that I had to go down to the basement to get my studying done.

[20]Well, this was the first weekend I spent at home in a long time, and if I could have anything to do about it, it will be the last.

EVALUATION: PUPIL K

1. *General Plan:* Excellent. The opening and concluding paragraphs are effective and interesting. The body of the composition is organized by the method of comparison (page 289): the second paragraph describes a weekend away from home; the third tells of a weekend at home.

2. *Thought Coherence:* Generally superior. One exception, however, is S18. The words "My restless cousins" give the impression of new arrivals. Actually, they are the "lovely children" of S17. For better coherence, Pupil K should have written: "My aunt and uncle came with their lovely children, who added to the excitement."

3. *Vocabulary:* Satisfactory, but contains many overworked words: *little* (S6 and 13), *good* (S11 and 12), *nice* (S9), *lovely* (S17), etc. The words "on a weekend" in S7 are unnecessary. S1 is a hasty, carelessly worded question. Doubtless there are things that Pupil K dislikes more than spending a weekend at home, were he only to think of the matter. It would have been more accurate to say: "Do you know *one of the things* I dislike most?"

4. *Capitalization: day* in S16 should have been capitalized because it is part of a proper noun—*Father's Day*.

5. *Spelling:* The only error is an obvious oversight in S7 (it should be *weekend*).

Rating: 24 (out of 30) or 80%

Pupil L

Spending the Weekend at Home

[1]"I'm home dear, and guess what? [2]I have the whole weekend off. [3]Isn't that great? [4]Now I can relax for two hole days. [5]Little does Dad know that his fate for the weekend is being planned by someone very superior to him—Mother!

[6]Dad thinks he is going to sleep late Saturday morning, but Mother has other plans. [7]She wants him to get up at eight o'clock to take the kids to the grand opening of the new supermarket. [8]There will be free gifts for everybody and special bargains. [9]It will be *so* much fun! [10]Dads afternoon assignment is the family trip to the dentist. [11]It takes Dad a long time to pursuade the kids that the dentist is really a very nice man. [12]He never hurts anybody. [13]To show the kids there is nothing to be afraid of, Dad gets into the dentists chair, and guess who has three bad cavaties?

[14]Sunday morning Dad is up bright and early for a few holes of golf with the boys. [15]It's a perfect day for golf. [16]The sun is shinning brightly. [17]There is not a cloud to be seen. [18]But it's also a perfect day for a picnic at Lake Oshingawa. [19]So off they go—two kids, one dog, a tired father, and a happy mother. [20]When the family returns home, there is a new addition to the family. [21]It is a little lizzard discovered in the picnic area.

[22]By this time Dad is quite glad that it is Sunday night and that he will be back at work the next day. [23]He has learned his lesson. [24]Now he knows that the best place to relax is at the office and not on a weekend at home.

EVALUATION: PUPIL L

1. *General Plan:* Excellent. The direct quotation in the first paragraph (S1-4) and the contrasting observation in S5 immediately arouse interest and state the topic. The body is organized by time-division (chronological) order (page 289): the second paragraph deals with Saturday, and the third with Sunday. The final paragraph sums up the weekend with a touch of humor.

2. *Unity:* The third paragraph is, strictly speaking, off the topic since it describes a day *away from* home. It would be more appropriate in a composition on "Spending the weekend with the family."

3. *Word Order:* Superior. S5, 19, and 24 show that Pupil L knows how to arrange word order for maximum emphasis.
4. *Punctuation:* There are two errors. In S1 there should be a comma before *dear* (as well as after) because *dear* is used in direct address. (See page 126.) In S4 there should be quotation marks after the period to close the direct quotation.
5. *Spelling:* Below average.

SENTENCE	ERROR	CORRECT SPELLING
4	"hole"	whole
10	"Dads"	Dad's
11	"pursuade"	persuade
13	"dentists"	dentist's
13	"cavaties"	cavities
16	"shinning"	shining
21	"lizzard"	lizard

Rating: 21 (out of 30) or 70%

Pupil M

Spending the Weekend at Home

¹Weekends usually pass very quickly for me. ²There's always something going on, a dance, a party, or just skating or bowling. ³My friends and I do a number of these things each weekend. ⁴Just so that we can all be together and pass the time away. ⁵This weekend, though, not only went slow, it draged.

⁶Oh, I could have gone to any of the places I just mentioned but, there were other more exciting things to do. ⁷Friday night, for instance, there was babysiting with cousins Bobby and Rita. ⁸It was to thrilling for words. ⁹While trying to study I was bombarded with railroad tracks and toy cars. ¹⁰Saturday turned out to be beautiful, it's too bad I couldn't enjoy it. ¹¹After finishing my housework, my father asked me if I could give him a hand for a while. ¹²I said "Yes" but, I didn't know what I was getting into. ¹³We skillfully moved the piano that was in the living room to the front porch. ¹⁴With a wrenched back, I went to my room limping up the stairs and studied till dinner time. ¹⁵Sunday I helped fix dinner, it was Fathers Day. ¹⁶Everything had to be just so. ¹⁷It was fun watching Dad opening a few presents for a change. ¹⁸My father allowed my sister and I to visit some friends in the afternoon. ¹⁹On the way home I felt my feet were going to melt from the

heat. ²⁰Into bed I fell and went to a wonderful place called "Dreamland" ²¹When I awoke the terrible thought came to me that it was Monday morning. ²²Butterflies began to take form in my stomack as I got ready my pens and pencils for the English examination I knew I must take.

Evaluation: Pupil M

1. *General Plan:* Poor. The opening paragraph deals with spending weekends; it makes no mention of the topic "Spending the weekend at home." Reread the opening paragraphs of Pupils J, K, and L to realize how weak Pupil M is in this respect. M's second paragraph is long and unwieldy. It is made up of several distinct thought units. S10, 15, and 21 are logical places to start new paragraphs.

2. *Sentence Structure:* Poor.

   S4 is a sentence fragment. It should be combined with S3 as follows: *My friends and I do a number of these things each weekend just so that we can all be together and pass the time away.*

   S5 is a run-on sentence. There are three ways to correct it:
   a. *This weekend, though, not only went slow. It dragged.* or
   b. *This weekend, though, not only went slow; it dragged.* or
   c. *This weekend, though, not only went slow but it dragged.*
   S10, also a run-on sentence, may be corrected similarly:
   a. *Saturday turned out to be beautiful. It's too bad I couldn't enjoy it.* or
   b. *Saturday turned out to be beautiful; it's too bad I couldn't enjoy it.* or
   c. *Saturday turned out to be beautiful, but it's too bad I couldn't enjoy it.*
   S15 is a run-on that may be corrected in one of these two ways:
   a. *Sunday I helped fix dinner. It was Father's Day.* or
   b. *Sunday I helped fix dinner; it was Father's Day.*

3. *Grammatical Correctness:* There are two serious errors.

   In S11, *After finishing my housework* is a dangling construction. It makes it appear that Father did Pupil M's housework. The sentence should be corrected as follows: *After I had finished my housework, my father asked me,* etc. (See page 115.)

In S18, *I* should be changed to *me*. The objective case (*me*)
is needed as subject of the infinitive *to visit*. (See page 85.)

4. *Punctuation:* There should be a period inside the final quotation marks in S20 in order to end the sentence. In S6 and 12,
there should be no comma after *but*. Since S6 is a long compound sentence, a comma should be inserted before *but*. In
S12, which is much shorter, a comma may be inserted before
but.

5. *Spelling:* Weak.

SENTENCE	ERROR	CORRECT SPELLING
5	"draged"	**drăgged**
7	"babysiting"	**babysitting**
8	"to"	**too**
15	"Fathers"	**Father's**
22	"stomack"	**stomach**

Rating: 16½ (out of 30) or 55%

EXERCISE

See how accurately you can evaluate the next three compositions.
They all deal with the same topic: "The bowling boom." Before as-
signing a rating to a composition, carefully consider its main strengths
and weaknesses. Make use of the evaluation aids that have been inserted below each composition.

(The teachers who graded these compositions rated them 87%, 70%,
and 60%. Can you tell which is which?)

Pupil N

The Bowling Boom

[1]Every ten years we find new fads which sweep our country. [2]Not
so long ago, miniature golf was the sensation of the day. [3]Today there
is no doubt that bowling is the most widely enjoyed indoor sport in
America. [4]In the following paragraphs I will try to explain some of
the reasons for this boom.

[5]Bowling is an inexpensive and enjoyable pastime. [6]In order to
bowl, you have to pay a small charge for each game. [7]It is not necessary to buy any expensive equipment. [8]The management provides you
free of charge with regulation bowling balls, and it charges only a few
cents for the rental of bowling shoes. [9]Once you have begun to bowl,

you will find that it is quite an easy sport to master. [10]Within three or four visits to your local alleys, you will find yourself giving pointers to the other bowlers. [11]All of these factors add to the widespread acceptance of bowling throughout the country.

[12]Bowling is also said to be good for physical fitness. [13]When you are in the process of bowling, every part of your body is in motion. [14]This can be very helpful if you have to watch your weight, especially if you can stay away from the fancy snack bar and restaurant that are also on the premises. [15]The surroundings are well ventilated. [16]It is a clean, wholesome place for the whole family. [17]The sport is open to all ages. [18]Thats why you can find people from six to seventy-six keeping physically fit by bowling.

[19]The next time you have time on your hands, just go down to your nearest bowling alley and see whether you don't agree that this sport deserves its widespread popularity.

EVALUATION AIDS: PUPIL N

1. What is your opinion of Pupil N's general plan for organizing his composition?
2. By what specific proofs does Pupil N support his statement in S5? in S12?
3. Find three sentences that are noteworthy for use of vocabulary. In S19, find an example of (*a*) vocabulary weakness, and (*b*) vocabulary strength.
4. Find a spelling error in S18. What is your opinion of Pupil N's spelling ability?

Rating: 60%, 70%, or 87%?

Pupil O

The Bowling Boom

[1]A sport that has caused great excitement among the American people is Bowling. [2]This sport originated some three thousand years ago, and was popular in the Near East. [3]Bowling has come a long way, it has captured the American frenzy.

[4]The big reason for the tremendous boom in bowling is the participation of any member of the family. [5]Upon entering a bowling establishment you would see people ranging from the age of six to ninety-six.

⁶This is a sport where the women can compete with the men. ⁷Bowling is played all year round, not like some sports, where it is just in the winter or the spring.

⁸Bowling attracts the weight watchers in this country, it is very good exercise and guaranteed to rid you of that ugly fat. ⁹The popularity of bowling has been evidenced by the expansion of bowling establishments from east to west. ¹⁰Bowling owners have arranged adequate facilities for their patrons. ¹¹If you have a car there is always a place to park in their spacious parking lots. ¹²People having small children have no worry about going bowling, in most establishments there is a special room where the children are cared for, free of charge. ¹³Don't worry about making supper if you have a bowling date, eat in the modern restaurant, and then stop in the snack bar before going home.

¹⁴Bowling is a sport for people who want to get out of the house and relax. ¹⁵Leaving all their problems home. ¹⁶In 1959 a census was taken and it was proven that more people participate in bowling than in any other sport.

EVALUATION AIDS: PUPIL O

1. Carefully examine the sentence structure of S3, 8, 12, 13, and 15.
2. Compare Pupil O's third paragraph with Pupil N's. Which is better? Why?
3. Study Pupil O's choice of words in S3 and 10.
4. Find an error in capitalization.

Rating: 60%, 70%, or 87%?

Pupil P

The Bowling Boom

¹Today bowling is a million dollar enterprize with more and more bowling alleys opening everyday.

²Ten or twenty years ago, if a person said "Let's go bowling," you would look at him as though he were some sort of shady character. ³This was due to the fact that bowling alleys in those days were a hangout for people with doughtful reputations and any respectible person wouldn't be seen in such a place. ⁴Today it is a healthy recreation center and wonderful new competitive sport.

⁵Today you can walk into a bowling alley, and if you have never been in one before, you will be amazed at what you will find. ⁶First you will be surprized at the wonderful and beautiful modern building which houses the alleys. ⁷Also to your amazement you will find how beautifully clean and lighted everything is. ⁸It is probably a lot different from what you might have thought it to look like. ⁹If you feel like freshing up a bit, there are rest rooms. ¹⁰If you feel famished after having played a few games there is a snack bar where you may purchase, food, drink or candy. ¹¹For the older participants there is a cocktail longue.

¹²These are some of the features of a modern bowling alley. ¹³From this I am sure you can tell why bowling has become one of Americas favorite games and why there is such a bowling boom.

EVALUATION AIDS: PUPIL P

1. What is your opinion of Pupil P's general plan for organizing his composition?
2. Carefully examine the spelling in S1, 3, 6, 11, and 13.
3. Study the use of the comma in S5 and 10.
4. Compare Pupil P's sentence structure with Pupil O's. Which is better? Why?

Rating: 60%, 70%, or 87%?

FORMER REGENTS QUESTIONS

Write a composition of 250 to 300 words on one of the topics below:　　[30]

1

A home I should like to own
Weren't you ever a teenager?
Observations of a caddie
A famous American document
Pets are like people.
Helping new Americans
The work of the coach
The modern prospector

Helping the farmer
Niagara's power
Report-card day
A new haircut
At Scout camp
The F.B.I.
Getting my license

2

Teachers as friends
It's later than you think.
Crusading for democracy
Comics and juvenile delinquency
New fabrics

The me nobody knows
Gum chewing in public gatherings
Party planning
A hole in my pocket
I like to eat.

Fluorine and tooth decay
The new look in schools

Organized charities
School can be fun.

3

Youth serves the community.
Water sports
I'd like to give an Oscar to
Young people's conferences
Fashions in cars
Songs to remember
Obeying the law
It's been fun.

To the suburbs!
Dramatics in high school
I've got a secret.
Souvenir hunting
Timesavers
Prevention is better than cure.
A college I should like to attend

4

From Edison to "hi-fi"
Winter in the country
Problems of desegregation
Traffic headaches
You and your clothes
Winter Olympics
Religion in our times
Automation: man vs. machines

A business I should like to own
Harnessing the sun's energy
New-term resolutions
Pen pals
Teamwork in the animal world
Male cooks
Hosts and guests

5

Flood control
Music for many moods
A good homemaker
The importance of student government
Parents' Night
Sports coverage on TV (*or* radio)
The city in early dawn
The manners of young people

Man-made satellites
"Giveaway" programs
Does Russia want peace?
Color in everyday life
To do or not to do it yourself
Summer work
The pleasures of convalescence

6

What is the farmer's problem?
Helping the people in backward countries
Behind the Russian smile
Mysteries uncovered by archaeology
The place of radar in peacetime
Our public library
A community project

How to meet people
Keeping fit all year round
Shopping wisely
Our school club program
I am an expert in a neglected field.
Studying a foreign language
Through the eyes of the artist
I changed my personality.

7

Unrest among Soviet satellites
A sport that deserves more popularity
Counting calories
No place to go
What's new in farm equipment?
A science fair
What businessmen expect of beginners

The value of a class trip
Community ambassadors
Improving a city's appearance
Top secret
Benefit shows
Car insurance for minors
The little things in life

8

The Fifth Amendment
New uses for the ocean's products
Sunday evening at our house
The price of being a public figure
The rights of an employer
To hear Dad tell it
The pleasures of skiing
Teenagers and the telephone

The farmer's wife speaks up.
How to be a well-groomed person
How to be a bore
The challenge of a difficult course (*or* courses)
A cruise I'd like to take
Preparing for an interview
How good is our national defense?

9

Education for a satellite age
Using animals for scientific research
Taking care of the sick
Labor has its troubles.
The farmer as a jack-of-all-trades
The intramural sports program
Music: make it yourself.
Protecting minority rights

If I had more time
I want to know why
Power conflicts in the Communist world
A look at American culture
Time out for laughter
The boss in our family
Parasites

10

The control of nuclear tests
Rocket fuels
Should billboards be abolished?
Insurance conscious
Storm clouds gather.
What the referee didn't see
Education in the home
I knew him (*or* her) when

The vanishing comedian
Background music
The need for adequate building codes
Modern art—what is it?
The case for reciprocal trade
Sidewalk observations
Shopping with a toddler in tow

Answer all six questions.

1. On the line at the right of *each* group below, write the *number* of the word or expression that most nearly expresses the meaning of the italicized word.   [15]

a. asset............ (1) false belief   (2) commission   (3) agreement   (4) raid   (5) resource

b. suppress......... (1) divide   (2) refine   (3) startle   (4) oversee (5) subdue

c. confound....... (1) perplex   (2) chat   (3) donate   (4) adjust (5) argue

d. integrate........ (1) make into a whole   (2) stir up   (3) strengthen (4) make identical   (5) question persistently

e. serenity.......... (1) kindliness   (2) seriousness   (3) self-satisfaction (4) simplicity   (5) calmness

f. incorrigible....... (1) inappropriate   (2) unmanageable   (3) honest (4) disconnected   (5) imperishable

g. curt............. (1) brief   (2) vulgar   (3) sly   (4) greedy (5) secretive

h. aloof............ (1) flexible   (2) watchful   (3) soundless   (4) reserved (5) spiteful

i. blight........... (1) conceal   (2) make happy   (3) ruin   (4) turn pale (5) wink

j. wane............. (1) joke   (2) reappear   (3) grieve   (4) decrease (5) rise

k. feint............ (1) pretense   (2) downfall   (3) achievement (4) dread   (5) threat

l. appellation....... (1) attire   (2) suspicion   (3) name   (4) prayer (5) phantom

m. nostalgia........ (1) patent medicine   (2) tactlessness   (3) sleepiness (4) fear of pain   (5) homesickness

n. enigmatic........ (1) strenuous   (2) alert   (3) puzzling   (4) attractive (5) feeble

o. cogent.......... (1) awake   (2) convincing   (3) cautious   (4) tardy (5) hidden

2. In each of the following, (1) through (10), only one of the words is misspelled. In *each* case spell correctly on the line at the right the misspelled word.   [5]

(1) delicious   wholly   geological   applys   furthered

(2) mountainous   partnership   ninty   participant   arterial

(3) entittled   mantle   analyst   pastime   pursuing

(4) minstrel   commentary   blossoming   appology   innumerable

(5) heresy   babyish   hatchet   refueled   vegatation

(6) discriminate   syndicate   greeness   aeronautics   accumulate

(7) fluency   rebellion   transitions   boycott   interchangable

(8) affable   siezure   influenza   deletion   descendant

(9) magnificent   suspension   butcher   ordinarily   vacume

(10) disability   forfeit   schedual   repentance   perforate

3. At the right of *each* of the following passages you will find one or more incomplete statements about the passage. Each statement is followed by five words or expressions numbered 1 through 5. Select the word or expression that most satisfactorily completes *each in accordance with the meaning of the passage* and write its *number* in the parentheses. [Two credits for each correct title; one credit for each other correct completion.]   [20]

a. We—all of us—exist to do creatively, in as craftsmanlike a fashion as we can, all things that must be done: great things like government, or mothering, or the healing of minds or bodies; small things like the making of beds, or hoeing corn, or driving a truck; things in the public eye like making speeches, or unleashing atomic energy, or making peace; obscure things like selling groceries, or running a bus, or teaching school. We find inner peace when we work at whatever is before us, not primarily for the pay we get or for what we can buy with that pay, not for applai e or gratitude, but for the sheer joy of creating, the pride we have in what we produce. There are a vast number of tasks to be performed, most of them neither romantic nor glamorous. They must be done in one of two ways: just to get them over with as quickly and painlessly as possible, in which case they become monotonous and hard to bear; or each as beautifully as possible, in which case life becomes rich and filled with nobility.

The title below that best expresses the ideas of this passage is:

1. The importance of great projects
2. The happy life
3. Dullness of everyday routine
4. Satisfactions from creative work
5. Working for the public ...... (   )

According to the passage, work brings us the greatest pleasure when we are motivated by   (1) pride in performance   (2) the desire to serve others   (3) recognition   (4) promotion to a higher position   (5) gratitude from others .... (   )

According to the author, the work of a teacher is   (1) glamorous   (2) important   (3) appreciated   (4) monotonous   (5) inconspicuous
.... (   )

b. Practically everybody has tried to analyze humor or to figure out just what makes a comedian funny. And everybody seems to have a different idea about the ingredients that constitute humor or make a comedian a comedian. However, there is one subject on which all the comedy experts seem to be in complete

The title below that best expresses the ideas of this passage is:

1. A laugh and a joke
2. A key to laughter
3. The nature of poor timing
4. What makes humor natural
5. The challenge of humor ..... (   )

agreement—a sense of timing. A good sense of timing is important in every field of endeavor—from when to buy or sell on the stock market to hitting a baseball. But nowhere is it more important than it is in comedy.

Timing is what makes a comedian know exactly when to say a line, or how long to wait between lines. It can be the difference between a laugh and no laugh. And, while good timing can make a mild joke get a big laugh, bad timing by the same token can ruin a fine joke. Obviously, every great comedian has to have a good sense of timing.

c. If an owner-publisher is seriously responsible for every word in his newspaper, he ought not to publish any columnist whose basic integrity he doubts— or with whose basic philosophy he disagrees. That is not the fashionable doctrine. The fashionable and convenient and profitable doctrine is that, in order to amuse the reader or "to give the readers various viewpoints," the owner-publisher has the right, even the duty, to print what personally he deplores or detests. In my view that is a childish evasion of a man's responsibility. It is worse than that: it is cynicism at the heart of American life. The Miltonian conception of Truth prevailing in open combat with Error did not, I think, have the modern press in mind. For Milton, surely, had in mind individual men speaking honestly their own truth—or their own lies. The Miltonian doctrine does not apply to a situation where one man feels justified in being the profitable vehicle of another man's lies or another man's distortions.

Good timing, according to the author, involves   (1) the use of a variety of techniques   (2) a knowledge of the use of the pause   (3) a cultivation of the actor's individuality   (4) an ability to find good comic material   (5) an analysis of humor . . . . ( )

This passage most probably first appeared in   (1) an article in an encyclopedia   (2) a novel   (3) an informal essay   (4) a book about American social patterns   (5) a diary of a comedian . . . . ( )

The title below that best expresses the main ideas of this passage is:

1. A responsibility of the owner-publisher
2. Giving the reading public what it wants
3. The privileges of publishers
4. The complaints of columnists
5. The Miltonian theory of truth

. . . . ( )

From the passage we may conclude that Milton   (1) defended the right of a journalist to have his opinions published at another's expense   (2) described the need for censorship under certain conditions   (3) believed that even a man who twisted the truth had a right to be heard   (4) thought that a man was justified in making money from another man's dishonesty   (5) conceived of Truth cynically

. . . . ( )

The author says that his point of view is   (1) popular with columnists   (2) identical with Milton's   (3) influenced by the results of a poll of readers   (4) different from that of many publishers   (5) agreeable to most newspaper owners . . . . ( )

According to this passage, the publisher of a newspaper should (1) ascertain the honesty of his columnists (2) give the public all conflicting opinions on a subject (3) avoid assuming a censor's role (4) place the profit motive above other motives (5) print comparatively few columns .... ( )

d. For Winston Churchill, painting has been a continuation of the war by other means. Visitors to an exhibition of his work may delude themselves that they are looking at a collection of peaceable, old-fashioned pictures in the manner of the impressionists, but the fact is that the beach or lake scenes are really items of battle. His campaign against the terrifying challenge of an empty canvas began more than forty years ago. The brush simply frightened him until a talented friend showed him that a brush is a weapon—a weapon capable of a carnage of colors, the joys of assault, and the no less stimulating stings of defeat, for Sir Winston has always admitted a taste for disaster. The statesman and warrior leads a strange, new army: the underground movement of the British Sunday painters. His war is a war against the most subtle corrosive of peacetime life: boredom.

The title that best expresses the ideas of this passage is:

1. Visiting a Churchill exhibition
2. A mighty weapon
3. Churchill's war paintings
4. Churchill as a painter
5. War and art .... ( )

By the end of the passage, the reader has *not* learned that (1) Churchill's paintings have been seen by exhibition-goers (2) Churchill has known defeats in his lifetime (3) the author considers Churchill's paintings artistic masterpieces (4) life during times of peace can be dull (5) Churchill frequently depicts peaceful scenes .... ( )

From this passage, one may most safely conclude that Churchill (1) was taught to paint by an impressionist (2) began painting before World War II (3) reserves Sundays for painting (4) uses glaringly bright colors on his canvases (5) is sensitive to the reactions of art critics

.... ( )

As used in lines 6-7, "in the manner of" most nearly means (1) in the style of (2) from the viewpoint of (3) with the directness of (4) in the state of (5) by way of ...... ( )

The "army" that Churchill now leads consists of (1) amateur artists (2) former soldiers (3) retired statesmen (4) bored churchgoers (5) underground workers .... ( )

The passage reveals that as a person Sir Winston is   (1) tasteless   (2) hesitant   (3) secretive   (4) subtle (5) aggressive . . . . (   )

4. Answer both *a* and *b*:

a. Each of the following involves related areas of English. Choose *five* only, and in the space provided write the *number* of the expression that best completes the statement or answers the question.   [5]

(1) In most organizations, when a meeting is held, which step precedes the others listed?   (1) secretary's report   (2) old business   (3) new business   (4) treasurer's report

(2) A by-line in a newspaper contains the name of the   (1) editor   (2) owner (3) author of an article   (4) person who edited the original story

(3) Which would most likely appear on the editorial page of a large city newspaper? (1) a book review   (2) an account of a wedding   (3) a political cartoon (4) the complete text of a speech by President Kennedy

(4) A library reference book which deals with parliamentary practice is edited by (1) Robert   (2) Lippincott   (3) Webster   (4) Brewer

(5) A primary purpose for including footnote references in a term paper (source theme) is to   (1) establish the fact that a source was read   (2) acknowledge the writer's debt to other sources   (3) indicate common facts of general knowledge familiar to most people   (4) indicate that certain materials are unimportant and irrelevant

(6) Which source contains pictures of important people?   (1) *Webster's Biographical Dictionary*   (2) *Current Biography*   (3) *Who's Who*   (4) *Reader's Cyclopedia*

b. Some of the underlined parts of the sentences below are incorrect in grammar, punctuation or usage. For each incorrect part, write your corrected answer in the space at the right. For each correct part, place a *C* in the space.   [5]

(1) He should not have received the prize, for he had <u>all ready</u> gone home.
(1)

(2) If he had had better training, he would have been <u>excepted</u> to play on the first
(2)

team.

(3) When <u>your</u> sure you know the answer, raise your hand.
(3)

(4) They disapproved of any council member<u>,</u> who did not attend meetings regularly.
(4)

(5) As the score rose, the <u>fans'</u> enthusiasm increased to almost a frenzy.
(5)

5. Choose either *a* or *b*:   [20]

a. A poet or an essayist may give the reader a new insight into an ordinary situation or may reveal some commonplace object in a new light. From the poems and essays you have read, choose a total of *four* selections (using at least *one* poem and *one* essay), and in *each* case show by definite references how the selection helped you to see an ordinary situation or a commonplace object in a new light. Give titles and authors.

b. In books, as in life, we encounter persons who have faults as well as virtues. From the novels and full-length biographies you have read, choose a total of *two* books. In *each* case point out a fault of a person in the book and show by definite references that the fault had an effect on the person's life. Give titles and authors.

6. Write a composition of 250 to 300 words on one of the topics below: [30]

Obstacles to Latin American progress

Controlling military strength

Imagination in the laboratory

Advantages to be gained by reaching the moon

Attracting new industry to a community

A career in nursing

Who should get scholarships?

The fun of being a pedestrian

Behind the scenes

What makes a good high school newspaper

A record-breaking performance

Camping out

Professional football

How to choose clothes

If I were not in summer school

Answer all six questions.

1. On the line at the right of *each* group below, write the *number* of the word or expression that most nearly expresses the meaning of the italicized word.   [15]

a. acute . . . . (1) keen   (2) bitter   (3) brisk   (4) genuine (5) certain

b. clientele . . . . (1) legal body (2) customers (3) board of directors (4) servants   (5) tenants

c. succumb . . . . (1) follow   (2) help   (3) respond   (4) yield (5) overthrow

d. sloth . . . . (1) selfishness   (2) hatred   (3) laziness (4) misery   (5) slipperiness

e. infringe . . . . (1) enrage (2) expand (3) disappoint (4) weaken (5) trespass

f. uncanny . . . . (1) ill-humored   (2) immature   (3) weird (4) unrestrained   (5) insincere

g. submissive . . . . (1) unintelligent (2) underhanded (3) destructive (4) enthusiastic   (5) meek

h. peer . . . . (1) ancestor   (2) teacher   (3) judge   (4) equal (5) assistant

i. eulogize . . . . (1) kill   (2) apologize   (3) glorify   (4) soften (5) imitate

j. innovation . . . . (1) change   (2) prayer   (3) hint   (4) restraint (5) inquiry

k. beguile . . . . (1) cheapen   (2) underestimate   (3) charm (4) sympathize   (5) forgive

l. avid . . . . (1) lighthearted   (2) eager   (3) cautious (4) insincere   (5) fast-moving

m. omnivorous . . . . . . (1) devouring everything   (2) many-sided   (3) powerful   (4) living on plants   (5) all-knowing

n. append . . . . (1) rely   (2) recognize   (3) arrest   (4) divide (5) attach

o. stratagem . . . . (1) sneak attack   (2) military command   (3) thin layer   (4) deceptive device   (5) narrow passage

2. In each of the following, *a* through *j*, only one of the words is misspelled. In *each* case spell correctly on the line at the right the misspelled word.   [5]

a. allowence interpreter supersonic imaginary mannerism
b. allegiance proffessor unbecoming snobbery perennial
c. metropolis partiality specimen fortunatly reservoir
d. suddenness chronicle skittish helicopter ilogical
e. declarative aboveboard affiliate plurality musicial
f. quarantine legitamate dimension corduroy reconnoiter
g. manualy flippant occasional adjournment stratosphere
h. misdemeanor autocracy exibition equilibrium indifferent
i. summation betrothal orthodox poisionous prescription
j. diphthong heighth stadium arrangement generosity

3. At the right of *each* of the following passages you will find one or more questions or incomplete statements about the passage. Each question or statement is followed by five words or expressions numbered 1 through 5. Select the word or expression that most satisfactorily completes *each in accordance with the meaning of the passage* and write its *number* in the parentheses. [Two credits for each correct title; one credit for each other correct completion.]   [20]

a. History is a fable agreed upon. At best, it is only a part-told tale. The conquerors tell their own story. The stage-hands never get the spotlight. The janitor and the night watchman remain in darkness. The names of the kings and caudillos monopolize attention.

When Jerusalem fell, who wielded the hammer and trowel to raise its walls again? Who actually watered the Hanging Gardens of Babylon? Were there no cooks and foot soldiers and ditch diggers and road makers in the conquering armies of the Caesars? Who taught Shakespeare the alphabet? Who thinks of the unknown heroes who created the alphabet itself and gave signs to sounds and made possible the memory of mankind in our libraries? The Presidents we know; the peasants are anonymous.

The locomotive engineer and the bus driver do their job to get us where we want to go — all unknown soldiers unless accident and death break the journey. Who ever thinks of the man in the front cab of the subway train unless a sudden jerk reminds us that he is human too? Can we spell out the debt we owe to those who give as well as get and put necessities and luxury within our reach? At least we should remember sometimes our collective debt to those who work in obscurity.

The title that best expresses the ideas of this passage is:

1. Heroes of history
2. A look at the past
3. Anonymous makers of history
4. The debts we owe
5. Our unknown soldiers . . . . . . ( )

The author indicates that   (1) man has a long memory   (2) most people do not know their history very well   (3) those who serve others are important to the world   (4) it is useless to expect recognition for one's work   (5) it is too bad that people have neglected historical records so shamefully . . . . ( )

This passage was probably written in observance of   (1) Thanksgiving Day   (2) Veterans Day   (3) Father's Day   (4) Independence Day   (5) Labor Day . . . . ( )

b. Foreign propagandists have a strange misconception of our national character. They believe that we Americans must be hybrid, mongrel, undynamic; and we are called so by the enemies of democracy because, they say, so many races have been fused together in our national life. They believe we are disunited and defenseless because we

The title below that best expresses the ideas of this selection is:
1. No common ideals
2. America's motivating force
3. American immigrants
4. The evils of foreign propaganda
5. Defenseless America . . . . ( )

argue with each other, because we engage in political campaigns, because we recognize the sacred right of the minority to disagree with the majority and to express that disagreement even loudly. It is the very mingling of races, dedicated to common ideals, which creates and recreates our vitality. In every representative American meeting there will be people with names like Jackson and Lincoln and Isaacs and Schultz and Kovacs and Sartori and Jones and Smith. These Americans with varied backgrounds are all immigrants or the descendants of immigrants. All of them are inheritors of the same stalwart tradition of unusual enterprise, of adventurousness, of courage — courage to "pull up stakes and git moving." That has been the great compelling force in our history. Our continent, our hemisphere, has been populated by people who wanted a life better than the life they had previously known. They were willing to undergo all conceivable hardships to achieve the better life. They were animated, just as we are animated today, by this compelling force. It is what makes us Americans.

c. A cliché is made, not born. The process begins when someone hits upon a bright new way of stating a common experience. At that point, the remark is an epigram. But if it is particularly apt as well as catchy, the saying receives wide circulation as verbal coin. Soon it is likely to be suffering from overwork. It has then arrived at clichéhood. The dictionary records the doom of the successful epigram in defining a cliché: "A trite phrase; a hackneyed expression." For the epigrammatist, the only cheer in this process is that it proves his expression was good. Even this situation is covered by a cliché: "Imitation is the sincerest form of flattery."

According to the paragraph, our national character thrives because we have (1) immigrant blood (2) majority groups (3) overcome hardships (4) driving ambition (5) minority rights .... ( )

Foreign propagandists believe that Americans (1) are enemies of democracy (2) lack a common heritage (3) have a unified national character (4) refuse to argue with each other (5) are ashamed of foreign descent .... ( )

Foreign propagandists and the author both agree that Americans (1) are disunited (2) have no common tradition (3) come from varied backgrounds (4) have the courage of their convictions (5) are deeply religious .... ( )

The title below that best expresses the ideas of this passage is:
1. A brilliant remark
2. The nature of an epigram
3. The way verbal coins circulate
4. The values of clichés
5. A fate of epigrams .... ( )

The writer suggests that an epigram is (1) fresh (2) trite (3) ordinary (4) cheerful (5) noble .... ( )

According to the author, the chief difference between an epigram and a cliché is in their (1) origin (2) length (3) meaning (4) use (5) purpose .... ( )

d. While the poll takers are most widely known for their political surveys, the greatest part of their work is on behalf of American business. There are three kinds of commercial surveys. One is public relations research, such as that done for banks, which finds out how the public feels about a company. Another is employee-attitude research, which learns from rank-and-file workers how they really feel about their jobs and their bosses, and which can avert strikes by getting to the bottom of grievances quickly. The third, and probably most spectacular, is marketing research, testing public receptivity to products and designs. The investment a company must make for a new product is enormous — $5,000,000 to $10,000,000, for instance, for just one new product. Through the surveys a company can discover in advance what objections the public has to competing products, and whether it really wants a new one. These surveys are actually a new set of signals permitting better communication between business and the general public — letting them talk, to each other. Such communication is vital in a complex society like our own. Without it, we would have not only tremendous waste but the industrial anarchy of countless new unwanted products appearing and disappearing.

An epigram is most likely to become a cliché if it (1) is coined by a careless writer (2) is insincere in tone (3) imitates more successful expressions (4) is recorded in the dictionary (5) makes its point briefly and effectively . . . . ( )

The title below which best expresses the ideas of this passage is:
1. The poll taker
2. Business asks questions
3. Behind the scenes in business
4. Our complex business world
5. Averting industrial anarchy . . ( )

The passage states that polls can benefit industry by (1) reducing waste (2) establishing fair prices (3) strengthening people's faith in business (4) saving small businesses (5) serving as a new form of advertising . . . . ( )

This paragraph is developed by means of (1) cause and effect (2) contrast (3) illustrations (4) anecdotes (5) vivid description . . ( )

Which is *not* mentioned as an area in which polls have been conducted? (1) new products (2) politics (3) public relations (4) labor-management relationships (5) family relationships . . . . ( )

The passage leads the reader to believe that for business purposes surveys are (1) overrated (2) too widely used (3) often deceptive (4) necessary (5) costly . . . . ( )

4. Answer both a and b:

a. Each of the following involves related areas of English. Choose *five* only, and in the space provided write the *number* of the expression that best completes the statement or answers the question. [5]

(1) Roget's *Thesaurus* serves the same general purpose as (1) *Who's Who* (2) *The World Almanac* (3) *New International Yearbook* (4) Webster's *Dictionary of Synonyms*

(2) The governmental body which regulates the broadcasting industry is the (1) FCC (2) FHA (3) FAO (4) FTC
(3) In a news story, which phrase would most strengthen the reader's belief in the report? (1) A reliable police court source indicated .... (2) Judging from the reports of the police, it is believed .... (3) According to Chief of Police Adams .... (4) In the opinion of the observers ....
(4) In a meeting, it is *not* necessary to wait for recognition by the chair in (1) making a nomination (2) rising to a point of order (3) moving that debate be limited (4) moving that a motion be tabled
(5) The abbreviation *ibid.* in a footnote means (1) compare with (2) around (3) see also (4) in the same place
(6) When he uses the expression "I'm one of you," a public speaker is using the technique known as (1) identification (2) personification (3) metonymy (4) allusion

b. In each of the following sentences that is incorrect, underline the word or expression that is incorrectly used and indicate your correction in the space provided. If you consider a sentence to be correct as it stands, place a *C* in the space provided. Do not change any correct part of a sentence. [5]

(1) Each of your papers is filed for future reference.
(2) I wish that he would take his work more serious.
(3) Last night the stranger lead us down the mountain.
(4) After the treasure's report had been read, the chairman called for the reports of the committees.
(5) It would not be safe for either you or I to travel in Tibet.

5. Answer *a* or *b* or *c*.   [20]

a. In writing poems or essays, authors reveal their experiences, their thoughts, their satisfactions or their disappointments. From the poems and essays you have read, choose a total of *four* selections (including at least *one* poem and *one* essay). In *each* case, show by definite references that the author reveals one or more of the above. Give titles and authors.

b. In literature, as in life, a person may make an error in judgment, such as in his estimate of another person or in his decision to take a certain course of action. From the books you have read, choose *one* novel and *one* full-length play. In *each* case show by definite references that a person in the book erred in his estimate of another person or in his decision to take a certain course of action. Give titles and authors.

c. Each of the statements or questions below involves a literary reference. Choose 20 only and on the line at the right of each of the 20 statements or questions write the *number* of the word or phrase that correctly completes the statement or answers the question.

1. Cassius and Brutus disagreed over (1) informing Portia of their plans (2) committing suicide after the battle (3) reading Caesar's will to the people (4) allowing Antony to speak
2. Tom Walker was not unduly concerned when the devil made off with Tom's (1) old horse (2) nagging wife (3) whining son (4) family Bible
3. When the witches tell Macbeth he will be harmed by no man of woman born,

they are referring to   (1) Malcolm   (2) Macduff   (3) Banquo   (4) Duncan

4. Who fell in love with the reflection of his own face?   (1) Cupid   (2) Endymion   (3) Narcissus   (4) Proteus

5. The "incident" in *The Ox-Bow Incident* was the   (1) discovery of gold in California   (2) mistreatment of a slave   (3) hanging of a group of men   (4) opening of the Oklahoma Territory

6. In "To An Athlete Dying Young," Housman points out that fame is   (1) difficult to achieve   (2) easy to achieve   (3) temporary   (4) useless

7. In "Stopping by Woods on a Snowy Evening," the poet leaves the scene because   (1) he is bored   (2) he has far to travel   (3) it is growing cold   (4) the storm is growing in intensity

8. A satire of totalitarianism is presented in   (1) *Animal Farm*   (2) *The Ides of March*   (3) *The Last Hurrah*   (4) *A Single Pebble*

9. In *The Good Earth,* Wang-Lung considered his most precious possession to be his   (1) wife   (2) sons   (3) land   (4) pride in his country

10. Which person blamed Fate for his misfortunes?   (1) Walter Simmons   (2) Bewick Finzer   (3) John Alden   (4) Miniver Cheevy

11. The subject of both "Crossing the Bar" and "Prospice" is   (1) death   (2) travel   (3) a loss of faith   (4) the dignity of work

12. The pen name used by Samuel Clemens had its origin in   (1) a pet phrase used by his mother   (2) an early occupation   (3) his habit of exaggeration   (4) his unusual size

13. The play *The Miracle Worker* dramatizes the life of the author of   (1) "My Financial Career"   (2) "Three Days to See"   (3) "Sinners in the Hands of an Angry God"   (4) "Self-Reliance"

14. The conclusion of Barrie's *Dear Brutus* suggests that we   (1) are all victims of fate   (2) create our own unhappiness   (3) would do better if given a second chance   (4) need money to enjoy life

15. One person who could successfully oppose Clarence Day, Sr., was   (1) his wife   (2) his oldest son   (3) the maid   (4) the minister

16. Gunga-Din served as a   (1) servant of the Maharajah   (2) guide for elephants   (3) spy for the British Army   (4) water carrier for the British

17. The hero of Homer's *Iliad* is   (1) Theseus   (2) Jason   (3) Achilles   (4) Troilus

18. "Here once the embattled farmers stood
    And fired the shot heard 'round the world"
    is an example of   (1) hyperbole   (2) metaphor   (3) alliteration   (4) personification

19. Mama pretended to have a bank account in order to   (1) increase Papa's self-respect   (2) silence her sisters' criticism   (3) give her children a feeling of security   (4) prevent Uncle Chris from making an unnecessary sacrifice

20. In "On Unanswering Letters," Christopher Morley says that there is something queer about people who   (1) put off answering letters   (2) find letter-writing dull   (3) answer letters the same day they receive them   (4) prefer writing letters to using the telephone

21. In *Silas Marner,* a weakness in Godfrey's character was that he depended too

much on   (1) chance   (2) his father's advice   (3) superstition   (4) Nancy's loyalty

22. Red Chief's ransom was finally paid by   (1) his parents   (2) Sitting Bull   (3) the kidnappers   (4) the tribal medicine man

23. Who first used the phrases "summer soldier" and "sunshine patriot" to describe those who shirk their duty to their country?   (1) Benjamin Franklin   (2) Thomas Paine   (3) Abraham Lincoln   (4) Woodrow Wilson

24. Passepartout was the servant of   (1) Roland   (2) Cyrano de Bergerac   (3) Gil Blas   (4) Phileas Fogg

25. Which character remarked that the time had come to talk of "cabbages and kings"?   (1) Father William   (2) the Snark   (3) the Walrus   (4) the Mad Hatter

26. The lines ". . . approach thy grave,
      Like one who wraps the drapery of his couch
      About him, and lies down to pleasant dreams"
are from   (1) "Thanatopsis"   (2) "Hymn to the Night"   (3) "Elegy Written in a Country Churchyard"   (4) "The Rhodora"

27. Caliban and Prospero are characters in   (1) *Othello*   (2) *The Tempest*   (3) *Romeo and Juliet*   (4) *Twelfth Night*

28. In *The Octopus,* the farmers' chief opponent is the   (1) locusts   (2) government's restrictions   (3) cattlemen   (4) railroad

29. In *A Doll's House,* Nora sacrificed for her husband by   (1) selling her family treasures   (2) opposing her sister   (3) working in a sweatshop   (4) borrowing money

30. According to Coleridge, the setting of Kubla Khan's palace is   (1) Lepanto   (2) Zipango   (3) Ultima Thule   (4) Xanadu

31. The bottle in "The Bottle Imp" could be sold only if   (1) its present owner had been granted three wishes   (2) its present owner sold it for less than he had paid for it   (3) its buyer were a complete stranger to the seller   (4) the Bottle Imp gave his permission

32. In "The Valiant," the convict revealed who he was to the audience when he   (1) took a crushed rose from his pocket   (2) talked to the chaplain   (3) recited lines from Shakespeare   (4) whispered the girl's name after the door had closed

33. Wouter Van Twiller earned a reputation for wisdom because he   (1) read a great deal   (2) often quoted from the Bible   (3) seldom spoke   (4) made a sizable fortune

34. *And Promenade Home* presents further experiences in the career of the author of   (1) *Family Circle*   (2) *My Lord, What a Morning!*   (3) *Bears in the Caviar*   (4) *Dance to the Piper*

35. Jabez Wilson sought the help of Sherlock Holmes to investigate the case of the   (1) Speckled Band   (2) Blue Carbuncle   (3) Norwood Builder   (4) Redheaded League

36. The short story "The Car" concerns a   (1) joyride with an unhappy ending   (2) boy's developing a sense of responsibility   (3) mother's scheme to teach her family a lesson   (4) conflict between a boy's love for his car and his love for a girl

37. Which word best describes Roger Chillingworth?   (1) vengeful   (2) misunderstood   (3) uneducated   (4) compassionate

38. Which is true of the ending of *Lord Jim?* (1) Lord Jim succeeds in killing the attacking pirates. (2) Lord Jim allows himself to be shot. (3) Lord Jim becomes a respected ship's officer. (4) Lord Jim finds peace in marriage to the chief's ward.

39. Thornfield Hall was the home of (1) Becky Sharp (2) Squire Cass (3) David Copperfield (4) Mr. Rochester

40. The setting of *Born Free* is (1) Africa (2) Louisiana (3) Israel (4) Guatemala

6. Write a composition of 250-300 words on one of the topics below: [30]

An essential government service

The threat of communism in Latin America

Our changing population

The importance of non-Western cultures

Nature's balanced world

Modern mathematics

Science fiction and reality

A school service club (*or* clubs)

The popularity of ice hockey

Who sets styles?

Making effective posters

Marketing farm products

Giant economy size

A proverb works for me.

Lights

Answer all six questions.

1. On the line at the right of *each* group below, write the *number* of the word or expression that most nearly expresses the meaning of the italicized word.   [15]

a. collaborate....... (1) condense   (2) converse   (3) arrange in order (4) provide proof   (5) act jointly

b. futility.......... (1) uselessness   (2) timelessness   (3) stinginess (4) happiness   (5) indistinctness

c. intact.......... (1) blunt   (2) fashionable   (3) hidden   (4) uninjured (5) attentive

d. fervor.......... (1) originality   (2) justice   (3) zeal   (4) productivity (5) corruption

e. unerring........ (1) modest   (2) illogical   (3) ghostly   (4) matchless (5) unfailing

f. refute.......... (1) polish   (2) disprove   (3) throw away   (4) break up   (5) shut out

g. consensus....... (1) steadfastness of purpose   (2) general agreement   (3) lack of harmony   (4) informal vote   (5) impressive amount

h. compliant....... (1) tangled   (2) grumbling   (3) self-satisfied   (4) treacherous   (5) submissive

i. access.......... (1) agreement   (2) rapidity   (3) welcome   (4) approach (5) surplus

j. prudent.......... (1) wise   (2) overcritical   (3) famous   (4) dull (5) early

k. incur............ (1) take to heart   (2) anticipate   (3) bring down on oneself   (4) impress by repetition   (5) attack

l. caustic......... (1) solemn   (2) puzzling   (3) biting   (4) influential (5) attentive

m. dilate.......... (1) retard   (2) fade   (3) wander   (4) expand (5) startle

n. apathy.......... (1) fixed dislike   (2) skill   (3) sorrow   (4) lack of feeling   (5) discontent

o. elicit........... (1) draw forth   (2) cross out   (3) run away   (4) lengthen   (5) revise

2. In each of the following, *a* through *j*, only one of the words is misspelled. In *each* case spell correctly on the line at the right the misspelled word.   [5]

a. anxiety   throttle   stirring   certianly   carriage
b. porcupine   boisterous   distroying   irrational   separately
c. prosprous   conceited   apprehensive   underwriter   terrorize
d. juvenile   ommitted   accusation   vinegar   ellipse
e. ballast   tapestry   journying   addict   temperature
f. zoologist   devastate   conciliatory   partiality   exsisted
g. audiance   extensively   comradeship   abundance   superintendency
h. degree   adhesive   integration   fragrance   gaurdian
i. overrated   sheriff   recognizable   weatherproof   veiwpoint
j. apprenticeship   cavernous   onslaught   predjudice   currant

3. At the right of *each* of the following passages you will find one or more questions or incomplete statements about the passage. Each question or statement is followed by five words or expressions numbered 1 through 5. Select the word or expression that most satisfactorily completes *each in accordance with the meaning of the passage* and write its *number* in the parentheses. [Two credits for each correct title; one credit for each other correct completion.]   [20]

a. Lamarck's theory of evolution, although at one time pretty generally discredited, has now been revived by a number of prominent biologists. According to Lamarck, changes in an animal occur through use and disuse. Organs which are specially exercised become specially developed. The need for this special exercise arises from the conditions in which the animal lives; thus a changing environment, by making different demands on an animal, changes the animal. The giraffe, for instance, has developed its long neck in periods of relative scarcity by endeavoring to browse on higher and higher branches of trees. On the other hand, organs that are never exercised tend to disappear altogether. The eyes of animals that have taken to living in the dark grow smaller and smaller, generation after generation, until the late descendants are born eyeless.

The great assumption made by this theory is that the effects of personal, individual effort are transmitted to the offspring of that individual. This is a doctrine that is very much in dispute among modern biologists.

The title below that best expresses the ideas of this passage is:
1. Why Lamarck's theory is valid
2. A changing environment
3. The modern biologist
4. The Lamarckian theory
5. An attack on Lamarck's theory
.... ( )

According to the passage, most scientists today regard Lamarck's theory of evolution as   (1) controversial   (2) disproved   (3) accepted   (4) important   (5) misunderstood .. ( )

The author's chief purpose in writing this passage was to   (1) discredit other theories of evolution   (2) indicate how heredity influences environment   (3) show why animals become extinct   (4) explain a concept of biology   (5) encourage the acceptance of Lamarck's theory ...... ( )

Which pattern do the ideas of this passage follow?   (1) general to particular, only   (2) particular to general, only   (3) general to particular to general   (4) particular to particular to general   (5) general to general to particular .... ( )

b. Disregard for odds and complete confidence in one's self have produced many of our great successes. But every young man who wants to go into business for himself should appraise himself as a candidate for the one percent to survive. What has he to offer that is new or better? Has he special talents, special know-how, a new invention or service, or more capital than the average competitor? Has he the most important qualification of all, a willingness to work harder than anyone else? A man who is working for himself without limitation of hours

The title below that best expresses the ideas of this passage is:
1. Overcoming obstacles
2. Running one's own business
3. How to become a success
4. Young men in industry
5. Why small businesses fail .... ( )

This passage suggests that   (1) small businesses are the ones that last   (2) salaried workers are untrustworthy   (3) a willingness to work will overcome loss of income   (4) small business failures cause depressions   (5) work-

or personal sacrifice can run circles around any operation that relies on paid help. But he must forget the eight-hour day, the forty-hour week, and the annual vacation. When he stops work, his income stops unless he hires a substitute. Most small operations have their busiest day on Saturday, and the owner uses Sunday to catch up on his correspondence, bookkeeping, inventorying, and maintenance chores. The successful self-employed man invariably works harder and worries more than the man on a salary. His wife and children make corresponding sacrifices of family unity and continuity; they never know whether their man will be home or in a mood to enjoy family activities.

ing for one's self may lead to success
.... ( )

The author of this passage would most likely believe in (1) individual initiative (2) socialism (3) corporations (4) government aid to small business (5) nonunion labor
.... ( )

c. The ability to express gratitude rests with the few. They are born with the gracious tongue and the right word, but the majority of us have to acquire the art of framing our gratitude in the most effective words.

Some go through life never passing the infantile stage of a mumble and grunt which leaves the giver standing awkward and empty-handed, questioning the wisdom of his gift. Others may reach the plateau where their plain, unvarnished "Thank you" is audible but scarcely adequate for the occasion.

But those who have achieved the art—and it is an art—of expressing in words the feeling of gratitude which is in their hearts, will leave the giver expanding in the joy he has created, convinced that the crown jewels themselves would have been no better choice. This pleasure alone is reward enough for the thought and time and cost that went into the gift. It then has double value—bringing joy to both the giver and the recipient.

The title below that best expresses the ideas of this passage is:
1. The gracious giver
2. The art of receiving
3. A dual gift
4. The simple "Thank you"
5. The art of pleasing others ... ( )

The writer states that a gift should (1) have a two-fold value (2) be a part of one's self (3) be immediately acknowledged (4) be profusely acknowledged (5) pay off an obligation .... ( )

The writer suggests that the ability to accept a gift graciously is dependent upon one's (1) formal education (2) intelligence (3) plainness (4) sense of fair play (5) gradual training .... ( )

What is the total number of ways of expressing gratitude that the author describes? (1) one (2) two (3) three (4) four (5) five .... ( )

d. No surveyor has been around a countryman's locality asking questions. If he had, he wouldn't have harvested many complaints about small kitchens. Most of the kitchens in a man's long-

Most farmers prefer that their kitchens especially be (1) up-to-date (2) inaccessible (3) enameled (4) compact (5) functional ..... ( )

settled neighborhood are as sizable as his own. This is fortunate, for there is a lot of living that has to go on in a farm kitchen. It can't be accomplished in a space 6 by 10, however much that space is enameled, chromiumed and cut up into huddled so-called conveniences. A country kitchen has to be big enough to allow room for an unslenderized housewife to sling around an old-fashioned tin dishpan, or maybe shoo away three kids when she is making doughnuts or frosting a cake.

A country kitchen is what a man steps into first when he gets back from a barn or all outdoors. He doesn't come into a living room, stamp snow on the rug and stick his head into a small laboratory where preparations are in progress to thaw out a package of frozen fish sticks or melt a chain-store chicken pie into warm mouthfuls. A kitchen without a good-sized center table is a dead loss. No hungry, well-wintered man is going to eat satisfactorily in a dining alcove. It cramps his style in more ways than one. There isn't space to stretch his legs or tilt back a chair. Abraham Lincoln could never have made out with a dining alcove, either in New Salem or Springfield.

The author implies that farm wives are (1) dissatisfied with their lot (2) lazy (3) well nourished (4) proud of their dining alcoves (5) contented with their lot .... ( )

The passage suggests that farm wives (1) dislike interference in the kitchen (2) like some modern decorations but not all (3) envy city housewives (4) need less working space than city wives (5) must discipline their children continually .... ( )

This passage is most probably taken from (1) a novel (2) a short story (3) a financial magazine (4) an atlas (5) an essay .... ( )

The author shows himself chiefly to possess (1) bias against the farmer (2) sympathy with dealers in chrome (3) admiration for the farmer (4) an intimate knowledge of the country (5) dislike for the size of farm kitchens .... ( )

The author is most probably (1) a pessimist (2) a savage critic of change (3) a sensitive observer (4) a defender of farmers' rights (5) an advocate of better working conditions for housewives .... ( )

4. Answer both *a* and *b*:

a. Each of the following involves related areas of English. Choose *five* only, and in the space provided write the *number* of the expression that best completes the statement or answers the question. [5]

(1) Which information about Sir Winston Churchill can be found in *Who's Who?* (1) a list of his honorary awards (2) his picture (3) his physical description (4) a lengthy statement of his present political beliefs

(2) Upon which technique do most political cartoons rely for their effect? (1) understatement (2) objectivity (3) alliteration (4) exaggeration

(3) An organizational meeting called to consider whether it might be desirable to form a French club requires (1) no elected officers (2) a sergeant at arms (3) a temporary president and a temporary secretary (4) a permanent president and a permanent secretary

(4) Which sentence contains a colloquial expression? (1) Justice will ultimately triumph. (2) The decision of the lower court is hereby overruled. (3)

There were lots of people at the game.   (4) Your presence is requested at the wedding.

(5) The magazine which is most similar to *Harper's* in format and content is   (1) *The Atlantic*   (2) *Look*   (3) *Life*   (4) *Architectural Forum*

(6) In a speech, a rhetorical question is one which is   (1) intended to puzzle the listeners   (2) included for special effect   (3) based upon a quotation   (4) directed at the most intelligent part of the listeners

b. In each of the following sentences that is incorrect, underline the word or expression that is incorrectly used and indicate your correction in the space provided. If a sentence is correct as it stands, place a *C* in the space provided. Do not change any correct part of a sentence.   [5]

(1) Both the body and the mind needs exercise.

(2) It's paw injured, the animal limped down the road.

(3) The butter tastes rancidly.

(4) Who do you think has sent me a letter?

(5) If more nations would have fought against tyranny, the course of history would have been different.

5. Answer *a* or *b* or *c*: [20]

a. Often in literature a person may be faced with a serious conflict. In some cases, he has a conflict with another person whose ideals or ideas are different from his own. In other cases, the person has a conflict within himself. From the novels and full-length plays you have read, choose a total of *two* books. For the first book, show by definite references that a person in that book had a serious conflict with another character as indicated above. For the second book, show by definite references that a character had a serious conflict within himself. Give titles and authors.

b. Reading may serve several purposes. It may broaden our knowledge, increase our understanding of today's world, or show how men and women have achieved almost unattainable goals. From the full-length biographies and books of true experience you have read, choose a total of *two* books. In *each* case show by definite references that the book served for you a purpose mentioned above. Give titles and authors.

c. Each of the statements or questions below involves a literary reference. Choose 20 only and on the line at the right of each of the 20 statements or questions write the *number* of the word or phrase that correctly completes the statement or answers the question.

1. In his essay "Of Studies," Francis Bacon states that the ability to write well makes a person   (1) more popular with his friends   (2) more argumentative about details   (3) more exact in his thinking   (4) better informed about life

2. In *PT-109*, the author recounts exploits during World War II in the   (1) South Seas   (2) North Atlantic   (3) South Atlantic   (4) Mediterranean Sea

3. In which selection does the author maintain that American food is losing its flavor?   (1) Philip Wylie's "Science Has Spoiled My Supper"   (2) Roald Dahl's "Taste"   (3) Darrell Huff's "How to Lie With Statistics"   (4) C. P. Snow's "The Future of Man"

4. In *The Bridge of San Luis Rey*, as the story nears the end the Marquesa becomes   (1) feeble   (2) bankrupt   (3) repentant   (4) unfeeling

5. The lines "Then look for me by moonlight,
        Watch for me by moonlight"
are from   (1) "My Lost Youth"   (2) "Love's Farewell"   (3) "Annabel Lee"   (4) "The Highwayman"

6. In *Walden*, Thoreau proposes that man can live more completely and enjoy life more fully by   (1) thinking positively about life's problems   (2) loving his neighbors unselfishly   (3) reading and studying the greatest books   (4) simplifying his manner of living

7. "Life's but a walking shadow" is an example of   (1) paradox   (2) metaphor   (3) onomatopoeia   (4) hyperbole

8. In *The Light in the Forest*, the central character finds his loyalties divided between the   (1) Tories and the Sons of Liberty   (2) North and the South   (3) Indians and the white settlers   (4) lumbermen and the conservationists

9. "Nightmare Number Three" describes what might happen if   (1) men became the really dominant sex   (2) machines became the masters of the world   (3) a city were attacked in a nuclear war   (4) every printing press were demolished

10. Which pair of lovers communicated by means of a signal fire?   (1) Eustacia and Wildeve   (2) Jane Eyre and Rochester   (3) Romeo and Juliet   (4) Scarlett O'Hara and Rhett Butler

11. King Lear was easily persuaded by appeals to his   (1) vanity   (2) ambition   (3) Christian sense of duty   (4) interest in the realm

12. Which commanding officer was most considerate of his men?   (1) Captain Queeg   (2) Captain Bligh   (3) Captain Larsen   (4) Captain Hornblower

13. The lines "I could not love thee, Dear, so much
        Lov'd I not Honour more"
were spoken by one about to   (1) depart for war   (2) enter prison   (3) renounce his king   (4) become a monk

14. Who spoke the lines "Your face, my thane, is as a book where men
        May read strange matters"?
(1) Banquo   (2) Banquo's ghost   (3) Duncan   (4) Lady Macbeth

15. A recent best seller by William Shirer is about life in   (1) modern Germany   (2) America in the Reconstruction Period   (3) Russia before the advent of the Czars   (4) 19th-century England

16. An eye-witness account of the Great Fire of London was recorded by   (1) Colonel William Byrd   (2) Samuel Sewall   (3) John Milton   (4) Samuel Pepys

17. In "In the Zone," Smitty battles his shipmates to defend his   (1) privacy   (2) family   (3) wealth   (4) friends

18. In *Our Town*, George Gibbs decided against going to college because   (1) his marks would not warrant his acceptance   (2) he wanted to marry and begin farming immediately   (3) he knew that his father could not afford to send him   (4) Emily begged him to stay home

19. In *The Glass Menagerie*, Amanda Wingfield was most concerned about her (1) son's education   (2) daughter's marriage possibilities   (3) own career as an actress   (4) husband's business

20. In "Old China," Charles Lamb emphasizes the point that   (1) distance lends enchantment   (2) true appreciation comes with maturity   (3) dreams are better than reality   (4) happiness depends very little on material things

21. Edmond Dantes and Captain Ahab had in common a   (1) loyalty to a lost love   (2) memory of a long imprisonment   (3) greed for power   (4) desire for vengeance

22. "Life has loveliness to sell" is the first line of the poem   (1) "Barter"   (2) "Patterns"   (3) "The Coin"   (4) "Silver"

23. Ántonia married   (1) Anton Cuzak   (2) Wick Cutter   (3) Jim Burden   (4) Otto Fuchs

24. In his courtship of Roxanne, Christian proved to be   (1) inconsiderate   (2) tardy   (3) uninspired   (4) faithless

25. At the end of *Hamlet*, which person is still living?   (1) Hamlet   (2) Gertrude   (3) Claudius   (4) Horatio

26. Which statement about *The Scarlet Letter* is true?   (1) Chillingworth died after disinheriting Pearl.   (2) Pearl returned to Boston to clear her mother's name.   (3) Dimmesdale persuaded the governor to let Hester keep Pearl.   (4) Pearl married the son of the governor of the colony

27. Tenzing Norgay was a climbing companion of   (1) Edmund Hillary   (2) Maurice Herzog   (3) William O. Douglas   (4) James Ramsey Ullman

28. Markheim reacted violently when the shopkeeper tried to sell him a   (1) mirror   (2) dagger   (3) paperweight   (4) green bottle

29. For his crimes Tantalus was condemned to   (1) roll a huge block of marble up Mt. Olympus   (2) carry water in a sieve   (3) be permanently chained to a wheel   (4) suffer constantly from hunger and thirst

30. In "Mending Wall," we are told that the attitude of the poet's neighbor was influenced by   (1) a recent argument   (2) his dislike for children   (3) his father's words   (4) his desire to preserve the beauty of the land

31. Dr. Manette was imprisoned in the Bastille because he had   (1) sympathized with the English   (2) known about a secret crime   (3) posed as a shoemaker   (4) taken up arms against the aristocracy

32. Which story is narrated in the third person?   (1) "The Fall of the House of Usher"   (2) "The Masque of the Red Death"   (3) "The Pit and the Pendulum"   (4) "The Tell-Tale Heart"

33. In Faulkner's "The Bear," when he encountered the bear, the boy   (1) ran from it in fear   (2) shot it with his last bullet   (3) pretended not to see it   (4) let it get away

34. In "My Last Duchess," the duke told his story to a man who had come to   (1) buy a portrait of the duchess   (2) sell the duke a piece of sculpture   (3) arrange the terms of a marriage settlement   (4) make inquiries about the disappearance of the duchess

35. At the end of "The Tooth, the Whole Tooth, and Nothing But the Tooth," Benchley's feeling for the dentist was one of   (1) pity   (2) horror   (3) fondness   (4) suspicion

36. In *Justice*, William Falder was sentenced to prison for   (1) forgery   (2) murder   (3) income tax evasion   (4) espionage

37. When helping aristocrats escape from France, the Scarlet Pimpernel used the sign of a   (1) feather   ·(2) flower   (3) scarf   (4) star

38. The theme of Carl Sandburg's poem "Four Preludes on Playthings of the Wind" is similar to that of   (1) "Ozymandias"   (2) "The Barrel-Organ"   (3) "When I Was One-and-Twenty"   (4) "The Prisoner of Chillon"

39. In the story "The Lagoon" by Conrad, the main character is chiefly motivated by   (1) greed   (2) vanity   (3) ambition   (4) remorse

40. Professor Barnhouse first learned about "dynamopsychism" while   (1) reading   (2) shooting dice   (3) studying mice   (4) testing his students

6. Write a composition of 250 to 300 words on one of the topics below: [30]

History in the making
If I could join the Peace Corps
A United States of Europe
Teamwork in science
Occupations for the space age
Moving day
Skin-diving
A poet laureate for America

Farmers' organizations
A career in music (*or* art)
Trials of a punctual person
In ten easy lessons
Time for myself
Trading stamps
Keys

Answer all six questions.

1. On the line at the right of *each* group below, write the *number* of the word or expression that most nearly expresses the meaning of the italicized word.   [15]

a. *appease* .... (1) attack   (2) soothe   (3) pray for   (4) estimate   (5) confess

b. *ruthless* .... (1) senseless   (2) sinful   (3) ruddy   (4) pitiless   (5) degrading

c. *muster* .... (1) rebel   (2) mask   (3) gather   (4) dampen   (5) grumble

d. *abduct* .... (1) embarrass   (2) desert   (3) omit   (4) kidnap   (5) resign

e. *knoll* .... (1) elf   (2) mound   (3) bell   (4) development   (5) technique

f. *irate* .... (1) evil   (2) wandering   (3) repetitious   (4) colorful   (5) angry

g. *grimace* .... (1) peril   (2) subtle suggestion   (3) signal   (4) wry face   (5) impurity

h. *acme* .... (1) layer   (2) summit   (3) edge   (4) pit   (5) interval

i. *covenant* ...... (1) solemn agreement   (2) formal invitation   (3) religious ceremony   (4) general pardon   (5) hiding place

j. *appall* .... (1) honor   (2) decorate   (3) calm   (4) bore   (5) dismay

k. *judicious* .... (1) wise   (2) dignified   (3) light-hearted   (4) confused   (5) respectful

l. *unscathed* ..... (1) unashamed   (2) uninjured   (3) unskilled   (4) unsuccessful   (5) unconscious

m. *chide* .... (1) misbehave   (2) cool   (3) select   (4) conceal   (5) scold

n. *charlatan* ...... (1) scholar   (2) acrobat   (3) quack   (4) faithful retainer   (5) fast talker

o. *disburse* .... (1) remove forcibly   (2) twist   (3) amuse   (4) vary slightly   (5) pay out

2. In each of the following, *a* through *j*, only one of the words is misspelled. In *each* case spell correctly on the line at the right the misspelled word.   [5]

a. temperary   ghastliness   duped   umbrella   righteous

b. midget   baptize   drapery   definitive   chosing

c. beneficiary   insomnia   formost   molasses   nostril *d.* unbiased   repellent   cruiser   icey   devotee

e. caramel   missionery   ruinous   asylum   amiable

f. annulment   dynamite   subterranean   placard   prisioner

g. handicaped   artificial   disadvantageous   attorneys   pennant

h. quizzing   abundance   brethren   compensatory   carraige

i. arbitary   coerce   fascination   abhorred   congratulation

j. mosquito   unchangeable   essentually   quarrelsome   balloon

3. At the right of *each* of the following passages you will find one or more questions or incomplete statements about the passage. Each question or statement is followed by five words or expressions numbered 1 through 5. Select the word or expression that most satisfactorily completes *each in accordance with the meaning of the passage* and write its *number* in the parentheses. [Two credits for each correct title; one credit for each other correct completion.] [20]

a. Every year, in November, the crowning and majestic hour of autumn, reverently I go to visit the chrysanthemums in the places where chance offers them to my sight. They are, indeed, the most universal, the most diverse of flowers. Yesterday I went to admire the year's gentle and gorgeous floral feast. They are there, under the immense transparent dome, the noble flowers of the month of fogs; they are there, at the royal meeting place, all the grave little autumn fairies, whose dances and attitudes seem to have been struck motionless with a single word. Go back for a moment to their modest origin; look at the poor buttercup of yore, the humble little crimson rose that still smiles sadly, along the roads full of dead leaves; compare with them these enormous masses and fleeces of snow, these disks and gloves of red copper, these spheres of old silver, this delirious prodigy of petals which seems to be trying to exhaust the world of autumnal shapes and shades which the winter entrusts to the bosom of the sleeping woods; let the unexpected varieties pass before your eyes; admire and appraise them.

The title below that best expresses the ideas in this selection is:

1. Fairy wonderlands
2. Autumn's buttercups
3. Enchantment in the fog
4. Admiration of floral beauty
5. Appreciation of universal variety

.... ( )

Which aspect of chrysanthemums does the author emphasize? (1) their resemblance to yesterday's roses (2) their classification as natural prodigies (3) their blooming in the fall (4) their modest appearance (5) their sameness in color the world over .... ( )

The author uses the phrase "crowning and majestic" (line 2) to describe a (1) dome (2) month (3) flower (4) season (5) meeting place .... ( )

The author uses the term *fairies* (line 13) to describe (1) woodland nymphs (2) autumn fogs (3) flowers (4) the royal family of the forest (5) gardeners .. ( )

b. Materials of construction of aircraft have gone through many cycles. For several years after World War I and in spite of the Zeppelin duralumin development, aluminum was suspect as a structural material. The famous specification 100-A of the Navy prohibited the use of aluminum in any structural part of aircraft. This is a pertinent example of how too-rigid specifications, based on what was good practice in previous years, can prevent future development.

Today we face a similar situation in prohibitions against Fiberglas or plastic stressed structures because it is so difficult, theoretically, to calculate and check the stressed condition. Yet plastics may well have as great a future in aircraft structures as dural stressed-skin "monocoques" and wing panels had thirty years ago. We hardly need to recapitulate how metal took over from wood and replaced a material that just could not stand the weathering difficulties of day-in, day-out air operation compared to aluminum alloy, so long-lasting and reliable. Now alloys—titanium and others—are also beckoning alluringly, like Fiberglas, for a chance to show their worth. Also "sandwich" materials are most promising. Will we still be slow to pick up the ball?

The title below that best expresses the ideas of this passage is:

1. The defects of aluminum in aircraft construction
2. Resistance to change in aircraft construction
3. Specification 100-A
4. The inadequacies of wood as structural material
5. The future of Fiberglas ..... ( )

As used in the passage, the word "recapitulate" (second paragraph, line 10) most nearly means   (1) reckon   (2) complain   (3) admit   (4) verify   (5) recount .... ( )

We may most safely conclude that the author's chief purpose in writing this passage is to (1) point out the superiorities of aluminum   (2) suggest the limitations of plastics (3) encourage the willingness to experiment   (4) show why aluminum was once suspect   (5) point out the value of specifications ..( )

The author's attitude toward the new materials for aircraft construction is one of   (1) grudging admiration (2) qualified approval   (3) qualified opposition   (4) definite opposition   (5) indifference ...... ( )

The author's thesis in the passage can be expressed as   (1) we can learn everything from the past (2) progress is a painless procedure (3) it is easier to build than to destroy   (4) we should profit from experience   (5) being conservative has its advantages .... ( )

c. The wealthy hunting societies of late glacial Europe might have maintained or even enriched their culture, or allowed it to stagnate and decline: they could hardly have advanced it to a higher form of civilization, for the environment forbade it. But their fu-

The title below that best expresses the ideas of this passage is:

1. Man's conflict with his environment
2. The effect of climate on man's way of life

ture was not left in their own hands. Inexorably, although no doubt to them imperceptibly, the climate changed: Summers grew longer and warmer, ice-sheets shrank and glaciers retreated. Enslaved to climate, plant and animal life had to change also. The mammoth, rhinoceros and reindeer in turn disappeared from western Europe, their going perhaps accelerated by the inroads of the human hunters themselves. On what had been open grassland or tundra with a scrub of dwarf birch and willow, forest spread, stocked with the appropriate forest animals—red deer, aurochs and wild pig. With the withdrawal or extinction of the great herds on which they had preyed, the economic basis of the hunting societies was cut away and their carefully adjusted culture made obsolete. This was one of the moments when early man was able to prove the full advantage of his self-made equipment over the biological specialization of the beasts: the reindeer found his coat intolerably hot and had to quit; man merely took his off and readjusted his habits.

3. Changes in plant and animal life in western Europe
4. Primitive hunting tribes and their culture
5. Extinct prehistoric animals .. ( )

The disappearance of certain animals from western Europe was (1) probably hastened by man, the hunter (2) disastrous to primitive man (3) the direct result of man's self-made equipment (4) the immediate result of a more advanced culture (5) caused by the glaciers
.... ( )

The primitive hunting societies were forced to change their way of life because (1) they were the victims of their biological specialization (2) they were incapable of enriching their lives (3) they were stagnating (4) the animals which they hunted disappeared (5) their culture was allowed to decline .... ( )

The writer apparently believes that levels of civilization are determined by (1) economic abundance (2) a balance of life (3) the ambitions of the people (4) the enrichment of a culture (5) climatic conditions .... ( )

d. Great men are more distinguished in range and extent, than by originality. If we require the originality which consists in weaving, like a spider, their web from their own bowels, in finding clay, and making bricks, and building the house, no great men are original. Nor does valuable originality consist in unlikeness to other men. The hero is in the press of knights, and the thick of events; and, seeing what men want, and sharing their desire, he adds the needful length of sight and of arm, to come at the desired point. The greatest genius is the most indebted man.

The title below that best expresses the ideas of this passage is:
1. A new use for originality
2. The activities of great men
3. The great man
4. Helping one's fellow man
5. The nonconformist .... ( )

In the passage the author maintains that (1) great men weave their originality from their inner being (2) great men are totally unlike other men (3) great men do not feel as their followers do (4) heroes sense the need in men (5) heroes are invariably distinguished in range .... ( )

"The needful length of sight and arm" can be defined as (1) strength and power (2) vision and power (3) discernment and attention to detail (4) sensitivity and emotion (5) arrival at the desired point .... ( )

4. Answer both a and b:

a. Choose only *five* of the following, and in the space provided write the *number* of the expression that best completes the statement or answers the question. [5]

(1) In good parliamentary practice, one should make a motion to "refer to a committee" when there is (1) an insufficient number of persons present (2) considerable opposition to a motion (3) insufficient information available on the topic (4) little opposition to a motion

(2) Which word is the most general in meaning? (1) trumpet (2) horse (3) electronics (4) education

(3) Which publication regularly contains critical essays on recordings? (1) *Popular Mechanics* (2) *Saturday Evening Post* (3) *Reader's Digest* (4) *Saturday Review*

(4) A summary of the most important news events of the past year can be found in (1) *Statesman's Year-Book* (2) *Lincoln Library* (3) *The World Almanac* (4) *Inside America*

(5) Which topic can be treated most effectively in a term paper (source theme) of 2,000 words? (1) The space age (2) Basic characteristics of the intercontinental ballistic missile (3) America's role in the space age, in war and in peace (4) The history of nuclear fission, rocketry and the race into space

(6) The introduction of a political candidate as "that great humanitarian" is an example of the propaganda technique known as (1) glittering generality (2) misleading association (3) card stacking (4) band wagon

b. In each of the following sentences that is incorrect, underline the word or expression that is incorrectly used and indicate your correction in the space provided. If you consider a sentence to be correct as it stands, place a *C* in the space provided. Do not change any correct part of a sentence. [5]

(1) Having considered the problem, the committee will submit its report.

(2) This action will effect the lives of hundreds of people.

(3) There's several reasons for that boy's popularity.

(4) The lawyer promised to notify my mother and I of any changes in the will.

(5) The notebook, not the textbooks, belong to me.

5. Answer either _a_ or _b_:　　[20]

_a._ In reading, as in life, characters struggle to improve their lot in life. Some succeed; some do not. From the books you have read, choose _one_ novel and _one_ full-length biography. In _each_ case, show by definite references that a character in the book was _or_ was not successful in improving his lot in life. Give titles and authors.

_b._ In writing about nature, a poet or essayist may show that in it he finds beauty, cruelty, inspiration, or a truth about life. From the poems and essays you have read, choose a total of _four_ selections. In each case, show by definite references that the poet or essayist found in nature one or more of the above. Give titles and authors.

6. Write a composition of 250-300 words on one of the topics below: [30]

Spheres of influence
A current issue in labor-management relations
Keeping up with the news
A breakthrough in science
Inside a laboratory
The future of professional boxing
Competition in the classroom

Cleaning up
What's in the attic?
A car of the future
Developing my musical taste
Cooling off
The trouble with names
The rewards of individualism
Windows

Answer all six questions.

1. On the line at the right of *each* group below, write the *number* of the word or expression that most nearly expresses the meaning of the italicized word. [15]

a. paramount .... (1) equal (2) supreme (3) well-known (4) difficult (5) ready

b. brochure .... (1) heavy shoe (2) weapon (3) pamphlet (4) trite remark (5) ornament

c. fidelity .... (1) happiness (2) bravery (3) prosperity (4) hardness (5) loyalty

d. diffuse .... (1) explain (2) scatter (3) differ (4) congeal (5) dart

e. aggressive .... (1) disgusting (2) impulsive (3) short-sighted (4) coarse-grained (5) self-assertive

f. amass .... (1) accumulate (2) encourage (3) comprehend (4) blend (5) astonish

g. diabolic .... (1) puzzling (2) uneducated (3) ornamental (4) fiendish (5) spinning

h. forbearance ..... (1) rejection (2) forgetfulness (3) sensitivity (4) patience (5) expectation

i. taint .... (1) snarl (2) infect (3) unite (4) annoy (5) list

j. disgruntled ...... (1) untidy (2) rambling (3) disabled (4) cheating (5) displeased

k. antipathy .... (1) exact opposite (2) intense dislike (3) high praise (4) tolerance (5) preventive medicine

l. homogeneous .... (1) numerous (2) healthful (3) similar (4) assorted (5) educational

m. archives .... (1) public records (2) models (3) supporting columns (4) tombs (5) large ships

n. infamy .... (1) anger (2) truth (3) disgrace (4) weakness (5) excitement

o. impinge .... (1) swear (2) involve (3) erase (4) encroach (5) beg

2. In each of the following, *a* through *j*, only one of the words is misspelled. In *each* case spell correctly on the line at the right the misspelled word. [5]

a. maintenance undoubtedly budgeting beautifuly promissory
b. negetive unilateral bacteriology dissenter encyclopedia
c. enthusastic translucent replaceable conglomeration unessential
d. choral utmost swerve ruffian strecher
e. incompetent jackknives cuticle recriminate charitible
f. consignment schedual riddance scourge millionaire
g. sophisticated underrate piteous appologetic delicacy
h. epedemic corollary financier irritable perspiration
i. customer analyses parcel exceedingly statute
j. ascertain economically impliment guarantee suppress

3. At the right of *each* of the following passages you will find one or more questions or incomplete statements about the passage. Each question or statement

is followed by five words or expressions numbered 1 through 5. Select the word or expression that most satisfactorily completes *each in accordance with the meaning of the passage* and write its *number* in the parentheses. [*One credit for each correct answer.*]   [20]

a. Vacations were once the prerogative of the privileged few, even as late as the 19th century. Now they are considered the right of all, except for such unfortunate masses as, for example, the bulk of China's and India's population, for whom life, save for sleep and brief periods of rest, is uninterrupted toil.

They are more necessary now than once because the average life is less well-rounded and has become increasingly departmentalized. I suppose the idea of vacations, as we conceive it, must be incomprehensible to primitive peoples. Rest of some kind has of course always been a part of the rhythm of human life, but earlier ages did not find it necessary to organize it in the way that modern man has done. Holidays, feast days, were sufficient.

With modern man's increasing tensions, with the stultifying quality of so much of his work, this break in the year's routine became steadily more necessary. Vacations became mandatory for the purpose of renewal and repair. And so it came about that in the United States, the most self-indulgent of nations, the tensest, and the most departmentalized, vacations have come to take a predominant place in domestic conversation.

The title below that best expresses the ideas of this passage is:
1. Vacation preferences
2. Vacations: the topic of conversation
3. Vacations in perspective
4. The well-organized vacation
5. Renewal, refreshment and repair
. . . . ( )

We need vacations now more than ever before because we have   (1) a more carefree nature   (2) much more free time   (3) little diversity in our work   (4) less emotional stability   (5) a higher standard of living . . . . ( )

It is implied in the passage that the lives of Americans are very   (1) habitual   (2) ennobling   (3) patriotic   (4) varied   (5) independent . . . . ( )

As used in the passage, the word "prerogative" (line 1) most nearly means   (1) habit   (2) distinction   (3) request   (4) demand   (5) hope . . . . ( )

b. In the ordinary course of nature, the great beneficent changes come slowly and silently. The noisy changes, for the most part, mean violence and disruption. The roar of storms and tornadoes, the explosions of volcanoes, the crash of thunder, are the result of a sudden break in the equipoise of the elements; from a condition of comparative repose and silence they become fearfully swift and audible. The still small voice is the voice of life and

The title below that best expresses the ideas of this passage is:
1. Upsetting nature's balance
2. Repose and silence
3. The voice of life and growth
4. Nature's intelligence
5. The violent elements . . . . . . ( )

As used in the passage, the word "equipoise" (line 8) most nearly means   (1) stress   (2) balance   (3) course   (4) slowness   (5)

growth and perpetuity. . . . In the history of a nation it is the same.

c. Fortunately it is as yet only through fantasy that we can see what the destruction of the scholarly and scientific disciplines would mean to mankind. From history we can learn what their existence has meant. The sheer power of disciplined thought is revealed in practically all the great intellectual and technological advances which the human race has made. The ability of the man of disciplined mind to direct this power effectively upon problems for which he was not specifically trained is proved by examples without number. The real evidence for the value of liberal education lies in history and in the biographies of men who have met the valid criteria of greatness. These support overwhelmingly the claim of liberal education that it can equip a man with fundamental powers of decision and action, applicable not only to boy-girl relationship, to tinkering hobbies, or to choosing the family dentist, but to all the great and varied concerns of human life—not least, those that are unforeseen.

condition .... ( )

The author implies that growth and perpetuity in nature and in history are the result of (1) quiet changes (2) a period of silence (3) undiscovered action (4) storms and tornadoes (5) violence and disruptions .... ( )

The title below that best expresses the ideas of this passage is:

1. The destruction of thinking
2. The advance of the human race
3. Facts vs. fantasies
4. The disciplined mind
5. The power of thought ..... ( )

The author indicates that the person with a liberal education has the ability to (1) read with more discernment than others (2) apply general principles (3) develop a clearer understanding of history than others (4) imagine a world without thought (5) gain prestige .... ( )

According to the passage, one of the evidences of the results of truly disciplined minds is found in (1) history (2) education itself (3) science (4) intellectual freedom (5) the beliefs of philosophers. . ( )

In this passage, the author stresses the importance of (1) increased interest in the study of history (2) technological advances (3) education for living (4) more training for students (5) satisfying the desire for security .... ( )

Which characteristic of great men is implied most strongly in the passage? (1) social consciousness (2) intellectual pride (3) self-respect (4) self-confidence (5) flexibility .... ( )

d. It is here, perhaps, that poetry may best act nowadays as corrective and complementary to science. When science tells us that the galaxy to which our solar system belongs is so enormous that light, traveling at 186,000 miles per second, takes between 60,000 and 100,000 years to cross from one rim to the other of the galaxy, we laymen accept the statement but find it meaningless—beyond the comprehension of heart or mind. When science tells us that the human eye has about 137 million separate "seeing" elements, we are no less paralyzed, intellectually and emotionally. Man is appalled by the immensities and the minuteness which science has disclosed for him. They are indeed unimaginable. But may not poetry be a possible way of mediating them to our imagination? of scaling them down to imaginative comprehension? Let us remember Perseus, who could not look directly at the nightmare Gorgon without being turned to stone, but could look at her image reflected in the shield the goddess of wisdom lent him.

The title below that best expresses the ideas of this passage is:
1. Poetry and imagination
2. A modern Gorgon
3. Poetry as a mediator
4. The vastness of the universe
5. Imaginative man . . . . ( )

According to the passage, the average man (1) should have a better memory (2) is impatient with science (3) cannot trust the scientists (4) is overwhelmed by the discoveries of science (5) does not understand either science or poetry
. . . . ( )

Perseus was most probably (1) a scientist (2) a legendary hero (3) an early poet (4) a horrible creature (5) a minor god . . . ( )

This passage is chiefly developed by means of (1) examples (2) cause and effect (3) narration (4) definition (5) anecdotes
. . . . ( )

e. Observe the dilemma of the fungus: it is a plant, but it possesses no chlorophyl. While all other plants can put the sun's energy to work for them combining the nutrients of ground and air into body structure, the chlorophylless fungus must look elsewhere for an energy source. It finds it in those other plants which, having received their energy free from the sun, relinquish it at some point in their cycle either to other animals (like us humans) or to fungi.

In this search for energy the fungus has become the earth's major source of rot and decay. Wherever you see mold forming on a piece of bread, or a pile of leaves turning to compost, or a blown-down tree becoming pulp on the ground, you are watching a fungus eating. Without fungus action the earth would be piled high with the dead plant life of

The title below that best expresses the ideas of this passage is:
1. Life without chlorophyl
2. The source of rot and decay
3. The harmful qualities of fungi
4. The strange world of the fungus
5. Utilization of the sun's energy
. . . . ( )

The statement ". . . you are watching a fungus eating" is best described as (1) figurative (2) ironical (3) parenthetical (4) joking (5) contradictory . . . . ( )

The author implies that fungi (1) are responsible for all the world's rot and decay (2) cannot live completely apart from other plants (3) attack plants in order to kill them (4) are poisonous to resin-producing

past centuries. In fact certain plants which contain resins that are toxic to fungi will last indefinitely; specimens of the redwood, for instance, can still be found resting on the forest floor centuries after having been blown down.

plants (5) can survive indefinitely under favorable conditions .... ( )

The author uses the word "dilemma" to indicate that (1) the fungus is both helpful and harmful in its effects (2) no one really understands how a fungus lives (3) fungi are not really plants (4) the function of chlorophyl in producing energy is a puzzle to scientists (5) the fungus seems to have its own biological laws .... ( )

4. Answer both *a* and *b*:

a. Choose *five* only of the following, and in the space provided write the *number* of the expression that best completes the statement or answers the question. [5]

(1) The Pulitzer Prize is an award for outstanding achievement in (1) science (2) journalism (3) television performance (4) radio acting

(2) Which magazine is devoted to travel? (1) *New York State Conservationist* (2) *Field and Stream* (3) *Foreign Affairs* (4) *Holiday*

(3) A sentence in a sales letter reads, "Italian movie star Maria Bella says that she keeps her skin smooth and glowing by frequent use of our product. If you use this preparation, your skin will glow as Miss Bella's does." This sentence uses the propaganda device known as (1) "card stacking" (2) the testimonial (3) the band wagon (4) the straw man

(4) Which word has the largest number of meanings? (1) foot (2) acre (3) triangle (4) hypotenuse

(5) In the library call number $\frac{620}{S23}$, the S indicates the (1) subject of the book (2) first letter of the title (3) first letter of the author's last name (4) identification letter of the bookshelf

(6) In good parliamentary practice, if a member feels that his rights are being violated, he may (1) request an adjournment (2) appeal to the sergeant-at-arms (3) rise to a point of order (4) call for a division of the house

b. In each of the following sentences that is incorrect, underline the word or expression that is incorrectly used and indicate your correction in the space provided. If you consider a sentence to be correct as it stands, place a *C* in the space provided. Do not change any correct part of a sentence. [5]

(1) She is more capable than any other girl in the office.

(2) At the picnic the young children behaved very good.

(3) I resolved to go irregardless of the consequences.

(4) The new movie has a number of actors which have been famous on Broadway.

(5) I am certain that those books are not our's.

5. Answer *a* or *b* or *c*:   [20]

a. Among the purposes of a writer is to call forth a reaction from a reader. This reaction may take the form of agreement, disagreement, or identification with a mood or an emotion. From the poems and essays you have read, choose a total of *four* selections (including at least *one* poem and *one* essay). In each case, show by specific references to the selection that you reacted to its idea, mood, or emotion in *one* of the ways mentioned above. Give titles and authors.

b. The theme (underlying idea) of a novel or full-length play may concern itself with a basic characteristic of man or with a problem of society. From the novels and full-length plays you have read, choose a total of *two* books, each of which has a theme of either kind mentioned above. In each case, make clear what the theme is and show by definite references that the book develops the theme you have indicated. Give titles and authors.

c. Each of the statements or questions below involves a literary reference. Choose 20 only and on the line at the right of each of the 20 statements or questions write the *number* of the word or phrase that correctly completes the statement or answers the question.

1. After Molly Farren's death, the only person who could betray Godfrey Cass was   (1) Mr. Bryce   (2) Mr. Macey   (3) Mr. Tookey   (4) Dunstan Cass

2. *Carry On, Mr. Bowditch* concerns the experiences of a young   (1) college professor   (2) naval officer   (3) lawyer   (4) minister

3. The father of Elizabeth Barrett Browning is best described as   (1) ambitious   (2) insincere   (3) indecisive   (4) tyrannical

4. Martin Arrowsmith finally found his life work in the field of   (1) general practice   (2) pediatrics   (3) radiology   (4) research

5. In *Strife*, both Mr. Roberts and Mr. Anthony proved to be   (1) more considerate of their followers than of themselves   (2) very sympathetic to the other's cause   (3) stubborn in their refusal to give in   (4) willing to take their wives' advice

6. In *Wuthering Heights*, which quality in Edgar Linton proved attractive to Cathy?   (1) gentility   (2) recklessness   (3) irresponsibility   (4) physical strength

7. Near the end of "Footfalls," Boaz Negro feared that he had   (1) revealed his son's guilt   (2) lost his skill as a cobbler   (3) killed an innocent man   (4) insulted an important customer

8. In "Ile," the chief problem confronting the Captain's wife is   (1) her loneliness   (2) her frail constitution   (3) the intense cold   (4) the mutinous crew

9. The hero of the "Leatherstocking Tales" is sometimes called   (1) Hawkeye   (2) Quasimodo   (3) Mowgli   (4) Brant

10. In *R. U. R.*, Helena fears that   (1) she is falling in love with a robot   (2) a female robot is stealing her husband's affections   (3) the robots will overpower mankind   (4) the robot factory is an unprofitable venture

11. In "A Liberal Education," Thomas Huxley compares life to a   (1) battle   (2) tug of war   (3) game of chess   (4) Chinese puzzle
12. In which ballad does a christening take place?   (1) "True Thomas"   (2) "Robin Hood and Little John"   (3) "The Cruel Brother"   (4) "King John and the Abbot of Canterbury"
13. In his biography of Queen Victoria, Lytton Strachey presents her as a woman of   (1) imperial greatness   (2) great intellect, yet inordinate pride   (3) few scruples   (4) boisterousness and fun
14. In the Bible, Ruth showed toward her mother-in-law a feeling of   (1) hatred   (2) jealousy   (3) patience   (4) affection
15. Which is most probably a quotation from *The Sea Around Us*?   (1) The ship stirred lazily in the breeze as the captain scanned the horizon.   (2) In 1956 there were over 200,000 passengers on ships bound for Europe.   (3) When pirates sailed the seas, the history of the sea as we know it began.   (4) Spring comes with a rhythm as the sea awakens from the long winter silence.
16. Jabez Stone made a bargain with the devil because   (1) he was too lazy to work   (2) his wife was dissatisfied   (3) he had had a series of misfortunes   (4) he wanted to run for Congress
17. Janus is usually represented as having   (1) two faces   (2) a thousand eyes   (3) winged feet   (4) hair of snakes
18. Which statement is true of Warburton in Maugham's story, "The Outstation"?   (1) He discharged Cooper.   (2) He dressed for dinner every night.   (3) He committed suicide.   (4) He became a native chieftain.
19. In *Macbeth,* about whom did Duncan say, "He was a gentleman upon whom I built an absolute trust"?   (1) Banquo   (2) Malcolm   (3) the thane of Cawdor   (4) the thane of Fife
20. "Life must go on; I forget just why" is quoted from   (1) "Ode on a Grecian Urn"   (2) "Recessional"   (3) "Lament"   (4) "Cool Tombs"
21. In *Cimarron,* one trait that *both* Yancey and Sabra possessed was   (1) courage   (2) patriotism   (3) a liking for elegant living   (4) a desire to lead the pioneers westward
22. In *The Heiress,* the central character was disillusioned to discover that her fiancé was   (1) a fortune hunter   (2) an atheist   (3) a murderer   (4) a potential bigamist
23. The lyric that begins
>   "The year's at the spring,
>   And day's at the morn"
ends on a note of   (1) optimism   (2) despair   (3) cynicism   (4) longing
24. In "Haircut," the barber reveals himself to be a   (1) practical joker   (2) confirmed gossip   (3) difficult employer   (4) champion of the underdog
25. Sydney Carton and Cyrano de Bergerac had in common   (1) an ability to write beautiful poetry   (2) a skill in dueling   (3) an unselfish devotion to another   (4) a lack of interest in their own professions
26. That all men have unfulfilled potential is an important idea in   (1) "Traits of Indian Character"   (2) "A New Jerusalem"   (3) "Elegy Written in a Country Churchyard"   (4) "God's Grandeur"
27. Hyman Kaplan helped himself by   (1) taking a correspondence course   (2) attending night school   (3) acting as a tutor   (4) teaching in a settlement house

28. Which Shakespearean hero was betrayed by a person he regarded as a friend? (1) Macbeth (2) Romeo (3) King Henry V (4) Othello
29. The Canterbury Pilgrims began their journey during the month of (1) January (2) March (3) April (4) May
30. In "Grass," which quality of nature does the poet praise? (1) its silent beauty (2) its power to heal and restore (3) its fickleness and changeability (4) its uncomplaining productivity
31. For Yeats, Innisfree was a symbol of (1) man's courage in the face of danger and death (2) the achievements of human ingenuity (3) the tranquillity needed in a complex civilization (4) the irresistible force of human progress
32. Which quality proved to be the undoing of Polonius? (1) greed (2) jealousy (3) curiosity (4) ambition
33. In "The Man with the Hoe," the poet states that the condition of the workingman is the result of (1) his own indifference to his fate (2) the centuries of war (3) the impersonal nature of modern technology (4) the attitude of the leaders and rulers of society
34. In *The Turmoil*, the chief desire of Mr. Sheridan was to train his sons to become (1) successful businessmen (2) conscientious citizens (3) wealthy farmers (4) cultured gentlemen
35. Walter Mitty's secret life included an adventure as a (1) garage mechanic (2) commander of a navy hydroplane (3) member of the Foreign Legion (4) detective
36. In "God Sees the Truth, But Waits," Aksënov was falsely accused of (1) murder (2) fraud (3) treason (4) desertion
37. In "The Pacing Goose," Jess Birdwell accused his hired man of (1) stealing the goose (2) conspiring with a neighbor (3) failing to count correctly (4) presenting false testimony in court
38. In which poem does the chief character criticize the younger generation for being too soft? (1) "Anne Rutledge" (2) "Reuben Bright" (3) "Bewick Finzer" (4) "Lucinda Matlock"
39. At the end of "The Cask of Amontillado," Montresor was (1) unrepentant (2) fearful of discovery (3) conscience-stricken (4) disillusioned
40. Horses were the only rational creatures in the land of (1) Brobdingnag (2) the Houyhnhnms (3) the Philistines (4) Titipu

6. Write a composition of 250 to 300 words on one of the topics below: [30]

Solidarity in the Western Hemisphere	America on skis
Developing rural areas	Operation hairdo
New York World's Fair—1964	Quiet things
Vanishing wildlife	A gift from the past
Helicopters	Art goes traveling
Progress in biochemistry	I wish I had said that
Fear in our world today	Countdown
The power of persuasion	

Answer all six questions.

1. On the line at the right of *each* group below, write the *number* of the word or expression that most nearly expresses the meaning of the italicized word.   [15]

a. placid .... (1) apparent (2) peaceful (3) wicked (4) unusual (5) absent-minded

b. evasive ... (1) emotional (2) effective (3) destructive (4) empty (5) shifty

c. chaos ..... (1) complete disorder (2) deep gorge (3) challenge (4) sudden attack (5) rejoicing

d. despicable . (1) insulting (2) ungrateful (3) contemptible (4) unbearable (5) jealous

e. deride .... (1) question (2) ignore (3) mock (4) unseat (5) produce

f. elude ..... (1) gladden (2) fascinate (3) mention (4) escape (5) ignore

g. mutable .. (1) colorless (2) harmful (3) uniform (4) changeable (5) invisible

h. indicative . (1) suggestive (2) curious (3) active (4) angry (5) certain

i. levity ..... (1) cleanness (2) tastiness (3) deadliness (4) sluggishness (5) lightness

j. excruciating (1) disciplinary (2) screaming (3) torturing (4) offensive (5) outpouring

k. depose ... (1) lay bare (2) deprive of office (3) empty (4) behead (5) blemish

l. ostentatious (1) unruly (2) showy (3) varied (4) scandalous (5) probable

m. conclave . (1) private meeting (2) covered passage (3) solemn vow (4) curved surface (5) ornamental vase

n. fray ...... (1) combat (2) trickery (3) unreality (4) madness (5) freedom

o. obsess .... (1) fatten (2) beset (3) make dull (4) exaggerate (5) interfere

2. In each of the following, *a* through *j*, only one of the words is misspelled. In *each* case spell correctly on the line at the right the misspelled word.   [5]

a. advertising peircing recommend convertible upholstery
b. gullible transparent survivor attendence partnership
c. reverence bulletin tremendous syllabic idenity
d. competetor medicine eligible creditable jamboree
e. expence holly minstrel cruising feudal
f. boundry municipal omission schemer brakeman
g. fraudulent allergy linoleum dazzling preformance
h. celebraty coefficient bodyguard nauseate meteorites
i. reliability anniversary conspicous argumentative preceding
j. disciple assemblage suicidal pamplet equipment

3. At the right of *each* of the following passages you will find one or more questions or incomplete statements about the passage. Each question or statement is followed by five words or expressions numbered 1 through 5. Select the word or expression that most satisfactorily completes *each in accordance with the meaning of the passage* and write its *number* in the parentheses. [*One credit for each correct answer.*]   [20]

a. John Greenleaf Whittier was the "Quaker-Puritan" scion of Massachusetts farmers. For this frail young man, however, farm life was too tough an existence. His early interest in books and legends led him toward journalism, with poetry as a pleasant side line. He became a Quaker firebrand and agitator, the politician among abolitionists, and a gadfly to New England Congressmen during the original "Great Debate." His impassioned prose and poetry against slavery were often directed at a clergy whose acceptance of it he fought as a Quaker and a Christian.

Only after the Civil War, when emancipation had been at least nominally won, did the aging Whittier emerge as the genial, easygoing "folk-bard" remembered today. Until recently the prominence given this last phase of his literary life by scholarly circles has obscured his earlier contributions to American literature and political freedom and tolerance.

The author of this passage indicates that Whittier's   (1) lifetime was one of invalidism   (2) nature caused him to detest farm life   (3) early writings were overlooked for some time   (4) ideas are similar to Robert Frost's   (5) chief desire was to lead the quiet life of the Quakers ....( )

The passage implies that Whittier showed a kind of personal courage when he   (1) fought in the Civil War   (2) attacked men in high places with his writings   (3) worked on the family farm in spite of his dislike for farming   (4) toned down his style because of his Quaker background   (5) gave up poetry to write political tracts ....( )

From reading the passage, we may infer that if Whittier were alive today he would most probably take up his pen in support of   (1) segregation   (2) politicians   (3) the United Nations   (4) desegregation   (5) folk literature ....( )

b. Many men can be of greatest service to a company by remaining in the laboratory. A single outstanding discovery may have a far greater impact on the company's profit picture five years hence than the activities of even the most able administrator. It is simply good sense—and good economics—to allow qualified researchers to continue their work. Granting these men maximum freedom to explore their scientific ideas is also eminently good sense.

Some years ago, the theory was rampant that after the age of about 40 the average researcher began losing his creative spark. The chance of his making a major discovery was believed to drop

According to the passage, research workers need   (1) less supervision by administrators   (2) good working conditions   (3) smaller budgets   (4) more assistants   (5) equal share in the company's profits ......( )

The author implies that the administrators are   (1) underpaid   (2) envious of the research workers   (3) well appreciated by the company   (4) able to hire sufficient research workers   (5) participating actively in research projects ....( )

Which factor once helped to determine the salary a research worker

off sharply. Hence, there really wasn't much point to encouraging a man of 45 or 50 to do research.

In recent years, however, this theory has fallen into wide disrepute. Companies find that many researchers continue to be highly productive throughout their careers. There is every reason to allow these men to continue their pioneering work.

Companies are also convinced that the traditional guideposts in establishing salaries are not completely valid. In former years, the size of a man's paycheck was determined primarily by such factors as the number of men he supervised or the size of his annual budget. On this basis, the researcher—however brilliant—who had perhaps one assistant and never spent much money made an extremely poor showing. Companies now realize that the two very important criteria that must also be considered are a man's actual contributions to the company and his creative potential.

In today's era of scientific manpower shortages, companies have more reason than ever to encourage scientists to do the work for which they are most qualified. They also have greater reason than ever to provide within the laboratory the environment in which the creative processes of research can be carried out most effectively.

received?   (1) his contributions to research   (2) the profits made on his discovery   (3) administrative considerations   (4) his creativeness (5) the number of administrators .. ..( )

The author's purpose in writing this passage is to   (1) describe a significant development in industry   (2) explore scientific ideas   (3) gain administrative responsibility for research workers   (4) encourage further education for research workers (5) defend the company administrators ....( )

According to the passage, companies should make the most effective use of research workers because   (1) otherwise America's scientific future is in danger   (2) research work is more important than any other kind of work   (3) the research worker's productive period is short   (4) research personnel are in short supply (5) the public needs must be satisfied ....( )

The author's tone in the passage is one of   (1) fierce indignation   (2) complaint   (3) calm appraisal   (4) sarcasm   (5) unconcern .....( )

Which idea is implied by the passage?   (1) A company must adapt itself to the times.   (2) A company's profits really are not as important as good human relations. (3) A company's annual budget is unnecessary.   (4) Men above 40 are a poor employment risk.   (5) Most research workers are brilliant ..( )

c. For though the terms are often confused, obscurity is not at all the same thing as unintelligibility. Obscurity is what happens when a writer undertakes a theme and method for which the reader is not sufficiently prepared. Unintelligibility is what happens when the writer undertakes a theme and

The title that best expresses the ideas of this passage is:

1. Enlarging experience
2. The cult of unintelligibility
3. The clarity of Robert Frost's poems
4. The familiar in poetry
5. The careful writer ....( )

method for which he himself is not sufficiently prepared.

A good creation is an enlarging experience, and the act of enlargement must require the reader to extend himself. Only the thoroughly familiar—which is to say, the already encompassed—may reasonably be expected to be immediately clear. True, the surface of a poem may seem deceptively clear, thus leading the careless reader to settle for an easy first-response as the true total. But even in work of such surface clarity as Frost's, it will be a foolish reader indeed who permits himself the illusion that one easy reading will reveal all of the poem. In this sense, indeed, there can be no great poetry without obscurity.

The author defines obscurity and unintelligibility in order to   (1) show his knowledge of literature   (2) please the reader   (3) set the stage for what follows   (4) clarify his own thinking   (5) defend unintelligibility .... (   )

According to this selection, good poetry   (1) has surface clarity   (2) has figurative language   (3) confuses the reader   (4) requires more than one reading   (5) can be appreciated only by college students .... (   )

Which quality would the author of this passage expect in a poet?   (1) sense of humor   (2) skill in rhyming   (3) use of the direct approach   (4) surface clarity   (5) knowledge of subject .... (   )

The author of this selection implies that   (1) the understanding of literature requires effort   (2) most readers of literature read carelessly   (3) most modern poems are unintelligible   (4) obscure poems are inevitably great poems   (5) familiar poems are the most popular ... (   )

As used in the passage, the word "encompassed" (line 15) most nearly means   (1) guided   (2) expected   (3) encountered   (4) described   (5) revised .... (   )

d. History has long made a point of the fact that the magnificent flowering of ancient civilization rested upon the institution of slavery, which released opportunity at the top for the art and literature which became the glory of antiquity. In a way, the mechanization of the present-day world produces the condition of the ancient in that the enormous development of labor-saving devices and of contrivances which amplify the capacities of mankind affords the base for the leisure necessary to widespread cultural pursuits. Mechanization is the present-day slave power,

The title below that best expresses the ideas of this passage is:
1. Slavery in the ancient world
2. Today's community
3. Worthwhile use of leisure
4. Ancient culture
5. Modern slave power .... (   )

Which factor has produced more leisure time?   (1) the abolition of slavery   (2) the glory of antiquity   (3) the development of art and literature   (4) an increase in inventions   (5) the development of the community .... (   )

with the difference that in the mechanized society there is no group of the community which does not share in the benefits of its inventions.

The flowering of any civilization has always depended on   (1) the galley slave   (2) leisure for the workingman   (3) mechanical power   (4) leisure for cultural pursuits   (5) transportation ....( )

The author's attitude toward mechanization is one of   (1) awe   (2) acceptance   (3) distrust   (4) fear   (5) devotion ....( )

4. Answer both *a* and *b*:

a. Choose *five* only of the following, and in the space provided write the *number* of the expression that best completes the statement or answers the question.   [5]

(1) Which word connotes the most extreme reaction?   (1) spectator   (2) fanatic   (3) adherent   (4) fan

(2) Which item in a newspaper contains an example of editorializing?   (1) The American economy is the most productive in the world.   (2) President Kennedy took office on January 20, 1961.   (3) The 1964 World's Fair will be held in New York.   (4) The Pirates defeated the Yankees, 11–10.

(3) Critical reviews of new movies and plays are a regular weekly feature of (1) *Time*   (2) *Life*   (3) *The Saturday Evening Post*   (4) *U. S. News and World Report*

(4) In writing a term paper on the subject "Strikes," one source to consult for the most recent information would be   (1) New York State *Legislative Manual*   (2) *New York Times Index*   (3) *Current Biography*   (4) *Reader's Encyclopedia*

(5) Which method of voting would be most accurate for a chairman of a meeting to use if he believed the results of the voting would be close?   (1) voice vote   (2) standing vote   (3) show of hands   (4) general consent

(6) Dependable information concerning the number of radio stations in the United States can most readily be found in   (1) *Variety* magazine   (2) *Readers' Guide to Periodical Literature*   (3) a dictionary   (4) *The World Almanac*

b. Each of the following sentences contains an underlined expression. Below each sentence are four suggested answers. Decide which answer is correct and place its *number* in the space provided.   [5]

(1) The general, with all his soldiers, was captured.

    1. Correct as is   3. , with all his soldiers; was
    2. , with all his soldier's were   4. with all his soldiers, was

(2) He is the boy who's poster was chosen for the contest.

    1. Correct as is   3. boy whose
    2. boy, whose   4. boy, who's

(3) Humbled by the loss of prestige, his plans changed.

    1. Correct as is   3. his plans were changed.
    2. a change in his plans occurred.   4. he changed his plans.

(4) We were not surprised at <u>him loosing</u> his way.
   1. Correct as is   3. him for loosing
   2. his losing   4. his loosing

(5) The prize money is to be divided <u>among you and I.</u>
   1. Correct as is   3. between you and me
   2. among you and me   4. between you and I

5. Answer *a* or *b* or *c*:   [20]

   a. In literature, as in life, a woman often has a major role in a man's life. In some books she helps a man; in other books, she hinders him. From the novels and full-length plays you have read, choose a total of *two* such books (two for either kind of woman *or* one for *each* kind). In each case, by referring specifically to the book, show how a woman helps a man to achieve success or happiness, *or* hinders him. Give titles and authors.

   b. In dealing directly or indirectly with such subjects as (1) war, (2) human rights, (3) national independence, (4) the search for a meaning in life, writers frequently reveal their own feelings and opinions. From the poems, essays and short stories you have read, choose a total of *four* selections. In each case, by referring specifically to the selection, show clearly the author's feeling or opinion about *one* of the subjects mentioned above. Give titles and authors.

   c. Each of the statements or questions below involves a literary reference. Choose 20 only and on the line at the right of each of the 20 statements or questions write the *number* of the word or phrase that correctly completes the statement or answers the question.

  1. In the Old Testament, Joseph was   (1) sold by his brothers   (2) disowned by his father   (3) adopted by the Queen   (4) betrayed by his wife
  2. In "The Open Window," Mr. Nuttel fled from the house because he   (1) feared the dog   (2) thought he was seeing ghosts   (3) was late for an important engagement   (4) had always had a fear of drafts
  3. 221B Baker Street is the address of   (1) Scotland Yard   (2) Sherlock Holmes   (3) Professor Moriarty   (4) Father Brown
  4. In "The U.S.A. from the Air," Langewiesche stresses America's   (1) confusion   (2) diversity   (3) independence   (4) monotony
  5. Which is the most apt description of Ethan Frome?   (1) a crag of a man, gaunt and bleak as the countryside   (2) as smooth as willow bark   (3) so wealthy that his money was a curse to him   (4) lazy and loose, his hair a shock of red like corn in a field
  6. In Arnold Bennett's "The Daily Miracle," he warns us against   (1) working too hard   (2) restricting our pleasures   (3) not saving for the future   (4) wasting time
  7. *This Hallowed Ground* is an account of   (1) World War I   (2) World War II   (3) the Civil War   (4) the American Revolution
  8. In "Sixteen," at the beginning of the story the heroine wishes to impress the reader with her   (1) sense of duty to her school   (2) excellent relationship with her parents   (3) fine scholastic record   (4) knowledge of proper conduct

9. Bryant's "Thanatopsis" suggests that one should approach death   (1) trustingly   (2) joyously   (3) longingly   (4) apprehensively

10. In *Riders to the Sea,* those who made their living at sea are   (1) members of the Coast Guard   (2) fishermen   (3) sailors in the British Navy   (4) deep-sea divers

11. Which two persons were unwilling witnesses to a murder?   (1) Jody and Penny Baxter   (2) Jim Hawkins and Squire Trelawney   (3) Tom Sawyer and Huckleberry Finn   (4) Penrod and Sam

12. "But screw your courage to the sticking-place" is advice given by   (1) King Lear   (2) Henry V   (3) Iago   (4) Lady Macbeth

13. Rachel Carson's *Silent Spring* is about the   (1) changes of the seasons in England   (2) erosion of the Continental Shelf on the Atlantic seaboard   (3) effects of man's war against insects   (4) exploration of the bottom of the sea

14. In Chekhov's "The Slanderer," the irony is that   (1) Akhineyev spread the rumor himself   (2) Akhineyev wasn't even married   (3) Vankin didn't really see Akhineyev with the maid   (4) the maid was unattractive

15. Which line completes the couplet below?
    ". . . Where ignorance is bliss,"
    (1) "A man must live on lies."   (2) "Darkness cloaks the eyes."   (3) " 'Tis folly to be wise."   (4) "Every fool replies."

16. In "The Open Boat," it was ironic that   (1) there were thirteen people aboard   (2) the captain was the only one with no insurance   (3) most of those aboard could not swim   (4) the boat was in plain sight of the shore

17. Keats' "Ode on a Grecian Urn" expresses the author's belief that   (1) all men are basically good   (2) beauty is a fleeting quality   (3) truth and beauty are inseparable   (4) only the art of the past is worthwhile

18. In his essay "How to Please," Lord Chesterfield gave advice to   (1) students   (2) nobility   (3) his wife   (4) his son

19. *The Ugly American* is based on the successes and failures of   (1) American industrialists   (2) United States citizens abroad   (3) people in suburbia   (4) a mythical United States dictator

20. Gluck cast into a river a flower containing three drops of dew upon the advice of the   (1) Knave of Hearts   (2) Red Queen   (3) Knight of the Burning Pestle   (4) King of the Golden River

21. In "The Leader of the People," the person most sympathetic to Grandfather was his   (1) son   (2) grandson   (3) wife   (4) daughter-in-law

22. The phrase "It takes life to love Life" appears in the poem   (1) "Richard Cory"   (2) "Miniver Cheevy"   (3) "Bewick Finzer"   (4) "Lucinda Matlock"

23. In *Ivanhoe,* the Black Knight proved to be   (1) Prince John   (2) King Richard   (3) Locksley   (4) Brian de Bois-Guilbert

24. *A Man for all Seasons* is a play based on the life of   (1) Abraham Lincoln   (2) William Shakespeare   (3) Oliver Cromwell   (4) Sir Thomas More

25. Dr. Heidegger's four friends discovered, if only for a fleeting instant,   (1) Truth   (2) Faith   (3) Life   (4) Youth

26. Kreton is the name of   (1) an atom-splitting machine   (2) a visitor from outer space   (3) a fairy prince   (4) a small boy's imaginary playmate

27. Which pairs a father and his son?   (1) Castor and Pollux   (2) Damon and Pythias   (3) Daedalus and Icarus   (4) Romulus and Remus

28. In "The Highwayman," the robber died at the hands of (1) Tim, the ostler (2) Bess' father (3) King George's men (4) the townspeople
29. At the end of *Our Town*, Emily's feeling toward George was one of (1) bitterness (2) pity (3) pride (4) admiration
30. The author of "Self-Reliance" believes that (1) inconsistency is to be avoided (2) genius is often misunderstood (3) imitation has its merits (4) to some extent, ignorance is desirable
31. Bottles Barton is the chief character in (1) "That's What Happened to Me" (2) "The Diving Fool" (3) "Spring over Brooklyn" (4) "The Slipover Sweater"
32. What advice was given to the poet in "When I Was One-and-Twenty"? (1) "Grow old along with me" (2) "Gather ye rosebuds while ye may" (3) "But keep your fancy free" (4) "Neither a borrower nor a lender be"
33. Which force in his life was Silas Lapham unable to overcome? (1) the disobedience of his sons (2) the wastefulness of his wife (3) the social distinctions of his time (4) his contempt for social barriers
34. In *Vanity Fair*, one of the main events is the battle of (1) Waterloo (2) Agincourt (3) Hastings (4) Moscow
35. In "Clean Curtains," the final winner in the struggle was the (1) new neighbors (2) laundry (3) slum (4) nuns
36. In *Lord Jim* by Conrad, the hero is motivated by a feeling of (1) patriotism (2) envy (3) guilt (4) haughtiness
37. When Romeo arrived at Juliet's grave, he was surprised by (1) her maid (2) her father (3) Count Paris (4) two gravediggers
38. In Maxwell Anderson's *Elizabeth the Queen*, Essex experienced a conflict between (1) loyalty and ambition (2) loyalty to his troops and regard for his own safety (3) love and fear (4) desire for power and religious conviction
39. Which group of characters appears in the same book by Dickens? (1) Bob Cratchit, Sam Weller, Jerry Cruncher (2) Joe Gargery, Abel Magwitch, Herbert Pocket (3) Mr. Fezziwig, Mr. Dick, Mr. Brownlow (4) Steerforth, Fagin, Smike
40. *The Making of the President* is an account of the (1) political career of Franklin D. Roosevelt (2) elections of American Presidents since the days of George Washington (3) election of John F. Kennedy as President (4) role of the presidency in American foreign affairs

6. Write a composition of 250 to 300 words on one of the topics below: [30]

The paradox of progress	Pencils
Taxes—burden or responsibility	Toys today
State (or national) parks	Crosscountry camping
Industry in our area	My part-time job
My science project	Farming as I know it
Miracles of modern surgery	The gift of silence
Juvenile decency	Safety in the home
A day in New York City	

Part I

Answer all questions in this part.

Directions (1–15): In the space provided on the separate answer sheet, write the *number* of the word or expression that most nearly expresses the meaning of the word in heavy black type. [15]

1. **meander**
   1 grumble
   2 wander aimlessly
   3 come between
   4 weigh carefully
   5 sing

2. **destitution**
   1 trickery
   2 fate
   3 lack of practice
   4 recovery
   5 extreme poverty

3. **malign**
   1 slander
   2 prophesy
   3 entreat
   4 approve
   5 praise

4. **impotent**
   1 unwise
   2 lacking strength
   3 free of sin
   4 without shame
   5 commanding

5. **snivel**
   1 crawl
   2 cut short
   3 whine
   4 doze
   5 giggle

6. **sojourn**
   1 court order
   2 nickname
   3 temporary stay
   4 slip of the tongue
   5 makeshift

7. **platitude**
   1 home remedy
   2 trite remark
   3 balance wheel
   4 rare animal
   5 protective film

8. **concord**
   1 brevity
   2 blame
   3 kindness
   4 worry
   5 agreement

9. **abominable**
   1 hateful
   2 ridiculous
   3 untamed
   4 mysterious
   5 boastful

10. **qualm**
    1 sudden misgiving
    2 irritation
    3 cooling drink
    4 deceit
    5 attention to detail

11. **careen**
    1 celebrate
    2 mourn
    3 ridicule
    4 lurch
    5 beckon

12. **convivial**
    1 formal
    2 gay
    3 rotating
    4 well-informed
    5 insulting

13. **rampant**
    1 playful
    2 crumbling
    3 roundabout
    4 unchecked
    5 defensive

14. **docile**
    1 delicate
    2 positive
    3 dreary
    4 obedient
    5 melodious

15. **vestige**
    1 bone
    2 test
    3 entrance
    4 cloak
    5 trace

Directions (16–25): In each of the following, 16 through 25, only one of the words is misspelled. In *each* case spell correctly in the space provided the misspelled word. [5]

16. predicament
    contagious
    transfered
    summarize
    serviceable

17. wilderness
    diameter
    formative
    lubricate
    excercise

18. favoritism
    offensive
    scissors
    approachs
    bridle

19. sluice
    ajacent
    columnist
    womanly
    shrubbery

20. survival
    inquirey
    lightning
    meanness
    mutually

21. laboratory
    clientele
    diagnosis
    antisipate
    competence

22. interferred
    physique
    anonymous
    supremacy
    pollution

23. electricity
    liesure
    disposable
    primeval
    emigrant

24. juvenile
    species
    adversly
    allegiance
    respectable

25. congradulate
    hilarious
    recommendation
    incriminate
    practically

Directions (26–45): Below each of the following passages you will find one or more questions or incomplete statements about the passage. Each question or statement is followed by five words or expressions numbered 1 through 5. Select the word or expression that most satisfactorily completes *each in accordance with the meaning of the passage* and write its *number* in the space provided on the separate answer sheet. [One credit for each correct completion.] [20]

Passage A

In the South American rain forest abide the greatest acrobats on earth. The monkeys of the Old World, agile as they are, cannot hang by their tails. It is only the monkeys of America that possess this skill. They are called ceboids and their unique group includes marmosets, owl monkeys, sakis, spider monkeys, squirrel monkeys and howlers. Among these the star gymnast is the skinny, intelligent spider monkey. Hanging head down like a trapeze artist from the loop of a liana, he may suddenly give a short swing, launch himself into space and, soaring outward and downward across a 50-foot void of air, lightly catch a bough on which he spied a shining berry. No owl monkey can match his leap, for their arms are shorter, their tails untalented. The marmosets, smallest of the tribe, tough noisy hoodlums that travel in gangs, are also capable of leaps into space, but their landings are rough: smack against a tree trunk with arms and legs spread wide.

26. The title below that best expresses the ideas of this selection is: (1) The star gymnast (2) Monkeys and trees (3) Travelers in space (4) The uniqueness of monkeys (5) Ceboid acrobats
27. The author states that the marmoset is (1) clannish (2) graceful (3) antisocial (4) shy (5) intelligent
28. Compared to monkeys of the Old World, American monkeys are (1) smaller (2) more quiet (3) more dexterous (4) more protective of their young (5) less at home in their surroundings

Passage B

To a philosopher, wisdom is not the same as knowledge. Facts may be known in prodigious numbers without the knower of them loving wisdom. Indeed, the person who possesses encyclopedic information may actually have a genuine contempt for those who love and seek wisdom. The philosopher is not content with a mere knowledge of facts. He desires to integrate and evaluate facts, and to probe beneath the obvious to the deeper orderliness behind the immediately given facts. Insight into the hidden depths of reality, perspective on human life and nature in their entirety, in the words of Plato, to be a spectator of time and existence—these are the philosopher's objectives. Too great an interest in the minutiae of science, may, and often does, obscure these basic objectives.

Philosophers assume that the love of wisdom is a natural endowment of the human being. Potentially every man is a philosopher because in the depths of his being there is an intense longing to fathom the mysteries of existence. This inner yearning expresses itself in various ways prior to any actual study of philosophy as a technical branch of human culture. Consequently every human being, in so far as he has ever been or is a lover of wisdom, has, to that extent, a philosophy of life.

29. The title below that best expresses the ideas of this passage is: (1) The potential philosopher (2) The philosophy of Plato (3) The philosopher versus the scientist (4) The philosopher defined (5) The natural endowments of mankind
30. According to the author, which statement concerning philosophers is most nearly accurate? (1) They are an impractical lot. (2) They are too radical. (3) They are a thoughtful group. (4) They have contempt for humanity. (5) They turn away from the findings of science.
31. The author indicates that a philosopher is a person who (1) disregards facts (2) loves wisdom (3) desires technical knowledge (4) collects all types of data (5) resents orderliness
32. A philosopher wishes to (1) systematize facts (2) work by himself (3) show his contempt for knowledge (4) have an encyclopedic mind (5) endow human beings with supernatural powers
33. The author suggests that a man becomes a philosopher when he (1) studies philosophy as a subject (2) collects all the facts (3) realizes obvious truths (4) seeks a meaning for life (5) develops natural skills
34. The passage suggests that the philosopher would probably be most opposed to (1) quiz shows on television (2) college courses in philosophy (3) courses in natural science (4) religious training (5) sales of encyclopedias

Passage C

It is no longer needful to labor Dickens' power as a portrayer of modern society nor the seriousness of his "criticism of life." But we are still learning to appreciate his supreme attainment as an artist. Richnesses of poetic imagery, modulations of emotional tone, subtleties of implication, complex unities of structure, intensities of psychological insight, a panoply of achievement, mount up to overwhelming triumph. Though contemporary readers perhaps still feel somewhat queasy about Dickens' sentiment, his comedy and his drama sweep all before them. Even his elaborate and multistranded plots are now seen as great symphonic compositions driving forward through theme and variation to the resolving chords on which they close.

35. The title below that best expresses the ideas of this passage is: (1) Dickens—a portrayer of modern society (2) Dickens as a critic of his times (3) The appeals of Dickens (4) Psychological insight (5) A weakness of Dickens

36. According to the passage, readers most recently have begun to appreciate Dickens' (1) feeling for culture (2) criticisms of life (3) rhythms (4) literary references (5) literary craftsmanship

37. The author suggests that Dickens was (1) a poet (2) a musician (3) a playwright (4) a wealthy man (5) an artist

38. According to the passage, the endings of Dickens' works are most probably characterized by (1) frequent use of comic relief (2) unexpected developments (3) visually effective symbols (4) a lack of sense of completion (5) dramatic power

39. In which sentence is the main idea of this passage stated? (1) first (2) second (3) third (4) fourth (5) fifth

Passage D

The operetta form of Offenbach, Herve and Lecocq was not essentially romantic. Like the music drama of Gilbert and Sullivan, it was pleasantly fantastic in its conception and completely realistic in its view of life. Its plots were simple but wide-ranging—it ransacked all literature, all history, for its subjects; and it ridiculed all that was hypocritical, pompous, solemn and bombastic. It was intended for an extremely sensitive and discriminating audience. It was chic, literate and in excellent taste. Exaggeration, anachronism, parody and surprise were its ordinary tools. Wit was its lifeblood, but wit expressed in a constantly refreshing stream of enchanting melody, pure, varied and seemingly effortless. In short it was young, first with youth, then with the youth of middle age, and it devastated its elders with all the malice of an *enfant terrible*.

40. The title that best expresses the ideas of this passage is: (1) The critical audience (2) A defense of Gilbert and Sullivan (3) Emotion in the operetta (4) A call to youth (5) A brilliant musical form

41. The passage suggests that the operettas of Offenbach, Herve and Lecocq were most appreciated by people who were (1) self-righteous (2) well informed (3) kind (4) honest (5) naive

42. An important purpose of the operettas was to (1) humble the rich (2) entertain the youth of the time (3) allow the audience to escape reality through fantasy (4) satirize human frailties (5) challenge the opinions of the critics

43. Which was the most distinguishing feature of the operettas? (1) lengthy dialogue (2) romantic plots (3) two-dimensional characters (4) historical accuracy (5) clever songs

44. The author's attitude toward his subject matter is one of   (1) skepticism
    (2) impatience   (3) enthusiasm   (4) mild disapproval   (5) nonchalance
45. Which word best describes the operettas of Offenbach, Herve and Lecocq?
    (1) conservative   (2) witty   (3) defensive   (4) romantic   (5) ordinary

Directions (46–50): **Each of the following sentences contains an underlined expression.   Below each sentence are four suggested answers.   Decide
which answer is correct and place its *number* in the space provided on the
separate answer sheet.   [5]**

46. How much has food costs raised during the past year?

    1 Correct as is   3 have food costs risen
    2 have food costs rose   4 has food costs risen
47. "Will you come too" she pleaded?

    1 Correct as is   3 too?" she pleaded.
    2 too,?" she pleaded.   4 too," she pleaded?
48. If he would have drank more milk, his health would have been better.

    1 Correct as is   3 had drank
    2 would drink   4 had drunk
49. Jack had no sooner laid down and fallen asleep when the alarm sounded.

    1 Correct as is
    2 no sooner lain down and fallen asleep than
    3 no sooner lay down and fell asleep when
    4 no sooner laid down and fell asleep than
50. Jackson is one of the few Sophomores, who has ever made the varsity team.

    1 Correct as is   3 one of the few sophomores, who has
    2 one of the few Sophomores, who have   4 one of the few sophomores who have

Directions (51–56): **Choose *five* only of the following, and in the space
provided on the separate answer sheet write the *number* of the expression
that best completes the statement or answers the question.   [5]**

51. The most abstract word in the following list is
    1 knife   2 culture   3 pillar   4 typewriter
52. Which library aid should be consulted *first* to find the address of Carl Sandburg?
    1 *Dictionary of American Biography*   3 *Readers' Guide to Periodical Literature*
    2 *Who's Who in America*   4 the card catalog
53. In parliamentary procedure, a motion to "lay on the table" means to
    1 set aside   3 arrange for a roll call
    2 filibuster   4 bring up for discussion
54. In a letter of application, which is the most effective close of the letter?
    1 It should be easy for you to see, then, why I am ideally suited for the position.
      My telephone number is 8-7191.
    2 I can come for an interview at any time, except on Thursdays, when I play
      volleyball.   My telephone number is 8-7191.
    3 I can come for an interview at your convenience, and my telephone number is
      8-7191.
    4 May I come for an interview at your convenience?   My telephone number is
      8-7191.
55. Which magazine is published once a month?
    1 *Harper's*   3 *The New Yorker*
    2 *The Saturday Evening Post* 4 *U.S. News and World Report*

56. Which is a national news service?

   1 AT & T   2 HNS   3 AP   4 NNS

Part II

57. **Answer *a* or *b* or *c*: [If you choose *a* or *b*, write your answer on paper supplied by the school.]   [20]**

   a. In literature, as in life, a person's response to a crisis may reveal his character. From the full-length books that you have read, choose *two* books. In each case indicate briefly a crisis faced by a person in the book, and by specific references show what his reaction to this crisis revealed about his character. Give titles and authors.

   b. A reader may like a short prose selection because it has one or more of these appeals: (1) an unusual setting, (2) humor, (3) a historical background, (4) a strange idea or custom, (5) suspense. From the short stories, essays, articles and one-act plays that you have read, choose a total of *four* selections. In each case, show by specific references that the selection might have *one* of the above appeals for a reader. [You may use the same appeal for any number of selections.] Give titles and authors.

   c. Each of the statements or questions below involves a literary reference. Choose 20 only and in the space provided on the separate answer sheet, write the *number* of the word or phrase that correctly completes the statement or answers the question.

1. That "the same person might not be master; the same person might not be servant" in a different situation is shown in the play
   1 *What Every Woman Knows*   3 *The Admirable Crichton*
   2 *The Twelve-Pound Look*   4 *Alice-Sit-by-the-Fire*

2. In *Jane Eyre,* Mr. Rochester faced a conflict between
   1 patriotism and ambition   3 family ties and friendships
   2 loyalty and civic-mindedness   4 love and duty

3. The Pyramus and Thisbe "play-within-a-play" may be found in Shakespeare's
   1 *The Tempest*   3 *Twelfth Night*
   2 *Antony and Cleopatra*   4 *A Midsummer-Night's Dream*

4. In *Shane,* which is a characteristic of the hero?
   1 ability to sway crowds to his viewpoint   3 indifference to pain
   2 hatred of poverty   4 reticence about his past

5. In "The Death of the Hired Man," Mary is shown to be
   1 carefree   2 hard-hearted   3 charitable   4 careless

6. "O world, I cannot hold thee close enough!" expresses Millay's response to
   1 her return to the scenes of her childhood   3 a great musical performance
   2 the outbreak of World War II   4 the beauties of autumn

7. "Lesser than Macbeth, and greater" was the prophecy made about
   1 Donalbain   2 Malcolm   3 Duncan   4 Banquo

8. The proverb "Death is a black camel, which kneels at the gates of all" is an example of
   1 alliteration   2 simile   3 metaphor   4 hyperbole

9. Walt Whitman's "O Captain! My Captain!" concerns the
   1 death of Abraham Lincoln   3 building of the *Constitution*
   2 naval victories of John Paul Jones   4 life of George Washington

10. In *My Fair Lady,* Higgins was a professor of
    1 anatomy   2 mathematics   3 language   4 history
11. In *A Doll's House,* Torvald Helmer regarded his wife as being
    1 holy   2 faithless   3 irresponsible   4 just
12. Father Damien addressed his congregation as "my brothers" rather than as "my children" after he had
    1 learned to love them in spite of their disease
    2 learned that he, too, was a leper
    3 decided to spend the rest of his life with them
    4 discussed with his Bishop his fear of contracting their disease
13. *The Prairie Years* is part of the title of a
    1 novel about the West   3 poem about Johnny Appleseed
    2 biography of Abraham Lincoln   4 play about a Norwegian farmer
14. "Either we live by accident and die by accident, or we live by plan and die by plan" is quoted from
    1 *Twenty Thousand Leagues Under the Sea*   3 *She*
    2 *The Bridge of San Luis Rey*   4 *Two Years Before the Mast*
15. In Greek mythology, Orpheus lost Eurydice forever when he
    1 looked back   3 cursed her
    2 could not charm Pluto   4 could not cross the river Styx
16. In *Great Expectations,* Pip believed at first that his unknown benefactor was
    1 Bentley Drummle   3 Miss Havisham
    2 Herbert Pocket   4 Joe Gargery
17. The final irony in *The Good Earth* is
    1 Wang Lung's second marriage   3 the sons' lack of respect for the land
    2 O-Lan's illness and death   4 the soldiers' desecration of the graves
18. In "The Method of Scientific Investigation," Thomas Huxley indicates that
    1 only trained scientists use induction successfully
    2 the scientific method should not be attempted by amateurs
    3 schools are responsible for teaching about the scientific method
    4 induction is actually used instinctively by most people
19. "The Sniper" shows the bitterness of the Irish Civil War by describing
    1 the torture of children
    2 party loyalty as more important than friendship or family affection
    3 a soldier's indifference to the suffering of civilians
    4 the looting and the senseless destruction of property
20. In "The Necklace," Mathilde Loisel learned too late that
    1 crime does not pay   3 cheap things are never worth the price
    2 love cannot be purchased   4 vanity is a costly fault
21. With which vessel is *Collision Course* concerned?
    1 R.M.S. *Titanic*   3 the *Andrea Doria*
    2 the *Lusitania*   4 the *Queen Mary*
22. *The Agony and the Ecstasy,* by Irving Stone, is about a
    1 painter in medieval France
    2 sculptor in Renaissance Italy
    3 religious leader during the Reformation
    4 playwright and actor in Elizabethan England
23. In Hawthorne's "The Ambitious Guest," the young man's plans were put to an end by a
    1 landslide   2 torrential flood   3 blizzard   4 hurricane
24. In "Trifles," Mrs. Hale and Mrs. Peters felt guilty because they had
    1 taken Mrs. Wright's canned cherries

    2 wrongly disliked John Wright
    3 not found the motive for the crime
    4 not been more neighborly toward Mrs. Wright

25. According to James W. Johnson's "The Creation," when God made the world He was
    1 desirous of companionship
    2 curious about His own strength
    3 determined to prove His mastery over the devil
    4 amazed at the reaction of the angels

26. The aggressive female and the retreating male are associated with the essays of
    1 James Thurber   3 George Santayana
    2 Stephen Leacock   4 Cornelia Otis Skinner

27. In Margaret Weymouth Jackson's story "The Stepmother," Arthur showed his affection for his stepmother by
    1 buying her a new hat
    2 giving her his sportsmanship award
    3 serving her breakfast in bed
    4 promising to do his chores without complaining

28. In the essay "Romance," the author takes a ride in
    1 a subway   2 an airplane   3 a train to Boston   4 an ocean liner

29. Which story is written in the form of a diary?
    1 "I Can't Breathe"   3 "Young Man Axelrod"
    2 "The Snob"   4 "The Stove"

30. "Up, lad: when the journey's over
     There'll be time enough to sleep"
    are the closing lines of a poem by
    1 Rupert Brooke   3 John Masefield
    2 A. E. Housman   4 W. B. Yeats

31. As Sir Launfal set out on his quest for the Holy Grail, he found at his gate
    1 a beggar girl   3 a leper
    2 an abandoned infant   4 a damsel in distress

32. John Steinbeck's main purpose in starting out on his "travels with Charley" was to
    1 obtain material for a new novel
    2 renew his acquaintance with the American people
    3 escape the monotony of his overcivilized life
    4 visit again the scenes of his early writings

33. Sire de Maletroit's cunning, treacherous nature explains his
    1 strange treatment of his niece   3 pride in his family's name
    2 readiness to use his sword   4 influence on the atmosphere of his home

34. "The best laid schemes o' mice an' men" is a quotation from
    1 Longfellow   2 Wordsworth   3 Keats   4 Burns

35. "Turkey Red" presents a vivid picture of the courage of
    1 a pioneer woman   3 an immigrant boy
    2 a Civil War soldier   4 a war correspondent

36. In "Cockles for Tea," Walter Ashcroft wins the respect of the other characters by
    1 being generous to Gommy Doakes
    2 proving himself shrewder than the villagers
    3 winning the village lottery
    4 winning Barbara Alice's affection

37. In *A Bell for Adano*, the Major's friends tried to prevent
    1 the closing of the bridge   3 the Major's demotion to captain
    2 the payment of the ransom   4 Purvis's letter from reaching the General

38. An author whose best known books deal with South African life is
    1 John Hersey   3 Thomas Costain
    2 MacKinlay Kantor   4 Alan Paton
39. That works of mankind cannot withstand the ravages of Nature is the theme of
    1 "Sea Fever"   2 "Futility"   3 "Ozymandias"   4 "Requiem"
40. In "Jim Bludso of the Prairie Belle," Jim is depicted as one who
    1 was thoroughly good
    2 played one too many jokes on others
    3 justly deserved the fate he met
    4 would go to heaven in spite of his faults

Part III

58. **Write a composition of 250 to 300 words on one of the topics below:**
    [30]

Problems facing the President	Responsible advertising
The plight of our cities	My idea of a luxury
The ideal ambassador	The two-year college
The power of the press	The library—its role in our school
Fluoridation of water	If I could abolish . . . .
The importance of the transistor	The personal qualities a farmer needs
Indifference—a modern enemy	Desk tops
Trailer living	

Part I

Answer all questions in this part.

Directions (1-15): In the space provided on the separate answer sheet, write the *number* of the word or expression that most nearly expresses the meaning of the word in heavy black type.   **[15]**

1. **impediment** (1) foundation   (2) conceit   (3) hindrance   (4) luggage   (5) instrument

2. **adhere** (1) pursue   (2) control   (3) arrive   (4) cling   (5) attend

3. **composure** (1) sensitiveness   (2) weariness   (3) stylishness   (4) hopefulness   (5) calmness

4. **provocation** (1) sacred vow   (2) formal announcement   (3) cause of irritation   (4) careful management   (5) expression of disgust

5. **savory** (1) thrifty   (2) wise   (3) appetizing   (4) warm   (5) uncivilized

6. **candid** (1) hidden   (2) shining   (3) straightforward   (4) critical   (5) warmhearted

7. **eclipse** (1) stretch   (2) obscure   (3) glow   (4) overlook   (5) insert

8. **correlate** (1) punish   (2) wrinkle   (3) conspire openly   (4) give additional proof   (5) connect systematically

9. **infirmity** (1) disgrace   (2) unhappiness   (3) rigidity   (4) hesitation   (5) weakness

10. **palpitate** (1) faint   (2) harden   (3) throb   (4) soothe   (5) taste

11. **imprudent** (1) reckless   (2) unexcitable   (3) poor   (4) domineering   (5) powerless

12. **dissension** (1) friction   (2) analysis   (3) swelling   (4) injury   (5) slyness

13. **disconcert** (1) separate   (2) cripple   (3) lessen   (4) upset   (5) dismiss

14. **rudimentary** (1) discourteous   (2) brutal   (3) displeasing   (4) elementary   (5) embarrassing

15. **autonomous** (1) self-governing   (2) self-important   (3) self-educated   (4) self-explanatory   (5) self-conscious

Directions (16-25): In each of the following, 16 through 25, only one of the words is misspelled. In *each* case spell correctly in the space provided the misspelled word.   **[5]**

16. disappointment   mournful   jubilant   tarriff   immigrant
17. anonymous   census   ridiculous   finially   miniature
18. absolutly   interpretation   nuclear   precipice   corrosive
19. contrivance   amunition   surrounded   practitioner   exaggerate
20. pioneers   concrete   sophomore   humane   loyality
21. antiquity   respectively   calendar   domicile   surgury
22. maintenance   enviroment   proceed   temperament   weird
23. excapade   effeminate   colossal   unveiling   tubular

24. forty-fourth   peculiarty   struggling   drought   platoon
25. theoretical   canvassed   neighborhood   excellence   polititian

Directions (26-45): Below *each* of the following passages you will find one or more questions or incomplete statements about the passage. Each question or statement is followed by five words or expressions numbered 1 through 5. Select the word or expression that most satisfactorily completes *each in accordance with the meaning of the passage* and write its *number* in the space provided on the separate answer sheet. [One credit for each correct completion.] [20]

Passage A

The traveler used to go about the world to encounter the natives. A function of travel agencies now is to prevent this encounter. They are always devising new ways of insulating the tourist from the travel world. In the old traveler's accounts, the colorful native innkeeper, full of sage advice and local lore, was a familiar figure. Now he is obsolete. Today on Main Street in your home town you can arrange transportation, food, lodging, and entertainment for Rome, Sydney, Singapore, or Tokyo.

No more chaffering. A well-planned tour saves the tourist from negotiating with the natives when he gets there. One reason why returning tourists nowadays talk so much about and are so irritated by tipping practices is that these are almost their only direct contact with the people. Even this may soon be eliminated. The Travel Plan Commission of the International Union of Official Travel Organization in 1958 was studying ways of standardizing tipping practices so that eventually all gratuities could be included in the tour package. Shopping, like tipping, is one of the few activities remaining for the tourist. It is a chink in the wall of prearrangements which separates him from the country he visits. No wonder he finds it exciting. When he shops he actually encounters natives, negotiates in their strange language, and discovers their local business etiquette. In a word, he tastes the thrill and "travail" which the old-time traveler once experienced all along the way—with every purchase of transportation, with every night's lodging, with every meal.

26. The title that best expresses the ideas of this passage is: (1) Current modes of travel   (2) Travel today and yesterday   (3) The services of travel bureaus   (4) The growing popularity of package tours   (5) The increasing isolation of modern tourists

27. According to the passage, the colorful native innkeeper has been made obsolete by   (1) the travel brochure   (2) the travel agency   (3) the experienced traveler   (4) the native shopkeeper   (5) an international commission

28. According to the writer, one of the purposes of the modern preplanned tour is to   (1) save money for the tourist   (2) leave the tourist time for spontaneous activities   (3) protect the tourist from supposed inconveniences   (4) provide pleasures unknown in the tourist's native country   (5) prevent the tourist from being victimized by greedy hotel employees

29. The author suggests that tourist shopping   (1) will soon be eliminated   (2) is a source of annoyance to travelers   (3) has become too standardized   (4) provides a chance to meet the unexpected   (5) has its own code of etiquette

30. The passage suggests that travel today has become   (1) less time-consuming

(2) less stimulating   (3) more irritating   (4) more strenuous   (5) less regimented

31. According to the passage, which statement is true?   (1) Tourists prefer to determine personally the amounts they will give in tips.   (2) Tourists will tend to reject the services of travel agencies in the future.   (3) Americans are traveling greater distances today than formerly.   (4) Travel agencies are comparatively modern institutions.   (5) Modern travel does not necessarily broaden a tourist's knowledge of foreign customs.

32. The author's attitude toward modern trends in travel arrangements can best be described as   (1) indifferent   (2) resigned   (3) optimistic   (4) amused   (5) regretful

33. As used in this passage, the word "chaffering" (line 8) most nearly means   (1) going by car   (2) bargaining   (3) taking chances   (4) traveling aimlessly   (5) tipping

Passage B

Next morning I saw for the first time an animal that is rarely encountered face to face. It was a wolverine. Though relatively small, rarely weighing more than 40 pounds, he is, above all animals, the one most hated by the Indians and trappers. He is a fine tree climber and a relentless destroyer. Deer, reindeer, and even moose succumb to his attacks. We sat on a rock and watched him come, a bobbing rascal in blackish-brown. Since the male wolverine occupies a very large hunting area and fights to the death any other male that intrudes on his domain, wolverines are always scarce, and in order to avoid extinction need all the protection that man can give. As a trapper, Henry wanted me to shoot him, but I refused, for this is the most fascinating and little known of all our wonderful predators. His hunchback gait was awkward and ungainly, lopsided yet tireless. He advanced through all types of terrain without change of pace and with a sense of power that seemed indestructible. His course brought him directly to us, and he did not notice our immobile figures until he was ten feet away. Obviously startled, he rose up on his hind legs with paws outstretched and swayed from side to side like a bear undecided whether to charge. Then he tried to make off at top speed and watch us over his shoulder at the same time, running headlong into everything in his path.

34. Wolverines are very scarce because   (1) their food supply is limited   (2) they are afraid of all humankind   (3) they are seldom protected by man   (4) trappers take their toll of them   (5) they suffer in the survival of the fittest

35. The reason the author did not kill the wolverine seems to be that   (1) the wolverine's ungainly gait made him miss the target   (2) conservation laws protected the animal   (3) the roughness of the terrain made tracking difficult   (4) he admired the skill of the animal   (5) he felt sorry for the animal

36. The wolverine ran headlong into everything in his path because of his   (1) anxiety and curiosity   (2) helplessness in the face of danger   (3) snow blindness   (4) ferocious courage   (5) pursuit by the trappers

37. The author of this selection is most probably   (1) an experienced hunter   (2) a conscientious naturalist   (3) an inexperienced trapper   (4) a young Indian   (5) a farmer

38. The author's chief purpose in writing this passage seems to be to   (1) defend

the wolverine from further attacks by man   (2) point out the fatal weakness of the wolverine   (3) show why the wolverine is scarce   (4) characterize a rarely seen animal   (5) criticize Henry's action

39. As a whole, this passage suggests that the wolverine   (1) is every bit as awesome as his reputation   (2) will eventually destroy the deer herds   (3) will one day be able to outwit man   (4) does not really need the protection of man   (5) is too smart for other animals

Passage C

I find it takes the young writer a long time to become aware of what language really is as a medium of communication. He thinks he should be able to put down his meaning at once and be done with it, and he puts it down and releases his feeling for it in language that is meaningless to anyone else. He has to learn that he can load almost any form of words with his meaning and be expressing himself but communicating nothing. He has to learn that language has grown naturally out of the human need to communicate, that it belongs to all those who use it, and its communicative capacities have developed to meet the general need, that it is most alive when it comes off the tongue supported as it always is by the look and action of the speaker, that the tongue use of it is universal but the written use of it is relatively rare. He must come to see that tongue use is filled with clichés which are the common counters best serving the general need. Words and phrases that come off his tongue made alive by the living presence of himself become on paper dead transcriptions. Somehow he must overcome the capacity of words to remain dead symbols of meaning as they are in the dictionary. He must breathe life into them as he sets them on paper.

40. The title below that best expresses the ideas of this passage is: (1) Why clichés are valueless   (2) The young writer speaks   (3) How speech aids the writer   (4) Writing: a universal language   (5) Why writing is difficult

41. The passage indicates that when words are spoken and then written   (1) they become more powerful   (2) they become more understandable   (3) their effect is different   (4) their capacity for communication is increased   (5) their dictionary definitions have no value

42. The author implies that young writers are   (1) in too much of a hurry to have their say   (2) lacking in confidence   (3) too critical in analyzing their own work   (4) too emotional in their approach to writing   (5) lacking in the ability to find topics

43. The passage suggests that   (1) the written word has more of a potential than the spoken word   (2) clichés will eventually disappear   (3) books are dead symbols   (4) words exist for a purpose   (5) words in themselves are accurate reflections of reality

44. The author implies that clichés   (1) are rarely used in writing   (2) have no place in speaking   (3) perform some functions usefully   (4) have equal value for writers and speakers   (5) brand their users as lazy

45. The passage suggests that   (1) writing is more difficult than speaking   (2) writing requires less creativity than speaking   (3) writing possesses distinct advantages over speaking   (4) the audience is not a factor for the writer as it is for the speaker   (5) effective writers are usually effective speakers

Directions (46-50): Each of the following sentences contains an underlined expression. Below each sentence are four suggested answers. Decide

which answer is correct and place its *number* in the space provided on the separate answer sheet. [5]

46. Henderson, the president of the class and who is also captain of the team, will lead the rally.

    (1) Correct as is   (3) captain of the team
    (2) since he is captain of the team   (4) also being captain of the team

47. Our car has always run good on that kind of gasoline.

    (1) Correct as is   (3) ran good
    (2) run well   (4) ran well

48. There was a serious difference of opinion among her and I.

    (1) Correct as is   (3) between her and I
    (2) among she and I   (4) between her and me

49. "This is most unusual," said Helen, "the mailman has never been this late before."

    (1) Correct as is   (3) Helen. "The
    (2) Helen, "The   (4) Helen; "The

50. The three main characters in the story are Johnny Hobart, a teenager, his mother a widow, and the local druggist.

    (1) Correct as is
    (2) teenager; his mother, a widow; and
    (3) teenager; his mother a widow; and
    (4) teenager, his mother, a widow and

Directions (51-56): Each of the following concerns related areas of English. Choose *five* only, and in the space provided on the separate answer sheet write the *number* of the expression that best completes each statement. [5]

51. In a club meeting, member A moves that the club purchase an outboard motor. Member B immediately gets recognition from the chairman and says, "I move that we purchase a small yacht." At this point the chairman should (1) ask A to withdraw his motion (2) ask B to second A's motion (3) rule A's motion out of order (4) rule B's motion out of order

52. An important fact about the English language is that it (1) undergoes changes (2) has relatively few synonyms (3) is based primarily upon writing, not speech (4) has borrowed from very few languages

53. As applied to a word, the term *colloquial* means that the word is (1) new (2) no longer in use (3) used only in writing (4) appropriate for informal writing and ordinary speech

54. The index in *The World Almanac* is unusual in that it (1) is printed and distributed separately (2) may be removed for independent use (3) is located in the front of the book (4) is not alphabetized

55. In the system generally used for outlining, main topics are preceded by Roman numerals and the subtopics preceded by capital letters. The sub-subtopics are preceded by (1) Arabic numerals (2) Arabic numerals in parentheses (3) small letters (4) small letters in parentheses

56. A function of a newspaper syndicate is to (1) collect foreign news (2) provide opportunities for inexperienced writers (3) sell columns to member newspapers (4) regulate a group of newspapers

Part II

57. Answer *a* or *b* or *c:*   [20]

a. In literature, as in life, the social, political, or economic conditions of the times in which a person lives may help him or hinder him. From the novels, biographies or full-length plays you have read, choose a total of *two* books. In each case, show by specific references that a person in the book was helped by one (or more) of the above conditions or that he was hindered by them. Give titles and authors.

b. A writer may use humor to make a serious point. From the humorous poems, essays and short stories you have read, choose a total of *four* selections. In each case indicate the serious idea or underlying truth about life that the author is presenting, and show by specific references that he has used humor to make his point. Give titles and authors.

c. Each of the statements or questions below involves a literary reference. Choose 20 only and in the space provided on the separate answer sheet write the *number* of the word or phrase that correctly completes the statement or answers the question.

(1) In *The Yearling,* Jody's parents acted as they did in the end of the story out of a desire to   (1) respect the law   (2) please Jody   (3) face the reality of survival   (4) encourage each other to push on

(2) The emotion that colors Walt Whitman's "When Lilacs Last in the Dooryard Bloom'd" is   (1) delight   (2) fear   (3) pride   (4) sorrow

(3) In "The Monkey's Paw," the third wish made possible   (1) great wealth for the White family   (2) Herbert's return from India   (3) the voiding of the second wish   (4) the return of Sergeant-Major Morris

(4) In "The Emperor's New Clothes," the Emperor pretends to see the clothes because he   (1) is afraid of public opinion   (2) does not want to hurt the tailor's feelings   (3) wants to surprise the little boy   (4) sees in them a way to make money

(5) In *What Every Woman Knows,* the Wylie brothers agreed to finance John Shand's education if he promised to   (1) enter the family business   (2) represent their district in Parliament   (3) abandon his plans to become a minister   (4) marry their sister

(6) Throughout his lifetime, Thoreau was noted for his intense   (1) cynicism   (2) individualism   (3) patriotism   (4) miserliness

(7) In *The Brothers Karamazov,* Dostoevski implies that man is   (1) neither good nor evil in his nature   (2) essentially good in his nature   (3) essentially evil in his nature   (4) torn by the conflict between good and evil in his nature

(8) "The Hound of Heaven" recounts the pursuit of   (1) a constellation   (2) a satellite   (3) an imaginary ideal   (4) a man's soul

(9) The setting of "The Pit and the Pendulum" is   (1) Spain during the Inquisition   (2) an insane asylum   (3) a jewelry store   (4) a mining camp

(10) In *To Kill a Mockingbird,* a possible lynching is averted because of the (1) escape of the prisoner   (2) appearance of the children   (3) intervention of the sheriff   (4) actions of a recluse

(11) Which statement best describes the theme of Robert Burns' "To a Louse"? (1) "Cleanliness is next to Godliness." (2) "Give not yourselves unto vanity." (3) "Honesty is the best policy." (4) "Go to the ant, thou sluggard."

(12) "Casey at the Bat" is not a true folk-ballad because (1) it deals with the subject of baseball (2) it is the product of a single, known author (3) its meter is not a traditional ballad meter (4) its main character does not die

(13) The ghost told Hamlet to (1) punish Gertrude for her faithlessness (2) use the players to trap Claudius (3) tell no one of the ghost's words (4) permit Fortinbras to cross Denmark

(14) The Ancient Mariner shot the albatross for (1) no reason (2) food (3) the bird's plumage (4) a reward

(15) In *Act One,* Moss Hart describes in detail his collaboration with (1) Ben Hecht (2) Marc Connelly (3) George Kaufman (4) Edna Ferber

(16) In Bret Harte's "The Outcasts of Poker Flat," the "outcasts" failed to reach Sandy Bar because they were (1) caught in a snowstorm (2) stopped by armed men (3) unwilling to desert Piney (4) abandoned by John Oakhurst

(17) William Faulkner's Nobel Prize acceptance speech stresses the theme of man's (1) isolationism (2) indestructibility (3) superstition (4) optimism

(18) "What, will the line stretch out to the crack of doom?" was said by Macbeth about the (1) royal descendants of Banquo (2) guests at the banquet (3) avenging forces at Dunsinane (4) trees of Birnam Wood

(19) The women of Marblehead accused Skipper Ireson of (1) failing to pay fair wages (2) neglecting to keep his ships in good repair (3) refusing to give his crew good food (4) deserting the crew on a sinking ship

(20) At the end of the play "In the Zone," Smitty's companions feel (1) ashamed (2) puzzled (3) justified (4) amused

(21) The former mistress of Manderley was (1) Becky Sharp (2) Melanie Wilkes (3) Rebecca de Winter (4) Sabra Cravat

(22) Dave's father in "Split Cherry Tree" changed his mind about (1) school (2) cars (3) farming (4) religion

(23) Unconventional use of capital letters is a characteristic of the poetry of (1) T. S. Eliot (2) E. E. Cummings (3) Richard Armour (4) Karl Shapiro

(24) In Galsworthy's *Strife,* the chief losers in the strike are (1) the followers of Roberts (2) the followers of Mr. Anthony (3) the labor mediators (4) all concerned in the strike

(25) Penelope agreed to marry the suitor who could (1) string and shoot her husband's bow (2) plow the most ground in a day (3) finish her weaving (4) tell the most entertaining story

(26) Jane, Elizabeth, Lydia and Mary are characters in a book by (1) Jane Austen (2) Louisa May Alcott (3) Maureen Daly (4) Dorothy Canfield Fisher

(27) The setting of *Antigone* is (1) Delphi (2) Sparta (3) Thebes (4) Troy

(28) In his essay "Old China," Lamb insists that pleasures in life are greatest

when we   (1) have the leisure to indulge ourselves   (2) have many friends with whom to share them   (3) are not overly concerned with the rules of society   (4) must sacrifice to obtain them

(29) At the end of *I Remember Mama*, Mama admitted that she   (1) was the author of a cookbook   (2) longed for a fur-trimmed coat   (3) had never been in a bank   (4) had borrowed money from Uncle Chris

(30) In Strachey's biography of Queen Victoria, he recounts how, after Victoria became Queen, she immediately threw off the influence of   (1) the Privy Council   (2) the Prime Minister   (3) her uncles   (4) her mother

(31) Lancelot was nursed back to health by   (1) Lynette   (2) Elaine   (3) Guinevere   (4) Morgan le Fay

(32) In "The Bet," the prisoner occupied his time by   (1) planning vengeance   (2) copying an encyclopedia   (3) reading great books   (4) making shoes

(33) Which story concludes with the words "You have better go for the police," said he: "I have killed your master"?   (1) "The Man Who Was"   (2) "The Outstation"   (3) "The Three Strangers"   (4) "Markheim"

(34) Esther Forbes and Catherine Drinker Bowen are contemporary   (1) humorists   (2) biographers   (3) dramatists   (4) newspaper columnists

(35) As a story, "The Gift of the Magi" turns, in part, upon   (1) a case of mistaken identity   (2) the activities of a jewel thief   (3) a haircut   (4) a valuable necklace

(36) In *Othello*, who was the real villain?   (1) Cassio   (2) Desdemona   (3) Iago   (4) Emilia

(37) A noted frontiersman created by James Fenimore Cooper is   (1) Boone Caudil   (2) Jim Deakins   (3) Natty Bumppo   (4) Nick o' the Pines

(38) The "native" referred to in the title *The Return of the Native* is   (1) Clym Yeobright   (2) Diggory Venn   (3) Eustacia Vye   (4) Damon Wildeve

(39) The Minotaur was slain by   (1) Achilles   (2) Jason   (3) Hercules   (4) Theseus

(40) An important character in *The Pearl Lagoon* is a boy from   (1) China   (2) India   (3) California   (4) Texas

Part III

58. Write a composition of 250 to 300 words on one of the topics below: [30]

Our role in Southeast Asia

Waging a war on poverty

Out-of-date laws

Smoking hazards

Our numerical world

Physics—passport to the future

It's a woman's (*or* a man's) world

An independent thinker

Reducing athletic injuries

The future of the Republican (*or* Democratic) party

Education in the news

Qualifications of a critic

Censorship of books (*or* movies *or* television *or* the theater)

Rules that we need in our family

I protest

INDEX

1

INDEX